Selected Essays

Rabindranath Tagore

Introduction by

Mohit K. Ray

PUBLISHERS & DISTRIBUTORS (P) LTD

Published by
ATLANTIC
PUBLISHERS & DISTRIBUTORS (P) LTD
7/22, Ansari Road, Darya Ganj,
New Delhi-110002
Phones : +91-11-40775252, 23273880, 23275880, 23280451
Fax : +91-11-23285873
Web : www.atlanticbooks.com
E-mail : orders@atlanticbooks.com

Branch Office
5, Nallathambi Street, Wallajah Road,
Chennai-600002
Phones : +91-44-64611085, 32413319
E-mail : chennai@atlanticbooks.com

Printed in India at Nice Printing Press, A-33/3A, Site-IV, Industrial Area, Sahibabad, Ghaziabad, U.P.

Foreword

On the auspicious occasion of the year-long celebrations of the 150th birth anniversary of Rabindranath Tagore we are pleased to place in the hands of the lovers of Tagore all over the world a collection of 37 essays gleaned from the rich repertoire of Tagore's original English writings which unfortunately have not received the attention they deserve. One possible reason for the neglect of Tagore's English writings is Tagore's prolific output, Shakespearean felicity and protean plasticity as a Bengali poet who chose to write in the medium of his mother tongue unless an occasion demanded otherwise.

Yet a close look at his English writings reveals his wide range of active interest in everything that mattered to man as a social being. The essays show that Tagore was a man who always kept his antennae out and registered every new movement in the contemporary cultural scenario and reacted to it. The essays, thus, constitute an important part of his total *oeuvre* and surprise us by the contemporary relevance of the ideas enshrined in them and the prophetic vision of a great humanist.

Mohit K. Ray
(Chief Editor)
Atlantic Publishers and Distributors (P) Ltd.

Contents

Foreword ... *iii*

Introduction ... *vii*

1. The Nobel Prize Acceptance Speech ... 1
2. What is Art? ... 10
3. Construction versus Creation ... 30
4. The Creative Ideal ... 43
5. The Religion of an Artist ... 50
6. The Artist ... 72
7. The Poet's Religion ... 81
8. The Principle of Literature ... 96
9. The Meaning of Art ... 104
10. My Pictures ... 117
11. Man's Nature ... 123
12. Man ... 132
13. The Surplus in Man ... 147
14. The Music Maker ... 156
15. Supreme Man ... 162
16. Woman ... 174
17. Woman and Home ... 183
18. Man's Universe ... 189
19. The Creative Spirit ... 197

20. The Religion of the Forest ... 213
21. City and Village ... 225
22. Judgment ... 238
23. The Teacher ... 252
24. Ideals of Education ... 262
25. Spiritual Union ... 267
26. The Man of My Heart ... 273
27. I Am He ... 280
28. Spiritual Freedom ... 291
29. The Message of the Forest ... 298
30. Nationalism in the West ... 322
31. The Nation ... 347
32. The Call of Truth ... 353
33. The Way to Unity ... 374
34. Race Conflict ... 391
35. The Meeting of the East and the West ... 398
36. A Cry for Peace ... 404
37. Crisis in Civilization ... 406
Notes ... 413
Bibliography ... 439
Index ... 441

Introduction

The epithet, “myriad-minded” which Coleridge used for Shakespeare is more eminently applicable to Tagore. Although he is best known as a poet, he has left his mark in all the branches of literature. He was a poet, and novelist, a short story writer, an essayist, and a dramatist who wrote all kinds of dramas including dance drama and musical drama. Yet he was not just a cloistered literary artist. The myriad minded genius as he was, he was not only a man of contemplation but also of action. He was also a distinguished educationist and a social thinker. His antennae were always out to register every movement that took place in the literary, cultural and political arena and he sharply reacted to it and left the indelible stamp of his genius on it.

As one goes through the writings of Tagore one is bound to be amazed by his contemporaneity. It is extremely fascinating and rewarding to see how the ideas that are scattered over the entire gamut of his writings and his utterances and actions on different occasions are so relevant and meaningful today. Quite often they are as topical as today’s newspaper. The ideas that he expressed about the unity of man, about nationalism and internationalism, about the woman question, about environmental awareness, humanism, untouchability and religion, about education, colonialism, Western notions of success and exploitation and violence, about music, painting, dance and drama, about rural reconstruction, and cooperative farming and handicraft, etc. only reveal the depth of his understanding of the malaise of modern civilization and his ability to see into the future with remarkable clarity and conviction. The Romans used to call a poet *vates*, a seer, and that is what his writings make us feel about him.

In this Introduction I have tried to confine myself mainly to the English writings of Tagore (both original and his own translations), which are not as well known as his Bengali writings and their translations by different scholars, although references to his Bengali writings have also been made wherever found necessary to reinforce a point.

As a humanist Tagore believed in the essential unity of man and the universality of the mind. To him the mind was more important than matter and under no circumstances should the mind be fettered by religion, materialism, greed or power, etc. He believed: "Uniformity is not unity. Those who destroy the independence of other races, destroy the unity of all races of humanity" (*EWT 6*: 579). He was critical if not contemptuous of the kind of unity that is claimed by Imperialism. In a sarcastic tone of ruthless banter he remarked: "Modern Imperialism is that idea of Unity, which the python has in swallowing other live creatures" (*EWT 6: 579*). It is true that people as individuals have distinctive differences in many respects: in physiognomy, complexion, passions and prejudices; but these differences are never inimical to the attainment of the universality of the mind. In other words, the universality of mind is manifested in the infinite variety of individual differences. In this connection Tagore had once said to H.G. Wells: "Our individual physiognomy need not be the same. Let the mind be universal. The individual should not be sacrificed" (*EWT 8*: 1237). And he regretted in "Nationalism in the West": "The history has come to a stage when the moral man, the complete man, is more and more giving way, almost without knowing it, to make room for the political and the commercial man, the man of the limited purpose" (*EWT 4*: 448).

The same concern for individual freedom is evident in his observations on the freedom of Europe—a kind of freedom which is not conducive to the development of the moral man. Tagore writes in "India and Europe": "The freedom that Europe has achieved today in action, in knowledge, in literature and in art, is a freedom from the rigid inanity of matter. The fetters that we forge in the name of religion, enchain the spiritual man more securely than even worldly ties. The home of freedom is in the spirit of man. That spirit refuses to recognize any limit to action, or to knowledge" (*EWT 7*: 845). His anxiety in the lack of moral links that can hold together the civilization is evident in his letter to Gilbert Murray where he writes:

> ...I find much that is deeply distressing in modern conditions, and I am in complete agreement with you again in believing that at no other period of history has mankind as a whole been more alive to the need of human cooperation, more conscious of the inevitable and inseparable moral links which hold together the fabric of human civilization. I cannot afford to lose my faith in this inner spirit of Man, nor in the sureness of human progress which following the upward path of struggle and travail is constantly achieving, through cyclic darkness and doubt, its ever widening ranges of fulfillment.
>
> (*EWT* 6: 455)

This faith is reaffirmed in his letter to Yone Nogichi where he writes: "Humanity in spite of its many failures, has believed in a fundamental moral structure of society" (*EWT 8*: 1140). Tagore had a feeling that the kind of human civilization that is prevailing in Europe is essentially a political civilization which is scientific but not human. It is based upon exclusiveness. He says in "Nationalism in Japan": "The political civilization which has sprung up from the soil of Europe and is overrunning the whole world, like some prolific weed, is based upon exclusiveness. It is carnivorous and cannibalistic in its tendencies, it feeds upon the resources of other peoples and tries to swallow their whole future.... *This political civilization is scientific, not human*. It is powerful because it concentrates all its forces upon one purpose, like a millionaire acquiring money at the cost of his soul" (*EWT 4*: 472. Emphasis added). Money is the anathema of modern civilization. In this connection Nandini Joshi writes in "Tagore and Gandhiji on

Village Reconstruction": "Money has ceased to be an instrument in the hands of man but has become a demonic power, before which the larger claims of humanity have become insignificant. Between money accumulated by the help of machinery and the natural powers of an ordinary man the difference is so great that the ordinary man must accept defeat at every step..." (Chaudhuri 199-200).

In *Muktadhārā* Tagore makes convincing dramatic evocation of the evils that machine can cause. He shows how the *Yantrāsura*, the demon of machine draws out man's diabolical skill in using machine for enslaving man rather than freeing him. Like the Renaissance humanists Tagore also believed that it is immaterial whether the world is geocentric or heliocentric; it is essentially anthropocentric. To him man is of the highest importance and the welfare of man is the most important thing. And by welfare he means the development of man in his fullness into a complete man. He believed that human society is "the best expression of man, and that expression, according to its perfection, leads him to the full realization of the divine in humanity" (*EWT 4*: 565). Mulk Raj Anand was right when he pointed out that when Tagore says in his "Conversations with Einstein" that the truth of the Universe is human truth, "he means that he is interested in concrete human beings and not in abstract man" (Chaudhuri 6). The human existence, for Tagore, is essentially co-existence. And this co-existence simultaneously operates on two levels: communication and communion. Communication takes place at an external, functional level. But communion that binds man to man and unites people in the universality of mind is inward and is bound not by any material need but by love. Love is an organic desire and it is not only the means of one's communion with others but also the means of fulfillment of oneself, and the fullest realization of the inherent potentialities that find expression in different forms. "The feeling of perfection in love, which is the feeling of the perfect oneness, opens for us the gate of the world of the Infinite One, who is revealed in the unity of all personalities; who gives truth to sacrifice of self, to death which leads to a larger life, and to loss which leads to a greater gain; who turns the emptiness of renunciation into fulfillment by his own fullness", Tagore writes in "Personality" (*EWT* 4: 385). It is not for nothing that the writings of Tagore are replete with glorification of love and paeans sung in its celebration. In one of his famous songs he says: "*Basiyā ācho kena āpana mane/ svārtha nimagana kī kārane?/ cāridike dekho cāhi hṛdaya prasāri,/ kṣudra duḥkha saba tuccha māni/ prema bhariyā laho śūnya jībane*" (*RR* 4: 105). [Roughly it means: Why are you sitting alone confined to yourself? Look around and see how the stream of joy flows around the world. Fill your empty life with love.] What the contemporary world needs most today is love in a profound sense.

Tagore sincerely believed that a better world can be formed on the principle of universality and sympathetic recognition of the problems and limitations of others by different countries. It could, then, lead to a Commonwealth of Nations bound by love and understanding, and where no nation would deprive another of its rightful place in the commonwealth and no nation would try to encroach into another's domain. The views are largely subscribed to by Noam Chomsky, though in a different context, in *Hegemony or Survival: America's Quest for Global Dominance* (New York, 2003). The world then, Tagore believes, would be ruled by the principle of love and cooperation and not by contempt and conflict. Tagore believed that "on each race is laid the duty to keep alight its own lamp of mind as its part of the illumination of the world. To break the lamp of any people is to deprive it of its rightful place in the illumination of the world" (Kripalani 282). Kripalani refers to a passage by Tagore which Romain Rolland quotes to call attention to Tagore's catholicity of approach: "*The infinite personality of man* (as the Upanishads say)", Tagore remarked, "can only come from the magnificent harmony of all human races" (Kripalani 305). In Tagore's scheme of things there should remain no dichotomy between the East and the West but a perfect symbiosis of the two functioning in complementary relationship, each benefiting from the other. But as it stood Tagore believed that the dichotomy between the East and the West was created by the West's contempt for the

East, stemming from the belief that European civilization has reached a height which India can never dream of—an attitude reflected in Kipling's notorious remark that the twain, the East and the West, can never meet or Macaulay's presumptuous claim that one shelf of English books is more valuable than the entire body of literature produced in India. Tagore writes: "While depriving us of our opportunities and reducing our education to a minimum required for conducting a foreign government, this Nation [of the West] pacifies its conscience by calling us names, by sedulously giving currency to the arrogant cynicism that the East is east and the West is west and never the twain shall meet" (*EWT 4*: 450).

Tagore clearly saw through the hypocrisy of the ideas of nationalism and colonialism and the so-called white man's burden. Tagore saw, like Conrad, long before the postcolonial critics made us conscious of it that both nationalism and colonialism were political strategies for self-aggrandizement and maximization of profit and power. He makes a fine anatomy of the essential nature of nationalism and defines a nation in "Nationalism in the West" thus:

> A nation in the sense of the political and economic union of a people, is that aspect which a whole population assumes when organized for a *mechanical purpose*. Society has no ulterior purpose. It is an end in itself. It is a spontaneous self-expression of man as a social being. It is a natural regulation of human relationships so that men can develop ideals of life in cooperation with one another.
>
> (*EWT 4*: 444. Emphasis added)

Tagore believes that the spirit of nationalism is inimical to the development of selfless personality and love. He writes: "The history has come to a stage when the moral man, the complete man, is more and more giving way, almost without knowing it, to make room for the political and the commercial man, the man of the limited purpose" (*EWT 4*: 448). He further remarks: "This, aided by the wonderful progress in science, is assuming gigantic proportions and power causing the upset of moral balance, obscuring his human side under the shadow of soul-less organisation" (*EWT 4*: 448). Nationalism, as Tagore sees it creates a fracture between the rhetoric and the reality, between the precept and the practice. Further it has also the fissiparous tendency to break into smaller units like race, clan, tribe or caste, and once the process of fragmentation is on one does not know where to stop. The noted postcolonial critic Frantz Fanon seems to confirm Tagore's apprehensions. In "National Culture" included in *The Postcolonial Studies Reader* (London, 1997) he writes: "National consciousness, instead of being the all-embracing crystallization of the innermost hopes of the whole people, instead of being the immediate and most obvious result of the mobilization of the people, will be in any case only an empty shell, a crude and fragile travesty of what it might have been. The faults that we find in it are quite sufficient explanation of the facility with which, when dealing with young and independent nations, the nation is passed over for the race, and the tribe is preferred to the state. These are the cracks in the edifice which show the process of retrogression that is so harmful and prejudicial to national effort and national unity" (156). Nationalism, many postcolonial critics believe, in its turn, often generates prejudice, hatred and terrorism. The Western nationalism, Tagore believes, "has evolved a perfect organization of power but not spiritual idealism. It is like a pack of predatory creatures that must have its victims" (*EWT 4*: 451). So Tagore's main objection to nationalism is that it was modeled on certain utilitarian objectives with an overemphasis on commercial and political aspects at the cost of moral and spiritual aspects of man. Thus it is "the continual and stupendous dead pressure of this unhuman upon the living human under whom the modern world is groaning" (*EWT 4*: 453). With unswerving faith in man Tagore affirms that man "in his fullness is not powerful, but perfect", and therefore "to turn him into mere power, you have to curtail his soul as much as possible. When we are fully human, we cannot fly at one another's throats; our instincts of social life, our traditions of moral ideals stand in the way" (*EWT 4*: 459).

From nationalism to colonialism is just one step forward. Colonialism, as the modern postcolonial studies reveal, is only a corollary to nationalism. Armed with the ideology of nationalism the colonizers went to different countries, colonized them and, on the pretext of carrying out the white man's burden to civilize the uncivilized, were able "to clutch in its titanic grip, the vitals of other races for whom it has no feeling of kinship" (*EWT* 7: 746), and it "displays its canine teeth in the barbed wire fencing round its inhospitable world, in the name of the inborn right to be supercilious, characteristic of a superior civilization" (*EWT* 7: 748). Conrad's *Heart of Darkness*, a critique of colonialism, at once comes to mind. In his poem "Africa" (*RR* 3: 381-83) Tagore lays bare the naked savagery of the civilized and makes a poetic evocation of the depravity to which colonialism can descend. He writes in course of the poem:

> *Elo orā lohār hātkaḍi niye/ nakh yāder tīkhṇa tomār nekḍer ceye,/elo mānuṣ dharār dal/ garbe yārā andha tomār sūryahārā araṇyer ceye.*
>
> *Sabhyer barbar lobh nagna karlo āpan nirlajja amānuṣatā.*

The poem in its short span succinctly sums up the evils and the atrocities of colonialism, which could not possibly be better done in any full length study. There is enough evidence in the writings of Tagore that he could clearly see through colonialism as a huge enterprise of exploitation at the economic, biological and cultural levels. In another poem, *Praśna* (*RR* 2: 898-99) Tagore deplores how justice is denied when the victim lacks the power of protest.

If all the ideas about nationalism, colonialism and exploitation are eminently relevant even today in the context of interconnected countries, no less relevant is Tagore's understanding of the basic human nature and acts of violence committed by man. Tagore concedes: "We must admit that evils there are in human nature, in spite of our faith in moral laws and our training in self-control" (*EWT* 4: 631). But men are children of God, *amṛtasya putrāh*, and therefore the glory of man consists in his endeavours and ability to transcend the evil and reach Godhead and experience the universality of mind. But the parochial notions of nationalism and, more blatantly, colonialism let loose the potential evils which find expression in all kinds of violence. And the great humanist as Tagore is, he has been deeply pained whenever there is an act of violence, irrespective of the place where it occurs, and has raised a strong voice of protest. Thus Tagore reacted sharply when the British force attacked China and were engaged in rampage, looting and arson and devastated three cities. He wrote in Naivedya (1901):

> *Śatādīr sūrya āji raktameghmājhe/ asta gela, hiṃsār utsabe āji bāje/ astre astre maraṇer unmād rāgiṇī/ bhayaṃkarī. Dayāhīn sabhyatānāginī,/ tuleche kutil phaṇā cakṣer nimeṣe/ gupta biṣdanta tār bhari tībra biṣe.*
>
> *Naivedya* 64 (*RR 1*: 890)

[Roughly it means: The sun of the century set down in bloody clouds. We hear the clanking of swords in the death dance of insane violence.] And again in 1937 he wrote: "*Nāginīrā cāridike pheliteche biṣakta nihśvās,/ śantir lalit vāni śonāibe byārtha parihās*" (*Prāntik* 18. *RR 3*: 546). [Roughly it means: The poisonous snakes are hissing around everywhere; talk about peace will sound like a mockery.]

And again he wrote in the same year: "*Yedin caitanya mor mukti pela suptiguhā hate/niye elo duhsaha bismayjhaḍe dāruṇ duryoge/ kon narakāgnigirigahvarer taṭe;...Dekhilām ekāler/ ātmaghātī mūḍha unmattatā, dekhinu sarbānge tār/ bikṛtir kadarya bidrūp*" (*Prāntik 17. RR 3*: 545). [Roughly it means: The day my sense was liberated from the dungeon of oblivion, it brought me to the brink of the ocean of hell fire in midst of some unbearable, turbulent storm. It was breathing the hot smoke of man's insult and it was polluting the atmosphere with sounds of evil. I saw the foolish and suicidal madness of this age and the signs of ugly perversions.]

Hence Tagore's untiring warnings about it. How relevant the warnings are today becomes abundantly clear when we look back at the recent history of the world which is marked by series of wars, attacks and acts of violence: the Kenyan war in the 1950s, the Algerian war (1954-62) for Algerian independence from France, the Vietnam war fought between 1964 and 1975 on the ground in South Vietnam and bordering areas of Cambodia and Laos and in bombing runs over North Vietnam, the Cuban missile crisis of 1962 which is supposed to be "the closest the world ever came to nuclear war", the Chinese aggression of India in 1962, Pakistani aggression of India in 1965, Pakistan war in Bangladesh in 1971, the Iran-Iraq war (1979-1988), terrorist attacks in different parts of the world, the fall of the World Trade towers on 9/11, war in Afghanistan, Taliban attacks on Pakistan, series of bomb blasts in different parts of the world, insurgencies in border states of India—the list is inexhaustible. Everywhere what Tagore calls "crowd psychology" has been in operation. Tagore's warnings keep on resonating: "Crowd psychology is a blind force. Like steam and other physical forces it can be utilized for creating a tremendous amount of power. And therefore rulers of men, who out of greed and fear, are bent upon turning their peoples into machine of power try to train this crowd psychology for their special purposes" (*EWT 4*: 631).

I have dwelt at length on the relevance of Tagore's utterances about nationalism, colonialism and violence because these areas have a global dimension and are concerned with a precarious situation when man's very existence on this planet is jeopardized.

There are many other important areas where Tagore is amazingly relevant. He may be said to be a precursor, in fact, of many ideas which are considered of vital importance today. Take, for example the issue of the environment. Now there is a global awareness of the importance of the environment in our life, leading to increasing concern for plants and forests, and the consequent plantation ceremony. But long, long ago, it was on 8th November 1926 in fact, that Tagore had planted a linden sapling at the sanatorium of Balaton Fured in commemoration of his recovery from temporary illness during his visit to Hungary. Incidentally that sapling has now grown into a huge tree. He had also written a poem in the sanatorium register. The poem runs as follows: "*He taru e dharātale rahibanā yabe/ sedin vasante nava pallave pallave/ tomār marmar dhvani pathikere kabe/ bhālobesechila kavi bẽcechila yabe"*. Tagore also wrote an English version of it. "When I am no longer on this earth my tree/ Let the ever renewed leaves of thy spring/ Murmur to all the wayfarers/ The poet did love while he lived". On 9th October 1956 Anil Kumar Chanda placed a bust of Tagore made by Ramkinnkar Bej, the famous sculptor of Santiniketan, at the foot of the tree with the inscription of the poem that Tagore had written on the sanatorium register.

Tagore, who was a great lover of nature, had always lamented the deforestations and in 1928 he introduced in Santiniketan the festival of *Brkṣharopaṇa* or the plantation ceremony, along with another seasonal festival, *Halakarṣaṇa* or ploughing. *Brkṣharopaṇa* was done quite ceremonially with dance and music and chanting of Vedic hymns invoking nature's fertility and celebrating its perennial vitality and youthfulness. In the introductory song of the plantation ceremony Tagore gave a call to hoist the victory flag marking the conquest of the desert. Since then the festival is celebrated every year, and in the process, Santiniketan, originally a barren land, gradually turned into a beautiful garden town. Thanks to Tagore now plantation ceremony has become an all India festival and every year the forest departments organize plantation ceremony during the rainy season. The entire book of *Vanavānī* (Message of the Forest) is devoted to various trees, shrubs and flowers. In the short introduction to this book of verse Tagore writes about the trees: "The language of the trees is the primordial language; it reaches the innermost chord of the heart; it stirs up the forgotten history of thousands of years; the response that it raises in the mind is also in the language of the tree—it has no definite meaning, yet it creates vague sensations about the bygone ages" (*RR* 2: 837. My translation). It reminds one of Baudelaire's epoch- makin poem, "Correspondances" [correspondences] where Baude writes: "*La nature est un temple où de vivants piliers/ I parfois sortir de confuses paroles;/ L'homme y passe des forêts de symbols/ Qui l'observent avec d familiers.*" [Nature is a temple where living pi allow confused words to escape; man passes there through forests of symbols that watch him with familiar glances. Trans. *Penguin Book of French Verse*].

There was a time when man was part of nature. Down the line somewhere man stepped out of nature and started exploiting it for his own benefit, little knowing that by so doing he was only bringing about his own ruin. Luckily good sense prevailed in recent years and man, now aware of the contribution of the trees to his life, has become conscious of the environment. Anyway, in the introduction Tagore refers to the Vedic hymn that says that the life on earth began with the trees: "*Yadicam kiñca sarvam prāṇa ejati nihsṛtam*". In the introductory poem, "Hymn to Trees" he writes:

> *Ogo sūryaraśmipāyī/ śataśata śatābdīr dinadhenu duhiyā sadāi/ ye-teje bharile majjā, mānabere tāi kari dān/ karecho jagatjayī; dile tāre parama sammān;....*
>
> (*RR* 2: 839-40)

[Roughly it means: O tree you have gifted man the strength that you gathered, by drinking rays of the sun for centuries of its diurnal motion]. The festival brought man, nature and culture into a healthy and harmonious relationship which, according to Tagore is supremely important for the development of man and the fulfillment of his self. The book is fittingly dedicated to Sir Jagadish Chandra Bose who discovered life in plants.

Tagore's care for the environment is also evident in his admiration for the mud houses of the Santhals with the thatched roof. A Santhal house is made almost wholly of natural things: mud, bamboo and dry hay, and the houses are generally surrounded not by any brick wall but by bamboo groves and natural fencing made of split bamboos and leaves and thus in perfect harmony with the sylvan settings. The way Tagore laid out the plans of Santiniketan and Sriniketan also bears eloquent testimony to his ecological awareness. There was always a conscious attempt to harmonize nature and culture in an eco-friendly way. It is really amazing how he foresaw the needs for an ecological consciousness and anticipated the modern awareness of the environmental problems.

Another important global issue is feminism or the woman question. It was in the 1960s—in 1963 to be very precise—that two books, *American Women* which was actually the report of the American President's Commission on the Status of Women, and Betty Friedan's best selling book, *Feminine Mystique,* which exposed "the ideology of domesticity that made women, particularly the upper class and the middle class women depend on men". As feminism developed into a movement and gathered momentum it addressed issues such as status of women in the society, traditional notions of gender and sexuality, relation of gender to power structures, etc.

Tagore was a great admirer of Raja Rammohun Roy, the great social reformer and was very much influenced by his ideas of social equality and attitude to women. A humanist and a very sensitive soul, Tagore saw how the women suffered in the patriarchal Indian society and became victims of various forms of exploitation—economic, social and cultural—and carried a lifelong crusade against the atrocities perpetrated on the helpless women. In his writings—poems, plays and novels—his liberal and humanistic ideas about women are embodied in characters and situations. We hear the voice of female protest in the poem "*Sabalā*" (1928. *RR* 2: 783-84): "*Nārīke āpan bhāgya jay karibār/ keno nāhi dibe adhikār/ he bidhātā? Nata kari māthā/ pathaprānte kena rabo jāgi/ klāntadhairya pratyāśār pūraṇer lāgi/ daibāgata dine*" (784). The persona demands of God why the woman should not be allowed to work out her own destiny. Why should she keep awake on the wayside waiting with tired patience for the fulfillment of her expectations? In the poem "*Aprakāś*" (1932. *RR* 3: 308-09) the poet exhorts the woman to tear the veil and come out into the open:

> *Mukta hao he sundarī./ Chinna karo rañgīn kuāśā,/ abanata dṛṣtir ābeś,/ ei abruddha bhāṣā/ ei abaguṇthita prakāś./ Sayatna lajjār chāyā/ tomāre beṣtan kari jaḍāyeche aspaṣter māyāy/ śatapāke,/ moha diye*

saundaryare karecho ābil;/ aprakāśe hayecho aśuci.Tāi tomāre nikhil/ rekheche sarāye.

The persona tells the fair lady that her shyness and the modesty of her submissive bearing have encouraged the world to ignore her.

In "*Kyāmeliā*" (Chamelia. 1932. *RR* 3: 47-52) the young girl when pursued by a young man takes care of herself and the man admits: "*O meye nijer dāy nijei pāre nite*" [That girl herself can take care of herself]. In the poem, '*Niṣkrti*' (Release. 1918. *RR* 2: 543-50) Manjulika, a very young girl is given in marriage to the 55 years old Panchanan, much against the will of her mother. Manjulika's mother wanted to marry her daughter to one doctor Pulin who was a playmate of Manjulika during her childhood days. Soon after the marriage the girl becomes widow, and returns to her parents' place. A few years later her mother also dies and she devotes all her attention to the care of her father, a widower now. But after some time her father decides to marry again. The girl does not like it; she protests. But the father stubbornly sticks to her decision and puts forward some scriptural recommendations in support of his decision. (*Kintu gṛhadharma/ strī nā hale apūrṇa ye ray/ manu hate mahābhārat sakal śāstre kay.*) [All the scriptures right from Manu to the Mahabharata say that domestic duties remain unfulfilled if one does not marry.] This time the girl who had made a verbal protest earlier takes an action. She marries Pulin during the absence of her father. From the feminist point of view the poem is significant in many ways. It shows the double standard of the society in regard to men and women, the exploitation of women, even if she is one's own daughter in the household in complete disregard of her emotional and biological needs. But what is remarkable about Tagore is the courage of conviction in getting the widow married and that too, to a person of her choice in 1918 when Western feminism was still a long way off.

A cursory look at his plays also reveals his concern with the woman question. Vasanti in *The Ascetic*, Aparna in *Sacrifice*, Chitra in *Chitra* and Prakriti in *Chandalika* bear testimony to Tagore's insight into the feminine mind and his concern for the position of women in the society. Devjani in "*Kac o Devyānī*" [Kacha and Devjani] refuses to surrender to male domination. The concern for the 'woman question' also underscores the stories like "*Denā-Pāonā*" [The Deal] (1891), "*Śāsti*" [Punishment] (1893) "*Vicārak*" [The Judge] (1894), "*Prāyaścitta*" [Atonement] (1894), "Didi" [The Elder Sister (1894)] and "*Strīr Patra*" [The Wife's Letter] (1914). Though the last one, "*Strīr Patra*", is written in the form of a long letter from the wife to her husband it is included in the collection of stories; it is a serious vindication of the woman's cause.

Another important aspect of Tagore's humanism which has a great relevance to the contemporary global situation is his concern for the subaltern. Tagore carried a lifelong crusade against untouchability and the discrimination against the poor and the downtrodden. All his writings bear eloquent testimony to his sincere solicitations for them. Taraknath Sen refers to an episode recorded by Nirmalkumari Mahalnobis. Tagore was "telling of his experiences in Bengal villages; and she found him shedding tears as he spoke feelingly of the sufferings of the villagers witnessed with his own eyes, due to scarcity of drinking water" (Sen 150). In the poem, "*Dūrbhāgā Deś*" (The Unfortunate Country 1317BS, 1911. *RR* 2: 283-84) he warns them that a time will come for retribution. He writes:

> *He mor dūrbhāgā deś, yāder karecha apamān,/ Apamāne hate habe tāhāder sabār samān./ Mānuṣer adhikāre baṇcita karecha yāre,/ Sammukhe dāḍāye rekhe tabu kole dāo nāi sthān/ Apamāne hate habe tāhāder sabār samān* [You will have to face the same insult that you have inflicted on others. Since you have deprived them of their human rights and you have forced them to keep on standing without drawing them into your fold a time is sure to come when you will be equal with them in humiliation.]

Tagore believed that God resides in the heart of man. To hate a man is to hate the god in him. In another poem "*Dhūlāmandir*". [The Temple of Dust, 119. *RR* 2: 291-92]

Tagore tells the ascetic that there is no point in worshipping God in the closed room of the temple. Tagore says that God does not reside in the temple. God is in the field where the peasant works hard round the year and tills the soil after breaking the earth, and where the workers break the stones to make a path. There God is with them in all the weathers and His hands are full of dust. He writes:

> *Bhajan pūjan sādhan ārādhanā/ samasta thāk paḍe. Ruddhadvāre devālayer koṇe/ kena āchis ore./ Andhakāre lukiye āpan mane/ kāhāre tui pūjis sañgopane, nayan mele dekh dekhi tui ceye/ devatā nāi ghare. Tini gechen yethāy māti bhenge karche; cāṣā cāṣ-/ pāthar bhenge kātche yethāy path, khātche bāro mās./ Raudre jale āchen sabār sāthe,/ Dhūlā tāhār legeche dui hāte;/ tāri matan śuci basan chāḍi/ āyere dhūlār pare.*

[Roughly it means: Leave aside your prayers, worship, penance and supplications. Why are you wasting your time sitting alone in the temple barring the doors? Hiding in the dark whom are you searching so secretly? If you open your eyes you will discover that God is not there in the room. He has gone to the field where the farmer is tilling the soil and cultivating the land. He is there where the worker is breaking stones to make a path labouring all the year round. He is there with them in all the seasons. His hands are covered with dust. Discard the sacred cloth and come out like Him to the field.]

Obviously Tagore's idea of religion stems from the same belief in the dignity of man and man's rightful place in the world. A radical humanist in the true sense of the term Tagore believed that every individual has a distinct identity, a dignified place in the world and each has a divine spark in him or her. He is reported to have told Humayun Kabir that "just as every cell in the human body has a distinct life of its own and yet shares in the corporate life of the body, each human being has his uniqueness and is at the same time a part of the divine personality" (*Centenary Volume* 145). In "Religion of Man" Tagore writes: "It is significant that all great religions have their historic origin in persons who represented in their life a truth which is not cosmic and unmoral, but human and good" (*EWT* 5: 136). God, to Tagore, is not just an abstract idea, enshrined in an Olympian altitude cut off from the activities of human life in supercilious disregard of the destiny of man but "a Being who is the infinite in Man, the Father, the Friend, the Lover, whose service must be realized through serving all mankind" (*EWT* 5: 136). He reminds us the question that was asked by the sages of the ancient India, "*Kasmai debāya havisā vidhema*? Who is the God to whom we must bring our oblation?", and Tagore remarks: "The question is still ours, and to answer it we must know in the depth of our love and the maturity of our wisdom what man is—know him not only in sympathy but in *science*, in the joy of creation and in the pain of heroism" (*EWT* 5: 136. Emphasis added). Although a great humanist Tagore was not averse to science as he was neither dogmatic nor obscurantist in his understanding of the contemporary human situation. He combined in a remarkable way the ideal and the practical. He never lived in an ivory tower. He knew that with the industrial revolution the West was able to cater to the material needs of the masses, improve the standard of living and give them comfort and complacence. Hence his acceptance of and emphasis on science. But he knew also that mechanical implantation of science dries up the soul. He observed in "Union of Cultures": "Commodities multiply, markets spread, and tall buildings pierce the sky. Not only so, but in education, healing and the amenities of life, man also gains success. That is because the machine has its own truth. But this very success makes the man who is obsessed by its mechanism, hanker for more and more mechanism. And as the greed continually increases, he has less and less compunction in lowering man's true value to the level of his own machine" (*EWT* 6: 575). We should not allow machine to be our master and control our life. Tagore believed that man, "the angel of the surplus" needs the joy of creation for the sustenance of the soul and fulfillment of the self. Hence his insistence on the creation and promotion of handicrafts which combine the aesthetic and the utilitarian and thereby help the artisan economically. The handicraft thus serves a number of purposes. It keeps the cultural heritage alive and promotes cultural nationalism. It gives the artisan a joy of creation and it helps him financially. It is with this end in view that Tagore established an organization at Sriniketan to promote handicrafts. The global demands for handicrafts today as valuable cultural artifacts only reaffirm Tagore's relevance to the modern world. It was Tagore, again, who in order to redress the sufferings of the peasants introduced cooperative farming and was one of the pioneers in community development and cooperative enterprises which have become part of modern existence in the world today.

Another important aspect of the myriad minded Tagore which has also a great relevance today is Tagore's theoretical and practical ideas of education. Tagore expresses his credo: "The highest education is that which does not merely give us information but makes our life in harmony with all existence" (*EWT 4*: 401). Incidentally the idea which later crystallized in the form of educational institution at Santiniketan was largely an influence of his family background. In this connection Tagore writes:

> We in our home sought freedom of power in our language, freedom of imagination in our literature, freedom of soul in our religious creeds and that of mind in our social environment. Such an opportunity has given me confidence in the *power of education which is one with life and only which can give us real freedom of moral communion in the human world.* (*EWT 7*: 832. Emphasis added)

This family environment played a significant role in Tagore's formulation of the ideals of education.

> "I refuse to believe that human society has reached its limit of moral possibility. And we must work all our strength for the seemingly impossible, and must believe that there is a constant urging in the depth of human soul for the attainment of the perfect, the urging which secretly helps us in our entire endeavour for the good. This faith has been my only asset in the educational mission which I have made my life's work, and almost unaided and alone, I struggle along my path. I try to

> assert in my words and works that *education has only its meaning and object in freedom*—freedom from ignorance about the laws of universe, and freedom from passion and prejudice in our communication with the human world. (*EWT* 7: 832-33. Emphasis added)

In Tagore's vision of education the learner was deeply rooted in the natural surroundings but receptive of other cultures of other countries. The learning must involve instruction and delight and be individualized to meet the needs of the learner. Education must be brought in harmony with nature and culture and be conducive to the aesthetic and intellectual development of the learner's personality. Music, literature, dance, drama, nature studies, bird watching and similar other activities are meant to draw out the latent talents of the learner and bring about a fullness of life.

As an educationist with his emphasis on the non-authoritarian approach and focus on the natural development of the learner he has some affinity with the ideas of Rousseau, Pestalozzi, Froebel, Russell, Illich, Monteswari and Knowles among others. For example, Johan Heinrich Pestalozzi (1746-1827) argued that instead of dealing with words the children should be made to learn through activities and things. Fiedrich Wilhelm August Froebel (1782-1852) believed that the purpose of education is "to encourage and guide man as a conscious, thinking and perceiving being in such a way that he becomes a pure and perfect representation of that divine inner law through his own personal choice; education must show him the ways and meanings of attaining that goal". Maria Monteswari also pleads for the child's right to explore the environment and develop his inner resources. Russell pleads for the development of the ability of the learner to think independently, and Illich pleads for "deschooling society". Tagore's ideals of education which absorb the insights of all distinguished educationists go beyond all of them, both in expansiveness and in inclusiveness. In his pleadings for the expansiveness of the learner's personality and his belief that the greatest glory of man lies in realizing the infinite in the finite self he outdistances all the educationists mentioned above. If put into practice in other parts of the world, it can revitalize the contemporary global scenario of educational practice. Luckily there is a growing awareness of the relevance of Tagore's educational ideas in educational circles in different parts of the world with the belief that learning should be a pleasant experience for a learner.

There are two other areas which also bear testimony to the myriad minded aspect of Tagore's genius. These are music and painting, and these also have some contemporary relevance. Tagore composed more than 2000 songs which in their depth and range run the entire gamut of human emotions. Tagore had a solid grounding in Indian classical music, but instead of composing songs in pure classical tunes he used a very wide variety of tunes. In his songs he used Bengali folk tunes, Western tunes, tunes generally used in devotional songs, and classical tunes in such a way that there was a perfect combination of emotive strength and beauty in keeping with the semantic content and the feeling content of the songs. In this connection Sisir Kumar Das writes:

> The greatest singular achievement of Tagore is his songs, his power to concentrate tremendous passion within the delicate frame of his lyrics. His world of poetry is not like a massive planet but like a night sky with thousand of tiny stars. There is as much abundance and light as there is agony and darkness, as much serenity and joy as there are tensions and torments. It is world of various experiences, each significant in its own right, where every sweet articulation is born out of great agony, every delicate movement out of great labour.
>
> (Chaudhuri 17).

In his fusion of different tunes to effectively evoke a particular mood or create a particular emotive atmosphere, Tagore partly anticipates the aesthetics of modern fusion music. On his own testimony Tagore broke away from "the canons of orthodox propriety" audaciously focusing more on the feeling-content of the song than on grammar of it, and he is happy that people have accepted them. With remarkable courage of conviction

Tagore says: "I do not hesitate to say that my songs have found their place in the heart of my land, along with her flowers that are never exhausted, and that the folk of the future, in days of joy or sorrow or festival, will have to sing them. This too is the work of a revolutionist" (*EWT* 7: 933-34).

Now about painting. It is late in life that Tagore took to painting after 60. In his paintings which were exhibited first in Paris and then in different parts of Europe, Tagore emulated various styles. At one stage he practiced what may be called abstract painting devoted entirely to form without any apparent meaning. According to Hiranmay Bandyopadhyay, many of his paintings are surrealistic in character expressing a free flow of thought unintruded by any conscious intellectual control. Many of his paintings, again, are visual expressions of certain definite ideas or objects. Prthwis Neogy writes in *Drawings and Paintings of Rabindranath Tagore* (Centenary Volume 198-202): "Rabindranath Tagore had come to belong fully to the world of his time, the modern world".

In fine we may say that the main thrust of Tagore in the huge body of his writings and multifarious activities is on freedom which alone can draw out the best in man, enable him to realize his unity with the world through love, joy and truth. Tagore had passed through two World Wars, in addition to the various wars fought in different parts of the world during his lifetime. Yet he never lost faith in man. In his last public address he emphatically declared with a remarkable courage of conviction; "And yet I shall not commit the grievous sin of losing faith in Man. I would rather look forward to the opening of a new chapter in his history after the cataclysm is over and the atmosphere rendered clean with the spirit of service and sacrifice" (*EWT* 7: 986).

The great poet as he was, he was not only a great artist and a great sentinel; he was also, at bottom, a great humanist. It is this humanism that informs all his writings and activities.

* * * * *

My special thanks go to my colleague, Professor Rama Kundu for her valuable suggestions and active cooperation in readying the volume.

I am grateful to Dr K.R. Gupta, Honorary Adviser, M/s Atlantic Publishers and Distributors (P) Ltd., New Delhi for the confidence evinced in me and for seeing the book through the press.

Mohit K. Ray

The Nobel Prize Acceptance Speech

I am glad that I have been able to come at last to your country and that I may use this opportunity for expressing my gratitude to you for the honour you have done to me by acknowledging my work and rewarding me by giving me the Nobel Prize.

I remember the afternoon when I received the cablegram from my publisher in England that the prize had been awarded to me. I was staying then at the school Shantiniketan, about which I suppose you know. At that moment we were taking a party over to a forest nearby the school, and when I was passing by the telegram office and the post office, a man came running to us and held up the telegraphic message. I had also an English visitor with me in the same carriage. I did not think that the message was of any importance, and I just put it into my pocket, thinking that I would read it, when I reached my destination. But my visitor supposed he knew the contents, and he urged me to read it, saying that it contained an important message. And I opened and read the message, which I could hardly believe. I first thought that possibly the telegraphic language was not quite correct and that I might misread the meaning of it, but at last I felt certain about it. And you can well understand how rejoicing it was for my boys at the school and for the teachers. What touched me more deeply than anything else was that these boys who loved me and for whom I had the deepest love felt proud of the honour that had been awarded to him for whom they had feeling of reverence, and I realized that my countrymen would share with me the honour which had been awarded to myself.

The rest of the afternoon passed away in this manner, and when the night came I sat upon the terrace alone, and I asked myself the question what the reason could be of my poems being accepted and honoured by the West—in spite of my belonging to a different race, parted and separated by seas and mountains from the children of the West. And I can assure you that it was not with a feeling of exaltation but with a searching of the heart that I questioned myself, and I felt humble at that moment.

I remember how my life's work developed from the time when I was very young. When I was about 25 years I used to live in utmost seclusion in the solitude of an obscure Bengal village by the river Ganges in a boat-house. The wild ducks which came during the time of autumn from the Himalayan lakes were my only living companions, and in that solitude I seem to have drunk in the open space like wine overflowing with sunshine, and the murmur of the river used to speak to me and tell me the secrets of nature. And I passed my days in the solitude dreaming and giving shape to my dream in poems and studies and sending out my thoughts to the Calcutta public through the magazines and other papers. You can well understand that it was a life quite different from the life of the West. I do not know if any of your Western poets or writers do pass the greatest part of their young days in such absolute seclusion. I am almost certain that it cannot be possible and that seclusion itself has no place in the Western world.

And my life went on like this. I was an obscure individual—to most of my countrymen in those days. I mean that my name was hardly known outside my own province, but I was quite content with that obscurity, which protected me from the curiosity of the crowds.

And then came a time when my heart felt a longing to come out of that solitude and to do some work for my human fellow-beings, and not merely give shapes to my dreams and meditate deeply on the problems of life, but try to give expression to my ideas through some definite work, some definitive service for my fellow-beings.

And the one thing, the one work which came to my mind was to teach children. It was not because I was specially fitted for this work of teaching, for I have not had myself the full benefit of a regular education. For some time I hesitated to take upon myself this task, but I felt that as I had a deep love for nature I had naturally love for children also. My object in starting this institution was to give the children of men full freedom of joy, of life and of communion with nature. I myself had suffered when I was young through the impediments which were inflicted upon most boys while they attended school and I have had to go through the machine of education which crushes the joy and freedom of life for which children have such insatiable thirst. And my object was to give freedom and joy to children of men.

And so I had a few boys around me, and I taught them, and I tried to make them happy. I was their playmate. I was their companion. I shared their life, and I felt that I was the biggest child of the party. And we all grew up together in this atmosphere of freedom.

The vigour and the joy of the children, their chats and songs filled the air with a spirit of delight, which I drank every day I was there. And in the evening during the sunset hour I used to sit alone watching the trees of the shadowing avenue, and in the silence of the afternoon I could hear distinctly the voices of the children coming up in the air, and it seemed to me that these shouts and songs and glad voices were like those trees, which come out from the heart of the earth like fountains of life towards the bosom of the infinite sky. And it symbolized, it brought before my mind the whole cry of human life all expressions of joy and aspirations of men rising from the heart of Humanity up to this sky. I could see that, and I knew that we also, the grown-up children, send up our cries of aspiration to the Infinite. I felt it in my heart of hearts.

In this atmosphere and in this environment I used to write my poems Gitanjali, and I sang them to myself in the midnight under the glorious stars of the Indian sky. And in the early morning and in the afternoon glow of sunset I used to write these songs till a day came when I felt impelled to come out once again and meet the heart of the large world.

I could see that my coming out from the seclusion of my life among these joyful children and doing my service to my fellow creatures was only a prelude to my pilgrimage to a larger world. And I felt a great desire to come out and come into touch with the Humanity of the West, for I was conscious that the present age belongs to the Western man with his superabundance of energy.

He has got the power of the whole world, and his life is overflowing all boundaries and is sending out its message to the great future. And I felt that I must before I die come to the West and meet the man of the secret shrine where the Divine presence has his dwelling, his temple. And I thought that the Divine man with all his powers and aspirations of life is dwelling in the West.

And so I came out. After my Gitanjali poems had been written in Bengali I translated those poems into English, without having any desire to have them published, being diffident of my mastery of that language, but I had—the manuscript with me when I came out to the West. And you know that the British public, when these poems were put before them, and those who had the opportunity of reading them in manuscript before, approved of them. I was accepted, and the heart of the West opened without delay.

And it was a miracle to me who had lived for fifty years far away from activity, far away from the West, that I should be almost in a moment accepted by the West as one of its own poets. It was surprising to me, but I felt that possibly this had its deeper significance and that those years which I had spent in seclusion, separated from the life and the spirit of the West, had brought with them a deeper feeling of rest, serenity and feeling of the eternal, and that these were exactly the sentiments that were needed by the Western people with their overactive life, who still in their heart of hearts have a thirst for the peace, for the infinite peace. My fitness was that training which my muse had from my young days in the absolute solitude of the beaches of the Ganges. The peace of those years had been stored in my nature so that I could bring it out and hold it up to the man of the West, and what I offered to him was accepted gratefully.

I know that I must not accept that praise as my individual share. It is the East in me which gave to the West. For is not the East the mother of spiritual Humanity and does not the West, do not the children of the West amidst their games and plays when they get hurt, when they get famished and hungry, turn their face to that serene mother, the East? Do they not expect their food to come from her, and their rest for the night when they are tired? And are they to be disappointed.

Fortunately for me I came in that very moment when the West had turned her face again to the East and was seeking for some nourishment. Because I represented the East I got my reward from my Eastern friends.

And I can assure you that the prize which you have awarded to me was not wasted upon myself. I as an individual had no right to accept it, and therefore I have made use of it for others. I have dedicated it to our Eastern children and students. But then it is like a seed which is put into the earth and comes up again to those who have sown it, and for their benefit it is producing fruits. I have used this money which I got from you for establishing and maintaining the university which I started lately, and it seemed to me, that this university should be a place where Western students might come and meet their Eastern brethren and when they might work together in the pursuit of truth and try to find the treasures that have lain hidden in the East for centuries and work out the spiritual resources of the East, which are necessary for all Humanity.

I can remind you of a day when India had her great university in the glorious days of her civilization. When a light is lighted it cannot be held within a short range. It is for the whole world. And India had her civilization with all its splendours and wisdom and wealth. It could not use it for its own children only. It had to open its gates in hospitality to all races of men. Chinese and Japanese and Persians and all different races of men, came, and they had their opportunity of gaining what was best in India, her best offering of all times and to all Humanity. And she offered it generously. You know the traditions of our country are never to accept any material fees from the students in return to the teaching, because we consider in India that he who has the knowledge has the responsibility to impart it to the students. It is not merely for the students to come and ask it from the master, but it is the master who must fulfil his mission of life by offering the best gift which he has to all who may need it. And thus it was that need of self-expression, of giving what had been stored in India and offering the best thing that she has in herself that made it possible and was the cause and the origin of these universities that were started in the different provinces of India.

And I feel that what we suffer from in the present day is no other calamity but this calamity of obscurity, of seclusion, that we have missed our opportunity of offering hospitality to Humanity and asking the world to share the best things we have got. We lost our confidence in our own civilization for over a century, when we came into contact with the Western races with their material superiority over the Eastern Humanity and Eastern culture, and in the educational establishments no provision was made for our own culture. And for over a century our students have been brought up in utter ignorance of the worth of their own civilization of the past. Thus we did not only lose touch of the great which lay hidden in our own inheritance, but also the great honour of being able to contribute to the civilization of Humanity, to have opportunity of giving what we have and not merely begging from others, not merely borrowing culture and living like eternal schoolboys.

But the time has come when we must not waste such our opportunities. We must try to do our best to bring out what we have, and not go from century to century, from land to land and display our poverty before others. We know what we have to be proud of, what we have inherited from our ancestors, and such opportunity of giving should not be lost—not only for the sake of our people, but for the sake of Humanity.

That is the reason, and that led me to the determination to establish an international institution where the Western and

Eastern students could meet and share the common feast of spiritual food.

And thus I am proud to say that your awarding me the prize has made some contribution to this great object which I had in my mind. This has made me come out once again to the West, and I have come to ask you, to invite you to the feast which is waiting for you in the Far East. I hope that my invitation will not be rejected. I have visited different countries of Europe, and I have accepted from them an enthusiastic welcome. That welcome has its own meaning, that the West has need of the East, as the East has need of the West, and so the time has come when they should meet.

I am glad that I belong to this great time, this great age, and I am glad that I have done some work to give expression to this great age, when the East and the West are coming together. They are proceeding towards each other. They are coming to meet each other. They have got their invitation to meet each other and join hands in building up a new civilization and the great culture of the future.

I feel certain that through my writing some such idea has reached you, even if obscurely through the translation, some idea which belongs both to the East and the West, some idea which proceeding from the East has been able to come to the West and claim its rest here, its dwelling, and to be able to receive its welcome, and has been accepted by the West. And if in my writings I have been fortunate enough to be able to interpret the voice of the need of the time I am deeply thankful to you for giving me this glorious opportunity. The acknowledgement I got from Sweden has brought me and my work before the Western public, though I can assure you that it has also given me some trouble. It has broken through the seclusion which I have been accustomed to. It has brought me out before the great public to which I have never been accustomed. And the adjustment has not been yet made. I shrink in my heart when I stand before the great concourse of Humanity in the West. I have not yet been accustomed to accept the great gift of your praise and your admiration in the manner in which you have given it to me. And I feel ashamed and shy when standing before you—I do so now. But I will only say that I am thankful to God that he has given me this great opportunity, that I have been an instrument to bring together, to unite the hearts of the East and the West. And I must to the end of my life carry on that mission. I must do all that I can. The feeling of resentment between the East and the West must be pacified. I must do something, and with that one object I have started this institution.

I do not think that it is the spirit of India to reject anything, reject any race, reject any culture. The spirit of India has always proclaimed the ideal of unity. This ideal of unity never rejects anything, any race, or any culture. It comprehends all, and it has been the highest aim of our spiritual exertion to be able to penetrate all things with one soul, to comprehend all things as they are, and not to keep out anything in the whole universe—to comprehend all things with sympathy and love. This is the spirit of India. Now, when in the present time of political unrest the children of the same great India cry for rejection of the West I feel hurt. I feel that it is a lesson which they have received from the West. Such is not our mission. India is there to unite all human races.

Because of that reason in India we have not been given the unity of races. Our problem is the race problem which is the problem of all Humanity. We have Dravidians, we have Mohammedans, we have Hindoos and all different sects and communities of men in India. Therefore, no superficial bond of political unity can appeal to us, can satisfy us, can ever be real to us. We must go deeper down. We must discover the most profound unity, the spiritual unity between the different races. We must go deeper down to the spirit of man and find out the great bond of unity, which is to be found in all human races. And for that we are well equipped. We have inherited the immortal works of our ancestors, those great writers who proclaimed the religion of unity and sympathy, in say: He who sees all beings as himself, who realizes all beings as himself, knows Truth. That has once again to be realized, not only by the children of the East but also by the children of the West. They also have to be reminded of these great immortal truths.

Man is not to fight with other human races, other human individuals, but his work is to bring about reconciliation and Peace and to restore the bonds of friendship and love. We are not like fighting beasts. It is the life of self which is predominating in our life, the self which is creating the seclusion, giving rise to sufferings, to jealousy and hatred, to political and commercial competition. All these illusions will vanish, if we go down to the heart of the shrine, to the love and unity of all races.

For that great mission of India I have started this university. I ask you now, when I have this opportunity, I invite you to come to us and join hands with us and not to leave this institution merely to us, but let your own students and learned men come to us and help us to make this university to a common institution for the East and the West may they give the contributions of their lives and may we all together make it living and representative of the undivided Humanity of the world.

For this I have come to you. I ask you this and I claim it of you in the name of the unity of men, and in the name of love, and in the name of God. I ask you to come. I invite you.

(26 May 1921, Stockholm)

What is Art?

2

We are face to face with this great world and our relations to it are manifold. One of these is the necessity we have to live, to till the soil, to gather food, to clothe ourselves, to get materials from nature. We are always making things that will satisfy our need, and we come in touch with Nature in our efforts to meet these needs. Thus we are always in touch with this great world through hunger and thirst and all our physical needs.

Then we have our mind; and mind seeks its own food. Mind has its necessity also. It must find out reason in things. It is faced with a multiplicity of facts, and is bewildered when it cannot find one unifying principle which simplifies the heterogeneity of things. Man's constitution is such that he must not only find facts, but also some laws which will lighten the burden of mere number and quantity.

There is yet another man in me, not the physical, but the personal man; which has its likes and dislikes, and wants to find something to fulfil its needs of love. This personal man is found in the region where we are free from all necessity,—above the needs, both of body and mind,—above the expedient and useful. It is the highest in man,—this personal man. And it has personal relations of its own with the great world, and comes to it for something to satisfy personality.

The world of science is not a world of reality, it is an abstract world of force. We can use it by the help of our intellect but cannot realize it by the help of our personality. It is like a swarm of mechanics who though producing things for ourselves as personal beings, are mere shadows to us.

But there is another world which is real to us. We see it, feel it; we deal with it with all our emotions. Its mystery is endless because we cannot analyse it or measure it. We can but say, 'Here you are.'

This is the world from which Science turns away, and in which Art takes its place. And if we can answer the question as to what art is, we shall know what this world is with which art has such intimate relationship.

It is not an important question as it stands. For Art, like life itself, has grown by its own impulse, and man has taken his pleasure in it without definitely knowing what it is. And we could safely leave it there, in the subsoil of consciousness, where things that are of life are nourished in the dark.

But we live in an age when our world is turned inside out and when whatever lies at the bottom is dragged to the surface. Our very process of living, which is an unconscious process, we must bring under the scrutiny of our knowledge,—even though to know is to kill our object of research and to make it a museum specimen.

The question has been asked, 'What is Art?' and answers have been given by various persons. Such discussions introduce elements of conscious purpose into the region where both our faculties of creation and enjoyment have been spontaneous and half-conscious. They aim at supplying us with very definite standards by which to guide our judgment of art productions. Therefore we have heard judges in the modern time giving verdict, according to some special rules of their own making, for the dethronement of immortals whose supremacy has been unchallenged for centuries.

This meteorological disturbance in the atmosphere of art criticism, whose origin is in the West, has crossed over to our own shores in Bengal bringing mist and clouds in its wake where there was a clear sky. We have begun to ask ourselves whether creations of art should not be judged either according to their fitness to be universally understood, or their philosophical interpretation of life, or their usefulness for solving the problems of the day, or their giving expression to something which is peculiar to the genius of the people to which the artist belongs. Therefore when men are seriously engaged in fixing the standard of value in art by something which is not inherent in it,—or, in other words, when the excellence of the river is going to be judged by the point of view of a canal, we cannot leave the question to its fate, but must take our part in the deliberations.

Should we begin with a definition? But definition of a thing which has a life growth is really limiting one's own vision in order to be able to see clearly. And clearness is not necessarily the only, or the most important, aspect of a truth. A bull's-eye lantern view is a clear view, but not a complete view. If we are to know a wheel in motion, we need not mind if all its spokes cannot be counted. When not merely the accuracy of shape, but velocity of motion, is important, we have to be content with a somewhat imperfect definition of the wheel. Living things have far-reaching relationships with their surroundings, some of which are invisible and go deep down into the soil. In our zeal for definition we may lop off branches and roots of a tree to turn it into a log, which is easier to roll about from classroom to classroom, and therefore suitable for a textbook. But because it allows a nakedly clear view of itself, it cannot be said that a log gives a truer view of a tree as a whole.

Therefore I shall not define Art, but question myself about the reason of its existence, and try to find out whether it owes its origin to some social purpose, or to the need of catering for our aesthetic enjoyment, or whether it has come out of some impulse of expression, which is the impulse of our being itself.

A fight has been going on for a long time round the saying, 'Art for Art's sake', which seems to have fallen into disrepute among a section of Western critics. It is a sign of the recurrence of the ascetic ideal of the puritanism age, when enjoyment as an end in itself was held to be sinful. But all puritanism is a reaction. It does not represent truth in its normal aspect. When enjoyment loses its direct touch with life, growing fastidious and fantastic in its world of elaborate conventions, then comes the call for renunciation which rejects happiness itself as a snare. I am not going into the history of your modern art, which I am not at all competent to discuss; yet I can assert, as a general truth, that when a man tries to thwart himself in his desire for delight, converting it merely into his desire to know, or to do good, then the cause must be that his power of feeling delight has lost its natural bloom and healthiness.

The rhetoricians in old India had no hesitation in saying, that enjoyment is the soul of literature,—the enjoyment which is disinterested. But the word 'enjoyment' has to be used with caution. When analysed, its spectrum shows an endless series of rays of different colours and intensity throughout its different worlds of stars. The art world contains elements which are distinctly its own and which emit lights that have their special range and property. It is our duty to distinguish them and arrive at their origin and growth.

The most important distinction between the animal and man is this, that the animal is very nearly bound within the limits of its necessities, the greater part of its activities being necessary for its self-preservation and the preservation of race. Like a retail shopkeeper, it has no large profit from its trade of life; the bulk of its earnings must be spent in paying back the interest to its bank. Most of its resources are employed in the mere endeavour to live. But man, in life's commerce, is a big merchant. He earns a great deal more than he is absolutely compelled to spend. Therefore there is a vast excess of wealth in man's life, which gives him the freedom to be useless and irresponsible to a great measure. There are large outlying tracts, surrounding his necessities, where he has objects that are ends in themselves.

The animals must have knowledge, so that their knowledge can be employed for useful purposes of their life. But there they stop. They must know their surroundings in order to be able to take their shelter and seek their food, some properties of things in order to build their dwellings, some signs of the different seasons to be able to get ready to adapt themselves to the changes. Man also must know because he must live. But man has a surplus where he can proudly assert that knowledge is for the sake of knowledge. There he has the pure enjoyment of his knowledge, because there knowledge is freedom. Upon this fund of surplus his science and philosophy thrive.

Then again, there is a certain amount of altruism in the animal. It is the altruism of parenthood, the altruism of the herd and the hive. This altruism is absolutely necessary for race preservation. But in man there is a great deal more than this. Though he also has to be good, because goodness is necessary for his race, yet he goes far beyond that. His goodness is not a small pittance, barely sufficient for a hand-to-mouth moral existence. He can amply afford to say that goodness is for the sake of goodness. And upon this wealth of goodness,—where honesty is not valued for being the best policy, but because it can afford to go against all policies,—man's ethics are founded.

The idea of 'Art for Art's sake' also has its origin in this region of the superfluous. Let us, therefore, try to ascertain what activity it is, whose exuberance leads to the production of Art.

For man, as well as for animals, it is necessary to give expression to feelings of pleasure and displeasure, fear, anger and love. In animals, these emotional expressions have gone little beyond their bounds of usefulness. But in man, though they still have roots in their original purposes, they have spread their branches far and wide in the infinite sky high above their soil. Man has a fund of emotional energy which is not all occupied with his self-preservation. This surplus seeks its outlet in the creation of Art, for man's civilization is built upon his surplus.

A warrior is not merely content with fighting which is needful, but, by the aid of music and decorations, he must give expression to the heightened consciousness of the warrior in him, which is not only unnecessary, but in some cases suicidal. The man who has a strong religious feeling not only worships his deity with all care, but his religious personality craves, for its expression, the splendour of the temple, the rich ceremonials of worship.

When a feeling is aroused in our hearts which is far in excess of the amount that can be completely absorbed by the object which has produced it, it comes back to us and makes us conscious of ourselves by its return waves. When we are in poverty, all our attention is fixed outside us,—upon the objects which we must acquire for our need. But when our wealth greatly surpasses our needs, its light is reflected back upon us, and we have the exultation of feeling that we are rich persons. This is the reason why, of all creatures, only man knows himself, because his impulse of knowledge comes back to him in its excess. He feels his personality more intensely than other creatures, because his power of feeling is more than can be exhausted by his objects. This efflux of the consciousness of his personality requires an outlet of expression. Therefore, in Art, man reveals himself and not his objects. His objects have their place in books of information and science, where he has completely to conceal himself.

I know I shall not be allowed to pass unchallenged when I use the word 'personality', which has such an amplitude of meaning. These loose words can be made to fit ideas which have not only different dimensions, but shapes also. They are like raincoats, hanging in the hall, which can be taken away by absent-minded individuals who have no claim upon them.

Man as a knower, is not fully himself,—his mere information does not reveal him. But, as a person, he is the organic man, who has the inherent power to select things from his surroundings in order to make them his own. He has his forces of attraction and repulsion by which he not merely piles up things outside him, but creates himself. The principal creative forces, which transmute things into our living structure, are emotional forces. A man, where he is religious, is a person, but not where he is a mere theologian. His feeling for the divine is creative. But his mere knowledge of the divine cannot be formed into his own essence because of this lack of the emotional fire.

Let us here consider what are the contents of this personality and how it is related to the outer world. This world appears to us as an individual, and not merely as a bundle of invisible forces. For this, as everybody knows, it is greatly indebted to our senses and our mind. This apparent world is man's world. It has taken its special features of shape, colour and movement from the peculiar range and qualities of our perception. It is what our sense limits have specially acquired and built for us and walled up. Not only the physical and chemical forces, but man's perceptual forces, are its potent factors,—because it is man's world, and not an abstract world of physics or metaphysics.

This world, which takes its form in the mould of man's perception, still remains only as the partial world of his senses and mind. It is like a guest and not like a kinsman. It becomes completely our own when it comes within the range of our emotions. With our love and hatred, pleasure and pain, fear and wonder, continually working upon it, this world becomes a part of our personality. It grows with our growth, it changes with our changes. We are great or small, according to the magnitude and littleness of this assimilation, according to the quality of its sum total. If this world were taken away, our personality would lose all its content.

Our emotions are the gastric juices which transform this world of appearance into the more intimate world of sentiments. On the other hand, this outer world has its own juices, having their various qualities which excite our emotional activities. This is called in our Sanskrit rhetoric *rasa,* which signifies outer juices having their response in the inner juices of our emotions. And a poem, according to it, is a sentence or sentences containing juices, which stimulate the juices of emotion. It brings to us ideas, vitalized by feelings, ready to be made into the life-stuff of our nature.

Bare information on facts is not literature, because it gives us merely the facts which are independent of ourselves. Repetition of the facts that the sun is round, water is liquid, fire is hot, would be intolerable. But a description of the beauty of the sunrise has its eternal interest for us,—because there, it is not the fact of the sunrise, but its relation to ourselves, which is the object of perennial interest.

It is said in the Upanishad, that 'Wealth is dear to us, not because we desire the fact of the wealth itself, but because we desire ourselves.' This means that we feel ourselves in our wealth,—and therefore we love it. The things which arouse our emotions arouse our own self-feeling. It is like our touch upon the harp-string: if it is too feeble, then we are merely aware of the touch, but if it is strong, then our touch comes back to us in tunes and our consciousness is intensified.

There is the world of science, from which the elements of personality have been carefully removed. We must not touch it with our feelings. But there is also the vast world, which is personal to us. We must not merely know it, and then put it aside, but we must feel it,—because, by feeling it, we feel ourselves.

But how can we express our personality, which we only know by feeling? A scientist can make known what he has learned by analysis and experiment. But what an artist has to say, he cannot express by merely informing and explaining. The plainest language is needed when I have to say what I know about a rose, but to say what I feel about a rose is different. There it has nothing to do with facts, or with laws,—it deals with taste, which can be realized only by tasting. Therefore the Sanskrit rhetoricians say, in poetry we have to use words which have got the proper taste,—which do not merely talk, but conjure up pictures and sing. For pictures and songs are not merely facts,—they are personal facts. They are not only themselves, but ourselves also. They defy analysis and they have immediate access to our hearts.

It has to be conceded, that man cannot help revealing his personality, also, in the world of use. But there self-expression is not his primary object. In everyday life, when we are mostly moved by our habits, we are economical in our expression; for then our soul-consciousness is at its low level,—it has just volume enough to glide on in accustomed grooves. But when our heart is fully awakened in love, or in other great emotions, our personality is in its flood-tide. Then it feels the longing to express itself for the very sake of expression. Then comes Art, and we forget the claims of necessity, the thrift of usefulness,—the spires of our temples try to kiss the stars and the notes of our music to fathom the depth of the ineffable.

Man's energies, running on two parallel lines,—that of utility and of self-expression—tend to meet and mingle. By constant human associations sentiments gather around our things of use and invite the help of art to reveal themselves,—as we see the warrior's pride and love revealed in the ornamental sword-blade, and the comradeship of festive gatherings in the wine goblet.

The lawyer's office, as a rule, is not a thing of beauty, and the reason is obvious. But in a city where men are proud of their citizenship, public buildings must in their structure express this love for the city. When the British capital was removed from Calcutta to Delhi, there was discussion about the style of architecture which should be followed in the new buildings. Some advocated the Indian style of the Moghal period,—the style which was the joint production of the Moghal and the Indian genius. The fact that they lost sight of was that all true art has its origin in sentiment. Moghal Delhi and Moghal Agra show their human personality in their buildings. Moghal emperors were men, they were not mere administrators. They lived and died in India, they loved and fought. The memorials of their reigns do not persist in the ruins of factories and offices, but in immortal works of art,—not only in great buildings, but in pictures and music and workmanship in stone and metal, in cotton and wool fabrics. But the British government in India is not personal. It is official and therefore an abstraction. It has nothing to express in the true language of art. For law, efficiency and exploitation cannot sing themselves into epic stones. Lord Lytton, who unfortunately was gifted with more imagination than was necessary for an Indian Viceroy, tried to copy one of the state functions of the Moghals,—the Durbar ceremony. But state ceremonials are works of art. They naturally spring from the reciprocity of personal relationship between the people and their monarch. When they are copies, they show all the signs of the spurious.

How utility and sentiment take different lines in their expression can be seen in the dress of a man compared with that of a woman. A man's dress, as a rule, shuns all that is unnecessary and merely decorative. But a woman has naturally selected the decorative, not only in her dress, but in her manners. She has to be picturesque and musical to make manifest what she truly is,—because, in her position in the world, woman is more concrete and personal than man. She is not to be judged merely by her usefulness, but by her delightfulness. Therefore she takes infinite care in expressing, not her profession, but her personality.

The principal object of art, also, being the expression of personality, and not of that which is abstract and analytical, it necessarily uses the language of picture and music. This has led to a confusion in our thought that the object of art is the production of beauty; whereas beauty in art has been the mere instrument and not its complete and ultimate significance.

As a consequence of this, we have often heard it argued whether manner, rather than matter, is the essential element in art. Such arguments become endless, like pouring water into a vessel whose bottom has been taken away. These discussions owe their origin to the idea that beauty is the object of art, and, because mere matter cannot have the property of beauty, it becomes a question whether manner is not the principal factor in art.

But the truth is, analytical treatment will not help us in discovering what is the vital point in art. For the true principle of art is the principle of unity. When we want to know the food-value of certain of our diets, we find in their component parts; but its taste-value is in its unity, which cannot be analysed. Matter, taken by itself, is an abstraction which can be dealt with by science; while manner, which is merely manner, is an abstraction which comes under the laws of rhetoric. But when they are indissolubly one, then they find their harmonics in our personality, which is an organic complex of matter and manner, thoughts and things, motives and actions.

Therefore we find all abstract ideas are out of place in true art, where, in order to gain admission, they must come under the disguise of personification. This is the reason why poetry tries to select words that have vital qualities,—words that are not for mere information, but have become naturalized in our hearts and have not been worn out of their shapes by too constant use in the market. For instance, the English word 'consciousness' has not yet outgrown the cocoon stage of its scholastic inertia, therefore it is seldom used in poetry; whereas its Indian synonym 'chetana' is a vital word and is of constant poetical use. On the other hand the English word 'feeling' is fluid with life, but its Bengali synonym 'anubhuti' is refused in poetry, because it merely has a meaning and no flavour. And likewise there are some truths, coming from science and philosophy, which have acquired life's colour and taste, and some which have not. Until they have done this, they are, for art, like uncooked vegetables, unfit to be served at a feast. History, so long as it copies science and deals with abstractions, remains outside the domain of literature. But, as a narrative of facts, it takes its place by the side of the epic poem. For narration of historical facts imparts to the time to which they belong a taste of personality. Those periods become human to us, we fell their living heartbeats.

The world and the personal man are face to face, like friends who question one another and exchange their inner secrets. The world asks the inner man,—'Friend, have you seen me? Do you love me?—not as one who provides you with foods and fruits, not as one whose laws you have found out, but as one who is personal, individual?'

The artist's answer is, 'Yes, I have seen you, I have loved and known you,—not that I have any need of you, not that I have taken you and used your laws for my own purposes of power. I know the forces that act and drive and lead to power, but it is not that. I see you, where you are what I am.'

But how do you know that the artist has known, has seen, has come face to face with this Personality?

When I first meet any one who is not yet my friend, I observe all the numberless unessential things which attract the attention at first sight: and in the wilderness of that diversity of facts the friend who is to be my friend is lost.

When our steamer reached the coast of Japan, one of our passengers, a Japanese, was coming back home from Rangoon; we on the other hand were reaching that shore for the first time in our life. There was a great difference in our outlook. We noted every little peculiarity, and innumerable small things occupied our attention. But the Japanese passenger dived at once into the personality, the soul of the land, where his own soul found satisfaction. *He* saw fewer things, *we* saw more things; but what he saw was the soul of Japan. It could not be gauged by any quantity or number, but by something invisible and deep. It could not be said, that because we saw those innumerable things, we saw Japan better, but rather the reverse.

If you ask me to draw some particular tree and I am no artist, I try to copy every detail, lest I should otherwise lose the peculiarity of the tree, forgetting that the peculiarity is not the personality. But when the true artist comes, he overlooks all details and gets into the essential characterization.

Our rational man also seeks to simplify things into their inner principle; to get rid of the details; to get to the heart of things where things are One. But the difference is this,—the scientist seeks an impersonal principle of unification, which can be applied to all things. For instance he destroys the human body which is personal in order to find out physiology, which is impersonal and general.

But the artist finds out the unique, the individual, which yet is in the heart of the universal. When he looks on a tree, he looks on that tree as unique, not as the botanist who generalizes and classifies. It is the function of the artist to particularize that one tree. How does he do it? Not through the peculiarity which is the discord of the unique, but through the personality which is harmony. Therefore he has to find out the inner concordance of that one thing with its outer surroundings of all things.

The greatness and beauty of Oriental art, especially in Japan and China, consist in this, that there the artists have seen this soul of things and they believe in it. The West may believe in the soul of Man, but she does not really believe that the universe has a soul. Yet this is the belief of the East, and the whole mental contribution of the East to mankind is filled with this idea. So, we, in the East need not go into details and emphasize them; for the most important thing is this universal soul, for which the Eastern sages have sat in meditation, and Eastern artists have joined them in artistic realization.

Because we have faith in this universal soul, we in the East know that Truth, Power, Beauty, lie in Simplicity,—where it is transparent, where things do not obstruct the inner vision. Therefore, all our sages have tried to make their lives simple and pure, because thus they have the realization of a positive Truth, which, though invisible, is more real than the gross and the numerous.

When we say that art only deals with those truths that are personal, we do not exclude philosophical ideas which are apparently abstract. They are quite common in our Indian literature, because they have been woven with the fibres of our personal nature. I give here an instance which will make my point clear. The following is a translation of an Indian poem written by a woman poet of mediaeval India,—its subject is Life.

I salute the Life which is like a sprouting seed,
With its one arm upraised in the air, and the other down in the soil;
The Life which is one in its outer form and its inner sap;
The Life that ever appears, yet ever eludes.
The Life that comes I salute, and the Life that goes;
I salute the Life that is revealed and that is hidden;
I salute the Life in suspense, standing still like a mountain,
And the Life of the surging sea of fire;
The Life that is tender like a lotus, and hard like a thunderbolt.
I salute the Life which is of the mind, with its one side in the dark and the other in the light.
I salute the Life in the house and the Life abroad in the unknown,
The Life full of joy and the Life weary with its pains,
The Life eternally moving, rocking the world into stillness,
The Life deep and silent, breaking out into roaring waves.

This idea of life is not a mere logical deduction; it is as real to the poetess as the air to the bird who feels it at every beat of its wings. Woman has realized the mystery of life in her child more intimately than man has done. This woman's nature in the poet has felt the deep stir of life in all the world. She has known it to be infinite,—not through any reasoning process, but through the illumination of her feeling. Therefore the same idea, which is a mere abstraction to one whose sense of the reality is limited, becomes luminously real to another whose sensibility has a wider range. We have often heard the Indian mind described by Western critics as metaphysical, because it is ready to soar in the infinite. But it has to be noted that the infinite is not a mere matter of philosophical speculation to India; it is as real to her as the sunlight. She must see it, feel it, make use of it in her life. Therefore it has come out so profusely in her symbolism of worship, in her literature. The poet of the Upanishad has said that the slightest movement of life would be impossible if the sky were not filled with infinite joy. This universal presence was as much of a reality to him as the earth under his feet, nay, even more. The realization of this has broken out in a song of an Indian poet who was born in the fifteenth century:

> There fall the rhythmic beat of life and death:
> Rapture wells forth, and all space is radiant with light.
> There the unstruck music is sounded; it is the love music
> of three worlds.
> There millions of lamps of sun and moon are burning;
> There the drum beats and the lover swings in play,
> There love songs resound, and light rains in showers.

In India, the greater part of our literature is religious, because God with us is not a distant God; He belongs to our homes, as well as to our temples. We feel His nearness to us in all the human relationship of love and affection, and in our festivities He is the chief guest whom we honour. In seasons of flowers and fruits, in the coming of the rain, in the fulness of the autumn, we see the hem of His mantle and hear His footsteps. We worship Him in all the true objects of our worship and love Him wherever our love is true. In the woman who is good we feel Him, in the man who is true we know Him, in our children He is born again and again, the Eternal

Child. Therefore religious songs are our love songs, and our domestic occurrences, such as the birth of a son, or the coming of the daughter from her husband's house to her parents and her departure again, are woven in our literature as a drama whose counterpart is in the divine.

It is thus that the domain of literature has extended into the region which seems hidden in the depth of mystery and made it human and speaking. It is growing, keeping pace with the conquest made by the human personality in the realm of truth. It is growing, not only into history, science and philosophy, but, with our expanding sympathy, into our social consciousness. The classical literature of the ancient time was only peopled by saints and kings and heroes. It threw no light upon men who loved and suffered in obscurity. But as the illumination of man's personality throws its light upon a wider space, penetrating into hidden corners, the world of art also crosses its frontiers and extends its boundaries into unexplored regions. Thus art is signalizing man's conquest of the world by its symbols of beauty, springing up in spots which were barren of all voice and colours. It is supplying man with his banners, under which he marches to fight against the inane and the inert, proving his living claims far and wide in God's creation. Even the spirit of the desert has owned its kinship with him, and the lonely pyramids are there as memorials of the meeting of Nature's silence with the silence of the human spirit. The darkness of the caves has yielded its stillness to man's soul, and in exchange has secretly been crowned with the wreath of art. Bells are ringing in temples, in villages and populous towns to proclaim that the infinite is not a mere emptiness to man. This encroachment of man's personality has no limit, and even the markets and factories of the present age, even the schools where children of man are imprisoned and jails where are the criminals, will be mellowed with the touch of art, and lose their distinction of rigid discordance with life. For the one effort of man's personality is to transform everything with which he has any true concern into the human. And art is like the spread of vegetation, to show how far man has reclaimed the desert for his own.

We have said before that where there is an element of the superfluous in our heart's relationship with the world, Art has its birth. In other words, where our personality feels its wealth it breaks out in display. What we devour for ourselves is totally spent. What overflows our need becomes articulate. The stage of pure utility is like the state of heat which is dark. When it surpasses itself, it becomes white heat and then it is expressive.

Take, for instance, our delight in eating. It is soon exhausted, it gives no indication of the infinite. Therefore, though in its extensiveness it is more universal than any other passion, it is rejected by art. It is like an immigrant coming to these Atlantic shores, who can show no cash balance in his favour.

In our life we have one side which is finite, where we exhaust ourselves at every step, and we have another side, where our aspiration, enjoyment and sacrifice are infinite. This infinite side of man must have its revealments in some symbols which have the elements of immortality. There it naturally seeks perfection. Therefore it refuses all that is flimsy and feeble and incongruous. It builds for its dwelling a paradise, where only those materials are used that have transcended the earth's mortality.

For men are the children of light. Whenever they fully realize themselves they feel their immortality. And, as they feel it, they extend their realm of the immortal into every region of human life.

This building of man's true world,—the living world of truth and beauty,—is the function of Art.

Man is true, where he feels his infinity, where he is divine, and the divine is the creator in him. Therefore with the attainment of his truth he creates. For he can truly live in his own creation and make out of God's world his own world. This is indeed his own heaven, the heaven of ideas shaped into perfect forms, with which he surrounds himself; where his children are born, where they learn how to live and to die, how to love and to fight, where they know that the real is not that which is merely seen and wealth is not that which is stored. If man could only listen to the voice that rises from the heart of his own creation, he would hear the same message that came from the Indian sage of the ancient time:

'Hearken to me, ye children of the Immortal, dwellers of the heavenly worlds, I have known the Supreme Person who comes as light from the dark beyond.'

Yes, it is that Supreme Person, who has made himself known to man and made this universe so deeply personal to him. Therefore, in India, our places of pilgrimage are there, where in the confluence of the river and the sea, in the eternal snow of the mountain peak, in the lonely seashore, some aspect of the infinite is revealed which has its great voice for our heart, and there man has left in his images and temples, in his carvings of stone, these words,—'Hearken to me, I have known the Supreme Person.' In the mere substance and law of this world we do not meet the person, but where the sky is blue, and the grass is green, where the flower has its beauty and fruit its taste, where there is not only perpetuation of race, but joy of living and love of fellow-creatures, sympathy and self-sacrifice, there is revealed to us the Person who is infinite. There, not merely are facts pelted down upon our heads, but we feel the bond of the personal relationship binding our hearts with this world through all time. And this is Reality, which is truth made our own,—truth that has its eternal relation with the Supreme Person. This world, whose soul seems to be aching for expression in its endless rhythm of lines and colours, music and movements, hints and whispers, and all the suggestion of the inexpressible, finds its harmony in the ceaseless longing of the human heart to make the Person manifest in its own creations.

The desire for the manifestation of this Person makes us lavish with all our resources. When we accumulate wealth, we have to account for every penny; we reason accurately and we act with care. But when we set about to express our wealthiness, we seem to lose sight of all lines of limit. In fact, none of us has wealth enough fully to express what we mean by wealthiness. When we try to save our life from an enemy's attack, we are cautious in our movements. But when we feel impelled to express our personal bravery, we willingly take risks and go to the length of losing our lives. We are careful of expenditure in our everyday life, but on festive occasions, when we express our joy, we are thriftless even to the extent of going beyond our means. For when we are intensely conscious of our own personality, we are apt to ignore the tyranny of facts. We are temperate in our dealings with the man with whom our relation is the relationship of prudence. But we feel we have not got enough for those whom we love. The poet says of the beloved:

'It seems to me that I have gazed at your beauty from the beginning of my existence, that I have kept you in my arms for countless ages, yet it has not been enough for me.'

He says, 'Stones would melt in tenderness, if touched by the breeze of your mantle.'

He feels that his 'eyes long to fly like birds to see his beloved.'

Judged from the standpoint of reason these are exaggerations, but from that of the heart, freed from limits of facts, they are true.

It is not the same in God's creation? There, forces and matters are alike mere facts—they have their strict accounts kept and they can be accurately weighed and measured. Only beauty is not a mere fact; it cannot be accounted for, it cannot be surveyed and mapped. It is an expression. Facts are like wine-cups that carry it, they are hidden by it, it overflows them. It is infinite in its suggestions, it is extravagant in its words. It is personal, therefore, beyond science. It sings as does the poet, 'It seems to me that I have gazed at you from the beginning of my existence, that I have kept you in my arms for countless ages, yet it has not been enough for me.'

So we find that our world of expression does not accurately coincide with the world of facts, because personality surpasses facts on every side. It is conscious of its infinity and creates from its abundance; and because, in art, things are challenged from the standpoint of the immortal Person, those which are important in our customary life of facts become unreal when placed on the pedestal of art. A newspaper account of some domestic incident in the life of a commercial magnate may create agitation in Society, yet would lose all its significance if placed by the side of great works of art. We can well imagine how it would hide its face in shame, if by some cruel accident it found itself in the neighbourhood of Keats's 'Ode on a Grecian Urn'.

Yet the very same incident, if treated deeply, divested of its conventional superficiality, might have a better claim in art than the negotiation for raising a big loan for China, or the defeat of British diplomacy in Turkey. A mere household event of a husband's jealousy of his wife, as depicted in one of Shakespeare's tragedies, has greater value in the realm of art than the code of caste regulations in Manu's scripture or the law prohibiting inhabitants of one part of the world from receiving human treatment in another. For when facts are looked upon as mere facts, having their chain of consequences in the world of facts, they are rejected by art.

When, however, such laws and regulations as I have mentioned are viewed in their application to some human individual, in all their injustice, insult and pain, then they are seen in their complete truth and they become subjects for art. The disposition of a great battle may be a great fact, but it is useless for the purpose of art. But what that battle has caused to a single individual soldier, separated from his loved ones and maimed for his life, has a vital value for art which deals with reality.

Man's social world is like some nebulous system of stars, consisting largely of a mist of abstractions, with such names as society, state, nation, commerce, politics and war. In their dense amorphousness man is hidden and truth is blurred. The one vague idea of war covers from our sight a multitude of miseries, and obscures our sense of reality. The idea of the nation is responsible for crimes that would be appalling, if the mist could be removed for a moment. The idea of society has created forms of slavery without number, which we tolerate simply because it has deadened our consciousness of the reality of the personal man. In the name of religion deeds have been done that would exhaust all the resources of hell itself for punishment, because with its creeds and dogmas it has applied an extensive plaster of anaesthetic over a large surface of feeling humanity. Everywhere in man's world the Supreme Person is suffering from the killing of the human reality by the imposition of the abstract. In our schools the idea of the class hides the reality of the school children;—they become students and not individuals. Therefore, it does not hurt us to see children's lives crushed, in their classes, like flowers pressed between book leaves. In government, the bureaucracy deals with generalizations and not with men. And therefore it costs it nothing to indulge in wholesale cruelties. Once we accept as truth such a scientific maxim as 'Survival of the Fittest' it immediately transforms the whole world of human personality into a monotonous desert of abstraction, where things become dreadfully simple because robbed of their mystery of life.

In these large tracts of nebulousness Art is creating its stars,—stars that are definite in their forms but infinite in their personality. Art is calling us the 'children of the immortal', and proclaiming our right to dwell in the heavenly worlds.

What is it in man that asserts its immortality in spite of the obvious fact of death? It is not his physical body or his mental organization. It is that deeper unity, that ultimate mystery in him, which, from the centre of his world, radiates towards its circumference; which is in his body, yet transcends his body; which is in his mind, yet grows beyond his mind; which through the things belonging to him, expresses something that is not in them; which, while occupying his present, overflows its banks of the past and the future. It is the personality of man, conscious of its inexhaustible abundance; it has the paradox in it that it is more than itself; it is more than as it is seen, as it is known, as it is used. And this consciousness of the infinite, in the personal man, ever strives to make its expressions immortal and to make the whole world its own. In Art the person in us is sending its answers to the Supreme Person, who reveals Himself to us in a world of endless beauty across the lightness world of facts.

Construction versus Creation 3

Construction is for a purpose, it expresses our wants; but creation is for itself, it expresses our very being. We make a vessel because water has to be fetched. It must answer the question why. But when we take infinite trouble to give it a beautiful form, no reason has to be assigned. It is something which is ultimate; it is for the realization of our own spirit which is free, which is glad. If, in the works of our life, needs make themselves too domineering, purposes too obtrusive, if something of our complete humanity is not expressed at the same time, then these works become ugly and unspiritual.

In love, in goodness, man himself is revealed; these express no want in him; they show the fulness of his nature which flows out of himself and therefore they are purely creative. They are ultimate—therefore, in our judgment of man's civilization, they give us the true criterion of perfection.

Creation is the revelation of truth through the rhythm of forms. It has a dualism consisting of the expression and the material. Of these two wedded companions the material must keep in the background and continually offer itself as a sacrifice to its absolute loyalty to the expression. And this is true of all things, whether in our individual life or in our society.

When the material makes itself too aggressive and furiously multiplies itself into unmeaning voluminousness, then the harmony of creation is disturbed and truth is obscured. If the lamp takes a perverse pride in displaying its oil, then the light remains unrevealed. The material must know that it has no idea of completeness in itself, that it must not hold out temptations to decoy men under its destination away from their creative activities.

The laws of grammar are necessary for the construction of a poem, but the readers must not be made conscious of their constant dictatorship. In classical India we have a Sanskrit poem in which all the complex grammatical rules are deliberately illustrated. This gives continual shocks of delight to a class of readers who, even in a work of art, seek some tangible proof of power almost physical in its manifestation. This proves that by special cultivation a kind of mentality can be produced which is strangely capable of taking delight in contemplating the mere spectacle of power manipulating materials, forgetting that materials are not the truth. And these people of an athletic habit of mind encourage artists to sacrifice art to the vanity of performance, simplicity of truth to the antics of cleverness.

What is the truth of the world? Its truth is not the mass of materials, but their universal relatedness. A drop of water is not a particular assortment of elements, it is their mutuality. In fact matter, as a mass, is an abstraction to us; we know it by a betrayal of secret through science. We do not directly perceive it. We see a flower, but not matter. Matter in a laboratory has its use but no expression. This expression alone is creation; it is an end in itself. So also does our civilization find its completeness when it expresses humanity, not when it displays its power to amass materials.

I have said that the truth of this world is in its law of relatedness, that is to say, the law of keeping step together. For the world is a movement, and this movement must not be retarded in any of its parts by a break of cadence. The world of men is suffering the agony of pain, because its movements are not in harmony with one another, because the relationship of races has not yet been established in a balance of beauty and goodness. This balance cannot be maintained by external regulation. It is a dance which must have music to regulate it. This great music is lacking in the historical meeting of man which has taken place in the present age, and all its movements in their discongruity are creating complexities of pain.

We know of an instance in our own history of India when a great personality* struck up in his life and voice the key-note of the solemn music of man-love for all creatures. And that music crossed the sea and the mountain and the desert, and races belonging to different climes and habits and languages were drawn together, not in a clash of arms or in the conflict of exploitation but in co-operation of life, in amity and peace. This was a creation. The great rhythm of this symphony was in the very heart of the world. This rhythm is what metre is to a poem, not a mere enclosure for keeping ideas from running off in disorder, but a vitalizing force, making them indivisible in a unity of creation.

When humanity lacks this music of soul, then society becomes a mechanical arrangement of compartments, of political and social classifications. Such a machine is a mere aping of creation, and not having unity at its heart it enforces it in its outer structure for mere convenience. In it the life that grows and feels is hurt, and either is crushed into insensibility or breaks out in constant convulsions.

The vital harmony is lacking today in unity of man, for the formalness of law and regulation has displaced the living ideal of personality from human affairs, and science has taken the office of religion in man's greatest creative work, his civilization.

The diversion of man's energy to the outside is producing an enormous quantity of materials which may give rise in us to the pride of power but not the joy of life. The hugeness of things is every day overawing the greatness of man, and the gap between matter and life is growing wider. For when things become too many, they refuse to be completely assimilated to life, thus becoming its most dangerous rival, as is an excessively large pile of fuel to the fire.

Expression belongs to a different plane from that of its material. Our physical body has its elaborate mechanism for its various vital needs. Yet the wholeness of our body, where it is an expression, where it is one with our personality, is

* Gautama Buddha.

absolutely different in its aspect and meaning from the muscular, vascular or nervous system, and it keeps its veil strictly drawn. The physiological mechanism as an organ of efficiency carefully exacts from its means and methods their full equivalents in results. But the body is more than this mechanism, it is divine. An exhaustive list of all its functions fails to give us its definiteness. It is a creation and not a mere construction, rising far above its purposes and composition. Creation is infinitely in excess of all measurements, it is the immaterial in matter.

In all art every display of power is vulgar, and a true artist is humble in his creation. He despises making a show of material in his work and a parade of the difficulties of its process. For the power which accumulates things and manipulates them is fundamentally different from the power which transmutes them into the perfection of a creative unity.

And God is humble in His creation. He does not keep His muscles bared, nor does He go out of His way to attract our attention to His store of things or account-book of their cost. He gives out Himself in the abundance of His nature.

It is the final object of man to prove his similarity of nature with God by his fulness of truth, by his creativeness. Whatever he does solely in obedience to natural law, goaded by hunger or other compulsions, he feels at heart to be alien to his own nature. He somehow feels a shame about their evidence in his life and tries to put a cover over it, some cover fashioned by his own creative mind.

For instance, in his necessity for eating there is no difference between man and other creatures, yet he seems unwilling fully to acknowledge this and consequently tries to hide away the hunger element from his meals till it is almost lost to sight. He takes endless care to make his food ornamental and likewise the vessel out of which he takes it. And so, with regulations and designs of his own make, he sets up an elaborate pretension that he is not busy satisfying any legitimate need of the physiological nature.

This is the process by which the unnecessary has assumed an enormously greater proportion than the necessary in our civilization. In its own turn it begets the danger of burdening us with fixed necessities of habit which have not the sanction of nature nor that of our creative freedom but get merely piled up into a refuse heap of conventionality.

It may be said that as life is a growth it cannot have a completeness of expression and, therefore, its only true expression is vigour. As intensity of passion leading to a variety of emotional experiences, and adventures of mind giving rise to a wealth of power and production, constitute what they call living, vigour of feeling and intellect is no doubt a great asset of life. But life, merely taken as a force, is elemental, it is not human. It has its use like steam and electricity, but there is no ideal of perfection in it. Those who make such life an object of their worship lose all pity for the personal man and have no compunction in sacrificing individuals to their blind infatuation for power and experiences. And I repeat it once again that life can only become an end in itself when it is a creation, just as the elements that go to the composition of a flower are fulfilled only when they are a flower.

Growth there must be in life. But growth does not mean an enlargement through additions. Things, such as masonry-structure, which have to be constructed by a gradual building up of materials, do not show their perfection until they are completed. But living things start with their wholeness from the beginning of their growth. Life is a continual process of synthesis. A child is complete in itself; it does not wait for the perfection of its lovability till it has come to the end of its childhood. The enjoyment of a song begins from the beginning of the singing and continually follows its course to the end. But the man whose sole concern is the acquisition of power or material deals with a task which is cursed with eternal incompleteness. For things find no meaning in themselves when their magnitude consists solely of accumulated bulk. They acquire truth only when they are assimilated to a living idea. This assimilation becomes impossible so long as the passion for acquisition occupies all our mind, when there is no large leisure for life force to pursue its own great work of self-creation.

There was a time when commerce was restricted to a narrow circle in society, and was meek enough to acknowledge its limitations. In spite of its usefulness men treated it with condescension, even with disrespect. This was because man tried to maintain an imperious aloofness from all exacting needs, and, while accepting their services, he refused to do homage to them. I believe and hope that in the range of all literature and art there is no single instance of a monied man being glorified for the mere sake of his money. Our Laxmi* is not the goodness of the cash balance in the bank: she is the symbol of that ideal plenitude which is never dissociated from goodness and beauty.

But in recent centuries has come a devastating change in our mentality with regard to the acquisition of money. We not only pursue it but bend our knees to it. For us its call has become the loudest of all voices, reaching even the sanctuaries of our temples. That it should be allowed a sufficiently large place in society there can be no question, but it becomes an outrage when it occupies those seats which are specially reserved for the immortals, by bribing us, by tampering with our moral pride, by recruiting the best strength of society on its side in a traitor's campaign against human ideals, disguising with the help of pageantry and pomp its innate insignificance.

Such a state has come to pass because, with the help of science, the possibility of profit has suddenly become immoderate. The whole of human society throughout its length and breadth has felt the gravitational pull of a giant planet of greed with its concentric rings of innumerable satellites. It has carried to our society a distinct deviation from its moral orbit, its mental balance being upset and its aspirations brought down to the dust. This is why never before in our history have our best instincts and endeavours been so openly flouted as a sickness of a rickety sentimentalism. And what is becoming a constant source of disaster for humanity is the incessant hypnotism of money and its secret action upon the mind. It manufactures opinions, it navigates newspapers through tortuous channels of suppression of truth and exaggeration, it

---

* The Hindu goddess of abundance and fortune, wife of Vishnu.

pulls most of the strings of politics, it secretly maintains all kinds of slavery under all varieties of masks. In former times the intellectual and spiritual powers of this earth upheld their dignity of independence, but today, as in the fatal stage of disease, the influence of money has got into our brain and affected our heart.

Any impetuosity of passion that tends to overwhelm social equilibrium not only produces moral callousness but destroys our reverence for beauty. The truth of this was made evident to us when I set out from Calcutta on my voyage to Japan. The first thing that shocked me with a sense of personal injury was the sight of the ruthless intrusion of factories on both banks of the Ganges, where they are most unbecoming in their brazier-faced effrontery. The blow which it gave to me was owing to the precious memory of the days of my boyhood when the scenery of this river was the only great thing near my birthplace reminding me of the existence of a world made by God's own hands. You all know that Calcutta is an upstart town with no depth of sentiment in her face or in her manners. It may truly be said about its genesis, that in the beginning there was the spirit of the shop which uttered through its megaphone, 'Let there be the office', and there was Calcutta. She brought with her no dowry of distinctions, no majesty of a noble or romantic origin. She never gathered round her any great historical associations, annals of brave sufferings or memory of mighty deeds done. The only thing which gave her the sacred baptism of beauty was the river, which carried the voice of the Genius of our race from an immortal past singing of its aspiration of the boundless. I was fortunate enough to be born before the smoke-belching Iron Dragon had devoured the greater part of the life on its banks; when the landing stairs descending into its water, caressed by its tide, appeared to me like the loving arms of the villages clinging to it.

I am afraid my complaint will evoke a feeling of pitying amusement in the minds of all sober people when these words reach them. To condemn the impairing of the beauty of a river bank and to overlook the substantial fact of the production of a prodigious quantity of gunny bags will sound too exquisitely unpractical to be able to cause any serious harm!

But as an instance of the contrast of the different ideal of a different age as incarnated in the form of a town, the memory of my last visit to Benares comes to my mind. What impressed me most deeply while I was there was the mother-call of the river Ganges which ever filled the atmosphere with an 'unheard melody', attracting the whole population to its bosom every hour of the day. I am proud of the fact that India has felt a most profound love for this river which nourished her civilization on its banks, guiding its course from the majestic silence of the Himalayas to the sea with its myriad voices of solitude. This feeling of love is different in a great measure from the modern sentiment of patriotism. It is not too definitely associated with a particular geography or a limited series of political events. It represents the subconscious memory of a whole country, of her ages of endeavour after spiritual emancipation.

But what about our gunny bags? Sentiments are fine, but gunny bags are indispensable. I admit it, and am willing to allow them a place in society (but in strictly modest moderation), if my opponent will only admit that even gunny bags should have their limits and acknowledge the full worth of man who needs leisure and space for his joy and worship. But if this concession to humanity be denied or curtailed, and if profit and production are allowed to run amuck, they play havoc with our love of beauty, of truth, of justice and with our love for our fellow-beings. That man is brave, that he is social, that he is religious, that he is the seeker of the unknown—these have some aspect of the complete in them; but that he is a manufacturer of gunny bags and other articles has not in itself any idea of an organic wholeness. Therefore utility should never forget its subordinate position in human affairs: it must not be permitted to occupy more than its legitimate place and powers in society, nor to have the liberty to desecrate the poetry of life, or to deaden our sensitiveness to ideals, bragging of our coarseness as a sign of virility and bespattering with the mud of mockery our spiritual nature. That would be like allowing a rugged boulder to sneer at and browbeat the living perfection of a flower.

We have our out-offices in the back yard of our houses. And because they disturb the unity of the idea which is our home, we keep a line of separateness between the outside help bought with money and services of kinship, between necessity and sentiment. But the home gives way to the office if the necessity becomes overwhelming. This has made our modern civilization all out-offices, to which home is an adjunct. Modern civilization has become Shudra* in its character.

For the name Shudra symbolizes one who is merely useful, in whom the man who is above usefulness is not recognized. The word Shudra denotes a classification which includes all named machines who have lost the decency of humanity, be their works manual of intellectual. They are like a walking stomach, or brain, and we feel, in pity, urged to call on God to make them into a man. When man adopted his ideals he did not give success a place of distinction; and even in war he held the ideal of honour above that of success. But success which is Shudra, and whose dwelling is in the office, has arrogantly come into the front. And if through its incessant touch of defilement we contract the ugly habit of deriding sentiments in favour of materials, then the slave dynasty will be confirmed for ever.

This is the root of the struggle of the present age. Man is refusing to accept for good his position as Shudra, and our civilization is feeling ashamed of the degradation imposed upon it by the lust of power and money.

In the old time when commerce was a member of the normal life of man, there ruled the spirit of Laxmi, who with her divine touch of humanity saved wealth from the unseemliness of rampant individualism, mean both in motive and method. Venice had very little that was deformed and discordant; Samarkand and Bokhara had in them the richness of human associations. We can imagine what Delhi and Agra

---

* Servile caste whose duty is to serve the three higher castes according to the Hindu code of Manu.

must have been in the time to which they belonged. They manifested in their development some creatively human aspect of a great empire. Whatever might have been its character, even in their decay they still retain their magnificence which was the true product of the self-respect of man.

Then think of Calcutta, which on one side has its squalid congeries of clerks clinging to the meagre and precarious livelihood short of all margin for beauty and joy accorded to them in a niggardly spirit of utilitarianism, and on the other its pompously formal rows of buildings sheltering a nomadic swarm of money-mongers—with no human link between them, with no common sharing of social amenities. This is the hideousness of modern commerce—it does not stimulate men into a healthy and normal activity of production but organizes and makes use of them by mixing and mangling their minds; it is shabbily parsimonious in all that is connected with human life and extravagant in all that tends to the multiplying of market wares.

I do not for a moment mean to imply that in any particular period of their history men were free from the disturbances of their lower passions. Selfishness ever had its share in their government and trade. Yet there was a struggle for maintaining a balance of forces in our society, and our passions with their rude strength cherished no delusions about their own rank and value, and contrived no clever devices to hoodwink our moral nature. For in those days our intellect was not so tempted to put its weight into the balance on the side of over-greed.

But now our passion for power and money has no equal in the field. It has not only science for its ally, but also other forces that have some semblance of religion, such as nation-worship and the idealizing of self-interest.

Science is producing a habit of mind which is ever weakening in us this spiritual standpoint of truth that has its foundation in our sense of a person as the ultimate and innermost reality of existence. Science has its true sphere in analysing this world as a construction just as a grammarian has his legitimate mission in analysing the syntax of a poem. But the world as a creation is not a construction; it is also more than its syntax. It is a poem, which we are apt to forget when, by exclusive attention, grammar takes complete possession of our mind.

Upon the loss of the sense of religion, the reign of the machine and of method has been firmly established. It is the simplification of man by jettisoning a great part of his treasure; spiritually speaking, he has been made a homeless tramp, getting a freedom which is negative because superficial. Its concentrated hurt had been felt by all the world in the late war. Freed from the bond of spiritual relationship as the medium of the brotherhood of man, the different sections of society are continually being resolved into their elemental character of forces. Labour is a force, and also capital; so are the Government and the people, the man and the woman. It is said that when the forces lying latent even in a handful of dust are liberated from their bond of unity, which is their bond of creation, they can lift St. Paul's Cathedral to the height of a mountain. Such disfranchised forces roving as irresponsible freebooters may be useful to us for certain purposes, but St. Paul's Cathedral is, generally speaking, better for us standing secure on its foundation than shattered into pieces and scattered in the void. To own the secret of mastering these forces is a proud fact for us, but the power of self-control and self-sacrifice within is a truer subject of exultation for mankind. The genii of the *Arabian Nights* may have their lure and fascination for us, but God is infinitely more precious for imparting to our society its spiritual power of creation. But these genii are abroad everywhere; and even after their death-dance in the late war, incantations addressed to them are secretly being muttered, and their red-robed devotees are still getting ready to play tricks upon humanity by suddenly spiriting it away to some hill-top of desolation. The thunder-clouds of revolution which are ominously gathering and flashing their angry teeth and growling, are the outcome of a long process of separation of human personality from human power, reducing man into a ghost of abstraction.

Modern science has outwardly brought all mankind close together. The situation requires the spiritual realization of some great truth of relationship to save human societies from constant conflict of interest and friction of pride. The people who are mere forces, when not organically united, must prove their humanity by some creative transfusion. This is not a mere problem of construction, and therefore does not chiefly fall within the province of science, which deals merely with discovery and invention and not with creation. The outer bonds of telegraph wires and railway lines have helped men all the more efficiently to tear one another to pieces and to rob their weaker fellow-beings of food, of freedom, and of self-respect. Must the sword continue to rule for ever and not the sceptre, and must science after her great achievement of mastering the geography of the earth remain at the head of the administration? Can she establish peace and unity in this world of diverse races? Has it not been sufficiently proved that her material law of ruthless skilfulness can only commandeer the genii of power for her agents but cannot conjure up that spirit of creation which is the love of God and man? And yet science does not show any sign of vacating her seat in favour of humanity or submit to any curtailment of her jurisdiction after her own proper work has been finished. The powerful races who have the scientific mind and method and machinery have taken upon themselves the immense responsibility of the present age. We complain not of their law and government, which are scientifically efficient, but of the desolating deadliness of their machine domination. These people in their dealings with subject races all over the world forget that science and law are not a perfect medium for human communication. They refuse to acknowledge what an ordeal it can be for human beings meekly to have to receive gifts from animated pigeon-holes or condescension from a steam-engine of the latest type. We feel the withering fierceness of the spirit of modern civilization all the more because it beats directly against our human sensibility; and it is we of the Eastern hemisphere who have the right to say that those who represent this great age of great opportunities are furiously building their doom by their renouncement of the divine ideal of personality; for the ultimate truth in man is not in his intellect or in his material wealth; it is in his imagination of sympathy, in his illumination of heart, in his activities of self-sacrifice, in his capacity for extending love far and wide across all barriers of caste and colour, in his realizing this world not as a storehouse of mechanical power but as a habitation of man's soul with its eternal music of beauty and its inner light of a divine presence.

(1920)

The Creative Ideal

4

In an old Sanskrit book there is a verse which describes the essential elements of a picture. The first in order is *Viúpa-bhédáh*—'separateness of forms'. Forms are many, forms are different, each of them having its limits. But if this were absolute, if all forms remained obstinately separate, then there would be a fearful loneliness of multitude. But the varied forms, in their very separateness, must carry something which indicates the paradox of their ultimate unity, otherwise there would be no creation.

So in the same verse, after the enumeration of separateness comes that of *Pramānāni*—proportions. Proportions indicate relationship, the principle of mutual accommodation. A leg dismembered from the body has the fullest licence to make a caricature of itself. But, as a member of the body, it has its responsibility to the living unity which rules the body; it must behave properly, it must keep its proportion. If, by some monstrous chance of physiological profiteering, it could outgrow by yards its fellow-stalker, then we know what a picture it would offer to the spectator and what embarrassment to the body itself. Any attempt to overcome the law of proportion altogether and to assert absolute separateness is rebellion; it means either running the gauntlet of the rest, or remaining segregated.

The same Sanskrit word *Pramānāni,* which in a book of aesthetics means proportions, in a book of logic means the proofs by which the truth of a proposition is ascertained. All proofs of truth are credentials of relationship. Individual facts have to produce such passports to show that they are not expatriated, that they are not a break in the unity of the whole.

The logical relationship present in an intellectual proposition, and the aesthetic relationship indicated in the proportions of a work of art, both agree in one thing. They affirm that truth consists, not in facts, but in harmony of facts. Of this fundamental note of reality it is that the poet has said, 'Beauty is truth, truth beauty.'

Proportions, which prove relativity, form the outward language of creative ideals. A crowd of men is desultory, but in a march of soldiers every man keeps his proportion of time and space and relative movement, which makes him one with the whole vast army. But this is not all. The creation of an army has, for its inner principle, one single idea of the General. According to the nature of that ruling idea, a production is either a work of art or a mere construction. All the materials and regulations of a joint-stock company have the unity of an inner motive. But the expression of this unity itself is not the end; it ever indicates an ulterior purpose. On the other hand, the revelation of a work of art is a fulfilment in itself.

The consciousness of personality, which is the consciousness of unity in ourselves, becomes prominently distinct when coloured by joy or sorrow, or some other emotion. It is like the sky, which is visible because it is blue, and which takes different aspect with the change of colours. In the creation of art, therefore, the energy of an emotional ideal is necessary; as its unity is not like that of a crystal, passive and inert, but actively expressive. Take, for example, the following verse:

> Oh, fly not Pleasure, pleasant-hearted Pleasure,
>   Fold me thy wings, I prithee, yet and stay,
>   For my heart no measure
> Knows, nor other treasure
> To buy a garland for my love to-day
>
> And thou too, Sorrow, tender-hearted Sorrow,
> Thou grey-eyed mourner, fly not yet away.
>   For I fain would borrow
>   Thy sad weeds to-morrow,
> To make a mourning for love's yesterday.

The words in this quotation, merely showing the metre, would have no appeal to us; with all its perfection and its proportion, rhyme and cadence, it would only be a construction. But when it is the outer body of an inner idea it assumes a personality. The idea flows through the rhythm, permeates the words and throbs in their rise and fall. On the other hand, the mere idea of the above-quoted poem, stated in unrhythmic prose, would represent only a fact, inertly static, which would not bear repetition. But the emotional idea, incarnated in a rhythmic form, acquires the dynamic quality needed for those things which take part in the world's eternal pageantry.

Take the following doggerel:

Thirty days hath September,
April, June, and November.

The metre is there, and it simulates the movement of life. But it finds no synchronous response in the metre of our heart-beats; it has not in its centre the living idea which creates for itself an indivisible unity. It is like a bag which is convenient, and not like a body which is inevitable.

This truth, implicit in our own works of art, gives us the clue to the mystery of creation. We find that the endless rhythms of the world are not merely constructive; they strike our own heart-strings and produce music.

Therefore it is we feel that this world is a creation; that in its centre there is a living idea which reveals itself in an eternal symphony, played on innumerable instruments, all keeping perfect time. We know that this great world-verse, that runs from sky to sky, is not made for the mere enumeration of facts—it is not 'Thirty days hath September'—it has its direct revelation in our delight. That delight gives us the key to the truth of existence; it is personality acting upon personalities through incessant manifestations. The solicitor does not sing to his client, but the bridegroom sings to his bride. And when our soul is stirred by the song, we know it claims no fees from us; but it brings the tribute of love and a call from the bridegroom.

It may be said that in pictorial and other arts there are some designs that are purely decorative and apparently have no living and inner ideal to express. But this cannot be true. These decorations carry the emotional motive of the artist, which says: 'I find joy in my creation; it is good.' All the language of joy is beauty. It is necessary to note, however, that joy is not pleasure, and beauty not mere prettiness. Joy is the outcome of detachment from self and lives in freedom of spirit. Beauty is that profound expression of reality which satisfies our hearts without any other allurements but its own ultimate value. When in some pure moments of ecstasy we realize this in the world around us, we see the world, not as merely existing, but as decorated in its forms, sounds, colours and lines; we feel in our hearts that there is One who through all things proclaims: 'I have joy in my creation.'

That is why the Sanskrit verse has given us for the essential elements of a picture, not only the manifoldness of forms and the unity of their proportions, but also *bhāvah,* the emotional idea.

It is needless to say that upon a mere expression of emotion—even the best expression of it—no criterion of art can rest. The following poem is described by the poet as 'An earnest Suit to his unkind Mistress':

> And wilt thou leave me thus?
> Say nay, say nay, for shame!
> To save thee from the blame
> Of all my grief and grame.
> And wilt thou leave me thus?
>   Say nay! say nay!

I am sure the poet would not be offended if I expressed my doubts about the earnestness of his appeal, or the truth of his avowed necessity. He is responsible for the lyric and not for the sentiment, which is mere material. The fire assumes different colours according to the fuel used; but we do not discuss the fuel, only the flames. A lyric is indefinably more than the sentiment expressed in it, as a rose is more than its substance. Let us take a poem in which the earnestness of sentiment is truer and deeper than the one I have quoted above:

The sun,
Closing his benediction,
Sinks, and the darkening air
Thrills with the sense of the triumphing night,—
Night with her train of stars
And her great gift of sleep.
So be my passing!
My task accomplished and the long day done,
My wages taken, and in my heart
Some late lark singing,
Let me be gathered to the quiet West,
The sundown splendid and serene,
Death.

The sentiment expressed in this poem is a subject for a psychologist. But for a poem the subject is completely merged in its poetry, like carbon in a living plant which the lover of plants ignores, leaving it for a charcoal-burner to seek.

This is why, when some storm of feeling sweeps across the country, art is under a disadvantage. In such an atmosphere the boisterous passion breaks through the cordon of harmony and thrusts itself forward as the subject, which with its bulk and pressure dethrones the unity of creation. For a similar reason most of the hymns used in churches suffer from lack of poetry. For in them the deliberate subject, assuming the first importance, benumbs or kills the poem. Most patriotic poems have the same deficiency. They are like hill streams born of sudden showers, which are more proud of their rocky beds than of their water currents; in them the athletic and arrogant subject takes it for granted that the poem is there to give it occasion to display its powers. The subject is the material wealth for the sake of which poetry should never be tempted to barter her soul, even though the temptation should come in the name and shape of public good or some usefulness. Between the artist and his art must be that perfect detachment which is the pure medium of love. He must never make use of this love except for its own perfect expression.

In everyday life our personality moves in a narrow circle of immediate self-interest. And therefore our feelings and events, within that short range, become prominent subjects for ourselves. In their vehement self-assertion they ignore their unity with the All. They rise up like obstructions and obscure their own background. But art gives our personality the disinterested freedom of the eternal, there to find it in its true perspective. To see our own home in flames is not to see fire in its verity. But the fire in the stars is the fire in the heart of the Infinite; there, it is the script of creation.

Matthew Arnold, in his poem addressed to a nightingale, sings:

> Hark! ah, the nightingale—
> The tawny-throated!
> Hark, from that moonlit cedar what a burst!
> What triumph! hark!—what pain!

But pain, when met within the boundaries of limited reality, repels and hurts; it is discordant with the narrow scope of life. But the pain of some great martyrdom has the detachment of eternity. It appears in all its majesty, harmonious in the context of everlasting life; like the thunder-flash in the stormy sky, not on the laboratory wire. Pain on that scale has its harmony in great love; for by hurting love it reveals the infinity of love in all its truth and beauty. On the other hand, the pain involved in business insolvency is discordant; it kills and consumes till nothing remains but ashes.

The poet sings again:

> How thick the bursts come crowding through the leaves!
> Eternal Passion!
> Eternal Pain!

And the truth of pain in eternity has been sung by those Vedic poets who had said, 'From joy has come forth all creation.' They say:

> Sa tapas tapatvá sarvam asrajata yadidam kincha.
> (God from the heat of his pain created all that there is.)

The sacrifice, which is in the heart of creation, is both joy and pain at the same moment. Of this sings a village mystic in Bengal:

My eyes drown in the darkness of joy,
My heart, like a lotus, closes its petals in the rapture of
the dark night.

That song speaks of a joy which is deep like the blue sea, endless like the blue sky; which has the magnificence of the night, and in its limitless darkness enfolds the radiant worlds in the awfulness of peace; it is the unfathomed joy in which all sufferings are made one.

A poet of mediaeval India tells us about his source of inspiration in a poem containing a question and an answer:

Where were your songs, my bird, when you spent your
nights in the nest?
Was not all your pleasure stored therein?
What makes you lose your heart to the sky, the sky that
is limitless?

The bird answers:

I had my pleasure while I rested within bounds.
When I soared into the limitless, I found my songs!

To detach the individual idea from its confinement of everyday facts and to give its soaring wings the freedom of the universal: this is the function of poetry. The ambition of Macbeth, the jealousy of Othello, would be at best sensational in police court proceedings; but in Shakespeare's dramas they are carried among the flaming constellations where creation throbs with Eternal Passion, Eternal Pain.

The Religion of an Artist

5

I was born in 1861: That is not an important date of history, but it belongs to a great epoch in Bengal, when the currents of three movements had met in the life of our country. One of these, the religious, was introduced by a very greathearted man of gigantic intelligence, Raja Rammohun Roy. It was revolutionary, for he tried to reopen the channel of spiritual life which had been obstructed for many years by the sands and debris of creeds that were formal and materialistic, fixed in external practices lacking spiritual significance. People who cling to an ancient past have their pride in the antiquity of their accumulations, in the sublimity of time-honoured walls around them. They grow nervous and angry when some great spirit, some lover of truth, breaks open their enclosure and floods it with the sunshine of thought and the breath of life. Ideas cause movement and all forward movements they consider to be a menace to their warehouse security.

This was happening about the time I was born. I am proud to say that my father was one of the great leaders of that movement, a movement for whose sake he suffered ostracism and braved social indignities. I was born in this atmosphere of the advent of new ideals, which at the same time were old, older than all the things of which that age was proud.

There was a second movement equally important. Bankimchandra Chatterjee, who though much older than myself, was my contemporary and lived long enough for me to see him, was the first pioneer in the literary revolution which happened in Bengal about that time. Before his arrival our literature had been oppressed by a rigid rhetoric that choked its life and loaded it with ornaments that became its fetters.

Bankimchandra was brave enough to go against the orthodoxy which believed in the security of tombstones and in that finality which can only belong to the lifeless. He lifted the dead weight of ponderous forms from our language and with a touch of his magic wand aroused our literature from her age-long sleep. A great promise and a vision of beauty she revealed to us when she awoke in the fulness of her strength and grace.

There was yet another movement started about this time called the National. It was not fully political, but it began to give voice to the mind of our people trying to assert their own personality. It was a voice of impatience at the humiliation constantly heaped upon us by people who were not oriental, and who had, especially at that time, the habit of sharply dividing the human world into the good and the bad according to the hemispheres to which they belong.

This contemptuous spirit of separatedness was perpetually hurting us and causing great damage to our own world of culture. It generated in our young men a distrust of all things that had come to them as an inheritance from their past. The old Indian pictures and other works of art were laughed at by our students in imitation of the laughter of their European schoolmasters of that age of philistinism.

Though later on our teachers themselves had changed their mind, their disciples had hardly yet fully regained confidence in the merit of our art. They have had a long period of encouragement in developing an appetite for third-rate copies of French pictures, for gaudy oleographs abjectly cheap, for the pictures that are products of mechanical accuracy of a stereotyped standard, and they still considered it to be a symptom of superior culture to be able disdainfully to refuse oriental works of creation.

The modern young men of that period nodded their heads and said that true originality lay not in the discovery of the rhythm of the essential in the heart of reality but in the full lips, tinted cheeks and bare breasts of imported pictures. The same spirit of rejection, born of utter ignorance, was cultivated in other departments of our culture. It was the result of the hypnotism exercised upon the minds of the younger generation by people who were loud of voice and strong of arm. The national movement was started to proclaim that we must not be indiscriminate in our rejection of the past. This was not a reactionary movement but a revolutionary one, because it set out with a great courage to deny and to oppose all pride in mere borrowings.

These three movements were on foot and in all three the members of my own family took active part. We were ostracized because of our heterodox opinions about religion and therefore we enjoyed the freedom of the outcast. We had to build our own world with our own thoughts and energy of mind.

I was born and brought up in an atmosphere of the confluence of three movements, all of which were revolutionary. My family had to live its own life, which led me from my young days to seek guidance for my own self-expression in my own inner standard of judgment. The medium of expression doubtless was my mother tongue. But the language which belonged to the people had to be modulated according to the urge which I as an individual had.

No poet should borrow his medium ready-made from some shop of orthodox respectability. He should not only have his own seeds but prepare his own soil. Each poet has his own distinct medium of language—not because the whole language is of his own make, but because his individual use of it, having life's magic touch, transforms it into a special vehicle of his own creation.

The races of man have poetry in their heart and it is necessary for them to give, as far as is possible, a perfect expression to their sentiments. For this they must have a medium, moving and pliant, which can freshly become their very own, age after age. All great languages have undergone and are still undergoing changes. Those languages which resist the spirit of change are doomed and will never produce great harvests of thought and literature. When forms become fixed, the spirit either weakly accepts its imprisonment within them or rebels. All revolutions consist of the fight of the within against invasion by the without.

There was a great chapter in the history of life on this earth when some irresistible inner force in man found its way out into the scheme of things, and sent forth its triumphant mutinous voice, with the cry that it was not going to be overwhelmed from outside by the huge brute beast of a body. How helpless it appeared at the moment, but has it not nearly won? In our social life also revolution breaks out when some power concentrates itself in outside arrangements and threatens to enslave for its own purpose the power which we have within us.

When an organization which is a machine becomes a central force, political, commercial, educational or religious, it obstructs the free flow of inner life of the people and waylays and exploits it for the augmentation of its own power. Today, such concentration of power is fast multiplying on the outside and the cry of the oppressed spirit of man is in the air which struggles to free itself from the grip of screws and bolts, of unmeaning obsessions.

Revolution must come and men must risk revilement and misunderstanding, especially from those who want to be comfortable, who put their faith in materialism, and who belong truly to the dead past and not to modern times, the past that had its age in distant antiquity when physical flesh and size predominated, and not the mind of man.

Purely physical dominance is mechanical and modern machines are merely exaggerating our bodies, lengthening and multiplying our limbs. The modern mind, in its innate childishness, delights in this enormous bodily bulk, representing an inordinate material power, saying: "Let me have the big toy and no sentiment which can disturb it." It does not realize that in this we are returning to that antediluvian age which revelled in its production of gigantic physical frames, leaving no room for the freedom of the inner spirit.

All great human movements in the world are related to some great ideal. Some of you may say that such a doctrine of spirit has been in its death-throes for over a century and is now moribund; that we have nothing to rely upon but external forces and material foundations. But I say, on my part, that your doctrine was obsolete long ago. It was exploded in the springtime of life, when mere size was swept off the face of the world, and was replaced by man, brought naked into the heart of creation, man with his helpless body, but with his indomitable mind and spirit.

When I began my life as a poet, the writers among our educated community took their guidance from their English textbooks which poured upon them lessons that did not fully saturate their minds. I suppose it was fortunate for me that I never in my life had the kind of academic training which is considered proper for a boy of respectable family. Though I cannot say I was altogether free from the influence that ruled young minds of those days, the course of my writings was nevertheless saved from the groove of imitative forms. In my versification, vocabulary and ideas, I yielded myself to the vagaries of an untutored fancy which brought castigation upon me from critics who were learned, and uproarious laughter from the witty. My ignorance combined with my heresy turned me into a literary outlaw.

When I began my career I was ridiculously young; in fact, I was the youngest of that band who had made themselves articulate. I had neither the protective armour of mature age, nor enough English to command respect. So in my seclusion of contempt and qualified encouragement I had my freedom. Gradually I grew up in years—for which, however, I claim no credit. Steadily I cut my way through derision and occasional patronage into a recognition in which the proportion of praise and blame was very much like that of land and water on our earth.

What gave me boldness when I was young was my early acquaintance with the old Vaishnava poems of Bengal, full of the freedom of metre and courage of expression. I think I was only twelve when these poems first began to be reprinted. I surreptitiously got hold of copies from the desks of my elders. For the edification of the young I must confess that this was not right for a boy of my age. I should have been passing my examinations and not following a path that would lead to loss of marks. I must also admit that the greater part of these lyrics was erotic and not quite suited to a boy just about to reach his teens. But my imagination was fully occupied with the beauty of their forms and the music of their words; and their breath, heavily laden with voluptuousness, passed over my mind without distracting it.

My vagabondage in the path of my literary career had another reason. My father was the leader of a new religious movement, a strict monotheism based upon the teachings of the Upanishads. My countrymen in Bengal thought him almost as bad as a Christian, if not worse. So we were completely ostracized, which probably saved me from another disaster, that of imitating our own past.

Most of the members of my family had some gift—some were artists, some poets, some musicians and the whole atmosphere of our home was permeated with the spirit of creation. I had a deep sense almost from infancy of the beauty of Nature, an intimate feeling of companionship with the trees and the clouds, and felt in tune with the musical touch of the seasons in the air. At the same time, I had a peculiar susceptibility to human kindness. All these craved expression. The very earnestness of my emotions yearned to be true to themselves, though I was too immature to give their expression any perfection of form.

Since then I have gained a reputation in my country, but till very late a strong current of antagonism in a large section of my countrymen persisted. Some said that my poems did not spring from the national heart; some complained that they were incomprehensible; others that they were unwholesome. In fact, I have never had complete acceptance from my own people, and that too has been a blessing; for nothing is so demoralizing as unqualified success.

This is the history of my career. I wish I could reveal it more clearly through the narration of my own work in my own language. I hope that will be possible some day or other. Languages are jealous. They do not give up their best treasures to those who try to deal with them through an intermediary belonging to an alien rival. We have to court them in person and dance attendance on them. Poems are not like market commodities transferable. We cannot receive the smiles and glances of our sweetheart through an attorney, however diligent and dutiful he may be.

I myself have tried to get at the wealth of beauty in the literature of the European languages, long before I gained a full right to their hospitality. When I was young I tried to approach Dante, unfortunately through an English translation. I failed utterly, and felt it my pious duty to desist. Dante remained a closed book to me.

I also wanted to know German literature and, by reading Heine in translation, I thought I had caught a glimpse of the beauty there. Fortunately I met a missionary lady from Germany and asked her help. I worked hard for some months, but being rather quick-witted, which is not a good quality, I was not persevering. I had the dangerous facility which helps one to guess the meaning too easily. My teacher thought I had almost mastered the language, which was not true. I succeeded, however, in getting through Heine, like a man walking in sleep crossing unknown paths with ease, and I found immense pleasure.

Then I tried Goethe. But that was too ambitious. With the help of the little German I had learnt, I did go through *Faust*. I believe I found my entrance to the palace, not like one who has keys for all the doors, but as a casual visitor who is tolerated in some general guest-room, comfortable but not intimate. Properly speaking, I do not know my Goethe, and in the same way many other great luminaries are dusky to me.

This is as it should be. Man cannot reach the shrine if he does not make the pilgrimage. So, one must not hope to find anything true from my own language in translation.

In regard to music, I claim to be something of a musician myself. I have composed many songs which have defied the canons of orthodox propriety and good people are disgusted at the impudence of a man who is audacious only because he is untrained. But I persist, and God forgives me because I do not know what I do. Possibly that is the best way of doing things in the sphere of art. For I find that people blame, but also sing my songs, even if not always correctly.

Please do not think I am vain. I can judge myself objectively and can openly express admiration for my own work, because I am modest. I do not hesitate to say that my songs have found their place in the heart of my land, along with her flowers that are never exhausted, and that the folk of the future, in days of joy or sorrow or festival, will have to sing them. This too is the work of a revolutionist.

If I feel reluctant to speak about my own view of religion, it is because I have not come to my own religion through the portals of passive acceptance of a particular creed owing to some accident of birth. I was born to a family who were pioneers in the revival in our country of a religion based upon the utterance of Indian sages in the Upanishads. But owing to my idiosyncrasy of temperament, it was impossible for me to accept any religious teaching on the only ground that people in my surroundings believed it to be true. I could not persuade myself to imagine that I had religion simply because everybody whom I might trust believed in its value.

My religion is essentially a poet's religion. Its touch comes to me through the same unseen and trackless channels as does the inspiration of my music. My religious life has followed the same mysterious line of growth as has my poetical life. Somehow they are wedded to each other, and though their betrothal had a long period of ceremony, it was kept secret from me. I am not, I hope, boasting when I confess to my gift of poesy, an instrument of expression delicately responsive to the breath that comes from depth of feeling. From my infancy I had the keen sensitiveness which always kept my mind tingling with consciousness of the world around me, natural and human.

I had been blessed with that sense of wonder which gives a child his right of entry into the treasure-house of mystery which is in the heart of existence. I neglected my studies because they rudely summoned me away from the world around me, which was my friend and my companion, and when I was thirteen I freed myself from the clutch of an educational system that tried to keep me imprisoned within the stone-walls of lessons.

I had a vague notion as to who or what it was that touched my heart's chords, like the infant which does not know its mother's name, or who or what she is. The feeling which I always had was a deep satisfaction of personality that flowed into my nature through living channels of communication from all sides.

It was a great thing for me that my consciousness was never dull about the facts of the surrounding world. That the cloud was the cloud, that a flower was a flower, was enough, because they directly spoke to me, because I could not be indifferent to them. I still remember the very moment, one afternoon, when coming back from school I alighted from the carriage and suddenly saw in the sky, behind the upper terrace of our house, an exuberance of deep, dark rain-clouds lavishing rich, cool shadows on the atmosphere. The marvel of it, the very generosity of its presence, gave me a joy which was freedom, the freedom we feel in the love of our dear friend.

There is an illusion I have made use of in another paper, in which I supposed that a stranger from some other planet has paid a visit to our earth and happens to hear the sound of a human voice on the gramophone. All that is obvious to him, and most seemingly active, is the revolving disk; he is unable to discover the personal truth that lies behind, and so might accept the impersonal scientific fact of the disk as final—the fact that could be touched and measured. He would wonder how it could be possible for a machine to speak to the soul. Then if in pursuing the mystery, he should suddenly come to the heart of the music through a meeting with the composer, he would at once understand the meaning of that music as a personal communication.

Mere information of facts, mere discovery of power, belongs to the outside and not to the inner soul of things. Gladness is the one criterion of truth as we know when we have touched Truth by the music it gives, by the joy of the greeting it sends forth to the truth in us. That is the true foundation of all religions; it is not in dogma. As I have said before, it is not as ether waves that we receive light; the morning does not wait for some scientist for its introduction to us. In the same way, we touch the infinite reality immediately within us only when we perceive the pure truth of love or goodness, not through the explanation of theologians, not through the erudite discussion of ethical doctrines.

I have already confessed that my religion is a poet's religion; all that I feel about it is from vision and not from knowledge. I frankly say that I cannot satisfactorily answer questions about the problem of evil, or about what happens after death. And yet I am sure that there have come moments when my soul has touched the infinite and has become intensely conscious of it through the illumination of joy. It has been said in our Upanishads that our mind and our words come away baffled from the supreme Truth, but he who knows That, through the immediate joy of his own soul, is saved from all doubts and fears.

In the night we stumble over things and become acutely conscious of their individual separateness, but the day reveals the great unity which embraces them. And the man, whose inner vision is bathed in an illumination of his consciousness, at once realizes the spiritual unity reigning supreme over all differences of race and his mind no longer awkwardly stumbles over individual facts of separateness in the human world, accepting them as final, he realizes that peace is in the inner harmony which dwells in truth, and not in any outer adjustments; and that beauty carries an eternal assurance of our spiritual relationship to reality, which waits for its perfection in the response of our love.

II

The renowned Vedic commentator, Sāyanāchārya, says:

> यज्ञे हुताशिष्टस्य ओदनस्य सर्वजगतकारणभूता
>
> ब्रह्माभेदेण स्तुतिः क्रियते।।

> The food offering which is left over after the completion of sacrificial rites is praised because it is symbolical of *Brahma,* the original source of the universe.

According to this explanation, *Brahma* is boundless in his superfluity which inevitably finds its expression in the eternal world process. Here we have the doctrine of the genesis of creation, and therefore of the origin of art. Of all living creatures in the world, man has his vital and mental energy vastly in excess of his need, which urges him to work in various lines of creation for its own sake. Like *Brahma* himself, he takes joy in productions that are unnecessary to him, and therefore representing his extravagance and not his hand-to-mouth penury. The voice that is just enough can speak and cry to the extent needed for everyday use, but that which is abundant sings, and in it we find our joy. Art reveals man's wealth of life, which seeks its freedom in forms of perfection which are an end in themselves.

All that is inert and inanimate is limited to the bare fact of existence. Life is perpetually creative because it contains in itself that surplus which ever overflows the boundaries of the immediate time and space, restlessly pursuing its adventure of expression in the varied forms of self-realization. Our living body has its vital organs that are important in maintaining its efficiency, but this body is not a mere convenient sack for the purpose of holding stomach, heart, lungs and brains; it is an image—its highest value is in the fact that it communicates its personality. It has colour, shape and movement, most of which belong to the superfluous, that are needed only for self-expression and not for self-preservation.

This living atmosphere of superfluity in man is dominated by his imagination, as the earth's atmosphere by the light. It helps us to integrate desultory facts in a vision of harmony and then to translate it into our activities for the very joy of its perfection, it invokes in us the Universal Man who is the seer and the doer of all times and countries. The immediate consciousness of reality in its purest form, unobscured by the shadow of self-interest, irrespective of moral or utilitarian recommendation, gives us joy as does the self-revealing personality of our own. What in common language we call beauty, which is in harmony of lines, colours, sounds, or in grouping of words or thoughts, delights us only because we cannot help admitting a truth in it that is ultimate. 'Love is enough', the poet has said; it carries its own explanation, the joy of which can only be expressed in a form of art which also has that finality. Love gives evidence to something which is outside us but which intensely exists and thus stimulates the sense of our own existence. It radiantly reveals the reality of its objects, though these may lack qualities that are valuable or brilliant.

The *I am* in me realizes its own extension, its own infinity whenever it truly realizes something else. Unfortunately, owing to our limitations and a thousand and one preoccupations, a great part of our world, though closely surrounding us, is far away from the lamp-post of our attention: it is dim, it passes by us, a caravan of shadows, like the landscape seen in the night from the window of an illuminated railway compartment: the passenger knows that the outside world exists, that it is important, but for the time being the railway carriage for him is far more significant. If among the innumerable objects in this world there be a few that come under the full illumination of our soul and thus assume reality for us, they constantly cry to our creative mind for a permanent representation. They belong to the same domain as the desire of ours which represents the longing for the permanence of our own self.

I do not mean to say that things to which we are bound by the tie of self-interest have the inspiration of reality; on the contrary, these are eclipsed by the shadow of our own self. The servant is not more real to us than the beloved. The narrow emphasis of utility diverts our attention from the complete man to the merely useful man. The thick label of market-price obliterates the ultimate value of reality.

That fact that we exist has its truth in the fact that everything else does exist, and the 'I am' in me crosses its finitude whenever it deeply realizes itself in the 'Thou art'. This crossing of the limit produces joy, the joy that we have in beauty, in love, in greatness. Self-forgetting, and in a higher degree, self-sacrifice, is our acknowledgement of this our experience of the infinite. This is the philosophy which explains our joy in all arts, the arts that in their creations intensify the sense of the unity which is the unity of truth we carry within ourselves. The personality in me is a self-conscious principle of a living unity; it at once comprehends and yet transcends all the details of facts that are individually mine, my knowledge, feeling, wish and will, my memory, my hope, my love, my activities, and all my belongings. This personality which has the sense of the *One* in its nature, realizes it in things, thoughts and facts made into units. The principle of unity which it contains is more or less perfectly satisfied in a beautiful face or a picture, a poem, a song, a character or a harmony of inter-related ideas or facts and then for it these things become intensely real, and therefore joyful. Its standard of reality, the reality that has its perfect revelation in a perfection of harmony, is hurt when there is a consciousness of discord—because discord is against the fundamental unity which is in its centre.

All other facts have come to us through the gradual course of our experience, and our knowledge of them is constantly undergoing contradictory changes through the discovery of new data. We can never be sure that we have come to know the final character of anything that there is. But such a knowledge has come to us immediately with a conviction which needs no arguments to support it. It is this, that all my activities have their sources in this personality of mine which is indefinable and yet about the truth of which I am more certain than anything in this world. Though all the direct evidence that can be weighed and measured support the fact that only my fingers are producing marks on the paper, yet no sane man ever can doubt that it is not these mechanical movements that are the true origin of my writings but some entity that can never be known unless known through sympathy. Thus we have come to realize in our own person the two aspects of activities, one of which is the aspect of law represented in the medium, and the other the aspect of will residing in the personality.

Limitation of the unlimited is personality: God is personal where he creates.

He accepts the limits of his own law and the play goes on, which is this world whose reality is in its relation to the Person. Things are distinct not in their essence but in their appearance; in other words, in their relation to one to whom they appear. This is art, the truth of which is not in substance or logic, but in expression. Abstract truth may belong to science and metaphysics, but the world of reality belongs to Art.

The world as an art is the play of the Supreme Person revelling in image making. Try to find out the ingredients of the image—they elude you, they never reveal to you the eternal secret of appearance. In your effort to capture life as expressed in living tissue, you will find carbon, nitrogen and many other things utterly unlike life, but never life itself. The appearance does not offer any commentary of itself through its material. You may call it *māyā* and pretend to disbelieve it, but the great artist, the *māyāvin,* is not hurt. For art is *māyā*, it has no other explanation but that it seems to be what it is. It never tries to conceal its evasiveness, it mocks even its own definition and plays the game of hide-and-seek through its constant flight in changes.

And thus life, which is an incessant explosion of freedom, finds its metre in a continual falling back in death. Every day is a death, every moment even. If not, there would be amorphous desert of deathlessness eternally dumb and still. So life is *māyā,* as moralists love to say, it *is* and *is not.* All that we find in it is the rhythm through which it shows itself. Are rocks and minerals any better? Has not science shown us the fact that the ultimate difference between one element and another is only that of rhythm? The fundamental distinction of gold from mercury lies merely in the difference of rhythm in their respective atomic constitution, like the distinction of the king from his subject which is not in their different constituents, but in the different metres of their situation and circumstance. There you find behind the scene the Artist, the Magician of rhythm, who imparts an appearance of substance to the unsubstantial.

What is rhythm? It is the movement generated and regulated by harmonious restriction. This is the creative force in the hand of the artist. So long as words remain in uncadenced prose form, they do not give any lasting feeling of reality. The moment they are taken and put into rhythm they vibrate into a radiance. It is the same with the rose. In the pulp of its petals you may find everything that went to make the rose, but the rose which is *māyā*, an image, is lost; its finality which has the touch of the infinite is gone. The rose appears to me to be still, but because of its metre of composition it has a lyric of movement within that stillness, which is the same as the dynamic quality of a picture that has a perfect harmony. It produces a music in our consciousness by giving it a swing of motion synchronous with its own. Had the picture consisted of a disharmonious aggregate of colours and lines, it would be deadly still.

In perfect rhythm, the art-form becomes like the stars which in their seeming stillness are never still, like a motionless flame that is nothing but movement. A great picture is always speaking, but news from a newspaper, even of some tragic happening, is still-born. Some news may be a mere commonplace in the obscurity of a journal; but give it a proper rhythm and it will never cease to shine. That is art. It has the magic wand which gives undying reality to all things it touches, and relates them to the personal being in us. We stand before its productions and say: I know you as I know myself, you are real.

A Chinese friend of mine, while travelling with me through the streets of Peking, suddenly, with great excitement, called my attention to a donkey. Ordinarily a donkey does not have any special force of truth for us, except when it kicks us or when we need its reluctant service. But in such cases, the truth is not emphasized in the donkey but in some purpose or bodily pain exterior to it. The behaviour of my Chinese friend at once reminded me of the Chinese poems in which the delightful sense of reality is so spontaneously felt and so simply expressed.

This sensitiveness to the touch of things, such abundant delight in the recognition of them, is obstructed when insistent purposes become innumerable and intricate in our society, when problems crowd in our path clamouring for attention, and life's movement is impeded with things and thoughts too difficult for a harmonious assimilation.

This has been growing evident every day in the modern age, which gives more time to the acquisition of life's equipment than to the enjoyment of it. In fact, life itself is made secondary to life's materials, even like a garden buried under the bricks gathered for the garden wall. Somehow the mania for bricks and mortar grows, the kingdom of rubbish dominates, the days of spring are made futile and the flowers never come.

Our modern mind, a hasty tourist, in its rush over the miscellaneous, ransacks cheap markets of curios which mostly are delusions. This happens because its natural sensibility for simple aspects of existence is dulled by constant preoccupations that divert it. The literature that it produces seems always to be poking her nose into out-of-the-way places for things and effects that are out of the common. She racks her resources in order to be striking. She elaborates inconstant changes in style, as in modern millinery; and the product suggests more the polish of steel than the bloom of life.

Fashions in literature that rapidly tire of themselves seldom come from the depth. They belong to the frothy rush of the surface, with its boisterous clamours for the recognition of the moment. Such literature, by its very strain, exhausts its inner development and quickly passes through outer changes like autumn leaves—produces with the help of paints and patches an up-to-dateness, shaming its own appearance of the immediately preceding date. Its expressions are often grimaces, like the cactus of the desert which lacks modesty in its distortions and peace in its thorns, in whose attitude an aggressive discourtesy bristles up, suggesting a forced pride of poverty. We often come across its analogy in some of the modern writings which are difficult to ignore because of their prickly surprises and paradoxical gesticulations. Wisdom is not rare in these works, but it is a wisdom that has lost confidence in its serene dignity, afraid of being ignored by crowds which are attracted by the extravagant and the unusual. It is sad to see wisdom struggling to seem clever, a prophet arrayed in caps and bells before an admiring multitude.

But in all great arts, literary or otherwise, man has expressed his feelings that are usual in a form that is unique and yet not abnormal. When Wordsworth described in his poem a life deserted by love, he invoked for his art the *usual* pathos expected by all normal minds in connection with such a subject. But the picture in which he incarnated the sentiment was unexpected and yet every sane reader acknowledges it with joy when the image is held before him of:

...a forsaken bird's nest filled with snow
Mid its own bush of leafless eglantine.

On the other hand, I have read some modern writing in which the coming out of the stars in the evening is described as the sudden eruption of disease in the bloated body of darkness. The writer seems afraid to own the feeling of a cool purity in the star-sprinkled night which is *usual,* lest he should be found out as commonplace. From the point of view of realism the image may not be wholly inappropriate and may be considered as outrageously virile in its unshrinking incivility. But this is not art; this is a jerky shriek, something like the convulsive advertisement of the modern market that exploits mob psychology against its inattention. To be tempted to create an illusion of forcefulness through an over-emphasis of abnormality is a sign of anaesthesia. It is the waning vigour of imagination which employs desperate dexterity in the present-day art for producing shocks in order to poke out into a glare the sensation of the unaccustomed. When we find that the literature of any period is laborious in the pursuit of a spurious novelty in its manner and matter, we must know that it is the symptom of old age, of anaemic sensibility which seeks to stimulate its palsied taste with the pungency of indecency and the tingling touch of intemperance. It has been explained too that these symptoms mostly are the outcome of a reaction against the last-century literature which developed a mannerism too daintily saccharine, unmanly in the luxury of its toilet and over-delicacy of its expressions. It seemed to have reached an extreme limit of refinement which almost codified its conventions, making it easy for the timid talents to reach a comfortable level of literary respectability. This explanation may be true; but unfortunately reactions seldom have the repose of spontaneity, they often represent the obverse side of the mintage which they try to repudiate as false. A reaction against a particular mannerism is liable to produce its own mannerism in a militant fashion, using the toilet preparation of the war paint, deliberately manufactured style of primitive rudeness. Tired of the elaborately planned flower-beds, the gardener proceeds with grim determination to set up everywhere artificial rocks, avoiding natural inspiration of rhythm in deference to a fashion of tyranny which itself is a tyranny of fashion. The same herd instinct is followed in a cult of rebellion as it was in the cult of conformity and the defiance, which is a mere counteraction of obedience, also shows obedience in a defiant fashion. Fanaticism of virility produces a brawny athleticism meant for a circus and not the natural chivalry which is modest but invincible, claiming its sovereign seat of honour in all arts.

It has often been said by its advocates that this show of the rudely loud and cheaply lurid in art has its justification in the unbiased recognition of facts as such; and according to them realism must not be shunned even if it be ragged and evil-smelling. But when it does not concern science but concerns the arts we must draw a distinction between realism and reality. In its own wide perspective of normal environment, disease is a reality which has to be acknowledged in literature. But disease in a hospital is realism fit for the use of science. It is an abstraction which, if allowed to haunt literature, may assume a startling appearance because of its unreality. Such vagrant spectres do not have a proper modulation in a normal surrounding; and they offer a false proportion in their feature because the proportion of their environment is tampered with. Such a curtailment of the essential is not art, but a trick which exploits mutilation in order to assert a false claim to reality. Unfortunately men are not rare who believe that what forcibly startles them allows them to see more than the facts which are balanced and restrained, which they have to woo and win.

Very likely, owing to the lack of leisure, such persons are growing in number, and the dark cellars of sex-psychology and drug-stores of moral virulence are burgled to give them the stimulus which they wish to believe to be the stimulus of aesthetic reality.

I know a simple line sung by some primitive folk in our neighbourhood which I translate thus: 'My heart is like a pebble-bed hiding a foolish stream.' The psycho-analyst may classify it as an instance of repressed desire and thus at once degrade it to a mere specimen advertising a supposed fact, as it does a piece of coal suspected of having smuggled within its dark the flaming wine of the sun of a forgotten age. But it is literature; and what might have been the original stimulus that startled this thought into a song, the significant fact about it is that it has taken the shape of an image, a creation of a uniquely personal and yet universal character. The facts of the repression of a desire are numerously common; but this particular expression is singularly uncommon. The listener's mind is touched not because it is a psychological fact, but because it is an individual poem, representing a personal reality, belonging to all time and place in the human world.

But this is not all. This poem no doubt owed its form to the touch of the person who produced it; but at the same time with a gesture of utter detachment, it has transcended its material—the emotional mood of the author. It has gained its freedom from any biographical bondage by taking a rhythmic perfection which is precious in its own exclusive merit. There is a poem which confesses by its title its origin in a mood of dejection. Nobody can say that to a lucid mind the feeling of despondency has anything pleasantly memorable. Yet these verses are not allowed to be forgotten, because directly a poem is fashioned, it is eternally freed from its genesis, it minimizes its history and emphasizes its independence. The sorrow which was solely personal in an emperor was liberated directly it took the form of verses in stone, it became a triumph of lament, an overflow of delight, hiding the black boulder of its suffering source. The same thing is true of all creation. A dewdrop is a perfect integrity that has no filial memory of its parentage.

When I use the word creation, I mean that through it some imponderable abstractions have assumed a concrete unity in its relation to us. Its substance can be analyzed but not this unity which is in its self-introduction. Literature as an art offers us the mystery which is in its unity.

We read the poem:

Never seek to tell thy love
  Love that never told can be;
For the gentle wind does move
  Silently, invisibly.
I told my love, I told my love,
  I told all my heart;
Trembling cold in ghastly fears
  Ah, she did depart.
Soon as she was gone from me
  A traveller came by;
Silently, invisibly,
  He took her with a sigh.

It has its grammar, its vocabulary. When we divide them part by part and try to torture out a confession from them, the poem which is *one* departs like the gentle wind, silently, invisibly. No one knows how it exceeds all its parts, transcends all its laws, and communicates with the person. The significance which is in unity is an eternal wonder.

As for the definite meaning of the poem, we may have our doubts. If it were told in ordinary prose, we might feel impatient and be roused to contradict it. We would certainly have asked for an explanation as to who the traveller was and why he took away love without any reasonable provocation. But in this poem we need not ask for an explanation unless we are hopelessly addicted to meaning-collection which is like the collection mania for dead butterflies. The poem as a creation, which is something more than as an idea, inevitably conquers our attention; and any meaning which we feel in its words is like the feeling in a beautiful face of a smile that is inscrutable, elusive and profoundly satisfactory.

The unity as a poem introduces itself in a rhythmic language in a gesture of character. Rhythm is not merely in some measured blending of words, but in a significant adjustment of ideas, in a music of thought produced by a subtle principle of distribution, which is not primarily logical but evidential. The meaning which the word character contains is difficult to define. It is comprehended in a special grouping of aspects which gives it an irresistible impetus. The combination it represents may be uncouth, may be unfinished, discordant; yet it has a dynamic vigour in its totality which claims recognition, often against our wishes for the assent of our reason. An avalanche has a character, which even a heavier pile of snow has not; its character is in its massive movement, its incalculable possibilities.

It is for the artist to remind the world that with the truth of our expression we grow in truth. When the man-made world is less an expression of man's creative soul than a mechanical device for some purpose of power, then it hardens itself, acquiring proficiency at the cost of the subtle suggestiveness of living growth. In his creative activities man makes Nature instinct with his own life and love. But with his utilitarian energies he fights Nature, banishes her from his world, deforms and defiles her with the ugliness of his ambitions.

This world of man's own manufacture, with its discordant shrieks and swagger, impresses on him the scheme of a universe which has no touch of the person and therefore no ultimate significance. All the great civilizations that have become extinct must have come to their end through such wrong expression of humanity; through parasitism on a gigantic scale bred by wealth, by man's clinging reliance on material resources; through a scoffing spirit of denial, of negation, robbing us of our means of sustenance in the path of truth.

It is for the artist to proclaim his faith in the everlasting yes—to say: 'I believe that there is an ideal hovering over and permeating the earth, an ideal of that Paradise which is not the mere outcome of fancy, but the ultimate reality in which all things dwell and move.'

I believe that the vision of Paradise is to be seen in the sunlight and the green of the earth, in the beauty of the human face and the wealth of human life, even in objects that are seemingly insignificant and unprepossessing. Everywhere in this earth the spirit of Paradise is awake and sending forth its voice. It reaches our inner ear without our knowing it. It tunes our harp of life which sends our aspiration in music beyond the finite, not only in prayers and hopes, but also in temples which are flames of fire in stone, in pictures which are dreams made everlasting, in the dance which is ecstatic meditation in the still centre of movement.

(1936)

6

The Artist

The fundamental desire of life is the desire to exist. It claims from us a vast amount of training and experience about the necessaries of livelihood. Yet it does not cost me much to confess that the food that I have taken, the dress that I wear, the house where I have my lodging, represent a stupendous knowledge, practice and organization which I helplessly lack; for I find that I am not altogether despised for such ignorance and inefficiency. Those who read me seem fairly satisfied that I am nothing better than a poet or perhaps a philosopher—which latter reputation I do not claim and dare not hold through the precarious help of misinformation.

It is quite evident in spite of my deficiency that in human society I represent a vocation, which though superfluous has yet been held worthy of commendation. In fact, I am encouraged in my rhythmic futility by being offered moral and material incentives for its cultivation. If a foolish blackbird did not know how to seek its food, to build its nest, or to avoid its enemies, but specialized in singing, its fellow creatures, urged by their own science of genetics, would dutifully allow it to starve and perish. That I am not treated in a similar fashion is the evidence of an immense difference between the animal existence and the civilization of man. His great distinction dwells in the indefinite margin of life in him which affords a boundless background for his dreams and creations. And it is in this realm of freedom that he realizes his divine dignity, his great human truth, and is pleased when I as a poet sing victory to him, to Man the self-revealer, who goes on exploring ages of creation to find himself in perfection.

Reality, in all its manifestations, reveals itself in the emotional and imaginative background of our mind. We know it, not because we can think of it, but because we directly feel it. And therefore, even if rejected by the logical mind, it is not banished from our consciousness. As an incident it may be beneficial or injurious, but as a revelation its value lies in the fact that it offers us an experience through emotion or imagination; we feel ourselves in a special field of realization. This feeling itself is delightful when it is not accompanied by any great physical or moral risk, we love to feel even fear or sorrow if it is detached from all practical consequences. This is the reason of our enjoyment of tragic dramas, in which the feeling of pain rouses our consciousness to a white heat of intensity.

The reality of my own self is immediate and indubitable to me. Whatever else affects me in a like manner is real for myself, and it inevitably attracts and occupies my attention for its own sake, blends itself with my personality, making it richer and larger and causing it delight. My friend may not be beautiful, useful, rich or great, but he is real to me; in him I feel my own extension and my joy.

The consciousness of the real within me seeks for its own corroboration the touch of the Real outside me. When it fails the self in me is depressed. When our surroundings are monotonous and insignificant, having no emotional reaction upon our mind, we become vague to ourselves. For we are like pictures, whose reality is helped by the background if it is sympathetic. The punishment we suffer in solitary confinement consists in the obstruction to the relationship between the world of reality and the real in ourselves, causing the latter to become indistinct in a haze of inactive imagination: our personality is blurred, we miss the companionship of our own being through the diminution of our self. The world of our knowledge is enlarged for us through the extension of our information; the world of our personality grows in its area with a large and deeper experience of our personal self in our own universe through sympathy and imagination.

At this world, that can be known through knowledge, is limited to us owing to our ignorance, so the world of personality, that can be realized by our own personal self, is also restricted by the limit of our sympathy and imagination. In the dim twilight of insensitiveness a large part of our world remains to us like a procession of nomadic shadows. According to the stages of our consciousness we have more or less been able to identify ourselves with this world, if not as a whole, at least in fragments; and our enjoyment dwells in that wherein we feel ourselves thus united. In art we express the delight of this unity by which this world is realized as humanly significant to us. I have my physical, chemical and biological self; my knowledge of it extends through the extension of my knowledge of the physical, chemical and biological world. I have my personal self, which has its communication with our feelings, sentiments and imaginations, which lends itself to be coloured by our desires and shaped by our imageries.

Science urges us to occupy by our mind the immensity of the knowable world; our spiritual teacher enjoins us to comprehend by our soul the infinite Spirit which is in the depth of the moving and changing facts of the world; the urging of our artistic nature is to realize the manifestation of personality in the world of appearance, the reality of existence which is in harmony with the real within us. Where this harmony is not deeply felt, there we are aliens and perpetually homesick. For man by nature is an artist; he never receives passively and accurately in his mind a physical representation of things around him. There goes on a continual adaptation, a transformation of facts into human imagery, through constant touches of his sentiments and imagination. The animal has the geography of its birthplace; man has his country, the geography of his personal self. The vision of it is not merely physical; it has its artistic unity, it is a perpetual creation. In his country, his consciousness being unobstructed, man extends his relationship, which is of his own creative personality. In order to live efficiently man must know facts and their laws. In order to be happy he must establish harmonious relationship with all things with which he has dealings. Our creation is the modification of relationship.

The great men who appear in our history remain in our mind not as a static fact but as a living historical image. The sublime suggestions of their lives become blended into a noble consistency in legends made living in the life of ages. Those men with whom we live we constantly modify in our minds, making them more real to us than they would be in a bare presentation. Men's ideal of womanhood and women's ideal of manliness are created by the imagination through a mental grouping of qualities and conducts according to our hopes and desires, and men and women consciously and unconsciously strive towards its attainment. In fact, they reach a degree of reality for each other according to their success in adapting these respective ideals to their own nature. To say that these ideals are imaginary and therefore not true is wrong in man's case. His true life is in his own creation, which represents the infinity of man. He is naturally indifferent to things that merely exist; they must have some ideal value for him, and then only his consciousness fully recognizes them as real. Men are never true in their isolated self, and their imagination is the faculty that brings before their mind the vision of their own greater being.

We can make truth ours by actively modulating its inter-relations. This is the work of art; for reality is not based in the substance of things but in the principal of relationship. Truth is the infinite pursued by metaphysics; fact is the infinite pursued by science, while reality is the definition of the infinite which relates truth to the person. Reality is human; it is what we are conscious of, by which we are affected, that which we express. When we are intensely aware of it, we are aware of ourselves and it gives us delight. We live in it, we always widen its limits. Our arts and literature represent this creative activity which is fundamental in man.

But the mysterious fact about it is that though the individuals are separately seeking their expression, their success is never individualistic in character. Men must find and feel and represent in all their creative works Man the Eternal, the creator. Their civilization is a continual discovery of the transcendental humanity. In whatever it fails it shows the failure of the artist, which is the failure in expression; and that civilization perishes in which the individual thwarts the revelation of the universal. For Reality is the truth of Man, who belongs to all times, and any individualistic madness of men against Man cannot thrive for long.

Man is eager that his feeling for what is real to him must never die; it must find an imperishable form. The consciousness of this self of mine is so intensely evident to me that it assumes the character of immortality. I cannot imagine that it ever has been or can be non-existent. In a similar manner all things that are real to me are for myself eternal, and therefore worthy of a language that has permanent meaning. We know individuals who have the habit of inscribing their names on the walls of some majestic monument of architecture. It is a pathetic way of associating their own names with some works of art which belong to all times and to all men. Our hunger for reputation comes from our desire to make objectively real that which is inwardly real to us. He who is inarticulate is insignificant, like a dark star that cannot prove itself. He ever waits for the artist to give him his fullest worth, not for anything specially excellent in him but for the wonderful fact that he is what he certainly is, that he carries in him the eternal mystery of being.

A Chinese friend of mine while travelling with me in the streets of Peking suddenly exclaimed with a vehement enthusiasm: 'Look, here is a donkey!' Surely it was an utterly ordinary donkey, like an indisputable truism, needing no special introduction from him. I was amused; but it made me think. This animal is generally classified as having certain qualities that are not recommendable and then hurriedly dismissed. It was obscured to me by an envelopment of commonplace associations; I was lazily certain that I knew it and therefore I hardly saw it. But my friend, who possessed the artist mind of China, did not treat it with a cheap knowledge but could see it afresh and recognize it as real. When I say real, I mean that it did not remain at the outskirt of his consciousness tied to a narrow definition, but it easily blended in his imagination, produced a vision, a special harmony of lines, colours and life and movement, and became intimately his own. The admission of a donkey into a drawing-room is violently opposed; yet there is no prohibition against its finding a place in a picture which may be admiringly displayed on the drawing-room wall.

The only evidence of truth in art exists when it compels us to say 'I see'. A donkey we may pass by in Nature, but a donkey in art we must acknowledge even if it be a creature that disreputably ignores all its natural history responsibility, even if it resembles a mushroom in its head and a palm-leaf in its tail.

In the Upanishad it is said in a parable that there are two birds sitting on the same bough, one of which feeds and the other looks on. This is an image of the mutual relationship of the infinite being and the finite self. The delight of the bird which looks on is great, for it is a pure and free delight. There are both of these birds in man himself, the objective one with its business of life, the subjective one with its disinterested joy of vision.

A child comes to me and commands me to tell her a story. I tell her of a tiger which is disgusted with the black stripes on its body and comes to my frightened servant demanding a piece of soap. The story gives my little audience immense pleasure, the pleasure of a vision, and her mind cries out, 'It is here, for I see!' She *knows* a tiger in the book of natural history, but she can *see* the tiger in the story of mine.

I am sure that even this child of five knows that it is an impossible tiger that is out on its untigerly quest of an absurd soap. The delightfulness of the tiger for her is not in its beauty, its usefulness, or its probability; but in the undoubted fact that she can see it in her mind with a greater clearness of vision than she can the walls around her—the walls that brutally shout their evidence of certainty which is merely circumstantial. The tiger in the story is inevitable, it has the character of a complete image, which offers its testimonial of truth in itself. The listener's own mind is the eye-witness, whose direct experience could not be contradicted. A tiger must be like every other tiger in order that it may have its place in a book of Science; there it must be a commonplace tiger to be at all tolerated. But in the story it is uncommon, it can never reduplicated. We *know* a thing because it belongs to a class; we *see* a thing because it belongs to itself. The tiger of the story completely detached itself from all others of its kind and easily assumed a distinct individuality in the heart of the listener. The child could vividly see it, because by the help of her imagination it became her own tiger, one with herself, and this union of the subject and object gives us joy. Is it because there is no separation between them in truth, the separation being the *Maya,* which is creation?

There come in our history occasions when the consciousness of a large multitude becomes suddenly illumined with the recognition of a reality which rises far above the dull obviousness of daily happenings. The world becomes vivid; we see, we feel it with all our soul. Such an occasion there was when the voice of Buddha reached distant shores across physical and moral impediments. Then our life and our world found their profound meaning of reality in their relation to the central person who offered us emancipation of love. Men, in order to make this great human experience ever memorable, determined to do the impossible; they made rocks to speak, stones to sing, caves to remember; their cry of joy and hope took immortal forms along the hills and deserts, across barren solitudes and populous cities. A gigantic creative endeavour built up its triumph in stupendous carvings, defying obstacles that were overwhelming. Such heroic activity over the greater part of the Eastern continents clearly answers the question: 'What is Art?' It is the response of man's creative soul to the call of the Real.

Once there came a time, centuries ago in Bengal, when the divine love drama that has made its eternal playground in human souls was vividly revealed by a personality radiating its intimate realization of God. The mind of a whole people was stirred by a vision of the world as an instrument, through which sounded out invitation to the meeting of bliss. The ineffable mystery of God's love-call, taking shape in an endless panorama of colours and forms, inspired activity in music that overflowed the restrictions of classical conventionalism. Our Kirtan music of Bengal came to its being like a star flung up by a burning whirlpool of emotion in the heart of a whole people, and their consciousness was aflame with a sense of reality that must be adequately acknowledged.

The question may be asked as to what place music occupies in my theory that art is for evoking in our mind the deep sense of reality in its richest aspect. Music is the most abstract of all the arts, as mathematics is in the region of science. In fact these two have a deep relationship with each other. Mathematics is the logic of numbers and dimensions. It is therefore employed as the basis of our scientific knowledge. When taken out of its concrete associations and reduced to symbols, it reveals its grand structural majesty, the inevitableness of its own perfect concord. Yet there is not merely a logic but also a magic of mathematics which works at the world of appearance, producing harmony—the cadence of inter-relationship. This rhythm of harmony has been extracted from its usual concrete context, and exhibited through the medium of sound. And thus the pure essence of expressiveness in existence is offered in music. Expressiveness finds the least resistance in sound, having freedom unencumbered by the burden of facts and thoughts. This gives it a power to arouse in us an intimate feeling of reality. In the pictorial, plastic and literary arts, the object and our feelings with regard to it are closely associated, like the rose and its perfumes. In music, the feeling distilled in sound, becoming itself an independent object. It assumes a tune-form which is definite, but a meaning which is undefinable, and yet which grips our mind with a sense of absolute truth.

It is the magic of mathematics, the rhythm which is in the heart of all creation, which moves in the atom and, in its different measures, fashions gold and lead, the rose and the thorn, the sun and the planets. These are the dance-steps of numbers in the arena of time and space, which weave the *maya,* the patterns of appearance, the incessant flow of change, that ever is and is not. It is the rhythm that churns up images from the vague and makes tangible what is elusive. This is *maya,* this is the art in creation, and art in literature, which is the magic of rhythm.

And must we stop here? What we know as intellectual truth, is that also not a rhythm of the relationship of facts, that weaves the pattern of theory, and produces a sense of convincingness to a person who somehow feels sure that he knows the truth? We believe any fact to be true because of a harmony, a rhythm in reason, the process of which is analysable by the logic of mathematics, but not its result in me, just as we can count the notes but cannot account for the music. The mystery is that I am convinced, and this also belongs to the *maya* of creation, whose one important, indispensable factor is this self-conscious personality that I represent.

And the Other? I believe it is also a self-conscious personality, which has its eternal harmony with mine.

The Poet's Religion

I

Civility is beauty of behaviour. It requires for its perfection patience, self-control, and an environment of leisure. For genuine courtesy is a creation, like pictures, like music. It is a harmonious blending of voice, gesture and movement, words and action, in which generosity of conduct is expressed. It reveals the man himself and has no ulterior purpose.

Our needs are always in a hurry. They rush and hustle, they are rude and unceremonious; they have no surplus of leisure, no patience for anything else but fulfilment of purpose. We frequently see in our country at the present day men utilising empty kerosene cans for carrying water. These cans are emblems of discourtesy; they are curt and abrupt, they have not the least shame for their unmannerliness, they do not care to be ever so slightly more than useful.

The instruments of our necessity assert that we must have food, shelter, clothes, comforts and convenience. And yet men spend an immense amount of their time and resources in contradicting this assertion, to prove that they are not a mere living catalogue of endless wants; that there is in them an ideal of perfection, a sense of unity, which is a harmony between parts and a harmony with surroundings.

The quality of the infinite is not the magnitude of extension, it is in the *advaitam,* the mystery of Unity. Facts occupy endless time and space; but the truth comprehending them all has no dimension; it is One. Wherever our heart touches the One, in the small or the big, it finds the touch of the infinite.

I was speaking to some one of the joy we have in our personality. I said it was because we were made conscious by it of a spirit of unity within ourselves. He answered that he had no such feeling of joy about himself, but I was sure he exaggerated. In all probability he had been suffering from some break of harmony between his surroundings and the spirit of unity within him, proving all the more strongly its truth. The meaning of health comes home to us with painful force when disease disturbs it; since health expresses the unity of the vital functions and is accordingly joyful. Life's tragedies occur, not to demonstrate their own reality, but to reveal that eternal principle of joy in life, to which they gave a rude shaking. It is the object of this Oneness in us to realize its infinity by perfect union of love with others. All obstacles to this union create misery, giving rise to the baser passions that are expressions of finitude, of that separateness which is negative and therefore *māyā*.

The joy of unity within ourselves, seeking expression, becomes creative; whereas our desire for the fulfilment of our needs is constructive. The water vessel, taken as a vessel only, raises the question, 'Why does it exist at all?' Through its fitness of construction, it offers the apology for its existence. But where it is a work of beauty it has no question to answer; it has nothing to do, but to be. It reveals in its form a unity to which all that seems various in it is so related that, in a mysterious manner, it strikes sympathetic chords to the music of unity in our own being.

What is the truth of this world? It is not in the masses of substance, not in the number of things, but in their relatedness, which neither can be counted, nor measured, nor abstracted. It is not in the materials which are many, but in the expression which is one. All our knowledge of things is knowing them in their relation to the Universe, in that relation which is truth. A drop of water is not a particular assortment of elements; it is the miracle of a harmonious mutuality, in which the two reveal the One. No amount of analysis can reveal to us this mystery of unity. Matter is an abstraction; we shall never be able to realize what it is, for our world of reality does not acknowledge it. Even the giant forces of the world, centripetal and centrifugal, are kept out of our recognition. They are the day-labourers not admitted into the audience-hall of creation. But light and sound come to us in their gay dresses as troubadours singing serenades before the windows of the senses. What is constantly before us, claiming our attention, is not the kitchen, but the feast; not the anatomy of the world, but its countenance. There is the dancing ring of seasons; the elusive play of lights and shadows, of wind and water; the many-coloured wings of erratic life flitting between birth and death. The importance of these does not lie in their existence as mere facts, but in their language of harmony, the mother tongue of our own soul, through which they are communicated to us.

We grow out of touch with this great truth, we forget to accept its invitation and its hospitality, when in quest of external success our works become unspiritual and unexpressive. This is what Wordsworth complained of when he said:

> The world is too much with us; late and soon,
> Getting and spending, we lay waste our powers.
> Little we see in Nature that is ours.

But it is not because the world has grown too familiar to us; on the contrary, it is because we do not see it in its aspect of unity, because we are driven to distraction by our pursuit of the fragmentary.

Materials are savage; they are solitary; they are ready to hurt one another. They are like our individual impulses seeking the unlimited freedom of wilfulness. Left to themselves they are destructive. But directly an ideal of unity raises its banner in their centre, it brings these rebellious forces under its sway and creation is revealed—the creation which is peace, which is the unity of perfect relationship. Our greed for eating is in itself ugly and selfish, it has no sense of decorum; but when brought under the ideal of social fellowship, it is regulated and made ornamental; it is changed into a daily festivity of life. In human nature sexual passion is fiercely individual and destructive, but dominated by the ideal of love, it has been made to flower into a perfection of beauty, becoming in its best expression symbolical of the spiritual truth in man which is his kinship of love with the Infinite. Thus we find it is the One which expresses itself in creation; and the Many, by giving up opposition, make the revelation of unity perfect.

II

I remember, when I was a child, that a row of cocoanut trees by our garden wall, with their branches beckoning the rising sun on the horizon, gave me a companionship as living as I was myself. I know it was my imagination which transmuted the world around me into my own world—the imagination which seeks unity, which deals with it. But we have to consider that this companionship was true; that the universe in which I was born had in it an element profoundly akin to my own imaginative mind, one which wakens in all children's natures the Creator, whose pleasure is in interweaving the web of creation with His own patterns of many-coloured strands. It is something akin to us, and therefore harmonious to our imagination. When we find some strings vibrating in unison with others, we know that this sympathy carries in it an eternal reality. The fact that the world stirs our imagination in sympathy tells us that this creative imagination is a common truth both in us and in the heart of existence. Wordsworth says:

> I'd rather be
> A pagan suckled in a creed outworn;
> So might I, standing on this pleasant lea,
> Have glimpses that would make me less forlorn;
> Have sight of Proteus rising from the sea,
> Or hear old Triton blow his wreathed horn.

In this passage the poet says we are less forlorn in a world which we meet with our imagination. That can only be possible if through our imagination is revealed, behind all appearances, the reality which gives the touch of companionship, that is to say, something which has an affinity to us. An immense amount of our activity is engaged in making images, not for serving any useful purpose or formulating rational propositions, but for giving varied responses to the varied touches of this reality. In this image-making the child creates his own world in answer to the world in which he finds himself. The child in us finds glimpses of his eternal playmate from behind the veil of things, as Proteus rising from the sea, or Triton blowing his wreathed horn. And the playmate is the Reality, that makes it possible for the child to find delight in activities which do not inform or bring assistance but merely express. There is an image-making joy in the infinite, which inspires in us our joy in imagining. The rhythm of cosmic motion produces in our mind the emotion which is creative.

A poet has said about his destiny as a dreamer, about the worthlessness of his dreams and yet their permanence:

I hang 'mid men my heedless head,
And my fruit is dreams, as theirs is bread:
The godly men and the sun-hazed sleeper,
Time shall reap; but after the reaper
The world shall glean to me, me the sleeper.

The dream persists; it is more real than even bread which has substance and use. The painted canvas is durable and substantial; it has for its production and transport to market a whole array of machines and factories. But the picture which no factory can produce is a dream, *māyā,* and yet it, not the canvas, has the meaning of ultimate reality.

A poet describes Autumn:

I saw old Autumn in the misty morn
Stand shadowless like Silence, listening
To silence, for no lonely bird would sing
Into his hollow ear from woods forlorn.

Of April another poet sings:

April, April,
Laugh thy girlish laughter;
Then the moment after
Weep thy girlish tears!
April, that mine ears
Like a lover greetest,
If I tell thee, sweetest,

All my hopes and fears.
April, April,
Laugh thy golden laughter.
But the moment after
Weep thy golden tears!

This Autumn, this April,—are they nothing but phantasy?

Let us suppose that the Man from the Moon comes to the earth and listens to some music in a gramophone. He seeks for the origin of the delight produced in his mind. The facts before him are a cabinet made of wood and a revolving disc producing sound; but the one thing which is neither seen nor can be explained is the truth of the music, which his personality must immediately acknowledge as a personal message. It is neither in the wood, nor in the disc, nor in the sound of the notes. If the Man from the Moon be a poet, as can reasonably be supposed, he will write about a fairy imprisoned in that box, who sits spinning fabrics of songs expressing her cry for a far-away magic casement opening on the foam of some perilous sea, in a fairyland forlorn. It will not be literally, but essentially true. The facts of the gramophone make us aware of the laws of sound, but the music gives us personal companionship. The bare facts about April are alternate sunshine and showers; but the subtle blending of shadows and lights, of murmurs and movements, in April, gives us not mere shocks of sensation, but unity of joy as does music. Therefore when a poet sees the vision of a girl in April, even a downright materialist is in sympathy with him. But we know that the same individual would be menacingly angry if the law of heredity or a geometrical problem were described as a girl or a rose—or even as a cat or a camel. For these intellectual abstractions have no magical touch for our lute-strings of imagination. They are no dreams, as are the harmony of bird-songs, rain-washed leaves glistening in the sun, and pale clouds floating in the blue.

The ultimate truth of our personality is that we are no mere biologists or geometricians; 'we are the dreamers of dreams, we are the music-makers'. This dreaming or music-making is not a function of the lotus-eaters, it is the creative impulse which makes songs not only with words and tunes, lines and colours, but with stones and metals, with ideas and men:

With wonderful deathless ditties
We build up the world's great cities,
And out of a fabulous story
We fashion an empire's glory.

I have been told by a scholar friend of mine that by constant practice in logic he has weakened his natural instinct of faith. The reason is, faith is the spectator in us which finds the meaning of the drama from the unity of the performance; but logic lures us into the greenroom where there is stagecraft but no drama at all; and then this logic nods its head and wearily talks about disillusionment. But the greenroom, dealing with its fragments, looks foolish when questioned, or wears the sneering smile of Mephistopheles; for it does not have the secret of unity, which is somewhere else. It is for faith to answer, 'Unity comes to us from the One, and the One in ourselves opens the door and receives it with joy.' The function of poetry and the arts is to remind us that the greenroom is the greyest of illusions, and the reality is the drama presented before us, all its paint and tinsel, masks and pageantry, made one in art. The ropes and wheels perish, the stage is changed; but the dream which is drama remains true, for there remains the eternal Dreamer.

III

Poetry and the arts cherish in them the profound faith of man in the unity of his being with all existence, the final truth of which is the truth of personality. It is a religion directly apprehended, and not a system of metaphysics to be analysed and argued. We know in our personal experience what our creations are and we instinctively know through it what creation around us means.

When Keats said in his "Ode to a Grecian Urn":

Thou, silent form, dost tease us out of thought,
As doth eternity, ...

he felt the ineffable which is in all forms of perfection, the mystery of the One, which takes us beyond all thought into the immediate touch of Infinite. This is the mystery which is for a poet to realise and to reveal. It comes out in Keats' poems with struggling gleams through consciousness of suffering and despair:

> Spite off despondence, of the inhuman dearth
>
> Of noble natures, of the gloomy days,
> Of all the unhealthy and o'er-darken'd ways
> Made for our searching : yes, in spite of all,
> Some shape of beauty moves away the pall
> From our dark spirits.

In this there is a suggestion that truth reveals itself in beauty. For if beauty were mere accident, a rent in the eternal fabric of things, then it would hurt, would be defeated by the antagonism of facts. Beauty is no phantasy, it has the everlasting meaning of reality. The facts that cause despondence and gloom are mere mist, and when through the mist beauty breaks out in momentary gleams, we realise that Peace is true and not conflict, Love is true and not hatred; and Truth is the One, not the disjointed multitude. We realize that Creation is the perpetual harmony between the infinite ideal of perfection and the eternal continuity of its realization; that so long as there is no absolute separation between the positive ideal and the material obstacle to its attainment, we need not be afraid of suffering and loss. This is the poet's religion.

Those who are habituated to the rigid framework of sectarian creeds will find such a religion as this too indefinite and elastic. No doubt it is so, but only because its ambition is not to shackle the Infinite and tame it for domestic use; but rather to help our consciousness to emancipate itself from materialism. It is as indefinite as the morning, and yet as luminous; it calls our thoughts, feelings, and actions into freedom, and feeds them with light. In the poet's religion we find no doctrine or injunction, but rather the attitude of our entire being towards a truth which is ever to be revealed in its own endless creation.

In dogmatic religion all questions are definitely answered, all doubts are finally laid to rest. But the poet's religion is fluid, like the atmosphere round the earth where lights and shadows play hide-and-seek, and the wind like a shepherd boy plays upon its reeds among flocks of clouds. It never undertakes to lead anybody anywhere to any solid conclusion; yet it reveals endless spheres of light, because it has no walls round itself. It acknowledges the facts of evil; it openly admits 'the weariness, the fever and the fret' in the world 'where men sit and hear each other groan'; yet it remembers that in spite of all there is the song of the nightingale, and 'haply the Queen Moon is on her throne', and there is:

> White hawthorn, and the pastoral eglantine,
> Fast-fading violets covered up in leaves;
> And mid-day's eldest child,
> The coming musk-rose, full of dewy wine,
> The murmurous haunt of flies on summer eves.

But all this has not the definiteness of an answer; it has only the music that teases us out of thought as it fills our being.

Let me read a translation from an Eastern poet to show how this idea comes out in a poem in Bengali:

> In the morning I awoke at the flutter of thy boat-sails,
> Lady of my Voyage, and I left the shore to follow the beckoning waves.
> I asked thee, 'Does the dream-harvest ripen in the island beyond the blue?'
> The silence of thy smile fell on my question like the silence of sunlight on waves.
> The day passed on through storm and through calm,
> The perplexed winds changed their course, time after time, and the sea moaned.
> I asked thee, 'Does thy sleep-tower stand somewhere beyond the dying embers of the day's funeral pyre?'
> No answer came from thee, only thine eyes smiled like the edge of a sunset cloud.
> It is night. Thy figure grows dim in the dark.
> Thy wind-blown hair flits on my cheek and thrills my sadness with its scent.

My hands grope to touch the hem of thy robe, and I ask
thee—'Is there thy garden of death beyond the stars, Lady of my Voyage, where thy silence blossoms into songs?'
Thy smile shines in the heart of the hush like the star-mist of midnight.

IV

In Shelley we clearly see the growth of his religion through periods of vagueness and doubt, struggle and searching. But he did at length come to a positive utterance of his faith, though he died young. Its final expression is in his 'Hymn to Intellectual Beauty'. By the title of the poem the poet evidently means a beauty that is not merely a passive quality of particular things, but a spirit that manifests itself through the apparent antagonism of the unintellectual life. This hymn rang out of his heart when he came to the end of his pilgrimage and stood face to face with the Divinity, glimpses of which had already filled his soul with restlessness. All his experiences of beauty had ever teased him with the question as to what was its truth. Somewhere he sings of a nosegay which he makes of violets, daisies, tender bluebells and—

That tall flower that wets,
Like a child, half in tenderness and mirth,
Its mother's face with heaven-collected tears.

He ends by saying:

And then, elate and gay,
I hastened to the spot whence I had come,
That I might there present it!—Oh! to whom?

This question, even though not answered, carries a significance. A creation of beauty suggests a fulfilment, which is the fulfilment of love. We have heard some poets scoff at it in bitterness and despair; but it is like a sick child beating its own mother—it is a sickness of faith, which hurts truth, but proves it by its very pain and anger. And the faith itself is this, that beauty is the self-offering of the One of the other One.

In the first part of his 'Hymn to Intellectual Beauty' Shelley dwells on the inconstancy and evanescence of the manifestation of beauty, which imparts to it an appearance of frailty and unreality:

Like hues and harmonies of evening,
    Like clouds in starlight widely spread,
    Like memory of music fled.

This, he says, rouses in our mind the question:

Why aught should fail and fade that once is shown,
    Why fear and dream and death and birth
    Cast on the daylight of this earth
    Such gloom,—why man has such a scope
For love and hate, despondency and hope?

The poet's own answer to this question is:

    Man were immortal, and omnipotent,
Didst thou, unknown and awful as thou art,
Keep with thy glorious train firm state within his heart.

This very elusiveness of beauty suggests the vision of immortality and of omnipotence, and stimulates the effort in man to realize it in some idea of permanence. The highest reality has actively to be achieved. The gain of truth is not in the end; it reveals itself through the endless length of achievement. But what is there to guide us in our voyage of realization? Men have ever been struggling for direction:

Therefore the names of Demon, Ghost, and Heaven
Remain the records of their vain endeavour,
Frail spells,—whose uttered charm might not avail to
    sever,
From all we hear and all we see,
Doubt, chance and mutability.

The prevalent rites and practices of piety, according to this poet, are like magic spells—they only prove men's desperate endeavour and not their success. He knows that the end we seek has its own direct call to us, its own light to guide us to itself. And truth's call is the call of beauty. Of this he says:

The light alone,—like mist o'er mountain driven,

Or music by the night wind sent,
Thro' strings of some still instrument,
Or moonlight on a midnight stream
Gives grace and truth to life's unquiet dream.

About this revelation of truth which calls us on, and yet which is everywhere, a village singer of Bengal sings:

My master's flute sounds in everything,
drawing me out of my house to everywhere.
While I listen to it I know that every step I take
is in my master's house.
For he is the sea, he is the river that leads to the sea,
and he is the landing place.

Religion, in Shelley, grew with his life; it was not given to him in fixed and ready-made doctrines; he rebelled against them. He had the creative mind which could only approach Truth through its joy in creative effort. For true creation is realization of truth through the translation of it into our own symbols.

V

For man, the best opportunity for such a realization has been in men's Society. It is a collective creation of his, through which his social being tries to find itself in its truth and beauty. Had that Society merely manifested its usefulness, it would be inarticulate like a dark star. But, unless it degenerates, it ever suggests in its concerted movements a living truth as its soul, which has personality. In this large life of social communion man feels the mystery of Unity, as he does in music. From the sense of that Unity, men came to the sense of their God. And therefore every religion began with its tribal God.

The one question before all others that has to be answered by our civilizations is not what they have and in what quantity, but what they express and how. In a society, the production and circulation of materials, the amassing and spending of money, may go on, as in the interminable prolonging of a straight line, if its people forget to follow some spiritual design of life which curbs them and transforms them into an organic whole. For growth is not that enlargement which is merely adding to the dimensions of incompleteness. Growth is the movement of a whole towards a yet fuller wholeness. Living things start with this wholeness from the beginning of their career. A child has its own perfection as a child; it would be ugly if it appeared as an unfinished man. Life is a continual process of synthesis, and not of additions. Our activities of production and enjoyment of wealth attain that spirit of wholeness when they are blended with a creative ideal. Otherwise they have the insane aspect of the eternally unfinished; they become like locomotive engines which have railway lines but no stations; which rush on towards a collision of uncontrolled forces or to a sudden breakdown of the overstrained machinery.

Through creation man expresses his truth; through that expression he gains back his truth in its fulness. Human society is for the best expression of man, and that expression, according to its perfection, leads him to the full realization of the divine in humanity. When that expression is obscure, then his faith in the Infinite that is within him becomes weak; then his aspiration cannot go beyond the idea of success. His faith in the Infinite is creative; his desire for success is constructive; one is his home, and the other is his office. With the overwhelming growth of necessity, civilization becomes a gigantic office to which the home is a mere appendix. The predominance of the pursuit of success gives to society the character of what we call *Shudra* in India. In fighting a battle, the *Kshatriya,* the noble knight, followed his honour for his ideal, which was greater than victory itself; but the mercenary *Shudra* has success for his object. The name Shudra symbolizes a man who has no margin round him beyond his bare utility. The word denotes a classification which includes all naked machines that have lost their completeness of humanity, be their work manual or intellectual. They are like walking stomachs of brains, and we feel, in pity, urged to call on God and cry, 'Cover them up for mercy's sake with some veil of beauty and life!'

When Shelley in his view of the world realized the Spirit of Beauty, which is the vision of the Infinite, he thus uttered his faith:

> Never joy illumed my brow
> Unlinked with hope that thou wouldst free
> This world from its dark slavery;
> That thou,—O awful Loveliness,—
> Wouldst give whate'er these words cannot express.

This was his faith in the Infinite. It led his aspiration towards the region of freedom and perfection which was beyond the immediate and above the successful. This faith in God, this faith in the reality of the ideal of perfection, has built up all that is great in the human world. To keep indefinitely walking on, along a zigzag course of change, is negative and barren. A mere procession of notes does not make music; it is only when we have in the heart of the march of sounds some musical idea that it creates song. Our faith in the infinite reality of Perfection is that musical idea, and there is that one great creative force in our civilization. When it wakens not, then our faith in money, in material power, takes its place; it fights and destroys, and in a brilliant fireworks of star-mimicry suddenly exhausts itself and dies in ashes and smoke.

VI

Men of great faith have always called us to wake up to great expectations, and the prudent have always laughed at them and said that these did not belong to reality. But the poet in man knows that reality is a creation, and human reality has to be called forth from its obscure depth by man's faith which is creative. There was a day when the human reality was the brutal reality. That was the only capital we had with which to begin our career. But age after age there has come to us the call of faith, which said against all the evidence of fact: 'You are more than you appear to be, more than your circumstances seem to warrant. You are to attain the impossible you are immortal.' The unbelievers had laughed and tried to kill the faith. But faith grew stronger with the strength of martyrdom and at her bidding higher realities have been created over the strata of the lower. Has not a new age come today, borne by thunderclouds, ushered in by a universal agony of suffering? Are we not waiting today for a great call of faith, which will say to us: 'Come out of your present limitations. You are to attain the impossible, you are immortal?' The nations who are not prepared to accept it, who have all their trust in their present machines of system, and have no thought or space to spare to welcome the sudden guest who comes as the messenger of emancipation, are bound to court defeat whatever may be their present wealth and power.

This great world, where it is a creation, an expression of the infinite—where its morning sings of joy to the newly awakened life, and its evening stars sing to the traveller, weary and worn, of the triumph of life in a new birth across death,—has its call for us. The call has ever roused the creator in man, and urged him to reveal the truth, to reveal the Infinite in himself. It is ever claiming from us, in our own creations, co-operation with God, reminding us of our divine nature, which finds itself in freedom of spirit. Our society exists to remind us, through its various voices, that the ultimate truth in man is not in his intellect or his possessions; it is in his illumination of mind, in his extension of sympathy across all barriers of caste and colour; in his recognition of the world, not merely as a storehouse of power, but as a habitation of man's spirit, with its eternal music of beauty and its inner light of the divine presence.

The Principle of Literature

8

In the world of our fairy tales, the son of the Detective, the son of the Merchant and the son of the King set forth in the adventurous quest of the Princess: the Truth, represented by her, is approached from three sides by three different types of mind.

The process which one of them follows is, by analysis, to find in her the secrets of body and mind; but in this region of science, she is of no more value than any other girl,—there is no difference between Princess and scullery-maid. The Detective, be he scientist or philosopher, has nothing to do with feeling, no sense even of utility, all he has is the spirit of Question.

The Princess has another aspect,—that in which she is useful. She spins, weaves and embroiders. The eyes with which the Merchant's son observes her,—turning her spindle, wielding her shuttle, plying her needle,—have in their gaze neither feeling, nor questioning, but only calculation.

The King's son is not physiologist or psychologist, nor has he passed any examination in economics. What he has passed, methinks, is just his twenty-fourth year, and also the impassable heath of the fairy tales. He has crossed difficult paths, not for learning, nor for riches, but for the Princess herself, whose palace is not in the laboratory, nor in the market place, but in that heart's paradise of Eternal Spring where bloom the flowers in the poet's bower of phantasy.

That which is not known by logic, which defies definition, whose value is not in any practical use, but which can only be intimately felt, finds its expression in Literature, is the subject of Aesthetics. No man who has the gift of enjoyment ever nags or pokes any creation of Art with the questions: *Why art thou here? What art thou?*—He exclaims: *It is enough for me that thou art thyself!* This was what the King's son whispered in the ear of the Princess, and it was for the proper utterance of these very words that Shahjahan was compelled to build the Taj Mahal.

We can only define that which can be measured: that which is immeasurable, which eludes all attempts at capture, is not attainable by reason, but by immediate perception. The Upanishad says of the Infinite Being that we can reach Him not with speech nor with the mind, but by our consciousness of delight, wherewith all fear departs from us. Our soul has her hunger for this immediateness of realization, whereby she is enabled also to know herself. The love, the contemplation, the vision that alone can satisfy this hunger finds its place in Literature, in Art.

The space enclosed within walls has been appropriated by my business office, which there buys and sells, pays and charges rent, by the yard. Outside, where is the assembly of stars, undivided space is realized by me through my sense of joy in the boundless. This vastness is superfluous for the purpose of mere physical life, as is proved by the worms that burrow underground. There are in this world also human worms for whom a dearth of sky is no privation; for in them has been killed the mind that cannot live without expanding its wings outside the prison bars of necessity. It was the tyranny of the ghosts of such dead souls that frightened the poet into the prayer:

> Doom me not to the futility
> Of offering things of joy to the callous!

But the heart of the King's son is fresh and sensitive. He realizes in the Princess that sweep of immensity which is in the sky lighted by the eternal stars; and his response to the sight of her is as befits such realization. The others behave differently. To measure the rhythm of the heart-throbs of the King's daughter, the scientist has no compunction in improvising a tube of tin. The Merchant finds his satisfaction in the tin can wherein he safe-keeps the cream churned by the Princess' own hand. But the King's son does not so much as dream of ordering tin armlets for the Princess,—should he perchance do so it would be for him a veritable nightmare. If, when he wakes, he happens to find gold scarce, he is forthwith impelled to sally forth in search of rose buds for her.

From this can be understood why, in Sanskrit, Rhetoric is called the Grammar of Ornament. Ornament is the symbol of the ultimate. The mother who finds the finality of her joy in her babe, translates this absolute consciousness of hers into the adornments wherewith she decks its body. We view our servant within fixed limits and our return for his service is likewise limited to a fixed salary. But we view our friend in the unlimited, so ornaments blossom forth in our language and behaviour, in the tone of our voice, our smile, our welcome. In literature we speak of him with decorated words, of which the significance is not in their meaning, but in their feeling the message whereof is brought home by the ring of their melody. The appearances, the thoughts, the dreams which are not made manifest through reasoning,—these are of Literature.

What in English is called *real,* is in our language called *sārthaka* (significant). Common truth is one thing, significant truth quite another. Common truth does not admit of selection; it is the significant that is select. Men of every sort come under the head of common truth, the man of significance is hardly to be found in a million. When, on the impulse of his profound pity, Valmiki was stirred to metrical utterance, it was only with the aid of Rishi Narada that he could find a real man, of a significance worthy of his metre.

Not that significantly real things are rare, but anything that is not significant to me is not real for me. Because the world of reality has more extensive boundaries for the Poet and the Artist, they can bring out the significance of a much larger variety of things. For in whatsoever we are made aware of some ideal of completeness, that becomes significant to us. A grain of sand is nothing to me, but a lotus flower has for me the full force of certitude. Though at every step the sand may obtrude itself on my attention,—grating on my feet, irritating my eye, setting my teeth on edge,—nevertheless it has not for me any fulness of truth. The lotus does not have to elbow its way into my notice, rather does my mind of its own accord go out to greet and welcome it.

Let me give an example of the sensitive fastidiousness of the mind when choosing the adornments for the object of its adoration. The flower of the *sajinā* is not lacking in beauty, but the poets, when celebrating the enthronement of the King of Seasons, do not by any chance include its name in their songs of acclamation. It has lost prestige with the poets because it happens to figure as an article of diet. For the same reason the flowers of the brinjal or the pumpkin stand with lowered heads outside the gates of poesy,—the kitchen has destroyed their caste. Not alone the poets, but also their sweethearts disdain these flowers as ornaments, though a spray of the delicate *sajinā* flower-clusters in their dark tresses would assuredly not have been ill-becoming. Neither the *kunda* nor *tagar* are gorgeous or scented, yet for them the door to the realm of adornment remains open, for they have not been tainted with the touch of the hunger of the body.

Here pictorial art is at an advantage. The artist's brush need not shrink from painting the superb foliage of the yam, whereas to bring that name, suggestive of a meal, into the description of any verdant scene would tax all the resources of the poet's pen. The sounds of words, moreover, sometimes have undignified associations, by reason of the way they are used in our everyday life, which are liable to give offence in the case of the word picture, for it is not shape or colour, but sound which is of the essence of poetry. I am not usually credited with any squeamish regard for convention, yet have I often to resort to a less usual name, or a round-about phrase, rather than use a word that has a utilitarian significance. I should say here, however, that these considerations do not apply with equal force in the case of the Western poet with whom it is the substance and not the name that dominates.

Be that as it may, it is a common experience that we fail to see in its entirety that which subserves our use, for it is eclipsed by the shadow of our need. The kitchen and pantry are of everyday necessity to the householder but, these are the rooms he fain would keep out of public view. His reception room, which he for himself can do without, is the one on which he lavishes all furniture and adornment, striving to the best of his means, by carpeting it, hanging it with pictures, stocking it with objects of exotic beauty, to give it a touch of the universal; for he would be known to the larger world outside, through this room of his choice, in all the glory of his own personality. In the facts that he eats and stores up food his personality finds no ultimate significance. That he has a special distinction is the tidings which he seeks to communicate through his reception rooms,—wherefore they are decorated.

In the realm of Biology man and beast are not distinct; as there viewed, self-preservation and race preservation are of equal importance in the nature of both. But man's spirit fails to find in these features the true significance of Man. So, however deep-seated or widespread man's desire to dine may be, his literature has but scanty recognition of it. Man's eating propensity may be an insistent, but it is not a significant truth; that is why the satisfaction of his hunger is not one of the joys that have found a place in the paradise of his Art-world.

The sexual relationship of man and woman stands on a higher plane than man's appetite for food, for it has achieved an intimate connection with the relationship of hearts. The sex instinct which, in a basic view of life, has only a secondary place, has risen, in the sex relations of the larger life of man, to a position transcending even the primary; for Love illumines man, within and without, into a supreme intensity of consciousness. That illumination is lacking in the primitive principle of race preservation, which therefore assumes importance only on the plane of science. The union of hearts, as seen by us, is abstracted from the primitive needs of Nature into the glory of its own finality. And hence it has come to occupy so vast a place in Literature and the Arts.

The supreme significance of the union of the sexes is, for man, not in procreation,—*prajanārtham* (for the sake of progeny) as our Lawgiver would have it,—for in that he is merely animal, but in love wherein he is truly man. I do not use the word *animal* with any implication of ethical judgment, but from the viewpoint of the progressive self-realization of man. Owing to their intimately close contact a natural spirit of rivalry prevails between the animal and the spiritual spheres of man's sex-life in their respective claims for the wreath of victory from art and literature. The psycho-analyst has introduced a further complication by asseverating that the animal sex-instinct is also a deep and potent factor in the mental life of man. But whatever practical utility or intellectual value this dictum of science may have, it can have no place in the realm of Literature and Art, which is concerned with the valuation of man's feeling of delight according to his standard of the eternal. The same is the case with considerations of social morality. The problems that have arisen with regard to the place of the sex-relation in Literature cannot be solved from the scientific or moral standpoint, but from that of Aesthetics, which alone can determine which of its two aspects man will adorn and raise on the pedestal of immortality.

We find in every age temporary extraneous circumstances occasionally creating obsessions that penetrate into the field of literature and overshadow for the time its true characteristics. It is not possible, however, for these temporary excitements to find any permanent place in literature, for, being volatile by nature, they soon evaporate. During the great European War, for instance, the war turbulence muddied even the streams of its poetry. When in England the Puritanic age was followed by one of license, its exhalations befogged the radiance of its literature, but even while such period lasted, the presence of this cloud testified not to its own significance, but to that of the light which it could not wholly obscure. In the Middle Ages of Europe the Church attained such power that it tried to throttle science, forgetting that, in its own sphere, science is supreme and owes no allegiance even to religion. Now the opposite phenomenon is at work, and it is science that seeks to establish its sway over every region of man's being: in the pride of its new prestige it has ceased to have misgivings about encroaching beyond its scope.

Science is impersonal. Its very essence is an impartial curiosity about truth. And yet the all-pervading net of this curiosity is gradually enmeshing modern literature within its folds; though of Literature, on the contrary, the essence is its partiality,—its supreme message is the freedom of choice according to the taste of man. It is this freedom which is being assailed by the invasion of science. The sensualism of which European literature is full today owes its origin to this *curiosity*, as its prototype in the Age of the Restoration had its impulse in *lust*. But just as the lust of that age failed to win the laurel which could secure it a permanent place in the Olympus of Literature, neither can the scientific curiosity of this age maintain its keenness for ever.

There was a day in our country when a heat wave of licentiousness passed over our society and stimulated our literature into an outburst of carnalism. It was a temporary aberration of which the modern reader refuses to take any serious notice, not by way of moral censure, but because he has ceased to accord it permanent value.

Of late, it is true, we notice the opposite tendency in some of our modern critics who would rank among the eternal verities the intemperance of the flesh that has been imported into our literature from the Western world. But they forget that the eternal cannot wholly contradict the past. The natural delicacy which has always been a feature of man's aesthetic enjoyment, the aristocracy which has always reigned in the realm of art,—these are eternal. It is only in the rantings of the science-intoxicated democracy of today that this modesty, this reticence, is dubbed a weakness, and a rude manifestation of physical hunger is proclaimed to constitute the virility of art.

I have seen an example of this begrimed pugilistic modernism in the form that our *Holi* play has taken amongst the roughs of Chitpore Road. There is no scattering of red powder, no spraying with rose-coloured perfumes, no laughter, no song. Rolling long pieces of wet cloth in the street mud and therewith bespattering one another and the unfortunate passers-by, to the accompaniment of unearthly yells, is the mad form which this old-time Spring Festival has here assumed. Not to tinge but to taint is the object. I do not say that such propensity is foreign to the mentality of man: the psycho-analyst is therefore welcome to revel in a study thereof. My objection to the importation of this common desire to soil into a festival inspired by man's aesthetic sense is not because it is not true, but because it is not appropriate.

Some of those who seek to defend the bringing in of such muddy carousals into the region of our literary enjoyment do so with the question—*But is it not true?* That question, as I say, does not arise. When our drug-befuddled *Bhojpuri* festive party storm the welkin with the unending clang of their intoxicated drums and cymbals, their demonaic shouts of an eternal repetition of the one line of their tuneless song, it is entirely beside the point to ask the suffering neighbours whether or not it is true; the only relevant question can be: *How is it music*? There is admittedly a kind of self-forgetful joy in inebriation; there is undoubtedly great forcefulness in an unrestrained exercise of lung power; and if the ugliness of incivility has to be taken as a sign of virility, then we must needs admire this athletic intoxication also. But what then? This forcefulness still remains of the slums of Chitpore, it cannot aspire to the Elysium of Art.

In conclusion it should be added that, if in the countries ridden by science, an indiscriminate curiosity should, Duhsāsana-like, seek to strip the goddess of Literature of her drapery, they have at least the excuse of science to offer for such conduct. But in our country, where neither within nor without, neither in thought nor in action, has science been permitted an entry, what excuse can serve to cover up the insolence of the spurious, borrowed immodesty that has come to infest its literature? If the question be sent to the other side of the seas: *Why this turmoil of the market-crowd in your literature?* The answer will come: *That is no fault of our literature; the cause lies in the markets that surround us*. When that same question is put on this side, the reply will be: *True, markets we have none; but the noisomeness of the market-place is all there; that is just the glory of our modernism!*

(1927)

The Meaning of Art

9

There is a remarkable verse in the Atharva Veda which attributes all that is great in the human world to superfluity. It says:

> *Ritam satyam tapo rashtram sramo dharmascha karmacha,*
> *Bhūtam bhavishyat ucchiste viryam lakshmīrbalam bale*
>
> Righteousness, truth, great endeavours, empire, religion, enterprise, heroism and prosperity, the past and the future dwell in the surpassing strength of the surplus.

The meaning of it is that man expresses himself through his superabundance which largely overlaps his absolute need.

The renowned Vedic commentator, Sāyaṇāchārya, says:

> *Yajñe hutasishtasya odanasya sarvajagatkāranabhūta*
> *Brahmābhedena stutih kriyate.*
>
> The food offering which is left over after the completion of sacrificial rites is praised because it is symbolical of Brahma, the original source of the universe.

According to this explanation, Brahma is boundless in his superfluity which inevitably finds its expression in the eternal world process. Here we have the doctrine of the genesis of creation, and therefore of the origin of art. Of all living creatures in the world man has his vital and mental energy vastly in excess of his need, which urges him to work in various lines of creation for its own sake. Like Brahma himself, he takes joy in productions that are unnecessary to him, and therefore representing his extravagance and not his hand-to-mouth penury. The voice that is just enough can speak and cry to the extent needed for every day use, but that which is abundant sings, and in it we find our joy. Art reveals man's wealth of life, which seeks its freedom in forms of perfection which are an end in themselves.

All that is inert and inanimate is limited to the bare fact of existence. Life is perpetually creative because it contains in itself that surplus which ever overflows the boundaries of the immediate time and space, restlessly pursuing its adventure of expression in the varied forms of self-realization. Our living body has its vital organs that are important in maintaining its efficiency, but this body is not a mere convenient sac for the purpose of holding stomach, heart, lungs and brains; it is an image,—its highest value is in the fact that it communicates its personality. It has colour, shape and movement, most of which belong to the superfluous, that are needed only for self-expression and not for self-preservation.

At the root of all creation there is a paradox, a logical contradiction. Its process is in the perpetual reconciliation of two contrary forces. We have already said that the natural urging of the surplus, the *ucchista,* is the motive force of all that makes for perfection. But the boundless overflow must yield to the bounds of finitude for its manifestation. Truth must become real by the definition of the infinite. We have two contradictory utterances in the Upanishad about the origin of all things. On the one hand, it has been said:

> *Anandādhyeva khalvimāni bhūtāni jāyante.*
> The universe has come out of joy.

On the other hand, there is the verse which says:

> *Sa tapo'tapyatah sa tapastaptvā sarvamasrijat yadidam kincha.*
> God made penance, and with the heat generated therefrom he created all that there is.

The freedom of joy and the restraint of *tapasyā,* both are equally true in the creative expression of Brahma.

This limitation of the unlimited is personality: God is personal where he creates.

Kavirmanīshī paribhūh svayambhūryatatathyāto'rthan
Vyadadhāt shāswatibhyah samābhyah.

Where he dispenses the inner necessities of existence in an accurate measure and for all time he is the poet, the lord of mind, the sovereign power, the self-creator.

He accepts the limits of his own law and the play goes on which is this world whose reality is in its relation to the Person. Things are distinct not in their essence but in their appearance, in other words, in their relation to one to whom they appear. This is art, the truth of which is not in substance or logic, but in expression. Abstract truth may belong to science and metaphysics, but the world of reality belongs to art.

The world as an art is the play of the Supreme Person revelling in image making. Try to find out the ingredients of the image—they elude you, they never reveal to you the eternal secret of appearance. In your effort to capture life as expressed in living tissue, you will find carbon, nitrogen and many other things utterly unlike life, but never life itself. The appearance does not offer any commentary of itself through its material. You may call it *māyā* and pretend to disbelieve it, but the great artist, the *Māyāvin,* is not hurt. For art is *maya,* it has no other explanation but that it seems to be what it is. It never tries to conceal its evasiveness, it mocks, even its own definition and plays the game of hide and seek through its constant flight in changes.

And thus life, which is an incessant explosion of freedom, finds its metre in a continual falling back in death. Every day is a death, every moment even. If not, there would be an amorphous desert of deathlessness eternally dumb and still. So life is *māyā,*—as moralists love to say, it *is* and *is not.* All that we find in it is the rhythm through which it shows itself. Are rocks and minerals any better? Has not science shown us the fact that the ultimate difference between one element and another is only that of rhythm? The fundamental distinction of gold from mercury lies merely in the difference of rhythm in their respective atomic constitution, like the distinction of the king from his subject which is not in their different constituents, but in the different metres of their situation and circumstance. There you find behind the scene the Artist, the Magician of rhythm, who imparts an appearance of substance to the unsubstantial.

What is this rhythm? It is the movement generated and regulated by harmonious restriction. This is the creative force in the hand of the artist. So long as words remain in uncadenced prose form, they do not give any lasting feeling of reality. The moment they are taken and put into rhythm they vibrate into a radiance. It is the same with the rose. In the pulp of its petals you may find everything that went to make the rose, but the rose which is *māyā,* an image, is lost; its finality which has the touch of the infinite is gone. The rose appears to me to be still, but because of its metre of composition it has a lyric of movement within that stillness, which is the same as the dynamic quality of a picture that has a perfect harmony. It produces a music in our consciousness by giving it a swing of motion synchronous with its own. Had the picture consisted of a disharmonious aggregate of colours and lines, it would be deadly still.

In perfect rhythm, the art-form becomes like the stars which in their seeming stillness are never still, like a motionless flame that is nothing but movement. A great picture is always speaking, but news from a newspaper, even of some tragic happening, is still-born. Some news may be a mere commonplace in the obscurity of a journal; but give it a proper rhythm and it will never cease to shine. That is art. It has the magic wand which gives undying reality to all things it touches, and relates them to the personal being in us. We stand before its productions and say: I know you as I know myself, you are real.

Let me repeat here my remark about the function of art from a previous paper of mine: 'When we talk of aesthetics in relation to arts we must know that it is not about beauty in its ordinary meaning but in that deeper meaning which a poet has expressed in his utterance: truth is beauty, beauty truth. An artist may paint a picture of a decrepit person not pleasing to the eye, and yet we call it perfect when we become deeply conscious of its reality.'

Hopeless tragedies of life can never technically be called beautiful, but when appearing on the background of art they delight us because of the convincingness of their reality. It only proves that every object which fully asserts its existence to us because of its inherent finality, is beautiful; it is what is called in Sanskrit *manohara,* the stealer of the mind,—the mind which stands between the knower and the known. We have our primal sympathy for all things that exist, for when realized they stimulate the consciousness of our own existence. The fact that we exist has its truth in the fact that everything else does exist.

The *I am* in me realizes its own extension, its own infinity whenever it truly realizes something else. Unfortunately, owing to our limitations and a thousand and one pre-occupations, a great part of our world, though closely surrounding us, is far away from the lamp-post of our attention; it is dim, it passes by us, a caravan of shadows, like the landscape seen in the night from the window of an illuminated railway compartment: the passenger knows that the outside world exists, that it is important, but for the time being the railway carriage for him is far more significant. If among the innumerable objects in this world there be a few that come under the full illumination of our soul and thus assume reality for us, they constantly cry to our creative mind for a permanent representation. They belong to the same domain as the desire of ours which represents the longing for the permanence of our own self.

I do not mean to say that things to which we are bound by the tie of self-interest have the inspiration of reality: on the contrary, these are eclipsed by the shadow of our own self. The servant is not more real to us than the beloved. The narrow emphasis of utility diverts our attention from the complete man to the merely useful man. The thick label of market price obliterates the ultimate value of reality. It has been said in the *Brihad-Aranyaka:*

> The desire for the son does not make him dear, the son is dear for the sake of the self.

That is to say, in the son the father becomes conscious of a reality which is immediately and profoundly within him. He is delighted not because his son is perfect and beautiful, but because his son is indubitably real to him,—our joy, as I have said before, being the disinterested perception of the real. This is the source of our delight in all arts and literature, where reality is presented to us on the pedestal of its own absolute value.

All the deep impressions in our mind are accompanied by some emotions which set up their own variety of tremors in our consciousness. This agitation modulates our voice and movements and impels us to all creative display of colours, forms and sounds. This reminds me of the occasion when I saw inscribed on the wall of a school building, in exaggerated characters: 'Bipin is an egregious ass!' It amused me, and at the same time offered me an answer to the question, *what is art*.

No one takes the least trouble to proclaim the information that Bipin is tall, or that he suffers from a cold. Ordinarily our mind is soberly grey in its impression of Bipin. But when we love him or hate him, the fact of Bipin's existence becomes glowingly evident on the agitated background of passion. Then our mind can no longer remain neutral; it detaches the idea of Bipin from the immense multitude of what is non-significant to us, and according to its own power our mind tries to make him as unavoidably real to others as he is to ourselves.

The boy who angrily longed to give permanence to his indignant estimate of Bipin and make it universally accepted had nothing but his inadequate charcoal and ineffectual training, whereas his forefathers of the primitive age, when excited to anger, not only could give vent to it effectively in action, but also in an expression of gorgeous ferocity by the help of pigments, feathers, tinsel and war dance. That writing on the school wall, craving immortality, sadly begged for colours and rhythmic lines to be like its glorious congeners, the fresco paintings of the world-renowned caves, where the artists attempted to emphasise their estimate of certain personalities, and of sundry incidents, into permanence.

As art creations are emotional representations of facts and ideas they can never be like the product of a photographic camera which is passively receptive of lights and shadows in all their indiscriminate details. Our scientific mind is unbiased; it accepts facts with a cold-blooded curiosity that has no preference. The artistic mind is strongly biased, and that bias not only guides it in its fastidious selection of the subject, but also in that of its details. It throws coloured lights of emphasis on its theme in such a manner that it attains a character which clearly distinguishes it from its fellows. The skylarks of science offer corroboration of their truth through their similarity, the skylarks of artists and poets through their dissimilarity. If Shelley's poem on this bird were just like that of Wordsworth, it should have been rejected for its lack of truth.

As art embodies our personal, estimate of a thing, or character, or circumstance, the artist in his work does not follow nature in its capacious heterogeneity, but his own human nature which is selective. By leaving out whatever is non-essential for his own purpose of expression and intensifying what is significant, he brings out the truth of his creation much more vividly than he would if he copied actuality which is strictly impartial to whatever exists. The wholeness of God's creation is immensely vast and it is not possible for any detail to be too defiantly discrepant in its relation to it. But the background of human expression is small and therefore it is never possible to accommodate nature's details in our art compositions. It is childish to expect the primeval forest in the perspective of our garden plot, or an illustration of natural history in our works which modulate fact to the tune of our personality.

Once the question had been asked to me as to the place I assigned to music in my theory of art. I am bound to answer it, and I take this opportunity to offer my explanation.

Music is the most abstract of all arts, as mathematics is in the region of science. In fact, these two have a deep relationship with each other. Mathematics as the logic of number and dimension is the basis of our scientific knowledge. When taken out of its concrete associations with cosmic phenomena and reduced to symbols it reveals its grand structural majesty, the inevitableness of its own perfect concord. But there is also such a thing as the magic of mathematics which works at the root of all appearances, producing harmony of unity,—the cadence of inter-relation of the parts bringing them under the dominion of the whole. This rhythm of harmony has been extracted from its usual context and exhibited through the medium of sound. And thus the pure essence of expressiveness in existence is offered in music. In sound it finds the least resistance and has a freedom unencumbered by the burden of facts and thoughts. It gives it a power to arouse in us an intense feeling of reality; it seems to lead us into the soul of all things and make us feel the very breath of inspiration flowing from the supreme creative joy.

In the pictorial, plastic and verbal arts the object and our feelings with regard to it are closely associated, like the rose and its perfume. In music the feeling, extracted in sound, becomes itself an independent object. It assumes a tune-form which is definite, but a meaning which is indefinable and yet grips our mind with a sense of absolute truth.

There came a time, centuries ago, in Bengal, when the divine love drama that had its eternal play in human souls was vividly revealed by a personality radiating its intimate realization of God. The mind of a whole people was stirred by the vision of the world as an instrument through which sounded our invitation to the meeting of bliss. The ineffable mystery of God's love-call taking shape in an endless panorama of colours and forms, finding its chorus in the symphony of human affections, inspired activity in a music that overflowed the restrictions of classical conventionalism. Our *kirtan* music in Bengal came to its being like a star flung up by a burning whirlpool of emotion in the heart of a whole people.

There come in our history occasions when the consciousness of a large multitude becomes suddenly illumined with the recognition of something which rises far above the triviality of daily happenings. Such an occasion there was when the voice of Buddha reached distant shores across all physical and moral impediments. Then our life and our world found their profound meaning of reality in their relation to the central person who offered us emancipation of love. And men, in order to make this great human experience ever memorable, determined to do the impossible; they made rocks to speak, stones to sing, caves to remember; the cry of joy and hope took immortal forms along hills and deserts, across barren solitudes and populous cities. A gigantic creative endeavour built up its triumph in stupendous carvings, defying obstacles that were overwhelming. Such heroic activity over the greater part of the Eastern continent clearly answers the question: *What is art?*—It is the response of man's creative soul to the call of the real.

But the individual mind according to its temperament and training has its own recognition or reality in some of its special aspects. We can see from the Gandhara figures of Buddha that the artistic influence of Greece put its emphasis on the scientific aspect, on anatomical accuracy, while the purely Indian mind dwelt on the symbolic aspect and tried to give expression to the soul of Buddha, never acknowledging the limitations of realism. For the adventurous spirit of the great European sculptor, Rodin, the most significant aspect of reality is the unceasing struggle of the incomplete for its freedom from the fetters of imperfection, whereas before the naturally introspective mind of the Eastern artist the real appears in its ideal form of fulfilment.

Therefore, when we talk of such a fact as Indian Art, it indicates some truth based upon the Indian tradition and temperament. At the same time we must know that there is no such thing as absolute caste restriction in human cultures; they ever have the power to combine and produce new variations, and such combinations have been going on for ages proving the truth of the deep unity of human psychology. It is admitted that in Indian art the Persian element found no obstacles, and there are signs of various other alien influences. China and Japan have no hesitation in acknowledging their debt to India in their artistic and spiritual growth of life. Fortunately for our civilizations all such intermingling happened when professional art critics were not rampant and artists were not constantly nudged by the warning elbow of classifiers in their choice of inspiration. Our artists were never tiresomely reminded of the obvious fact that they were Indian; and in consequence they had the freedom to be naturally Indian in spite of all the borrowings that they indulged in.

The sign of greatness in great geniuses is their enormous capacity for borrowing, very often without their knowing it; they have unlimited credit in the world market of culture. Only mediocrities are ashamed and afraid of borrowing, for they do not know how to pay back the debt in their own coin. Even the most foolish of critics does not dare blame Shakespeare for what he openly appropriated from outside his own national inheritance. The human soul is proud of its comprehensive sensitiveness; it claims its freedom of entry everywhere when it is fully alive and awake. We congratulate ourselves on the fact, and consider it a sign of our being alive in soul, that European thoughts and literary forms found immediate hospitality in Bengali literature from the very beginning of its contact with our mind. It ushered in a great revolution in the realm of our literary expression.

Enormous changes have taken place, but our Indian soul has survived the shock and has vigorously thriven upon this cataclysm. It only shows that though human mentality, like the earth's atmosphere, has undoubtedly different temperatures in different geographical zones, yet it is not walled up into impassable compartments and the circulation of the common air over the entire globe continues to have its wholesome effect. So let us take heart and make daring experiments, venture out into the open road in the face of all risks, go through experiences in the great world of human mind defying unholy prohibitions preached by prudent little critics, laughing at them when in their tender solicitude for our safety they ask our artists to behave the good children and never to cross the threshold of their school-room.

Fearfully trying always to conform to a conventional type is a sign of immaturity. Only in babies is individuality of physiognomy blurred, and therefore personal distinction not strongly marked. Childishness is a mentality that can easily be generalised: children's babbling has the same sound-tottering everywhere, their toys are very nearly similar. But adult age is difficult of classification, it is composed of individuals who claim recognition of their personal individuality which is shown not only in its own uniqueness of manner but also in its own special response to all stimulations from outside.

I strongly urge our artists, vehemently to deny their obligation carefully to produce something that can be labelled as Indian art according to some old world mannerism. Let them proudly refuse to be herded into a pen like branded beasts that are treated as cattle and not as cows. Science is impersonal, it has its one aspect which is merely universal and therefore abstract; but art is personal and, therefore, through it the universal manifests itself in the guise of the individual, physiology expresses itself in physiognomy, philology in literature. Science is a passenger in a railway train of generalization; there reasoning minds from all directions come to make their journey together in a similar conveyance. Art is a solitary pedestrian, who walks alone among the multitude, continually assimilating various experiences, unclassifiable and uncatalogued.

There was a time when human races lived in comparative segregation and therefore the art adventurers had their experience within a narrow range of limits deeply-cut grooves of certain common characteristics. But today that range has vastly widened, claiming from us a much greater power of receptivity than what we were compelled to cultivate in former ages. If today we have a living soul that is sensitive to ideas and to beauty of form, let it prove its capacity by accepting all that is worthy of acceptance, not according to some blind injunction of custom or fashion, but in following one's instinct for eternal value—the instinct which is a God-given gift to all real artists. Even then our art is sure to have a quality which is Indian, but it must be an inner quality and not an artificially fostered formalism, and therefore not be too obtrusively obvious and abnormally self-conscious.

When in the name of Indian art we cultivate with deliberate aggressiveness a certain bigotry born of the habit of a past generation, we smother our soul under idiosyncrasies unearthed from buried centuries. These are like masks with exaggerated grimaces, that fail to respond to the ever changing play of life.

Art is not a gorgeous sepulchre immovably brooding over a lonely eternity of vanished years. It belongs to the procession of life, making constant adjustment with surprises, exploring unknown shrines of reality along its path of pilgrimage to a future which is as different from the past as the tree from the seed. Art represents the inexhaustible magnificence of creative spirit; it is generous in its acceptance and generous in its bestowal; it is unique in its manner and universal in its appeal; it is hospitable to the All because it has the wealth which is its own; its vision is new though its view may be old; it carries its special criterion of excellence within itself and therefore contemptuously refuses to be brow-beaten into conformity with a rhetoric manufactured by those who are not in the secret of the subtle mysteries of creation, who want to simplify through their academic code of law that which is absolutely simple through its spontaneity.

The art ideal of a people may take fixed root in a narrow soil of tradition developing a vegetable character, producing a monotonous type of leaves and flowers in a continuous round of repetitions. Because it is not disturbed by a mind which ever seeks the unattained, and because it is held firm by a habit which piously discourages allurements of all adventures, it is neither helped by the growing life of the people nor does it help to enrich that life. It remains confined to coteries of specialists who nourish it with delicate attention and feel proud of the ancient flavour of its aristocratic exclusiveness. It is not a stream that flows through and fertilises the soil, but a rare wine stored in a dark cellar underground, acquiring a special stimulation through its artificially nurtured, barren antiquity. In exchange for a freedom of movement which is the prerogative of vigorous youth, we may gain a static perfection of senility that has minted its wisdom into hard and rounded maxims. Unfortunately, there are those who believe it an advantage for a child to be able to borrow its grandparents' age and be spared the trouble and risk of growing, and think that it is a sign of wealthy respectability for an artist lazily to cultivate a monotonously easy success by means of some hoarded patrimony of tradition.

And yet we may go too far if we altogether reject tradition in the cultivation of art, and it is an incomplete statement of truth to say that habits have the sole effect of deadening our mind. The tradition which is helpful is like a channel that helps the current to flow. It is open where the water runs onward, guarding it only where there is danger in deviation. The bee's life in its channel of habit has no opening,—it revolves within a narrow circle of perfection. Man's life has time-honoured institutions which are its organized habits. When these act as enclosures, then the result may be perfect, like a beehive of wonderful precision of form, but unsuitable for the mind which has unlimited possibilities of progress.

Before I close my address let me take this opportunity to ask our artists to realize the greatness of their vocation: it is to take a creative part in the festival of life, the festival which is to give expression to the infinite in man. In our everyday world we live in poverty; our resources have to be husbanded with care; our strength becomes exhausted and we come to our God as beggars. On festival days, we display our wealth and say to Him that we are even as He is; and we are not afraid to spend. This is the day when we bring to Him our gift of joy. For we truly meet God, when we come to Him, with our offerings and not our wants, and such offerings need Art for its vehicle.

I need have no anxiety about the great world to which I have been born. The sun does not wait to be trimmed by me. But from the early morning all my thoughts are occupied by the little world of my *self*. Its importance is owing to the fact that I have a world given to me which is *mine,* which depends for its perfection on my own creative soul. It is great because I have the power to make it worthy of its relationship with me; it is great, because by its help I can offer my own hospitality to the God of all the world.

(1926)

My Pictures

I

An apology is due from me for my intrusion into the world of pictures and thus offering a perfect instance to the saying that those who do not know that they know not are apt to be rash where angels are timidly careful. I, as an artist, cannot claim any merit for my courage; for it is the unconscious courage of the unsophisticated, like that of one who walks in dream on a perilous path, who is saved only because he is blind to the risk.

The only training which I had from my young days was the training in rhythm in thought, the rhythm in sound. I had come to know that rhythm gives reality to that which is desultory, which is insignificant in itself. And therefore, when the scratches in my manuscript cried, like sinners, for salvation, and assailed my eyes with the ugliness of their irrelevance, I often took more time in rescuing them into merciful finality of rhythm than in carrying on what was my obvious task. In the process of this salvage work I came to discover one fact, that in the universe of forms there is a perpetual activity of natural selection in lines, and only the fittest survives which has in itself the fitness of cadence, and I felt that to solve the unemployment problem of the homeless heterogeneous into interrelated balance of fulfilment is creation itself.

My pictures are my versification, in lines. If by chance they are entitled to claim recognition, it must be primarily for some rhythmic significance of form which is ultimate and not for any interpretation of an idea or representation of a fact.

(May 1930)

II

When, at the age of five, I was compelled to learn and to repeat the lessons from my textbook, I had the notion that literature had its mysterious manifestation on the printed pages, that it represented some supernatural tyranny of an immaculate perfection. Such a despairing feeling of awe was dissipated from my mind when by chance I discovered in my own person that verse-making was not beyond the range of an untrained mind and tottering handwriting. Since then my sole medium of expression has been words, followed at sixteen by music, which also came to me as a surprise.

In the meanwhile the modern art movement, following the line of the oriental tradition, was started by my nephew Abanindranath. I watched his activities with an envious mood of self-diffidence, being thoroughly convinced that my fate had refused me passport across the strict boundaries of letters.

But one thing which is common to all arts is the principle of rhythm which transforms inert materials into living creations. My instinct for it and my training in its use led me to know that lines and colours in art are no carriers of information; they seek their rhythmic incarnation in pictures. Their ultimate purpose is not to illustrate or to copy some outer fact or inner vision, but to evolve a harmonious wholeness which finds its passage through our eyesight into imagination. It neither questions our mind for meaning nor burdens it with unmeaningness, for it is, above all, meaning. Desultory lines obstruct the freedom of our vision with the inertia of their irrelevance. They do not move with the great march of all things. They have no justification to exist and therefore they rouse up against them their surroundings; they perpetually disturb peace. For this reason the scattered scratches and corrections in my manuscripts cause me annoyance. They represent regrettable mischance, like a gapingly foolish crowd stuck in a wrong place, undecided as to how or where to move on. But if the spirit of a dance is inspired in the heart of the crowd, the unrelated many would find a perfect unity and be relieved of its hesitation between to be and not to be. I try to make my corrections dance, connect them in a rhythmic relationship and transform accumulation into adornment.

This has been my unconscious training in drawing. I find disinterested pleasure in this work of reclamation, often giving to it more time and care than to my immediate duty in literature that has the sole claim upon my attention, often aspiring to a permanent recognition from the world. It interests me deeply to watch how lines find their life and character, as their connection with each other develops in varied cadences, and how they begin to speak in gesticulations. I can imagine the universe to be a universe of lines which in their movements and combinations pass on their signals of existence along the interminable chain of moments. The rocks and clouds, the trees, the waterfalls, the dance of the fiery orbs, the endless procession of life send up across silent eternity and limitless space a symphony of gestures with which mingles the dumb wail of lines that are widowed gypsies roaming about for a chance union of fulfilment.

In the manuscript of creation there occur erring lines and erasures, solitary incongruities, standing against the world principle of beauty and balance, carrying perpetual condemnation. They offer problems and therefore material to the *Visvakarma,* the Great Artist, for they are the sinners whose obstreperous individualism has to be modulated into a new variation of universal concord.

And this was my experience with the casualties in my manuscripts, when the vagaries of the ostracized mistakes had their conversion into rhythmic inter-relationship, giving birth to unique forms and characters. Some assumed the temperature exaggeration of a probable animal that had unaccountably missed its chance of existence, some a bird that only can soar in our dreams and find its nest in some hospitable lines that we may offer it in our canvas. Some lines showed anger, some placid benevolence, through some lines ran an essential laughter that refused to apply for its credential to the shape of a mouth which is a mere accident. These lines often expressed passions that were abstract, evolved characters that hung upon subtle suggestions. Though I did not know whether such unclassified apparitions of non-deliberate origin could claim their place in decent art, they gave me intense satisfaction and very often made me neglect my important works. In connection with this came to my mind the analogy of music's declaration of independence. There can be no question that originally melody accompanied words, giving interpretation to the sentiments contained in them. But music threw off this bond of subservience and represented moods abstracted from words, and characters that were indefinite. In fact, this liberated music does not acknowledge that feelings which can be expressed in words are essential for its purpose, though they may have their secondary place in musical structure. This right of independence has given music its greatness, and I suspect that evolution of pictorial and plastic art develops on this line, aiming to be freed from an absolute alliance with natural facts or incidents.

However, I need not formulate any doctrine of art but be contented by simply saying that in my case my pictures did not have their origin in trained discipline, in tradition and deliberate attempt at illustration, but in my instinct for rhythm, my pleasure in harmonious combination of lines and colours.

(July 1930)

III

The world of sound is a tiny bubble in the silence of the infinite. The Universe has its only language of gesture, it talks in the voice of pictures and dance. Every object in this world proclaims in the dumb signal of lines and colours the fact that it is not a mere logical abstraction or a mere thing of use but is unique in itself, it carries the miracle of its existence.

There are countless things which we know but do not recognize their own dignity of truth, independent of the fact that they are injurious or beneficial. It is enough that a flower exists as a flower, but my cigarette has no other claim upon me for its recognition but as being subservient to my smoking habit.

But there are other things which in their dynamic quality of rhythm or character make us insistently acknowledge the fact that they are. In the book of creation they are the sentences that are underlined with coloured pencil and we cannot pass them by. They seem to cry to us, 'See, here I am', and our mind bows its head and never question, 'Why are you?'

A Painting by Rabindranath Tagore
(*Courtesy*: Rabindra Bhavan, Visva-Bharati)

In a picture the artist creates the language of undoubted reality, and we are satisfied that we see. It may not be the representation of a beautiful woman but that of a commonplace donkey, or of something that has no external credential of truth in nature but only in its own inner artistic significance.

People often ask me about the meaning of my pictures. I remain silent even as my pictures are. It is for them to express and not to explain. They have nothing ulterior behind their own appearance for the thoughts to explore and words to describe, and if that appearances carries its ultimate worth, then they remain, otherwise they are rejected and forgotten even though they may have some scientific truth or ethical justification.

It is related in the drama of *Shakuntala,* how one busy morning there stood humbly before the maiden of the forest-hermitage a stranger youth who did not give his name. Her soul acknowledged him at once without question. She did know him not but only saw him and for her he was the artist God's masterpiece to which must be offered the full value of love.

Days passed. There came at her gate another guest, a venerable sage who was formidable. And, sure of his claim to a dutiful welcome, proudly he announced. 'I am here!' But she missed his voice, for it did not carry with it an inherent meaning, it needed a commentary of household virtue, pious words of sanction which could assign a sacred value to a guest, the value that was not of the irresponsible art, but of moral responsibility.

Love is kindred to art, it is inexplicable. Duty can be measured by the degree of its benefit, utility by the profit and power it may bring, but art by nothing but itself. There are other factors of life which are visitors that come and go. Art is the guest that comes and remains. The others may be important but art is inevitable.

(1930)

Man's Nature

11

From the time when Man became truly conscious of his own self he also became conscious of a mysterious spirit of unity which found its manifestation through him in his society. It is a subtle medium of relationship between individuals, which is not for any utilitarian purpose but for its own ultimate truth, not a sum of arithmetic but a value of life. Somehow Man has felt that this comprehensive spirit of unity has a divine character which could claim the sacrifice of all that is individual in him, that in it dwells his highest meaning transcending his limited self, representing his best freedom.

Man's reverential loyalty to this spirit of unity is expressed in his religion it is symbolized in the names of his deities. That is why, in the beginning, his gods were tribal gods, even gods of the different communities belonging to the same tribe. With the extension of the consciousness of human unity his God became revealed to him as one and universal, proving that the truth of human unity is the truth of Man's God.

In the Sanskrit language, religion goes by the name *dharma,* which in the derivative meaning implies the principle of relationship that holds us firm, and in its technical sense means the virtue of a thing, the essential quality of it; for instance, heat is the essential quality of fire, though in certain of its stages it may be absent.

Religion consists in the endeavour of men to cultivate and express those qualities which are inherent in the nature of Man the Eternal, and to have faith in him. If these qualities were absolutely natural in individuals, religion could have no purpose. We begin our history with all the original promptings of our brute nature which helps us to fulfil those vital needs of ours that are immediate. But deeper within us there is a current of tendencies which runs in many ways in a contrary direction, the life current of universal humanity. Religion has its function in reconciling the contradiction, by subordinating the brute nature to what we consider as the truth of Man. This is helped when our faith in the Eternal Man, whom we call by different names and imagine in different images, is made strong. The contradiction between the two natures in us is so great that men have willingly sacrificed their vital needs and courted death in order to express their *dharma*, which represents the truth of the Supreme Man.

A page from the manuscript of *The Religion of Man*
(*Courtesy*: Rabindra Bhavan, Visva-Bharati)

The vision of the Supreme Man is realized by our imagination, but not created by our mind. More real than individual men, he surpasses each of us in his permeating personality which is transcendental. The procession of his ideas, following his great purpose, is ever moving across obstructive facts towards the perfected truth. We, the individuals, having our place in his composition, may or may not be in conscious harmony with his purpose, may even put obstacles in his path bringing down our doom upon ourselves. But we gain our true religion when we consciously co-operate with him, finding our exceeding joy through suffering and sacrifice. For through our own love for him we are made conscious of a great love that radiates from his being, who is Mahātma, the Supreme Spirit.

The great Chinese sage Lao-tze has said: 'One who may die, but will not perish, has life everlasting.' It means that he lives in the life of the immortal Man. The urging for this life induces men to go through the struggle for a true survival. And it has been said in our scripture: 'Through *adharma* (the negation of *dharma*) man prospers, gains what appears desirable, conquers enemies, but he perishes at the root.' In this saying it is suggested that there is a life which is truer for men than their physical life which is transient.

Our life gains what is called 'value' in those of its aspects which represent eternal humanity in knowledge, in sympathy, in deeds, in character and creative works. And from the beginning of our history we are seeking often at the cost of everything else, the value for our life and not merely success; in other words, we are trying to realize in ourselves the immortal Man, so that we may die but not perish. This is the meaning of the utterance in the Upanishad: *Tam vedyam purusham veda, yatha ma vo mrityuh parivyathah*—'Realize the Person so that thou mayst not suffer from death.'

The meaning of these words is highly paradoxical, and cannot be proved by our senses or our reason, and yet its influence is so strong in men that they have cast away all fear and greed, defied all the instincts that cling to the brute nature, for the sake of acknowledging and preserving a life which belongs to the Eternal Person. It is all the more significant because many of them do not believe in its reality, and yet are ready to fling away for it all that they believe to be final and the only positive fact.

We call this ideal reality 'spiritual'. That word is vague; nevertheless, through the dim light which reaches us across the barriers of physical existence, we seem to have a stronger faith in the spiritual Man than in the physical; and from the dimmest period of his history, Man has a feeling that the apparent facts of existence are not final; that his supreme welfare depends upon his being able to remain in perfect relationship with some great mystery behind the veil, at the threshold of a larger life, which is for giving him a far higher value than a mere continuation of his physical life in the material world.

Our physical body has its comprehensive reality in the physical world, which may be truly called our universal body, without which our individual body would miss its function. Our physical life realizes its growing meaning through a widening freedom in its relationship with the physical world, and this gives it a greater happiness than the mere pleasure of satisfied needs. We become aware of a profound meaning of our own self at the consciousness of some ideal of perfection some truth beautiful or majestic which gives us an inner sense of completeness, a heightened sense of our own reality. This strengthens man's faith, effective even if indefinite—his faith in an objective ideal of perfection comprehending the human world. His vision of it has been beautiful or distorted, luminous or obscure, according to the stages of development that his consciousness has attained. But whatever may be the name and nature of his religious creed, man's ideal of human perfection has been based upon a bond of unity running through individuals culminating in a supreme Being who represents the eternal in human personality. In his civilization the perfect expression of this idea produces the wealth of truth which is for the revelation of Man and not merely for the success of life. But when this creative ideal which is *dharma* gives place to some overmastering passion in a large body of men civilization bursts out in an explosive flame, like a star that has lighted its own funeral pyre of boisterous brilliancy.

When I was a child I had the freedom to make my own toys out of trifles and create my own games from imagination. In my happiness my playmates had their full share, in fact the complete enjoyment of my games depended upon their taking part in them. One day, in this paradise of our childhood, entered the temptation from the market world of the adult. A toy brought from an English shop was given to one of our companions; it was perfect, it was big and wonderfully life-like. He became proud of the toy and less mindful of the game; he kept that expensive thing carefully away from us, glorying in his exclusive possession of it, feeling himself superior to his playmates whose toys were cheap. I am sure if he could use the modern language of history he would say that he was more civilized than ourselves to the extent of his owning that ridiculously perfect toy.

One thing he failed to realize in his excitement—a fact which at the moment seemed to him insignificant—that this temptation obscured something a great deal more perfect than his toy, the revelation of the perfect child whichever dwells in the heart of man, in other words, the *dharma* of the child. The toy merely expressed his wealth but not himself, not the child's creative spirit, not the child's generous joy in his play, his identification of himself with others who were his compeers in his play world. Civilization is to express Man's *dharma* and not merely his cleverness, power and possession.

Once there was an occasion for me to motor down to Calcutta from a place a hundred miles away. Something wrong with the mechanism made it necessary for us to have a repeated supply of water almost every half-hour. At the first village where we were compelled to stop, we asked the help of a man to find water for us. It proved quite a task for him, but when we offered him his reward, poor though he was, he refused to accept it. In fifteen other villages the same thing happened. In a hot country, where travellers constantly need water and where the water supply grows scanty in summer, the villagers consider it their duty to offer water to those who need it. They could easily make a business out of it, following the inexorable law of demand and supply. But the ideal which they consider to be their *dharma* has become one with their life. They do not claim any personal merit for possessing it.

Lao-tze, speaking about the man who is truly good, says: 'He quickens but owns not. He acts but claims not. Merit he accomplishes but dwells not in it. Since he does not dwell in it, it will never leave him.' That which is outside ourselves we can sell; but that which is one with our being we cannot sell. This complete assimilation of truth belongs to the paradise of perfection; it lies beyond the purgatory of self-consciousness. To have reached it proves a long process of civilization.

To be able to take a considerable amount of trouble in order to supply water to a passing stranger and yet never to claim merit or reward for it seems absurdly and negligibly simple compared with the capacity to produce an amazing number of things per minute. A millionaire tourist, ready to corner the food market and grow rich by driving the whole world to the brink of starvation, is sure to feel too superior to notice this simple thing while rushing through our villages at sixty miles an hour.

Yes, it is simple, as simple as it is for a gentleman to be a gentleman; but that simplicity is the product of centuries of culture. That simplicity is difficult of imitation. In a few years' time, it might be possible for me to learn how to make holes in thousands of needles simultaneously by turning a wheel, but to be absolutely simple in one's hospitality to one's enemy, or to a stranger, requires generations of training. Simplicity takes no account of its own value, claims no wages, and therefore those who are enamoured of power do not realize that simplicity of spiritual expression is the highest product of civilization.

A process of disintegration can kill this rare fruit of a higher life, as a whole race of birds possessing some rare beauty can be made extinct by the vulgar power of avarice which has civilized weapons. This fact was clearly proved to me when I found that the only place where a price was expected for the water given to us was a suburb at Calcutta, where life was richer, the water supply easier and more abundant and where progress flowed in numerous channels in all directions. It shows that a harmony of character which the people once had was lost—the harmony with the inner self which is greater in its universality than the self that gives prominence to its personal needs. The latter loses its feeling of beauty and generosity in its calculation of profit; for there it represents exclusively itself and not the universal man.

There is an utterance in the Atharva Veda, wherein appears the question as to who it was that gave Man his music. Birds repeat their single notes, or a very simple combination of them, but Man builds his world of music and establishes ever new rhythmic relationship of notes. These reveal to him a universal mystery of creation which cannot be described. They bring to him the inner rhythm that transmutes facts into truths. They give him pleasure not merely for his sense of hearing, but for his deeper being, which gains satisfaction in the ideal of perfect unity. Somehow man feels that truth finds its body in such perfection; and when he seeks for his own best revelation he seeks a medium which has the harmonious unity, as has music. Our impulse to give expression to Universal Man produces arts and literature. They in their cadence of lines, colours, movements, words, thoughts, express vastly more than what they appear to be on the surface. They open the windows of our mind to the eternal reality of man. They are the superfluity of wealth of which we claim our common inheritance whatever may be the country and time to which we belong; for they are inspired by the universal mind. And not merely in his arts, but in his own behaviour, the individual must for his excellence give emphasis to an ideal which has some value of truth that ideally belongs to all men. In other words, he should create a music of expression in his conduct and surroundings which makes him represent the supreme Personality. And civilization is the creation of the race, its expression of the universal Man.

When I first visited Japan I had the opportunity of observing where the two parts of the human sphere strongly contrasted; one, on which grew up the ancient continents of social ideal, standards of beauty, codes of personal behaviour; and the other part, the fluid element, the perpetual current that carried wealth to its shores from all parts of the world. In half a century's time Japan has been able to make her own the mighty spirit of progress which suddenly burst upon her one morning in a storm of insult and menace. China also has had her rousing, when her self-respect was being knocked to pieces through series of helpless years, and I am sure she also will master before long the instrument which hurt her to the quick. But the ideals that imparted life and body to Japanese civilization had been nourished in the reverent hopes of countless generations through ages which were not primarily occupied in an incessant hunt for opportunities. They had those large tracts of leisure in them which are necessary for the blossoming of Life's beauty and the ripening of her wisdom.

On the one hand we can look upon the modern factories in Japan with their numerous mechanical organizations and engines of production and destruction of the latest type. On the other hand, against them we may see some fragile vase, some small piece of silk, some architecture of sublime simplicity, some perfect lyric of bodily movement. We may also notice the Japanese expression of courtesy daily extracting from them a considerable amount of time and trouble. All these have come not from any accurate knowledge of things but from an intense consciousness of the value of reality which takes time for its fullness. What Japan reveals in her skilful manipulation of telegraphic wires and railway lines, of machines for manufacturing things and for killing men, is more or less similar to what we see in other countries which have similar opportunity for training. But in her art of living, her pictures, her code of conduct, the various forms of beauty which her religious and social ideals assume Japan expresses her own personality, her *dharma,* which, in order to be of any worth, must be unique and at the same time represent Man of the Everlasting Life.

Lao-tze has said: 'Not knowing the eternal causes passions to rise; and that is evil.' He has also said: 'Let us die, and yet not perish.' For we die when we lose our physical life, we perish when we miss our humanity. And humanity is the *dharma* of human beings.

What is evident in this world is the endless procession of moving things; but what is to be realized, is the supreme human Truth by which the human world is permeated.

We must never forget today that a mere movement is not valuable in itself, that it may be a sign of a dangerous form of inertia. We must be reminded that a great upheaval of spirit, a universal realization of true dignity of man once caused by Buddha's teachings in India, started a movement for centuries which produced illumination of literature, art, science and numerous efforts of public beneficence. This was a movement whose motive force was not some additional accession of knowledge or power or urging of some overwhelming passion. It was an inspiration for freedom, the freedom which enables us to realize *dharma,* the truth of Eternal Man.

Lao-tze in one of his utterances has said: 'Those who have virtue (*dharma*) attend to their obligations; those who have no virtue attend to their claims.' Progress which is not related to an inner *dharma*, but to an attraction which is external, seeks to satisfy our endless claims. But civilization, which is an ideal, gives us the abundant power to renounce which is the power that realizes the infinite and inspires creation.

This great Chinese sage has said: 'To increase life is called a blessing.' For, the increase of life realizes the eternal life and yet does not transcend the limits of life's unity. The mountain pine grows tall and great, its every inch maintains the rhythm of an inner balance, and therefore even in its seeming extravagance it has the reticent grace of self-control. The tree and its productions belong to the same vital system of cadence; the timber, the flowers, leaves and fruits are one with the tree; their exuberance is not a malady of exaggeration, but a blessing.

Man

12

The road is ever extended to the outside and has no meaning within itself. Its significance is reached when it reaches the home where begins the manifestation of the inward. When the course of evolution advanced to the stage of Man its character changed, it shifted its emphasis mainly from the body to the mind. There is relentless competition among them, where creatures struggle to preserve their physical integrity. But in their mind it becomes possible for them to realize their unity and their fulfilment in mutual co-operation. In the world of Man individuals are conscious of a comprehensive truth which is spiritual and whose members they are themselves. The best expression of Man therefore is that which does not exclusively represent an isolated mind, but can be accepted by the minds of men of all times. To set up creeds and practices to which the universal mind cannot respond is what we call barbarism.

Once, seeking perfection, Man engaged in external forms, in rituals and ceremonies. At last, in the language of the *Gita,* he declared that the sacrifice which is comprehended in the inner culture (ज्ञान यज्ञ) is superior to material sacrifices (द्रव्यमय यज्ञ). In the words of Christ, he heard that purity lies, not in external commands and prohibitions, but in the sanctifying of the heart. This was the invocation of the universal Personality in the mind of the individual person. The final utterance of this very consciousness is that he alone knows Truth who realizes in his own soul those of others, and in the soul of others, his own.

The aspect of man which has surpassed the animal grows with its ideal. It is an aspiration for that which is not evident in his material world nor urgent for his physical life, it belongs to his universal self.

In the *Rigveda* we find of this universal Being:

पादोऽस्य विश्वाभूतानि।
त्रिपादस्यामृतं दिवि।।

A quarter of him is in the apparent world, the remainder subsists above in the form of immortality. This is proved when the individual man at a great cost of himself thinks the thoughts of all men, fulfils the desire of the many and gives form to the joy that is for every one. The extent to which his trend is in the opposite direction, towards the narrow distinctions of time and place, to that extent he is a barbarian.

The human body is a universe inhabited by millions of cells. Each of them is instinct with its own individual life and yet with a deep direction towards a mystery of unity. If they had self-consciousness they would have been conscious of their separateness and at the same time of their identity with the whole body. The latter fact could only have been possible through an unaccountable indication of relationship, though the complete and direct knowledge of the whole body would surely be beyond the power of those cells.

For, this body exists not only here and now, but its past persists in it, its future awaits it. There is also a common element of general felicity pervading the whole system which cannot be analysed and which is what we mean by health. Besides this each cell embodies a spirit of self-dedication to the purpose of the maintenance of life's wholeness. If we try to grasp the mystery of this career, we can understand that the truest nature of these minute bodies centres round something which we can call their universal aspect.

It is the same with Man. He has observed the deeper endeavour of his own heart and felt that he is not exclusively an individual: he is also one in spirit with the universal Man, under whose inspiration the individual engages in expressing his ultimate truth through crossing nature's limitations. To these expressions he gives the name of the true, the good, the beautiful, not only from the point of view of the preservation and enrichment of society, but from the completeness of his own self.

Let us imagine the creature as if he is born, lives and dies in a railway carriage. This train travels towards a fixed destination along a definite narrow route. The head of the animal is parallel to the floor of the carriage, his vision is stretched downward, and he carries on his quest of food and recreation within the limits of the car. Even in this restricted sphere, opposition and danger are many, and his time is taken up in struggling with them. He cannot lift up his head and stand up-right like man. His vision does not reach up to the window above. The impulse of his mind does not take him beyond the needs of the security of life.

Man has stood up and found the window in front. He has come to know that the universe is not confined within the carriage. Outside it, vistas on vistas open out. Would it have mattered if he had remained indifferent to the 'beyond' which serves no immediate need? But in defiance of the sharply-mapped dominion of the Life Force he ventured out to find his own autonomy. In this triumphal march, his natural instincts do not side with him. On this path, he knows neither comfort nor rest, and yet hundreds of explorers are continually widening the path and opening it up even at the cost of their own lives.

By stooping downward, the animal sees things piecemeal and separate and his smell is allied to his sight. Visual perception is relatively disinterested and is therefore the more important in the kingdom of knowledge. Affection through smell is within the borders of the physical faculties. The awareness of objects which animals obtain through smell and sight is essentially in the interest of immediate needs. By lifting up his head, man no longer saw merely separate and distinct objects; he also had a complete view of the unity of manifold things. He saw himself at the centre of an undivided extension. The erect man prized the distant more than the near. His mind turned towards the unknown and unexpected. It is not only his sight, but also his two hands that have found liberation. If the hands had not gained exemption from the tasks of the feet, they would have been in a subordinate position in the body, a fourth caste with the indignity attached to the untouchable. In the human body, the *śūdra* was elevated to *Kṣattriyahood.* He found the dignity of the hand and entered into partnership with the mind. He no longer remained a whole-time servant in the routine of daily life. He became busy with experiments on the unexpected, with construction of the unthought of, with largely the useless. Animals also have plenty of leisure when they can play, but in their life, play is secondary. Besides, their play also represents the tendencies of their life's needs. The sport of the kitten is to play at catching imaginary rats, and the pup finds its joy in the loud pretence of fighting its own tail. But what may be called recreation of man, what serves no useful purpose in his life, only too often becomes primary and becomes even more insistent than the routine of his daily life. In the foreground of his leisure, man is everywhere busy in building up his paradise,—there lies the garden of his imaginings. From this we infer that Nature may control man's supply of food, and for the sake of the body, he may be forced to meet her exactions; but the freehold temple-land where man has his spiritual home is outside nature's domain. There is no risk of urgent summons there from many overlord. The greatest obligation there is a voluntary obligation. It is the challenge of the ideal, the challenge of humanity, the ignoring of the greed of things in the endeavour after the realization by man, of his universal self.

In the animal world, the nebula of consciousness is diffused in indistinct light. That nebula was concentrated in man and declared in the language of radiant light, अयमहं भो—'Here am I.' In the history of man there began from that day in many forms, in many ways and many languages the answers to the one fundamental question, 'What am I?' In the true answer to this question lies his joy, his glory. He has understood that he is not simple, but hides a mystery of depth within himself, and that he will finally know himself only when the veils of the mystery have been pierced. Through centuries he has persisted in this attempt. He has founded innumerable religions and institutions. He protests against his natural instincts and tried to force on himself the recognition that, in truth, he is far greater than what he externally appears to be. He is trying to accept in his mind the idea of Being who is ideally far greater than himself and yet intimately related to him. It is by what he adores that he proves wherein, in his own estimation, lies his truth. Needless to say, that sometimes in the attempt to answer this question, the object of adoration that he imagines, reveals a mind which is blind in its intelligence, vulgar in its morality and deformed in its ideal of beauty. Such answer we shall regard as mistaken. Like all mistakes, these must also be rectified by a universal standard of truth, goodness and beauty.

When the physical side was of primary importance in the evolution of animal life, many animals degenerated or died out as the result of some maladjustment in their bodily constitution. When in the course of evolution the conscious self, or 'I' appeared in man, any mistake about this self led and leads to a death far greater than bodily destruction. All great prophets have given the same strange answer that the mistake lies in the obstacles to knowing the self in the not-self. The unceasing attempt of man to remove such obstacles and to find his truth beyond himself is represented in most of his institutions.

Animals live on the terrestrial globe, but man lives in what he calls his country. This country is not geographic, but spiritual. It is enriched with the currents of thought and love that have flowed through the ages. Countless is the number of those who have gone through suffering and death in order to prove the truth of the Person who is immortal in them, and the country is the creation of their sacrifice. Irrespective of caste or colour, their thoughts and their achievements belong to all men. Human beings live in a country which means a region where each man exists beyond the boundaries of his time and place, a region where his learning and his endeavours become true in the communion of all men of all times. The past and the future equally belong to the World-Man. Man likes to think that his ideal of perfection has already been realized in same departed past. This is why we find that in the mythologies of almost all races the golden age is imagined in the past. These legends express the aspiration of man that what is established before the beginnings of time, shall be continuously tested throughout its limitless flow. Though man no longer admits that the golden age is in the past, yet in all his strivings after excellence there is an implicit expectation of the golden age to come in future. A person may be an atheist and yet there is no lack of instance that he does not consider it a loss to sacrifice his immediate present, only because he feels that he exists more truly in that unarrived future.

The major aspects of the Supreme man are yet unrevealed. The hope of revealing him extends continually to the future. The Supreme man is to come. His chariot is on the move, but He has not yet arrived. The marriage party is continually gathering, its members are waiting for ages in the distance one hears the music of the bridegroom's march. Messengers go forward on the difficult path to receive Him and lead Him to the feast. This urgency of man towards the indefinite future counts no cost of life, this quest of his final certainty in the midst of the uncertain and the unarrived knows no rest. Man meets with obstacles again and again on his dangerous way; again and again he finds himself baffled and yet he cannot give up his quest. This perseverance might have been called mere madness, but man has given to it the name of greatness. We find man's mind continually attracted by a sense of perfection not yet attained, like the natural groping of the plant in a dark room towards the light beyond the walls. The light is true. If the source from which the attraction of the perfect continually radiates be not equally true, the thoughts that men think, the tasks they undertake for the refinement of the spirit over and above the needs of bare existence, all become utterly meaningless. From time to time we reach this truth in our resolves, in our meditations, in our ideals. In the glow of suffering, in the glory of death, we perceive this ineffable spirit of perfection. It has taken our knowledge out of its narrow roost and given it freedom in a wider field. Otherwise the art of cookery would have found from men more acceptance than the science of the molecule. Today man's final physical analysis has arrived at mathematical symbols. Once man had placed the theory of light beyond intelligibility. He made the curious statement that vibrations in the ether are felt by us as light. Light which reveals all material things in the field of our vision turned out to be the manifestation of something which is utterly beyond our comprehension. We only know through experience that waves of different rhythms form it. It is further reported now that to call it mere wave-radiation does not give a full account of the nature of light; it also radiates minute corpuscles. All these contradictory statements are beyond the simple language of the ordinary intelligence of man. But man was not to be frightened by the deep water of the unintelligible. He declared the stone wall to be the unceasing dance of electrons and never for a moment suspected that he had perhaps turned insane. It never occurred to him that perhaps Reason is an acrobat in the circus of the mind, that is profession is to turn everything upside down. If animals were placed in judgment over man, they would have characterized him as born insane. In fact, human science has proved all men to be creatures possessed by a universal dementia. It prompts them to say that things are not at all what they appear to be, but just the reverse. Animals never declare such libel about themselves. To their instinct a thing is what is, in other words, for them only facts exist. The area of their world is confined to its surface. All their obligations are at its groundfloor.

As with other animal fact constitutes man's resources, and yet his wealth consists in truth. The ultimate aim of wealth is not to satisfy needs but to convey the sense of splendour. That is why man declares भूमैव सुखम्—that there is no happiness in littleness, it lies in immensity.

These are after all the words of a spendthrift. Caution tells us that it is a matter for congratulation when our needs agree in measure with what we have. There is a proverb in English that the enough is as good as a feast. Our *Śāstras* also tell us सुखार्थी संयतो भवेत्—that he who seeks happiness must be contented.

We thus seem to meet the two contradictory statements that happiness does and does not lie in contentment. The reason for this apparent contradiction is that there is a basic duality in man's being. In the aspect of man which belongs to animal life, the satisfaction of his necessities is adequate to his happiness. But in his heart of hearts, man the animal reaches up to the World-Man. There he no longer wants mere happiness, but something greater. He wants magnificence. That is why of all animals man alone is intemperate. He wants profusely and has to give profusely, for in him there is the Infinite man. This Infinite Man does not hanker after happiness, nor is he afraid of suffering. This Infinite Man shatters the shelters of comfort which men build, and continuously calls them out to an architecture of a difficult design. The little man who is also in us laughs in mockery at this wasting of our substance in wild-goose chase. But he laughs in vain.

In the Upanishad there is a question and answer about God: सभगव: कस्मिन् प्रतिष्ठित इति—'Where does God have his seat?' The answer comes, स्वे महिम्नि—'In his own glory.' This glory is his nature, and his nature is his joy.

Man's delight is also in his glory. That is why it is said that happiness is in immensity. But the nature to which glory belongs is realized by man only through strain and struggle. Only through great suffering is measured the truth of his happiness. There is continual tension between man's natural condition and his true character. That is why the path of religion, the path dictated by his inmost nature is called the path that is difficult of crossing,—दुर्गं पथस्तत् कवयो वदन्ति।

The nature of an animal conforms to its condition. Its claims never exceed what is due to it. But with man it is different. He puts forward claims far beyond what was due to him by nature. The portion allotted to one can be fixed, but there is no limit to the extras one may demand. Man finds sustenance for life from his allotted portion. But it is his extras that reveal his glory. Even in respect of keeping himself alive, man exacts many extras. He must live magnificently, for this

his sustenance must not be commonplace. It is not enough that his dress and his dwelling should merely serve their barest purposes: they must also reveal his greatness, reveal something which is worthy of man; and a greater portion of the activities of his life is engaged in crossing the boundaries of a passive existence where there is a provision for enough, but none for the feast. Man has an inherent distrust of what is offered to his senses, what lies spread before his instincts on the surface of existence. For he himself is not superficial, he realizes that deep within him there is something which he calls truth and which is often the opposite of what seems to be the fact.

The friction of trees produces fire. If the human intellect had accepted the merest fact that the fire is produced, and asked no further questions, we could not take it to task. It is not known because there is nothing to know, is a statement whose propriety cannot be doubted. But man must have extras in his department of knowledge, the extras, which at least for the time being is utterly unnecessary. And like a child, man repeatedly asked, 'Why should friction produce fire?' Thus began for intelligence its labour of love. Perhaps the first answers given were childish. Perhaps he said that an angry spirit dwelt invisibly within the tree and its fury flames up when it is provoked. Human mythology is full of answers like this. Those whose intelligence refuses to grow beyond that of a child, for ever cling to such answers. But inspite of the stupidity which is easily satisfied, man's questioning surmounts all obstacles and slowly pushes forward. As a result, the amount of energy he has spent in order to find out the answer to the perfectly useless question 'why fire burns' has certainly not been less than that spent for lighting the fire in his kitchen. Perhaps this has led to the kitchen fire dying out before the food was ready, while the pangs of hunger became keener and keener: but he persisted in his question, 'Why does fire burn?' The fire before him cannot give any answer, for the answer can be found only by going far beyond the experienced fact.

The foolhardiness of this strange intelligence becomes clearest when it disturbs man himself and asks, 'Who are *you*?' It does not even hesitate to tell him, 'you may think you exist, but do you really do so? And if you do, where is your existence?' We have quoted before the answer which the Atharvaveda gives to this question. It says, one aspect of Man's self is seen directly here, but the other is the vast unseen.

Let us try to understand this clearly:

Here is land, here is water. Here is this and here is that. In like manner we may point at all objects and use the pronoun इदं 'This' with regard to it. We must understand clearly and know all objects whatsoever to which we can point and say 'this', be it water, be it land, be it this or that. Otherwise we cannot live properly. But simultaneously man declares, तद्विद्धि—'Know That.' But what? नेदं यदिदमुपासते—That is not that which we can define as इदं, as 'this'. It is a simple statement of a fact, that *I hear*. Yet man insists that its final analysis takes us where the pronoun 'it' cannot reach. Like one possessed he asks 'Where is श्रोत्रस्य श्रोत्रं—the audition of the hearing?' His physical researches lead him to vibrations in the air. But even here we have इदं the pronoun, we have 'this vibration'. But the vibration is not hearing. We attain to him who says, '*I hear*.' But in what does the truth of that *I* lie?

A stone falls down from above. The keeper who guards the gates of wisdom gives the report of the news—it has fallen. With regard to it the downward attraction is manifested. Here the task of the gatekeeper ends. But in the inner courts, the cry rings out, 'Transcending all the instances of इदं of this fall and his other fall, *one* attraction alone pervades throughout the universe.'

To know this one among the many is what the *Upaniṣad* calls प्रतिबोध विदितं, to know the one unique as true in the perception of each one unique as true in the perception of each particular hearing,—yours and mine, then and now—it is this universal, श्रोत्रस्य श्रोत्रं the truth which is the audition of hearing. About it, the *Upaniṣad* says, अन्यदेव तद्विदितादथों अविदितादधि। It is distinct from all that we know and all that we do not know. Even in the physical science, it is not only that we cannot reconcile its hidden secrets with our direct experience, but we are forced to admit that they are contrary to it.

Man's discovery and utilization of the hidden forces of nature contribute to his well-being. The truth which constitutes the well-being of his soul is also hidden: it can be realized only through endeavour. To this endeavour man give the name spiritual discipline (धर्मसाधना).

The root-meaning of the word *dharma* is nature. It sounds self-contradictory to say that one's *nature* is to be realized through *effort*, through discipline; this seems like finding nature by transcending it. The Christian Scriptures have condemned the nature of man, for its original sin and disobedience. The Indian Scriptures also prescribe the repudiation of nature in order to realize truth in us. Man has no respect for what he is by nature.

It is said:

श्रेयश्च प्रेयश्च मनुष्य मेतस्
तौ सम्परीत्य विविनक्ति धीरः।

* * *

तयोः श्रेय आददानस्य साधु भवति
दीयतेऽर्थाद् य उ प्रेयो वृणीते।

In human nature there is that which is desirable and the other which is desired. The wise man keeps the two separate.

* * *

He who accepts the good is pure, he who accepts evil falls short of his true worth.

These statements we regard as familiar maxims of morality, we think they have value only as principles of human conduct. But this verse was not uttered in reference to social conduct of man. This verse discusses how we can truly know the soul.

The desire for that which satisfies our animal instincts is active in human nature. But striving for the good which *ought* to be desired is also to be found there. It is not that man adds to his possessions by accepting the good: it is that he *becomes* something. This is called 'being साधु'. This does not make him rich, it does not make him powerful, it may or may not bring honour in society, in fact it may very possibly bring insult and indignity. Complete understanding of goodness is not possible in the realm of nature. On the other hand, acceptance of evil makes man something else—something which the Upanisads call 'falling short of one's true meaning'. The truth which we understand by the term man is degraded in one who identifies himself with evil. Goodness lies in realizing in oneself the humanity which is universal and of all times: degradation is in the failure to realize the Universal Man. All this would have no meaning unless man had a spiritual self over and above his natural self.

Man's endeavour strives from one nature towards another. It is only when his enquiries go beyond individual inclinations that his science is founded on universal knowledge. It is only when his efforts take him beyond all personal interests and the inertia of customary habit that he becomes विश्वकर्मा, a world-worker. It is only when his love transcends his self-seeking that man becomes a Mahatma—a great soul—through his relationship with all creatures. One nature of man obscures him, the other gives freedom.

The astronomer observed that a planet had deviated from its orbit. He asserted with conviction that it was due to the attraction of some other unseen planet. It was observed that the mind of man also did not move along the course prescribed by its nature for the preservation of life. It deviated towards the uncertain, towards the transcendent. This led man to imagine the realm of the Spirit. He asserted that commands came from there, it was there that his centre of being lay. Men wrangle and fight to decide who it is that presides over that realm. Whoever He maybe and whatever name we might give to Him, He did not let man rest within the limits of animal life.

The sea becomes restless. There is the continual ebb and flow of the tides. The restlessness of the sea would by itself prove the attraction of the moon, even if that remained invisible. Even the new-born babe knows instinctively that the hunger which indubitably is in him has an object that is real also in the external world. Man's lifelong efforts have often been directed to things which have no connections whatever with his immediate physical needs. A life transcending death leads him on to the paths of adventure, not for the sake of self-preservation, but for the sake of immortality.

In Vedic language God has been called *Avih*, denoting that his nature is Revelation. About him it has been said—यस्य नाम महद्यशः—His great glory is His name: His truth is in his great expression. It is the same with the nature of man: it is to reveal the glory of his soul. The creature preserves his life by taking in food from outside, the soul reveals itself by pouring itself out, and crossing nature's limits. Even the savage in his own way wants to transcend nature for the sake of his self-glorification, which according to him is the expression of his truth. He pierces his own nose and sticks in it a rod. Through a painful process he sharpens his teeth. He flattens his infant skull between wooden boards and deforms it. He concocts strange garments and hideous ornaments and endures insufferable pain and discomfort in putting them on. In all this he attempts to declare that he is potentially greater than what he can normally be. This greater self of man is contrary to nature. The God whom he exalts as his ideal is equally strange. A nursling of nature and yet man has this fighting attitude which always seeks to defy nature. Here in India we see people, some with lifted arm, some lying on a bed of thorns, some hanging with head down towards a raging fire. They declare in this way their superiority, their saintliness, only because they are unnatural. In the modern European countries also, there are people who glory in facing unnecessary hardship, which are called breaking records. Most of these they perform in order to glorify unnaturalness. The peacock feels proud in being peacock: ferocious animals exalt in the success of their ferocity. But Man prides that in his exaggerations he is more real than in his normal reality.

There is no limit to man's presumption in the economic as in the physical sphere. Here also breaking records means to vault over all the barriers prescribed by the past history of past achievements. The effort in this field is not exactly for the unnatural, rather it is for the unusual. Here we find impatience with limitations. But whatever is material and external, must in its very nature be limited. These limits can be extended, but they cannot be transcended. Jesus has said that the kingdom of heaven is as inaccessible to the rich as the eye of a needle for a camel to pass through. The reason for this is that the rich man is accustomed to realize and reveal his humanity through something which is the opposite to the immeasurable. To be huge like the elephant is not regarded by man as being a great man, though perhaps some savages might think so.

In the world which is the field of his ego, man boasts of his bulk, but in the world where his spirit dwells, his perfection is in greatness which cannot be measured by dimension. Beauty and excellence, heroism and sacrifice reveal the soul of man: they transcend the isolated man and realize the Universal Man who dwells in the inmost heart of all individuals.

All around him, other creatures roam about in search of the means of livelihood. Man goes about for ages to seek the *One* in his inmost heart who निहितार्थो दधाति, who gives to him his inner meaning. It signifies that man is great and he must prove that in him dwells the Eternal Man, the Universal Man, the Man who is beyond the bounds of death. We attain our unity with this dweller of our heart to the extent that we realize truth in knowledge and feeling. All the misfortunes of man are caused by the obscuration of the Inner Man, through searching Him in external forms, in making strangers of our ownselves. Then we seek ourselves in money, in fame, and in the physical means of enjoyment. Once I heard a wandering beggar sing the lament of the man who scatters himself and loses the touch of the Eternal within him:

> Where shall I find Him; Him who is the Man of my heart. Because I have lost him, I wander in strange and far-off lands in his quest.

It is from one of these illiterate villagers that I heard the line तोरि भितर अतल सागर—an unfathomed sea is there within you. It was the same *Baul* who sang: मनेर मध्ये मनेर मानुष करो अन्वेषसा,—

Seek for the inner man in your inner heart. It is the same as the prayer of the quest which is in the *Upaniṣad:* आविरावीर्म एधि—May his manifestation in me be completely fulfilled whose nature is self-revelation.

The Surplus in Man

13

There are certain verses from the Atharva Veda in which the poet discusses his idea of Man, indicating some transcendental meaning that can be translated as follows:

> Who was it that imparted form to man, gave him majesty, movement, manifestation and character, inspired him with wisdom, music and dancing? When his body was raised upwards he found also the oblique sides and all other directions in him—he who is the Person, the citadel of the infinite being.
>
> *Tasmād vai vidvān purushamidan brahmēti manyatē.*
>
> And therefore the wise man knoweth this person as Brahma.
>
> *Sanātanam ēnam āhur utādya syāt punarnavah.*
>
> Ancient they call him, and yet he is renewed even now today.

In the very beginning of his career Man asserted in his bodily structure his first proclamation of freedom against the established rule of Nature. At a certain bend in the path of evolution he refused to remain a four-footed creature, and the position which he made his body to assume carried with it a permanent gesture of insubordination. For there could be no question that it was Nature's own plan to provide all land-walking mammals with two pairs of legs, evenly distributed along their lengthy trunk heavily weighted with a head at the end. This was the amicable compromise made with the earth when threatened by its conservative downward force, which extorts taxes for all movements. The fact that man gave up such an obviously sensible arrangement proves his inborn mania for repeated reforms of constitution, for pelting amendments at every resolution proposed by Providence.

If we found a four-legged table stalking about upright upon two of its stumps, the remaining two foolishly dangling by its sides, we should be afraid that it was either a nightmare or some supernormal caprice of that piece of furniture, indulging in a practical joke upon the carpenter's idea of fitness. The like absurd behaviour of Man's anatomy encourages us to guess that he was born under the influence of some comet of contradiction that forces its eccentric path against orbits regulated by Nature. And it is significant that Man should persist in his foolhardiness, in spite of the penalty he pays for opposing the orthodox rule of animal locomotion. He reduces by half the help of an easy balance of his muscles. He is ready to pass his infancy tottering through perilous experiments in making progress upon insufficient support, and followed all through his life by liability to sudden downfalls resulting in tragic or ludicrous consequences from which law-abiding quadrupeds are free. This was his great venture, the relinquishment of a secure position of his limbs, which he could comfortably have retained in return for humbly salaaming the all-powerful dust at every step.

This capacity to stand erect has given our body its freedom of posture, making it easy for us to turn on all sides and realize ourselves at the centre of things. Physically, it symbolizes the fact that while animals have for their progress the prolongation of a narrow line Man has the enlargement of a circle. As a centre he finds his meaning in a wide perspective, and realizes himself in the magnitude of his circumference.

As one freedom leads to another, Man's eyesight also found a wider scope. I do not mean any enhancement of its physical power, which in many predatory animals has a better power of adjustment to light. But from the higher vantage of our physical watch-tower we have gained our *view,* which is not merely information about the location of things but their inter-relation and their unity.

But the best means of the expression of his physical freedom gained by Man in his vertical position is through the emancipation of his hands. In our bodily organization these have attained the highest dignity for their skill, their grace, their useful activities, as well as for those that are above all uses. They are the most detached of all our limbs. Once they had their menial vocation as our carriers, but raised from their position as *shudras*, they at once attained responsible status as our helpers. When instead of keeping them underneath us we offered them their place at our side, they revealed capacities that helped us to cross the boundaries of animal nature.

This freedom of view and freedom of action have been accompanied by an analogous mental freedom in Man through his imagination, which is the most distinctly human of all our faculties. It is there to help a creature who has been left unfinished by his designer, undraped, undecorated, unarmoured and without weapons, and, what is worse, ridden by a Mind whose energies for the most part are not tamed and tempered into some difficult ideal of completeness upon a background which is bare. Like all artists he has the freedom to make mistakes, to launch into desperate adventures contradicting and torturing his psychology or physiological normality. This freedom is a divine gift lent to the mortals who are untutored and undisciplined; and therefore the path of their creative progress is strewn with debris of devastation, and stages of their perfection haunted by apparitions of startling deformities. But, all the same, the very training of creation ever makes clear an aim which cannot be in any isolated freak of an individual mind or in that which is only limited to the strictly necessary.

Just as our eyesight enables us to include the individual fact of ourselves in the surrounding view, our imagination makes us intensely conscious of a life we must live which transcends the individual life and contradicts the biological meaning of the instinct of self-preservation. It works at the surplus, and extending beyond the reservation plots of our daily life builds there the guest chambers of priceless value to offer hospitality to the world-spirit of Man. We have such an honoured right to be the host when our spirit is a free spirit not chained to the animal self. For free spirit is godly and alone can claim kinship with God.

Every true freedom that we may attain in any direction broadens our path of self-realization, which is in superseding the self. The unimaginative repetition of life within a safe restriction imposed by Nature may be good for the animal, but never for Man, who has the responsibility to outlive his life in order to live in truth.

And freedom in its process of creation gives rise to perpetual suggestions of something further than its obvious purpose. For freedom is for expressing the infinite; it imposes limits in its works, not to keep them in permanence but to break them over and over again, and to reveal the endless in unending surprises. This implies a history of constant regeneration, a series of fresh beginnings and continual challenges to the old in order to reach a more and more perfect harmony with some fundamental ideal of truth.

Our civilization, in the constant struggle for a great Further, runs through abrupt chapters of spasmodic divergences. It nearly always begins its new ventures with a cataclysm; for its changes are not mere seasonal changes of ideas gliding through varied periods of flowers and fruit. They are surprises lying in ambuscade provoking revolutionary adjustments. They are changes in the dynasty of living ideals—the ideals that are active in consolidating their dominion with strongholds of physical and mental habits, of symbols, ceremonials and adornments. But however violent may be the revolutions happening in whatever time or country, they never completely detach themselves from a common centre. They find their places in a history which is one.

The civilizations evolved in India or China, Persia or Judaea, Greece or Rome, are like several mountain peaks having different altitude, temperature, flora and fauna, and yet belonging to the same chain of hills. There are no absolute barriers of communication between them; their foundation is the same and they affect the meteorology of an atmosphere which is common to us all. This is at the root of the meaning of the great teacher who said he would not seek his own salvation if all men were not saved; for we all belong to a divine unity, from which our great-souled men have their direct inspiration; they feel it immediately in their own personality, and they proclaim in their life, 'I am one with the Supreme, with the Deathless, with the Perfect.'

Man, in his mission to create himself, tries to develop in his mind an image of his truth according to an idea which he believes to be universal, and is sure that any expression given to it will persist through all time. This is a mentality absolutely superfluous for biological existence. It represents his struggle for a life which is not limited to his body. For our physical life has its thread of unity in the memory of the past, whereas this ideal life dwells in the prospective memory of the future. In the records of past civilizations, unearthed from the closed records of dust, we find pathetic efforts to make their memories uninterrupted through the ages, like the effort of a child who sets adrift on a paper boat his dream of reaching the distant unknown. But why is this desire? Only because we feel instinctively that in our ideal life we must touch all men and all times through the manifestation of a truth which is eternal and universal. And in order to give expression to it materials are gathered that are excellent and a manner of execution that has a permanent value. For we mortals must offer homage to the Man of the everlasting life. In order to do so, we are expected to pay a great deal more than we need for mere living, and in the attempt we often exhaust our very means of livelihood, and even life itself.

The ideal picture which a savage imagines of himself requires glaring paints and gorgeous fineries, a rowdiness in ornaments and even grotesque deformities of over-wrought extravagance. He tries to sublimate his individual self into a manifestation which he believes to have the majesty of the ideal Man. He is not satisfied with what he is in his natural limitations; he irresistibly feels something beyond the evident fact of himself which only could give him worth. It is the principle of power, which, according to his present mental stage, is the meaning of the universal reality whereto he belongs, and it is his pious duty to give expression to it even at the cost of his happiness. In fact, through it he becomes one with his God, for him his God is nothing greater than power. The savage takes immense trouble, and often suffers tortures, in order to offer in himself a representation of power in conspicuous colours and distorted shapes, in acts of relentless cruelty and intemperate bravado of self-indulgence. Such an appearance of rude grandiosity evokes a loyal reverence in the members of his community and a fear which gives them an aesthetic satisfaction because it illuminates for them the picture of a character which, as far as they know, belongs to ideal humanity. They wish to see in him not an individual, but the Man in whom they all are represented. Therefore, in spite of their sufferings, they enjoy being overwhelmed by his exaggerations and dominated by a will fearfully evident owing to its magnificent caprice in inflicting injuries. They symbolize their idea of unlimited wilfulness in their gods by ascribing to them physical and moral enormities in their anatomical idiosyncracy and virulent vindictiveness crying for the blood of victims, in personal preferences indiscriminate in the choice of recipients and methods of rewards and punishments. In fact, these gods could never be blamed for the least wavering in their conduct owing to any scrupulousness accompanied by the emotion of pity so often derided as sentimentalism by virile intellects of the present day.

However crude all this may be, it proves that Man has a feeling that he is truly represented in something which exceeds himself. He is aware that he is not imperfect, but incomplete. He knows that in himself some meaning has yet to be realized. We do not feel the wonder of it, because it seems so natural to us that barbarism in Man is not absolute, that its limits are like the limits of the horizon. The call is deep in his mind—the call of his own inner truth, which is beyond his direct knowledge and analytical logic. And individuals are born who have no doubt of the truth of this transcendental Man. As our consciousness more and more comprehends it, new valuations are developed in us, new depths and delicacies of delight, a sober dignity of expression through elimination of tawdriness, of frenzied emotions, of all violence in shape, colour, words, or behaviour, of the dark mentality of Ku-Klux-Klanism.

Each age reveals its personality as dreamer in its great expressions that carry it across surging centuries to the continental plateau of permanent human history. These expressions may not be consciously religious, but indirectly they belong to Man's religion. For they are the outcome of the consciousness of the greater Man in the individual men of the race. This consciousness finds its manifestation in science, philosophy and the arts, in social ethics, in all things that carry their ultimate value in themselves. These are truly spiritual and they should all be consciously co-ordinated in one great religion of Man, representing his ceaseless endeavour to reach the perfect in great thoughts and deeds and dreams, in immortal symbols of art, revealing his aspiration for rising in dignity of being.

I had the occasion to visit the ruins of ancient Rome, the relics of human yearning towards the immense, the sight of which teases our mind out of thought. Does it not prove that in the vision of a great Roman Empire the creative imagination of the people rejoiced in the revelation of its transcendental humanity? It was the idea of an Empire which was not merely for opening an outlet to the pent-up pressure of over-population, or widening its field of commercial profit, but which existed as a concrete representation of the majesty of Roman personality, the soul of the people dreaming of a world-wide creation of its own for a fit habitation of the Ideal Man. It was Rome's titanic endeavour to answer the eternal question as to what Man truly was, as Man. And any answer given in earnest falls within the realm of religion, whatever may be its character; and this answer, in its truth, belongs not only to any particular people but to us all. It may be that Rome did not give the most perfect answer possible when she fought for her place as a world-builder of human history, but she revealed the marvellous vigour of the indomitable human spirit which could say, *Bhumaiva sukkam*, 'Greatness is happiness itself'. Her Empire has been sundered and shattered, but her faith in the sublimity of man still persists in one of the vast strata of human geology. And this faith was the true spirit of her religion, which had been dim in the tradition of her formal theology, merely supplying her with an emotional pastime and not with spiritual inspiration. In fact this theology fell far below her personality, and for that reason it went against her religion, whose mission was to reveal her humanity on the background of the eternal. Let us seek the religion of this and other people not in their gods but in Man, who dreamed of his own infinity and majestically worked for all time, defying danger and death.

Since the dim nebula of consciousness in Life's world became intensified into a centre of self in Man, his history began to unfold its rapid chapters; for it is the history of his strenuous answers in various forms to the question rising from this conscious self of his, 'What am I?' Man is not happy or contented as the animals are; for his happiness and his peace depend upon the truth of his answer. The animal attains his success in a physical sufficiency that satisfies his nature. When a crocodile finds no obstruction in behaving like an orthodox crocodile he grins and grows and has no cause to complain. It is truism to say that Man also must behave like a man in order to find his truth. But he is sorely puzzled and asks in bewilderment: 'What is it to be like a man? What am I?' It is not left to the tiger to discover what is his own nature as a tiger, nor, for the matter of that, to choose a special colour for his coat according to his taste.

But Man has taken centuries to discuss the question of his own true nature and has not yet come to a conclusion. He has been building up elaborate religions to convince himself, against his natural inclinations, of the paradox that he is not what he is but something greater. What is significant about these efforts is the fact that in order to know himself truly Man in his religion cultivates the vision of a Being who exceeds him in truth and with whom also he has his kinship. These religions differ in details and often in their moral significance, but they have a common tendency. In them men seek their own supreme value, which they call divine, in some personality anthropomorphic in character. The Mind, which is abnormally scientific, scoffs at this; but it should know that religion is not essentially cosmic or even abstract; it finds itself when it touches the Brahma in man; otherwise it has no justification to exist.

It must be admitted that such a human element introduces into our religion a mentality that often has its danger in aberrations that are intellectually blind, morally reprehensible and aesthetically repellent. But these are wrong answers; they distort the truth of man and, like all mistakes in sociology, in economics or politics, they have to be fought against and overcome. Their truth has to be judged by the standard of human perfection and not by some arbitrary injunction that refuses to be confirmed by the tribunal of the human conscience. And great religions are the outcome of great revolutions in this direction causing fundamental changes of our attitude. These religions invariably made their appearance as a protest against the earlier creeds which had been unhuman, where ritualistic observances had become more important and outer compulsions more imperious. These creeds were, as I have said before, cults of power; they had their value for us, not helping us to become perfect through truth, but to grow formidable through possessions and magic control of the deity.

But possibly I am doing injustice to our ancestors. It is more likely that they worshipped power not merely because of its utility, but because they, in their way, recognized it as truth with which their own power had its communication and in which it found its fulfilment. They must have naturally felt that this power was the power of will behind nature, and not some impersonal insanity that unaccountably always stumbled upon correct results. For it would have been the greatest depth of imbecility on their part had they brought their homage to an abstraction, mindless, heartless and purposeless; in fact, infinitely below them in its manifestation.

The Music Maker

14

A particle of sand would be nothing if it did not have its background in the whole physical world. This grain of sand is known in its context of the universe where we know all things through the testimony of our senses. When I say the grain of sand *is,* the whole physical world stands guarantee for the truth which is behind the appearance of the sand.

But where is that guarantee of truth for this personality of mine that has the mysterious faculty of knowledge before which the particle of sand offers its credential of identification? It must be acknowledged that this personal self of mine also has for its truth a background of personality where knowledge, unlike that of other things, can only be immediate and self-revealed.

What I mean by personality is a self-conscious principle of transcendental unity within man which comprehends all the details of facts that are individually his in knowledge and feeling, wish and will and work. In its negative aspect it is limited to the individual separateness, while in its positive aspect it ever extends itself in the infinite through the increase of its knowledge, love and activities.

And for this reason the most human of all facts about us is that we *do* dream of the limitless unattained—the dream which gives character to what *is* attained. Of all creatures man lives in an endless future. Our present is only a part of it. The ideas unborn, the unbodied spirits, tease our imagination with an insistence which makes them more real to our mind than things around us. The atmosphere of the future must always surround our present in order to make it life-bearing and suggestive of immortality. For he who has the healthy vigour of humanity in him has a strong instinctive faith that ideally he is limitless. That is why our greatest teachers claim from us a manifestation that touches the infinite. In this they pay homage to the Supreme Man. And our true worship lies in our indomitable courage to be great and thus to represent the human divine and ever to keep open the path of freedom towards the unattained.

We Indians have had the sad experience in our own part of the world how timid orthodoxy, its irrational repressions and its accumulation of dead centuries, dwarfs man through its idolatry of the past. Seated rigid in the centre of stagnation, it firmly ties the human spirit to the revolving wheels of habit till faintness overwhelms her. Like a sluggish stream choked by rotting weeds, it is divided into shallow slimy pools that shroud their dumbness in a narcotic mist of stupor. This mechanical spirit of tradition is essentially materialistic, it is blindly pious but not spiritual, obsessed by phantoms of unreason that haunt feeble minds in the ghastly disguise of religion. For our soul is shrunken when we allow foolish days to weave repeated patterns of unmeaning meshes round all departments of life. It becomes stunted when we have no object of profound interest, no prospect of heightened life, demanding clarity of mind and heroic attention to maintain and mature it. It is destroyed when we make fireworks of our animal passions for the enjoyment of their meteoric sensations, recklessly reducing to ashes all that could have been saved for permanent illumination. This happens not only to mediocre individuals hugging fetters that keep them irresponsible or hungering for lurid unrealities, but to generations of insipid races that have lost all emphasis of significance in themselves, having missed their future.

The continuous future is the domain of our millennium, which is with us more truly than what we see in our history in fragments of the present. It is in our dream. It is in the realm of the faith which creates perfection. We have seen the records of man's dreams of the millennium, the ideal reality cherished by forgotten races in their admiration, hope and love manifested in the dignity of their being through some majesty in ideals and beauty in performance. While these races pass away one after another they leave great accomplishments behind them carrying their claim to recognition as dreamers—not so much as conquerors of earthly kingdoms, but as the designers of paradise. The poet gives us the best definition of man when he says:

> We are the music-makers,
> We are the dreamers of dreams.

Our religious present for us the dreams of the ideal unity which is man himself as he manifests the infinite. We suffer from the sense of sin, which is the sense of discord, when any disruptive passion tears gaps in our vision of the One in man, creating isolation in our self from the universal humanity.

The Upanishad says, *mā gridah*, 'covet not'. For coveting diverts attention from the infinite value of our personality to the temptation of materials. Our village poet sings: 'Man will brightly flash into your sight, my heart, if you shut the door of desires.'

We have seen how primitive man was occupied with his physical needs, and thus restricted himself to the present which is the time boundary of the animal; and he missed the urge of his consciousness to seek its emancipation in a world of ultimate human value.

Modern civilization for the same reason seems to turn itself back to that primitive mentality. Our needs have multiplied so furiously fast that we have lost our leisure for the deeper realization of our self and our faith in it. It means that we have lost our religion, the longing for the touch of the divine in man, the builder of the heaven, the music-maker, the dreamer of dreams. This has made it easy to tear into shreds our faith in the perfection of the human ideal, in its wholeness, as the fuller meaning of reality. No doubt it is wonderful that music contains a fact which has been analysed and measured, and which music shares in common with the braying of an ass or of a motor-car horn. But it is still more wonderful that music has a truth, which cannot be analysed into fractions; and there the difference between it and the bellowing impertinence of a motor-car horn is infinite. Men of our own times have analysed the human mind, its dreams, its spiritual aspirations,—most often caught unawares in the shattered state of madness, disease and desultory dreams—and they have found to their satisfaction that these are composed of elemental animalities tangled into various knots. This may be an important discovery; but what is still more important to realize is the fact that by some miracle of creation man infinitely transcends the component parts of his own character.

Suppose that some psychological explorer suspects that man's devotion to his beloved has at bottom our primitive stomach's hankering for human flesh, we need not contradict him; for whatever may be its genealogy, its secret composition, the complete character of our love, in its perfect mingling of physical, mental and spiritual associations, is unique in its utter difference from cannibalism. The truth underlying the possibility of such transmutation is the truth of our religion. A lotus has in common with a piece of rotten flesh the elements of carbon and hydrogen. In a state of dissolution there is no difference between them, but in a state of creation the difference is immense; and it is that difference which really matters. We are told that some of our most sacred sentiments hold hidden in them instincts contrary to what these sentiments profess to be. Such disclosures have the effect upon certain persons of the relief of a tension, even like the relaxation in death of the incessant strenuousness of life.

We find in modern literature that something like a chuckle of an exultant disillusionment is becoming contagious, and the knights-errant of the cult of arson are abroad, setting fire to our time-honoured altars of worship, proclaiming that the images enshrined on them, even if beautiful, are made of mud. They say that it has been found out that the appearances in human idealism are deceptive, that the underlying mud is real. From such a point of view, the whole of creation may be said to be a gigantic deception, and the billions of revolving electric specks that have the appearance of 'you' or 'me' should be condemned as bearers of false evidence.

But whom do they seek to delude? If it be beings like ourselves who possess some inborn criterion of the real, then to them these very appearances in their integrity must represent reality, and not their component electric specks. For them the rose must be more satisfactory as an object than its constituent gases, which can be tortured to speak against the evident identity of the rose. The rose, even like the human sentiment of goodness, or ideal of beauty, belongs to the realm of creation, in which all its rebellious elements are reconciled in a perfect harmony. Because these elements in their simplicity yield themselves to our scrutiny, we in our pride are inclined to give them the best prizes as actors in that mystery-play, the rose. Such an analysis is really only giving a prize to our own detective cleverness.

I repeat again that the sentiments and ideals which man in his process of self-creation has built up, should be recognized in their wholeness. In all our faculties or passions there is nothing which is absolutely good or bad; they all are the constituents of the great human personality. They are notes that are wrong when in wrong places; our education is to make them into chords that may harmonize with the grand music of Man. The animal in the savage has been transformed into higher stages in the civilized man—in other words has attained a truer consonance with Man the divine, not through any elimination of the original materials, but through a magical grouping of them, through the severe discipline of art, the discipline of curbing and stressing in proper places, establishing a balance of lights and shadows in the background and foreground, and thus imparting a unique value to our personality in all its completeness.

So long as we have faith in this value, our energy is steadily sustained in its creative activity that reveals the eternal Man. This faith is helped on all sides by literature, arts, legends, symbols, ceremonials, by the remembrance of heroic souls who have personified it in themselves.

Our religion is the inner principle that comprehends these endeavours and expressions and dreams through which we approach Him in whose image we are made. To keep alive our faith in the reality of the ideal perfection is the function of civilization, which is mainly formed of sentiments and the images that represent that ideal. In other words, civilization is a creation of art, created for the objective realization of our vision of the spiritually perfect. It is the product of the art of religion. We stop its course of conquest when we accept the cult of realism and forget that realism is the worst form of untruth, because it contains a minimum of truth. It is like preaching that only in the morgue can we comprehend the reality of the human body—the body which has its perfect revelation when seen in life. All great human facts are surrounded by an immense atmosphere of expectation. They are never complete if we leave out from them what might be, what should be, what is not yet proven but profoundly felt, what points towards the immortal. This dwells in a perpetual surplus in the individual, that transcends all the desultory facts about him.

The realism in Man is the animal in him, whose life is a mere duration of time; the human in him is his reality which has life everlasting for its background. Rocks and crystals being complete definitely in what they are, can keep as 'mute insensate things' a kind of dumb dignity in their stolidly limited realism; while human facts grow unseemly and diseased, breeding germs of death, when divested of their creative ideal—the ideal of Man the divine. The difference between the notes as mere facts of sound and music as a truth of expression is immense. For music though it comprehends a limited number of notes yet represents the infinite. It is for man to produce the music of the spirit with all the notes which he has in his psychology and which, through inattention or perversity, can easily be translated into a frightful noise. In music man is revealed and not in a noise.

Supreme Man

15

The scientist solves the mystery of a piece of iron and says that it is nothing but the constant movements of electric particles of a special rhythm. The intervals between them in such a system are, in proportion to their size, immense. If our unaided eyes could see what has been discovered by scientific vision, then, like the individuals in human society, we should have seen the particles as distinct and separate. However distinct these may be, a force,—for let us call it a force—is working among them. It is a relating force,—the community force of the piece of iron. When we see the piece of iron, we do not see the multitude of electrons, we see the mass. In fact, the visible appearance of the iron is a symbol; it is not what it ultimately is. To take an analogy we are given a ten-rupee note. He knows it truly who at sight recognizes the piece of paper as a symbol of unity that represents ten separate silver coins.

We see the piece of iron to be iron, and yet it is only a physical symbol revealing the mysterious spirit of relationship which cannot be seen by the bodily eye. Likewise, the distinctions of time and place between individual men are very great, and yet there is a large and deep unity encompassing all men. This unity, imperceptible by the senses, is not that of a numerical aggregate, for it transcends all aggregates. Those who have in them the great capacity of feeling within themselves the one Spirit in all men, are the people to whom we give the name *Mahātmā* or Great Soul. It is they who can lay down their lives for the good of all men. It is they who can address the comprehensive spirit within and without them and say:

तदेतत् प्रेयः पुत्रात् प्रेयो वित्तात् प्रयोऽन्यस्मात् सर्वस्मादन्तरतरं यदयमात्मा

> He is dearer than a son, dearer than wealth, dearer than all else is this spirit who is in our inmost heart.

The scientist condemns such statements. He says that we attribute humanity to God in calling Him our Beloved. I reply that it is not *attributing*, but *realizing* humanity. It is by developing the sense of the dignity of his human truth that man has attained to his God. The human mind cannot therefore protest against the attribution of humanity to his God, and it would not be at all true if he did so. Man does not attribute lighthood to the vibrations of ether, he feels and uses the vibrations themselves as light and is not deceived in such use.

There is the ultimate world entity even beyond the immediate entity of man, as we have the stellar sphere beyond the solar system. But it is primarily the solar system of which the earth is a part, it is solar heat that is the life of the earth, and it is the solar connection that governs the earth's movements and its day and night. We have knowledge of the stellar sphere, but it is the solar system we fully comprehend with our body and our mind. Similarly, the greatness which is supremely cosmical is for us an object of knowledge, but the greatness which is human is a matter for the fulfilment of all our body, mind and character.

But even the impersonal world with regard to which we can trace no distinctions of good and evil, beautiful and ugly, about which nothing more can be said beyond the fact that it exists, is bounded by human knowledge. And therefore by knowing it we become aware of the extension of our own consciousness and we are glad. The world we know or hope to know sometime through scientific experience is itself a human world. *Man* alone perceives this world in the form of *his* thought within the scaffoldings of *his* Understanding and Reason. It is possible to conceive of a mind which perceives a world that is beyond the range of our mathematical measurements and does not exist in the space which *we* know. But how shall we call extra-human the world whose fundamental truths are found by man in conformity with the innate principles of his thought? That is why a modern scientist describes the universe as the creation of mathematical mind.

But even this mathematical mind is not beyond the bounds of the human mind. If it were, then we could not have at all known the scientific theory of the world, like the dogs and cats who can never reach it.

The true character of Him who is the Qualified Reality, *Saguṇa Brahma*, is defined in our scripture as *Sarvendriyaguṇbāhāsam*. All the qualities which belong to the external and internal faculties of man have their suggestion in Him. The very meaning of this is that the ultimate Truth for us is *human* Truth, and that is why this world we know is necessarily a *human* world. Even if there be any other world beside this, it is non-existent for us, not only for today, but for ever.

We give the name Love to that relation of one soul to another which is the deepest and truest. Our actual acquaintance with the physical world is through sense perception, but our true comprehension of the spiritual world is through love. In the love of his parents, man begins his acquaintance with the spiritual world from the very moment of his birth. Here we find immeasurable mystery,—the contact of the indescribable. The question may arise, wherein lies the basis of the truth of parenthood. It must be in Him, who is पितृतमः पितृणाम् who contains the perfection of the fatherhood of all fathers. We can understand the characteristics of this earth to which we are born by scrutinizing it from outside, but the mystery of parenthood we can comprehend only in the depth of our own spirit, and it is there in this depth that we realize the Supreme Father. This Supreme Father does not dwell in any particular heaven, nor is He to be found in the history of any particular time or country. He has not expressed Himself once and for good in any particular individual but extends His love over the past and future of humanity and pervades the whole world of man.

We hear of the God of man:

> यद् यद् विभूतिमत् सत्त्वं श्रीमद् ऊर्जितमेव वा
> तत्तदेवोवगच्छ त्वं मम तेजोंशसम्भवम्।

> Whatever has splendour, has beauty and excellence, is born of an aspect of my own divine energy.

In the universe there are many things great and small. So far as bare existence is concerned, they all have the same worth. From the point of view of mere actuality, there is no distinction for better or worse between the lotus and the clod of earth. But man has in his mind a standard of value, which does not judge by need nor by the measurement of size or degree. In man, there is the sense of perfection transcending all quantitative standards—a consciousness of the inmost satisfaction. This is what he means by excellence, and yet we find no unanimity of opinion about this excellence. How then can we say that this excellence is based upon an impersonal and eternal truth which is in the universal man.

We know all scientific truths have passed through innumerable errors. In fact, the errors are many, the truth is one. The errors are personal, the truth belongs to the all. The astronomer wants to study the planet with his telescope, but he has many obstacles to overcome. In our sky there are the dust of the earth, the enveloping atmosphere, the veils of vapour and many kinds of disturbances all around. Defects are possible in the instrument, and the mind which observes is clouded by its predispositions. Pure truth can be attained only when all the obstacles—internal and external—have been overcome.

It is easy to admit that the realization of pure truth is the manifestation of the universal mind, but it is possible to doubt whether in aesthetic experience, we realize the universal mind. How can there be an absolute standard of beauty when our sense of joy in it often varies with the country, time and the individual? And yet, when we look at human history over a large period, we find that the minds of all artists of all times tend to agree in their judgment of the merit of artistic beauty. It has to be admitted that it is not absolutely every man that finds complete joy in an artistic creation. Many have minds blind to beauty: their personal preferences do not agree with universal appreciation. There are also among men many who are naturally impervious to science. Their conceptions of the world are confusingly irrelevant and antagonistic, because their minds are prejudiced, for the prejudice of one does not agree with that of another. Yet they are so inordinately vain of the truth of their own particular wrong view that they are prepared to go to any lengths in support of their doctrine. Similarly, there is no lack of persons in the world with naturally deficient taste. In their case also, differences of opinion become dangerous. We cannot question the universal perfection of knowledge simply because there are different levels of born stupidity, of every variety, from the lowest to the highest. It is the same with regard to the ideal of beauty.

Bertrand Russell has expressed in some writing of his, that Beethoven's symphonies cannot be regarded as creations of the Universal Mind, for they are personal to him. Russell means that a symphony is not like a mathematical truth, which is an object to all minds and has the mind of the individual as merely the occasion of its formulation. But it has to be admitted that everyone ought to appreciate Beethoven's creation, that if there is no natural deficiency of the mind, everyone must appreciate it when with proper training the opposition of ignorance and unaccustomedness have been dispelled, then it must also be admitted that the appreciation of the best composer is to be fully met with in the mind of Man and is impeded only in some particular men as listeners.

The intellect is indispensable for the preservation of life, but there are many instances of worldly success in spite of an imperfect sense of beauty. The sense of beauty has no sanction of vital urgency, nor does licence in this sphere carry with it its own necessary punishment. And yet a stupendous amount of effort is being applied to the task of creating beauty although in the maintenance of life it serves no purpose: only its influence is for transforming our inner being.

In the *Upaniṣads* we again and again find mention of this attainment through being. From these we understand that man is one in spirit with the Supreme Object of his strivings.

नाविरतो दुश्चरितान् नाशान्तो नासमाहितः।
नाशान्तमानसो वापि प्रज्ञानेनैनमाप्नुयात्।।

It is said that He cannot be reached through mere knowledge. He has to be realized through the perfection of being, by refraining from evil conduct, by achieving a steadfast mind through the control of the passions. In other words, this realization is the attainment of one's eternal truth.

I have stated before that we must remove all impurities and disturbances of the environment and all individual idiosyncrasies if we want to see physical truth in its purity. This applies even more to spiritual truth. It is when we attribute to spiritual truth the perversions arising out of our lower nature that our mistakes become most dangerous. We can understand how much more ruinous that mistakes in knowledge are our mistakes in being when we find that the very forces which we have brought under our control through science become our medium of the hatred and avarice of man and extend the sphere of his self-destruction from one end of the earth to the other. It is for this reason that perversion of the nature of some particular individual or group in the name of the community or religion incites man's will to evil far more than scientific mistakes or conflicts of material interest. The communal god thus becomes the receptacle of hatred, vanity, snobbishness and stupidity. Insulted Godhead degrades man and keeps him in constant fear of his own fellows. This calamity strikes at the very root of power and fortune in our country.

There are instances of this in other countries as well. The traditional Christians express their contempt for the degradation and cruelty in the characters of the traditional gods and modes of worship of some Indian communities. On account of habit they cannot however see that their own conception of God is equally possessed by the evil genius of man. The community whose sacred books condemn to eternal hell a child that has died before its baptism, has attributed to God a degree of cruelty that is perhaps unparalleled anywhere else. In fact, the conception of eternal hell, for any sin however heinous, is the most potent invention of human cruelty. Herein lies the explanation of the anti-scientific and anti-religious persecution practised in mediaeval Europe in order to preserve intact the faith in scriptural religion. Even today that conception of hell pervades with horror the prisons of civilized man, where there is no principle of reformation, but only the ferocity of punishment.

It is with the development of humanity that the realization of God gradually grows free of prejudice, at any rate, it ought to be so. The reason that it is not always so is due to the fact that we take anything and everything connected with religion to be eternal. It does not follow from our reverence for the eternal ideal of religion, that we must accept any particular religious dogma as also eternal. If we were fanatically to assert that every scientific opinion is eternally true, because there is eternal truth as the foundation of physical science, then we should have to assert, even today, that the sun is revolving round the earth. It is this mistake we generally make with regard to religion. The community gives the name of religion to its own traditional opinion, and thus strikes at Religion itself. The conflict, the cruelty, the unreasoning and unintelligent superstition, which then emerge, are without parallel in any other sphere of human life.

Mistakes in science, or in our code of conduct, arise from our inability to comprehend the wholeness of truth. In spiritual life we realize the wholeness of our being when it is conscious of a centre in a great and eternal meaning.

The earth revolves round its own axis and yet it circles round the sun along its vast orbit. Whatever happens in human society also exhibits these two tendencies. On the one hand, the paraphernalia of wealth and power are accumulated through the urge of the individual ego, and yet on the other, under the inspiration of the Universal Man, men unite with one another in their activity and their joy and make sacrifices for one another's sake.

Some years ago there was a report published in the *London Times*, which I came to know through the *Nation* of America. The British air-force was destroying from the air a Mahsud village in Afghanistan. One of the bombing planes was damaged and came down. An Afghan girl led the airmen into a neighbouring cave, and to protect them, a Malik remained on guard at the entrance of the cave. Forty men with brandished knives rushed forward to attack them, but the Malik dissuaded them. All this time, bombs were dropping from above and people were crowding into take shelter in the cave. Some Maliks of the neighbourhood and a Mollah proposed to help the Britishers and some of the women offered to feed them. After some time they at last disguised the airmen as Mahsuds and brought them out to a safe place.

In this incident, we find the two aspects of human nature revealed in their extremest forms. In the bombing from aeroplanes we have an instance of the wonderful development of human power—the vast expanse of his mailed fist from earth to heaven. But to forgive and protect the enemy engaged in dealing death reveals another aspect of man. The natural instinct to kill enemies is the prompting of man's animal nature; but he transcended it and uttered the strange command: Forgive your enemies.

Our scriptures lay down that at the time of battle a charioteer must not attack the man who is not in a chariot but on the ground. Nor must he kill one who is impotent, or a supplicant, nor one who is seated or has his hair untied, nor one who humbly offers to submit. Nor yet must he kill one who is asleep or unprotected, naked or unarmed, a spectator or a non-combatant, or engaged in fighting another. He must remember the teachings of virtue and refrain from killing one whose weapons are broken, one who is afflicted with sorrow, one who is wounded or frightened.

We have heard Man say 'Do not sin against those that sin against you.' Whether or not the individual conforms in his conduct to this law he does not laugh it away as the ravings of a lunatic. In human life, we only occasionally find conformity to this principle and generally we find its opposite. In other words, its truth is hardly seen in a mere count of heads, and yet its truth is acknowledged. Where lies the basis of the aspect of man which realizes it? Let us see what answers have been given by man to this question.

यस्यात्मा विरतः पापात् कल्याणे च निवेशितः।
तेन सर्वमिदं बुद्धं प्रकृतिर्विकृतिश्च या।।

He whose spirit refrains from evil and attends to the good has comprehended the *sarvam*, the totality. He therefore knows what is natural to him and what is an aberration.

Man comprehends his nature only when he abstains from evil and works for the good of all. This means that only the great among men understand human nature. How do they know it?

With a transparent heart, they comprehend the totality. The true and the good are in the totality. It is when man refrains from the sin which belongs to his nature as limited by the ego that he knows his own spiritual wholeness—it is then that he understands his own nature. His nature does not concern the individual alone: it concerns Him of Whom the *Gita* says, पूरुषः नृषु 'He is the humanity in Men.'

All that we have said so far about the good and evil is not from the point of view of the preservation of society. The code based on the solid foundation of praise and blame, which society promulgates through commands and percepts for its own preservation, gives but a secondary importance to the eternal principle of Truth: the preservation of the traditional society is its primary object. We are therefore told that it is harmful to introduce into society the Religion of Truth in all its purity. It is often said that there is a great deal of stupidity in the common man. To keep him away from evil, he must therefore, if need be, be kept engaged with delusions, frightened or comforted with false fears or hopes, in short, treated as eternally a child or a brute. It is with society as with religious communities. The opinions and customs prevalent at some previous time are loath to give up their rights even at a later age. In the insect-world, we find some harmless insects that adopt the disguise of terrible ones and thus secure themselves. It is the same with social laws. They try to make themselves powerful and permanent by disguising themselves as eternal truths. On the one hand, they have the external show of piety, and on the other, the terrors of torture in the afterlife, various strict and sometimes unjust means of social punishment, compelling blind conformity to needless conventions under the threat of a made-to-order Hell. The Andamans, the Devil Islands of France, and the Lipari Isles of Italy, are the symbols of this very attitude in the field of politics. The inner truth about them is that the pure law of Truth and man-made laws do not move with the same rhythm. Those who revere the True, the Good, the Human as the ultimate goals of man have throughout the ages fought against this attitude.

It is not the object of this lecture to estimate the value of the good as conformity to society or the State. I want to discuss the basis of man's acceptance of the Truth, to discuss wherein Truth lies. In the many fields of interest in society and the State, we find at every step contradiction of the Truth in daily conduct, and yet man has given to it the highest place in his self-knowledge, called it his *dharma* which means his ultimate nature. In spite of the many differences of opinion with regard to the ideal of the good that different countries, times and individuals have, all men have honoured the reality of the good. What I have discussed are the implications of this fact with regard to the nature of the Religion of Man. The conflict of 'It is' and 'It ought to be' has raged from the very beginnings of human history. In discussing the reason of this conflict, I have said that in the mind of man, there is, on the one hand, the Universal Man, and on the other, the animal man limited by his self-seeking. It is the attempts at harmonizing the two that reveal themselves in different forms according to different religious systems. Otherwise, only advantage and disadvantage, the pleasant and the unpleasant, could have prevailed in the law of life. There would have been no significance at all of sin and virtue, of good and evil.

The question has been asked about the truth, in the Universal Mind, of the pain and pleasure one feels in his individual mind. If we think about it, we find that the pleasure and pain within the limits of the ego are transformed at the borders of the spirit. The man who dedicates his life for Truth, for the sake of his country and for the good of man, who thinks of himself against a vast background of ideals, finds that personal happiness and misery have changed their meaning for him. Such a man gives up his happiness with ease, and by accepting pain, he transcends it. In the life of self-seeking, the burden of pleasure and pain is very great, but when man transcends his self-interest he feels the burden so light that his patience when faced with the bitterest suffering and his forgiveness in spite of the heaviest insults seems to us to be superhuman.

Discords become too evident when the tuning of the instrument is going on, but they are not a part of the music itself. Discords jar on us, and if they did not, we should not progress on our quest after harmony. That is why we give the name *Rudra* or Terrible to the Infinite—He draws us towards freedom along the path of the pain of disharmony.

The *Upaniṣad* declares:

एषास्य परमागतिरेषास्य परमा सम्पत्
एषोऽस्य परमो लोक एषोऽस्य परम आनन्दः।

Here we have the dualism of He and this, the individual man and the other One who is within him and beyond him. It is said that *He* is the ultimate aim of *this*, its richest possession, its final rest and supreme joy. In other words, it is in Him that *this* has its perfection.

He is not a mere abstraction. He is an immediate object of the most intimate awareness, just as much as the self which I call my own. When my devotion yearns after Him and in Him I find my joy, it is my self-consciousness that is enlarged, deepened and extended to the Truth beyond the limits of my narrow existence. It is *Eṣaḥ*, this great He who challenges man to strike after perfection through endeavours to struggle from the unreal to the real, from darkness towards the light, from death towards immortality.

This challenge never allowed man to stop anywhere; it made of him an eternal wayfarer. Tired and worn out, those who abandon the road and build themselves a permanent house have in fact built their own mausoleums. Animals have their lairs, but man has taken to the road. Those who are great among men are the road-builders and the path-finders. The lure of the call of the infinite the path-finders. The lure of the call of the infinite in him has brought man out on the way in quest of the unattained. Empires rose and fell by the roadside of his journey, riches were amassed and then lost beneath the dust. Man built many an image to give form to his desire and again smashed them to pieces, like childhood's toys when childhood is over. He tried again and again to construct the magic key and open with it nature's treasure-house and again he discarded them all and started anew to search out the secret path leading to its depths. Age follows age in human history, and man continues in his ceaseless search, not for the satisfaction of his material needs, but in order to strive with all his might for the revelation of the Universal Man in the world of men, to rescue his own inmost truth from the crude obstacles set up by himself. That is the Truth which is greater than all his accumulated wealth, greater than all his achievements, greater than all his traditional beliefs and knows no death nor decay. Man's mistakes and failures have been many, leaving their ruins on the way along which he came. The strain of his sorrow and suffering has been infinite, but they mark his strong perseverance to shatter the bonds of his imprisoned ideals. Who could have, even for a moment, endured all this struggle, if it did not have an eternal significance in an inspiration which ever urges him to realize a greater unity in wisdom and love with him who can lead his heart and mind into the truth of all things. Who among men can seek for comfort and where for him is rest? The only goal of human life is to offer freedom and be free, the freedom that guides it to be life.

Woman

16

When male creatures indulge in their fighting propensity to kill one another Nature connives at it, because comparatively speaking, females are needful to her purpose, while males are barely necessary. Being of an economic disposition she does not specially care for the hungry broods who are quarrelsomely voracious and who yet contribute very little towards the payment of Nature's bill. Therefore, in the insect world we witness the phenomenon of the females taking it upon themselves to keep down the male population to the bare limit of necessity.

But because greatly relieved of their responsibility to Nature, the males in the human world have had the freedom of their occupation and adventures. The definition of the human being is said to be that he is the tool-making animal. This tool-making is outside of Nature's scope. In fact, with our tool-making power we have been able to defy Nature. The human male, having the most part of his energies free, developed this power, and became formidable. Thus, though in the vital department of humanity woman still occupies the throne given to her by Nature, man in the mental department has created and extended his own dominion. For this great work detachment of mind and freedom of movement were necessary.

Man took advantage of his comparative freedom from the physical and emotional bondage, and marched unencumbered towards his extension of life's boundaries. In this he has travelled through the perilous path of revolutions and ruins. Time after time his accumulations have been swept away and the current of progress has disappeared at its source. Though the gain has been considerable yet the waste in comparison has been still more enormous, especially when we consider that much of the wealth, when vanished, has taken away the records with it. Through this repeated experience of disasters man has discovered, though he has not fully utilized, the truth, that in all his creations the moral rhythm has to be maintained to save them from destruction; that a mere unlimited augmentation of power does not lead to real progress, and there must be balance of proportion, must be harmony of the structure with its foundation, to indicate a real growth in truth.

This ideal of stability is deeply cherished in woman's nature. She is never in love with merely going on, shooting wanton arrows of curiosity into the heart of darkness. All her forces instinctively work to bring things to some shape of fulness,—for that is the law of life. In life's movement though nothing is final yet every step has its rhythm of completeness. Even the bud has its ideal of rounded perfection, so has the flower, and also the fruit. But an unfinished building has not that ideal of wholeness in itself. Therefore if it goes on indefinitely in its growth of dimensions, it gradually grows out of its standard of stability. The masculine creations of intellectual civilization are towers of Babel, they dare to defy their foundations and therefore topple down over and over again. Thus human history is growing up over layers of ruins; it is not a continuous life growth. The present war is an illustration of this. The economic and political organizations, which merely represent mechanical power, born of intellect, are apt to forget their centres of gravity in the foundational world of life. The cumulative greed of power and possession which can have no finality of completeness in itself, which has no harmony with the ideal of moral and spiritual perfection, must at last lay a violent hand upon its own ponderousness of material.

At the present stage of history civilization is almost exclusively masculine, a civilization of power, in which woman has been thrust aside in the shade. Therefore it has lost its balance and it is moving by hopping from war to war. Its motive forces are the forces of destruction, and its ceremonials are carried through by an appalling number of human sacrifices. This one-sided civilization is crashing along a series of catastrophes at a tremendous speed because of its one-sidedness. And at last the time has arrived when woman must step in and impart her life rhythm to this reckless movement of power.

For woman's function is the passive function of the soil, which not only helps the tree to grow but keeps its growth within limits. The tree must have life's adventure and send up and spread out its branches on all sides, but all its deeper bonds of relation are hidden and held firm in the soil and this helps it to live. Our civilization must also have its passive element, broad and deep and stable. It must not be mere growth but harmony of growth. It must not be all tune but it must have its time also. This time is not a barrier, it is what the banks are to the river; they guide into permanence the current which otherwise would lose itself in the amorphousness of morass. It is rhythm, the rhythm which does not check the world's movements but leads them into truth and beauty.

Woman is endowed with the passive qualities of chastity, modesty, devotion and power of self-sacrifice in a greater measure than man is. It is the passive quality in nature which turns its monster forces into perfect creations of beauty—taming the wild elements into die delicacy to tenderness fit for the service of life. This passive quality has given woman that large and deep placidity which is so necessary for the healing and nourishing and storing of life. If life were all spending, then it would be like a rocket, going up in a flash and coming down the next moment in ashes. Life should be like a lamp where the potentiality of light is far greater in quantity than what appears as the flame. It is in the depth of passiveness in woman's nature that this potentiality of life is stored.

I have said elsewhere that in the woman of the Western world a certain restlessness is noticed which cannot be the normal aspect of her nature. For women who want something special and violent in their surroundings to keep their interests active only prove that they have lost touch with their own true world. Apparently, numbers of women as well as men in the West condemn the things that are commonplace. They are always hankering after something which is out of the common, straining their powers to produce a spurious originality that merely surprises though it may not satisfy. But such efforts are not a real sign of vitality. And they must be more injurious to women than to men, because women have the vital power more strongly in them than men have. They are the mothers of the race, and they have a real interest in the things that are around them, that are the common things of life; if they did not have that, then the race would perish.

If, by constantly using outside stimulation, they form something like a mental drug habit, become addicted to a continual dram-drinking of sensationalism, then they lose the natural high sensibility which they have, and with it the bloom of their womanhood, and their real power to sustain the human race with what it needs the most.

A man's interest in his fellow-beings becomes real when he finds in them some special gift of power of usefulness, but a woman feels interest in her fellow-beings because they are living creatures, because they are human, not because of some particular purpose which they can serve, or some power which they possess and for which she a special admiration. And because woman has this power, she exercises such charm over our minds; her exuberance of vital interest is so attractive that it makes her speech, her laughter, her movement, everything graceful; for the note of gracefulness is in this harmony with all our surrounding interests.

Fortunately for us, our everyday world has the subtle and unobtrusive beauty of the commonplace, and we have to depend upon our own sensitive minds to realize its wonders which are invisible because spiritual. If we can pierce through the exterior, we find that the world in its commonplace aspects is a miracle.

We realize this truth intuitively through our power of love; and women, through this power, discover that the object of their love and sympathy, in spite of its ragged disguise of triviality, has infinite worth. When women have lost the power of interest in things that are common, then leisure frightens them with its emptiness, because, their natural sensibilities being deadened, there is nothing in their surroundings to occupy their attention. Therefore they keep themselves frantically busy, not in utilizing the time, but merely in filling it up. Our everyday world is like a reed, its true value is not in itself,—but those who have the power and the serenity of attention can hear the music which the Infinite plays through its very emptiness. But when women form the habit of valuing things for themselves, then they may be expected furiously to storm your mind, to decoy your soul from her love-tryst of the eternal and to make you try to smother the voice of the Infinite by the unmeaning rattle of ceaseless movement.

I do not mean to imply that domestic life is the only life for a woman. I mean that the human world is the woman's world, be it domestic or be it full of the other activities of life, which are human activities, and not merely abstract efforts to organize.

Wherever there is something which is concretely personal and human, there is woman's world. The domestic world is the world where every individual finds his worth as an individual, therefore his value is not the market value, but the value of love; that is to say, the value that God in his infinite mercy has set upon all his creatures. This domestic world has been the gift of God to woman. She can extend her radiance of love beyond its boundaries on all sides, and even leave it to prove her woman's nature when the call comes to her. But this is a truth which cannot be ignored, that the moment she is born in her mother's arms, she is born in the centre of her own true world, the world of human relationship.

Woman should use her power to break through the surface and go to the centre of things, where in the mystery of life dwells an eternal source of interest. Man has not this power to such an extent. But woman has it, if she does not kill it,—and therefore she loves creatures who are not lovable for their uncommon qualities. Man has to do his duty in a world of his own where he is always creating power and wealth and organizations of different kinds. But God has sent woman to love the world, which is a world of ordinary things and events. She is not in the world of the fairy tale where the fair woman sleeps for ages till she is touched by the magic wand. In God's world women have their magic wands everywhere, which keep their hearts awake,—and these are not the golden wands of wealth nor the iron rods of power.

All our spiritual teachers have proclaimed the infinite worth of the individual. It is the rampant materialism of the present age which ruthlessly sacrifices individuals to the bloodthirsty idols of organization. When religion was materialistic, when men worshipped their gods for fear of their malevolence, or for greed of wealth and power, then the ceremonies of worship were cruel and sacrifices were claimed without number. With the growth of man's spiritual life, our worship has become the worship of love.

At the present stage of civilization, when the mutilation of individuals is not only practised, but glorified, women are feeling ashamed of their own womanliness. For God, with his message of love, has sent them as guardians of individuals, and, in this their divine vocation, individuals are more to them than army and navy and parliament, shops and factories. Here they have their service in God's own temple of reality, where love is of more value than power.

But because men in their pride of power have taken to deriding things that are living and relationships that are human, a large number of women are screaming themselves hoarse to prove that they are not women, that they are true where they represent power and organization. In the present age they feel that their pride is hurt when they are taken as mere mothers of the race, as the ministers to the vital needs of its existence, and to its deeper spiritual necessity of sympathy and love.

Because men praise with pious unctuousness the idolatry of their manufactured images of abstractions, women in shame are breaking their own true god, who is waiting for his worship of self-sacrifice in love.

Changes have been going on for a long time underneath the solid crust of society on which woman's world has its foundation. Of late, with the help of science, civilization has been growing increasingly masculine, so that the full reality of the individual is more and more ignored. Organization is encroaching upon the province of personal relationship, and sentiment is giving way to law. In some societies, too much dominated by masculine ideals, infanticide prevailed, which ruthlessly kept down the female element of the population as low as possible. The same thing in another form has taken place in modern civilization. In its inordinate lust for power and wealth it has robbed woman of the most part of her world, and the home is every day being crowded out by the office. It is taking the whole world for itself, leaving hardly any room for woman. It is not merely inflicting injury but insult upon her.

But woman cannot be pushed back for good into the mere region of the decorative by man's aggressiveness of power. For she is not less necessary in civilization than man but possibly more so. In the geological history of earth the periods of gigantic cataclysms have passed when the earth had not attained that mellowness of maturity which despises all violent exhibition of force. And the civilization of competing commerce and fighting powers must also make room for that stage of perfection whose power lies deep in beauty and beneficence. Too long has ambition been at the helm of our history so that every right of the individual has had to be wrenched by force from the party in power and man has had to invoke the help of evil to attain what was good for him. But such an arrangement cannot be lasting, but must give way time after time; for the seeds of violence lie in wait in its cracks and crevices, and roots of disruption spread in the dark and cause breakdown when it is least expected.

Therefore although in the present stage of history man is asserting his masculine supremacy and building his civilization with stone blocks, ignoring the living principle of growth, he cannot altogether crush woman's nature into dust or into his dead building materials. Woman's home may have been shattered, but woman is not, and cannot, herself be killed. It is not that woman is merely seeking her freedom of livelihood, struggling against man's monopoly of business, but against man's monopoly of civilization where he is breaking her heart every day and desolating her life. She must restore the lost social balance by putting the full weight of the woman into the creation of the human world. The monster car of organization is creaking and growling along life's highway, spreading misery and mutilation, for it must have speed before everything else in the world. Therefore woman must come into the bruised and maimed world of the individual; she must claim each one of them as her own, the useless and the insignificant. She must protect with her care all the beautiful flowers of sentiment from the scorching laughter of the science of proficiency. The growing impurities, born of the deprivation of its normal conditions imposed upon life by the organized power of greed, she must sweep away. The time has come when woman's responsibility has become greater than ever before, when her field of work has far transcended the domestic sphere of life. The world with its insulted individuals has sent its appeal to her. These individuals must find their true value, raise their heads once again in the sun, and renew their faith in God's love through her love.

Men have seen the absurdity of today's civilization, which is based upon nationalism,—that is to say, on economics and politics and its consequent militarism. Men have been losing their freedom and their humanity in order to fit themselves for vast mechanical organizations. So the next civilization, it is hoped, will be based not merely upon economical and political competition and exploitation but upon worldwide social co-operation; upon spiritual ideals of reciprocity, and not upon economic ideals of efficiency. And then women will have their true place.

Because men have been building up vast and monstrous organizations they have got into the habit of thinking that this turning-out power has something of the nature of perfection in itself. The habit is ingrained in them, and it is difficult for them to see where truth is missing in their present ideal of progress.

But woman can bring her fresh mind and all her power of sympathy to this new task of building up a spiritual civilization, if she will be conscious of her responsibilities. Of course, she can be frivolous or very narrow in her outlook, and then she will miss her great mission. And just because woman has been insulated, has been living in a sort of obscurity, behind man, I think she will have her compensation in the civilization which is waiting to come.

And these human beings who have been boastful of their power, and aggressive in their exploitation, who have lost faith in the real meaning of the teaching of their Master, that the meek shall inherit the earth, will be defeated in the next generation of life. It is the same thing that happened in the ancient days, in the prehistoric times, to those great monsters like the mammoths and dinosaurs. They have lost their inheritance of the earth. They had the gigantic muscles for mighty efforts but they had to give up to creatures who were much feebler in their muscles and who took up much less space with their dimensions. And in the future civilization and the women, the feebler creatures,—feebler at least in their outer aspects,—who are less muscular, and who have been behind hand, always left under the shadow of those huge creatures, the men,—they will have their place, and those bigger creatures will have to give way.

Woman and Home

17

Creative expressions attain their perfect form through emotions modulated. Woman has that expression natural to her—a cadence of restraint in her behaviour, producing poetry of life. She has been an inspiration to man, guiding, most often unconsciously, his restless energy into an immense variety of creations in literature, art, music and religion. This is why, in India, woman has been described as the symbol of Shakti, the creative power.

But if woman begins to believe that, though biologically her function is different from that of man, psychologically she is identical with him; if the human world in its mentality becomes exclusively male, then before long it will be reduced to utter inanity. For life finds its truth and beauty, not in any exaggeration of sameness, but in harmony.

If woman's nature were identical with man's, if Eve were a mere tautology of Adam, it would only give rise to a monotonous superfluity. But that she was not so was proved by the banishment she secured from a ready-made Paradise. She had the instinctive wisdom to realize that it was her mission to help her mate in creating Paradise of their own on earth, whose ideal she was to supply with her life, whose materials were to be produced and gathered by her comrade.

However, it is evident than an increasing number of women in the West are ready to assert that their difference from men is unimportant. The reason for the vehement utterance of such a paradox cannot be ignored. It is rebellion against a necessity, which is not equal for both the partners.

Love in all forms has its obligations, and the love that binds women to their children binds them to their homes. But necessity is a tyrant, making us submit to injury and indignity, allowing advantage over us to those who are wholly or comparatively free from its burden. Such has been the case in the social relationship between man and woman. Along with the difference inherent in their respective natures, there have grown up between them inequalities fostered by circumstances. Man is not handicapped by the same biological and psychological responsibilities as woman, and therefore he has the liberty to give her the security of home. This liberty exacts payment when it offers its boon, because to give to withhold the gift is within its power. It is the unequal freedom in their mutual relationships which has made the weight of life's tragedies so painfully heavy for woman to bear.

Some mitigation of her disadvantage has been effected by her rendering herself and her home a luxury to man. She has accentuated those qualities in herself which insidiously impose their bondage over her mate, some by pandering to his weakness, and some by satisfying his higher nature, till the sex-consciousness in our society has grown abnormal and overpowering. There is no actual objection to this in itself, for it offers a stimulus, acting in the depth of life, which leads to creative exuberance. But a great deal of it is a forced growth of compulsion bearing seeds of degradation. In those ages when men acknowledged spiritual perfection to be their object, women were denounced as the chief obstacle in their way. The constant and conscious exercise of allurements, which gave women their power, attacked the weak spots in man's nature, and doing so added to its weakness. For all relationships tainted with repression of freedom must become sources of degeneracy to the strong who impose such repressions.

Balance of power, however, between man and woman was in a measure established when home wielded a strong enough attraction to make men accept its obligations. But at last the time has come when the material ambition of man has assumed such colossal proportions that home is in danger of losing its centre of gravity for him, and he is receding farther and farther from its orbit.

The arid zone in the social life is spreading fast. The simple comforts of home, made precious by the touch of love, are giving way to luxuries that can only have their full extension in the isolation of self-centred life. Hotels are being erected on the ruins of homes; productions are growing more stupendous than creations; and most men have, for the materials of their happiness and recreation, their dogs and horses, their pipes, guns, and gambling clubs.

Reactions and rebellions, not being normal in their character, go on hurting truth until peace is restored. Therefore, when woman refuses to acknowledge the distinction between her life and that of man, she does not convince us of its truth, but only proves to us that she is suffering. All great suffering indicate some wrong somewhere. In the present case, the wrong is in woman's lack of freedom in her relationship with man, which compels her to turn her disabilities into attractions, and to use untruths as her allies in the battle of life, while she is suffering from the precariousness of her position.

From the beginning of our society, women have naturally accepted the training which imparts to their life and to their home a spirit of harmony. It is their instinct to perform their services in such a manner that these, through beauty, might be raised from the domain of slavery to the realm of grace. Women have tried to prove that in the building up of social life they are artists and not artisans. But all expressions of beauty lose their truth when compelled to accept the patronage of the gross and the indifferent. Therefore when necessity drives women to fashion their lives to the taste of the insensitive or the sensual, then the whole thing becomes a tragedy of desecration. Society is full of such tragedies. Many of the laws and social regulations guiding the relationships of man and woman are relics of a barbaric age, when the brutal pride of an exclusive possession had its dominance in human relations, such as those of parents and children, husbands and wives, masters and servants, teachers and disciples. The vulgarity of it still persists in the social bond between the sexes because of the economic helplessness of woman. Nothing makes us so stupidly mean as the sense of superiority which the power of the purse confers upon us.

The powers of muscle and of money have opportunities of immediate satisfaction, but the power of the ideal must have infinite patience. The man who sells his goods, or fulfils his contract, is cheated if he fails to realize payment, but he who gives form to some ideal may never get his due and be fully paid. What I have felt in the women of India is the consciousness of this ideal—their simple faith in the sanctity of devotion lighted by love which is held to be divine. True womanliness is regarded in our country as the saintliness of love. It is not merely praised there, but literally worshipped; and she who is gifted with it is called *Devi,* as one revealing in herself Woman, the Divine. That this has not been a mere metaphor to us is because, in India, our mind is familiar with the idea of God in an eternal feminine aspect. Thus the Eastern woman, who is deeply aware in her heart of the sacredness of her mission, is a constant education to man. It has to be admitted that there are chances of such an influence failing to penetrate the callousness of the coarse-minded; but that is the destiny of all manifestations whose value is not in success or reward in honour.

Woman, has to be ready to suffer. She cannot allow her emotions to be dulled or polluted, for these are to create her life's atmosphere, apart from which her world would be dark and dead. This leaves her heart without any protection of insensibility, at the mercy of the hurts and insults of life. Women of India, like women everywhere, have their share of suffering, but it radiates through the ideal, and becomes, like sunlight, a creative force in their world. Our women know by heart the legends of the great women of the epic age—Savitri who by the power of love conquered death, and Sita who had no other reward for her life of sacrifice but the sacred majesty of sorrow. They know that it is their duty to make this life an image of the life eternal, and that love's mission truly performed has a spiritual meaning. It is a religious responsibility for them to live the life which is their own. For their activity is not for money-making, or organizing power, or intellectually probing the mystery of existence, but for establishing and maintaining human relationships requiring the highest moral qualities. It is the consciousness of the spiritual character of their life's work, which lifts them above the utilitarian standard of the immediate and the passing, surrounds them with the dignity of the eternal, and transmutes their suffering and sorrow into a crown of light.

I must guard myself from the risk of a possible misunderstanding. The permanent significance of home is not in the narrowness of its enclosure, but in an eternal moral idea. It represents the truth of human relationship; it reveals loyalty and love for the personality of man. Let us take a wider view, in a perspective truer than can be found in its present conventional associations. With the discovery and development of agriculture there came a period of settled life in our history. The nomad ever moved on with his tents and cattle; he explored space and exploited its contents. The cultivator of land explored time in its immensity, for he had leisure. Comparatively secured from the uncertainty of his outer resources, he had the opportunity to deal with his moral resources in the realm of human truth. This is why agricultural civilization, like that of India and China, is essentially a civilization of human relationship, of the adjustment of mutual obligations. It is deep-rooted in the inner life of man. Its basis is co-operation and not competition. In other words, its principle is the principle of home, to which all its outer adventures are subordinated.

In the meanwhile, the nomadic life with its predatory instinct of exploitation has developed into a great civilization. It is immensely proud and strong, killing leisure and pursuing opportunities. It minimises the claims of personal relationship and is jealously careful of its unhampered freedom for acquiring wealth and asserting its will upon others. Its burden is the burden of things, which grows heavier and more complex every day, disregarding the human and the spiritual. Its powerful pressure from all sides narrows the limits of home, the personal region of the human world. Thus, in this region of life, women are every day hustled out of their shelter for want of accommodation.

But such a state of things can never have the effect of changing woman into man. On the contrary, it will lead her to find her place in the unlimited range of society, and the Guardian Spirit of the personal in human nature will extend the ministry of woman over all developments of life. Habituated to deal with the world as machine, man is multiplying his materials, banishing away his happiness and sacrificing love to comfort, which is an illusion. At last the present age has sent its cry to women, asking her to come out from her segregation in order to restore the spiritual supremacy of all that is human in the world of humanity. She has been aroused to remember that womanliness is not chiefly decorative. It is like that vital health, which not only imparts the bloom of beauty to the body, but joy to the mind and perfection to life.

Man's Universe

18

Light, as the radiant energy of creation, started the ring-dance of atoms in a diminutive sky, and also the dance of the stars in the vast, lonely theatre of time and space. The planets came out of their bath of fire and basked in the sun for ages. They were the thrones of the gigantic Inert, dumb and desolate, which knew not the meaning of its own blind destiny and majestically frowned upon a future when its monarchy would be menaced.

Then came a time when life was brought into the arena in the tiniest little monocycle of a cell. With its gift of growth and power of adaptation it faced the ponderous enormity of things, and contradicted the unmeaningness of their bulk. It was made conscious not of the volume but of the value of existence, which it ever tried to enhance and maintain in many-branched paths of creation, overcoming the obstructive inertia of Nature by obeying Nature's law.

But the miracle of creation did not stop here in this isolated speck of life launched on a lonely voyage to the Unknown. A multitude of cells were bound together into a larger unit, not through aggregation, but through a marvellous quality of complex interrelationship maintaining a perfect co-ordination of functions. This is the creative principle of unity, the divine mystery of existence, that baffles all analysis. The larger co-operative units could adequately pay for a greater freedom of self-expression, and they began to form and develop in their bodies new organs of power, new instruments of efficiency. This was the march of evolution ever unfolding the potentialities of life.

But this evolution which continues on the physical plane has its limited range. All exaggeration in that direction becomes a burden that breaks the natural rhythm of life, and those creatures that encouraged their ambitious flesh to grow in dimensions have nearly all perished of their cumbrous absurdity.

Before the chapter ended Man appeared and turned the course of this evolution from an indefinite march of physical aggrandizement to a freedom of a more subtle perfection. This has made possible his progress to become unlimited, and has enabled him to realize the boundless in his power.

The fire is lighted, the hammers are working, and for laborious days and nights amidst dirt and discordance the musical instrument is being made. We may accept this as a detached fact and follow its evolution. But when the music is revealed, we know that the whole thing is a part of the manifestation of music in spite of its contradictory character. The process of evolution, which after ages has reached man, must be realized in its unity with him; though in him it assumes a new value and proceeds to a different path. It is a continuous process that finds its meaning in Man; and we must acknowledge that the evolution which Science talks of is that of Man's universe. The leather binding and title-page are parts of the book itself; and this world that we perceive through our senses and mind and life's experience is profoundly one with ourselves.

The divine principle of unity has ever been that of an inner interrelationship. This is revealed in some of its earliest stages in the evolution of multicellular life on this planet. The most perfect inward expression has been attained by man in his own body. But what is most important of all is the fact that man has also attained its realization in a more subtle body outside his physical system. He misses himself when isolated; he finds his own larger and truer self in his wide human relationship. His multicellular body is born and it dies; his multi-personal humanity is immortal. In this ideal of unity he realizes the eternal in his life and the boundless in his love. The unity becomes not a mere subjective idea, but an energizing truth. Whatever name may be given to it, and whatever form it symbolizes, the consciousness of this unity is spiritual, and our effort to be true to it is our religion. It ever waits to be revealed in our history in a more and more perfect illumination.

We have our eyes, which relate to us the vision of the physical universe. We have also an inner faculty of our own which helps us to find our relationship with the supreme self of man, the universe of personality. This faculty is our luminous imagination, which in its higher stage is special to man. It offers us that vision of wholeness which for the biological necessity of physical survival is superfluous; its purpose is to arouse in us the sense of perfection which is our true sense of immortality. For perfection dwells ideally in Man the Eternal, inspiring love for this ideal in the individual, urging him more and more to realize it.

The development of intelligence and physical power is equally necessary in animals and men for their purposes of living; but what is unique in man is the development of his consciousness which gradually deepens and widens the realization of his immortal being, the perfect, the eternal. It inspires those creations of his that reveal the divinity in him—which is his humanity—in the varied manifestations of truth, goodness and beauty, in the freedom of activity which is not for his use but for his ultimate expression. The individual man must exist for Man the great, and must express him in disinterested works, in science and philosophy, in literature and arts, in service and worship. This is his religion, which is working in the heart of all his religions in various names and forms. He knows and uses this world where it is endless and thus attains greatness, but he realizes his own truth where it is perfect and thus finds his fulfilment.

The idea of the humanity of our God, or the divinity of Man the Eternal, is the main subject of this book. This thought of God has not grown in my mind through any process of philosophical reasoning. On the contrary, it has followed the current of my temperament from early days until it suddenly flashed into my consciousness with a direct vision. The experience which I have described in one of the chapters which follow convinced me that on the surface of our being we have the ever-changing phases of the individual self, but in the depth there dwells the Eternal Spirit of human unity beyond our direct knowledge. It very often contradicts the trivialities of our daily life, and upsets the arrangements made for securing our personal exclusiveness behind the walls of individual habits and superficial conventions. It inspires in us works that are the expressions of a Universal Spirit; it invokes unexpectedly in the midst of a self-centred life a supreme sacrifice. At its call, we hasten to dedicate our lives to the cause of truth and beauty, to unrewarded service of others, in spite of our lack of faith in the positive reality of the ideal values.

During the discussion of my own religious experience I have expressed my belief that the first stage of my realization was through my feeling of intimacy with Nature—not that Nature which has its channel of information for our mind and physical relationship with our living body, but that which satisfies our personality with manifestations that make our life rich and stimulate our imagination in their harmony of forms, colours, sounds and movements. It is not that world which vanishes into abstract symbols behind its own testimony to Science, but that which lavishly displays its wealth of reality to our personal self having its own perpetual reaction upon our human nature.

I have mentioned in connection with my personal experience some songs which I had often heard from wandering village singers, belonging to a popular sect of Bengal, called Baüls, who have no images, temples, scriptures, or ceremonials, who declare in their songs the divinity of Man, and express for him an intense feeling of love. Coming from men who are unsophisticated, living a simple life in obscurity, it gives us a clue to the inner meaning of all religions. For it suggests that these religions are never about a God of cosmic force, but rather about the God of human personality.

At the same time it must be admitted that even the impersonal aspect of truth dealt with by Science belongs to the human Universe. But men of Science tell us that truth, unlike beauty and goodness, is independent of our consciousness. They explain to us how the belief that truth is independent of the human mind is a mystical belief, natural to man but at the same time inexplicable. But may not the explanation be this, that ideal truth does not depend upon the individual mind of man, but on the universal mind which comprehends the individual? For to say that truth, as we see it, exists apart from humanity is really to contradict Science itself; because Science can only organize into rational concepts those facts which man can know and understand, and logic is a machinery of thinking created by the mechanic man.

The table that I am using with all its varied meanings appears as a table for man through his special organ of senses and his special organ of thoughts. When scientifically analysed the same table offers an enormously different appearance to him from that given by his senses. The evidence of his physical senses and that of his logic and his scientific instruments are both related to his own power of comprehension; both are true and true for him. He makes use of the table with full confidence for his physical purposes, and with equal confidence makes intellectual use of it for his scientific knowledge. But the knowledge is his who is a man. If a particular man as an individual did not exist, the table would exist all the same, but still as a thing that is related to the human mind. The contradiction that there is between the table of our sense perception and the table of our scientific knowledge has its common centre of reconciliation in human personality.

The same thing holds true in the realm of idea. In the scientific idea of the world there is no gap in the universal law of causality. Whatever happens could never have happened otherwise. This is a generalization which has been made possible by a quality of logic which is possessed by the human mind. But this very mind of Man has its immediate consciousness of will within him which *is* aware of its freedom and ever struggles for it. Every day in most of our behaviour we acknowledge its truth; in fact, our conduct finds its best value in its relation to its truth. Thus this has its analogy in our daily behaviour with regard to a table. For whatever may be the conclusion that Science has unquestionably proved about the table, we are amply rewarded when we deal with it as a solid fact and never as a crowd of fluid elements that represent a certain kind of energy. We can also utilize this phenomenon of the measurement. The space represented by a needle when magnified by the microscope may cause us no anxiety as to the number of angels who could be accommodated on its point or camels which could walk through its eye. In a cinema-picture our vision of time and space can be expanded or condensed merely according to the different technique of the instrument. A seed carries packed in a minute receptacle a future which is enormous in its contents both in time and space. The truth, which is Man, has not emerged out of nothing at a certain point of time, even though seemingly it might have been manifested then. But the manifestation of Man has no end in itself—not even now. Neither did it have its beginning in any particular time we ascribe to it. The truth of Man is in the heart of eternity, the fact of it being evolved through endless ages. If Man's manifestation has round it a background of millions of light-years, still it is his own background. He includes in himself the time, however long, that carries the process of his becoming, and he is related for the very truth of his existence to all things that surround him.

Relationship is the fundamental truth of this world of appearance. Take, for instance, a piece of coal. When we pursue the fact of it to its ultimate composition, substance which seemingly is the most stable element in it vanishes in centres of revolving forces. These are the units, called the elements of carbon, which can further be analysed into a certain number of protons and electrons. Yet these electrical facts are what they are, not in their detachment, but in their interrelationship, and though possibly some day they themselves may be further analysed, nevertheless the pervasive truth of interrelation which is manifested in them will remain.

We do not know how these elements, as carbon, compose a piece of coal; all that we can say is that they build up that appearance through a unity of interrelationship, which unites them not merely in an individual piece of coal, but in a comradeship of creative co-ordination with the entire physical universe.

Creation has been made possible through the continual self-surrender of the unit to the universe. And the spiritual universe of Man is also ever claiming self-renunciation from the individual units. This spiritual process is not so easy as the physical one in the physical world, for the intelligence and will of the units have to be tempered to those of the universal spirit.

It is said in a verse of the Upanishad that this world which is all movement is pervaded by one supreme unity, and therefore true enjoyment can never be had through the satisfaction of greed, but only through the surrender of our individual self to the Universal Self.

There are thinkers who advocate the doctrine of the plurality of worlds, which can only mean that there are worlds that are absolutely unrelated to each other. Even if this were true it could never be proved. For our universe is the sum total of what Man feels, knows, imagines, reasons to be, and of whatever is knowable to him now or in another time. It affects him differently in its different aspects, in its beauty, its inevitable sequence of happenings, its potentiality; and the world proves itself to him only in its varied effects upon his senses, imagination and reasoning mind.

I do not imply that the final nature of the world depends upon the comprehension of the individual person. Its reality is associated with the universal human mind which comprehends all time and all possibilities of realization. And this is why for the accurate knowledge of things we depend upon Science that represents the rational mind of the universal Man, and not upon that of the individual who dwells in a limited range of space and time and the immediate needs of life. And this is why there is such a thing as progress in our civilization; for progress means that there is an ideal perfection which the individual seeks to reach by extending his limits in knowledge, power, love, enjoyment, thus approaching the universal. The most distant star, whose faint message touches the threshold of the most powerful telescopic vision, has its sympathy with the understanding mind of man, and therefore we can never cease to believe that we shall probe further and further into the mystery of their nature. As we know the truth of the stars we know the great comprehensive mind of man.

We must realize not only the reasoning mind, but also the creative imagination, the love and wisdom that belong to the Supreme Person, whose Spirit is over us all, love for whom comprehends love for all creatures and exceeds in depth and strength all other loves, leading to difficult endeavours and martyrdoms that have no other gain than the fulfilment of this love itself.

The *Isha* of our Upanishad, the Super Soul, which permeates all moving things, is the God of this human universe whose mind we share in all our true knowledge, love and service, and whom to reveal in ourselves through renunciation of self is the highest end of life.

The Creative Spirit

19

Once, during the improvisation of a story by a young child, I was coaxed to take my part as the hero. The child imagined that I had been shut in a dark room locked from the outside. She asked me, 'What will you do for your freedom?' and I answered, 'Shout for help.' But, however desirable that might be if it succeeded immediately, it would be unfortunate for the story. And thus she in her imagination had to clear the neighbourhood of all kinds of help that my cries might reach. I was compelled to think of some violent means of kicking through this passive resistance; but for the sake of the story the door had to be made of steel. I found a key, but it would not fit, and the child was delighted at the development of the story jumping over obstructions.

Life's story of evolution, the main subject of which is the opening of the doors of the dark dungeon, seems to develop in the same manner. Difficulties were created, and at each offer of an answer the story had to discover further obstacles in order to carry on the adventure. For to come to an absolutely satisfactory conclusion is to come to the end of all things, and in that case the great child would have nothing else to do but to shut her curtain and go to sleep.

The Spirit of Life began her chapter by introducing a simple living cell against the tremendously powerful challenge of the vast Inert. The triumph was thrillingly great which still refuses to yield its secret. She did not stop there, but defiantly courted difficulties, and in the technique of her art exploited an element which still baffles our logic.

This is the harmony of self-adjusting interrelationship impossible to analyse. She brought close together numerous cell units and, by grouping them into a self-sustaining sphere of co-operation, elaborated a larger unit. It was not a mere agglomeration. The grouping had its caste system in the division of functions and yet an intimate unity of kinship. The creative life summoned a larger army of cells under her command and imparted into them, let us say, a communal spirit that fought with all its might whenever its integrity was menaced.

This was the tree which has its inner harmony and inner movement of life in its beauty, its strength, its sublime dignity of endurance, its pilgrimage to the Unknown through the tiniest gates of reincarnation. It was a sufficiently marvellous achievement to be a fit termination to the creative venture. But the creative genius cannot stop exhausted; more windows have to be opened; and she went out of her accustomed way and brought another factor into her work, that of locomotion. Risks of living were enhanced, offering opportunities to the daring resourcefulness of the Spirit of Life. For she seems to revel in occasions for a fight against the giant Matter, which has rigidly prohibitory immigration laws against all newcomers from Life's shore. So the fish was furnished with appliances for moving in an element which offered its density for an obstacle. The air offered an even more difficult obstacle in its lightness; but the challenge was accepted, and the bird was gifted with a marvellous pair of wings that negotiated with the subtle laws of the air and found in it a better ally than the reliable soil of the stable earth. The Arctic snow set up its frigid sentinel; the tropical desert uttered in its scorching breath a gigantic 'No' against all life's children. But those peremptory prohibitions were defied, and the frontiers, though guarded by a death penalty, were triumphantly crossed.

This process of conquest could be described as progress for the kingdom of life. It journeyed on through one success to another by dealing with the laws of Nature through the help of the invention of new instruments. This field of life's onward march is a field of ruthless competition. Because the material world is the world of quantity, where resources are limited and victory waits for those who have superior facility in their weapons, therefore success in the path of progress for one group most often runs parallel to defeat in another.

It appears that such scramble and fight for opportunities of living among numerous small combatants suggested at last an imperialism of big bulky flesh—a huge system of muscles and bones, thick and heavy coats of armour and enormous tails. The idea of such indecorous massiveness must have seemed natural to life's providence; for the victory in the world of quantity might reasonably appear to depend upon the bigness of dimension. But such gigantic paraphernalia of defence and attack resulted in an utter defeat, the records of which every day are being dug up from the desert sands and ancient mud flats. These represent the fragments that strew the forgotten paths of a great retreat in the battle of existence. For the heavy weight which these creatures carried was mainly composed of bones, hides, shells, teeth and claws that were non-living, and therefore imposed its whole huge pressure upon life that needed freedom and growth for the perfect expression of its own vital nature. The resources for living which the earth offered for her children were recklessly spent by these megalomaniac monsters of an immoderate appetite for the sake of maintaining a cumbersome system of dead burdens that thwarted them in their true progress. Such a losing game has now become obsolete. To the few stragglers of that party, like the rhinoceros or the hippopotamus, has been allotted a very small space on this earth, absurdly inadequate to their formidable strength and magnitude of proportions, making them look forlornly pathetic in the sublimity of their incongruousness. These and their extinct forerunners have been the biggest failures in life's experiments. And then, on some obscure dusk of dawn, the experiment entered upon a completely new phase of a disarmament proposal, when little Man made his appearance in the arena, bringing with him expectations and suggestions that are unfathomably great.

We must know that the evolution process of the world has made its progress towards the revelation of its *truth*—that is to say some inner value which is not in the extension in space and duration in time. When life came out it did not bring with it any new materials into existence. Its elements are the same which are the materials for the rocks and minerals. Only it evolved a value in them which cannot be measured and analysed. The same thing is true with regard to mind and the consciousness of self; they are revelations of a great meaning, the self-expression of a truth. In man this truth has made its positive appearance, and is struggling to make its manifestation more and more clear. That which is eternal is realizing itself in history through the obstructions of limits.

The physiological process in the progress of Life's evolution seems to have reached its finality in man. We cannot think of any noticeable addition or modification in our vital instruments which we are likely to allow to persist. If any individual is born, by chance, with an extra pair of eyes or ears, or some unexpected limbs like stowaways without passports, we are sure to do our best to eliminate them from our bodily organization. Any new chance of a too obviously physical variation is certain to meet with a determined disapproval from man, the most powerful veto being expected from his aesthetic nature, which peremptorily refuses to calculate advantage when its majesty is offended by any sudden license of form. We all know that the back of our body has a wide surface practically unguarded. From the strategic point of view this oversight is unfortunate, causing us annoyances and indignities, if nothing worse, through unwelcome intrusions. And this could reasonably justify in our minds regret for retrenchment in the matter of an original tail, whose memorial we are still made to carry in secret. But the least attempt at the rectification of the policy of economy in this direction is indignantly resented. I strongly believe that the idea of ghosts had its best chance with our timid imagination in our sensitive back—a field of dark ignorance; and yet it is too late for me to hint that one of our eyes could profitably have been spared for our burden-carrier back, so unjustly neglected and haunted by undefined fears.

Thus, while all innovation is stubbornly opposed, there is every sign of a comparative carelessness about the physiological efficiency of the human body. Some of our organs are losing their original vigour. The civilized life, within walked enclosures, has naturally caused in man a weakening of his power of sight and hearing along with subtle sense of the distant. Because of our habit of taking cooked food we give less employment to our teeth and a great deal more to the dentist. Spoilt and pampered by clothes, our skin shows lethargy in its function of adjustment to the atmospheric temperature and in its power of quick recovery from hurts.

The adventurous Life appears to have paused at a crossing in her road before Man came. It seems as if she became aware of wastefulness in carrying on her experiments and adding to her inventions purely on the physical plane. It was proved in Life's case that four is not always twice as much as two. In living things it is necessary to keep to the limit of the perfect unit within which the interrelationship must not be inordinately strained. The ambition that seeks power in the augmentation of dimension is doomed; for that perfection which is in the inner quality of harmony becomes choked when quantity overwhelms it in a fury of extravagance. The combination of an exaggerated nose and arm that an elephant carries hanging down its front has its advantage. This may induce us to imagine that it would double the advantage for the animal if its tail also could grow into an additional trunk. But the progress which greedily allows Life's field to be crowded with an excessive production of instruments becomes a progress towards death. For Life has its own natural rhythm which a multiplication table has not; and proud progress that rides roughshod over Life's cadence kills it at the end with encumbrances that are unrhythmic. As I have already mentioned, such disasters did happen in the history of evolution.

The moral of that tragic chapter is that if the tail does not have the decency to know where to stop, the drag of this dependency becomes fatal to the body's empire.

Moreover, evolutionary progress on the physical plane inevitably tends to train up its subjects into specialists. The camel is a specialist of the desert and is awkward in the swamp. The hippopotamus which specializes in the mudlands of the Nile is helpless in the neighbouring desert. Such one-sided emphasis breeds professionalism in Life's domain, confining special efficiencies in narrow compartments. The expert training in the aerial sphere is left to the bird; that in the marine is particularly monopolized by the fish. The ostrich is an expert in its own region and would look utterly foolish in an eagle's neighbourhood. They have to remain permanently content with advantages that desperately cling to their limits. Such mutilation of the complete ideal of life for the sake of some exclusive privilege of power is inevitable; for that form of progress deals with materials that are physical and therefore necessarily limited.

To rescue her own career from such a multiplying burden of the dead and such constriction of specialization seems to have been the object of the Spirit of Life at one particular stage. For it does not take long to find out that an indefinite pursuit of quantity creates for Life, which is essentially qualitative, complexities that leads to a vicious circle. These primeval animals that produced an enormous volume of flesh had to build a gigantic system of bones to carry the burden. This required in its turn a long and substantial array of tails to give it balance. Thus their bodies, being compelled to occupy a vast area, exposed a very large surface which had to be protected by a strong, heavy and capacious armour. A progress which represented a congress of dead materials required a parallel organization of teeth and claws, or horns and hooves, which also were dead.

In its own manner one mechanical burden links itself to other burdens of machines, and Life grows to be a carrier of the dead, a mere platform for machinery, until it is crushed to death by its interminable paradoxes. We are told that the greater part of a tree is dead matter; the big stem, except for a thin covering, is lifeless. The tree uses it as a prop in its ambition for a high position and the lifeless timber is the slave that carries on its back the magnitude of the tree. But such a dependence upon a dead dependant has been achieved by the tree at the cost of its real freedom. It had to seek the stable alliance of the earth for the sharing of its burden, which it did by the help of secret underground entanglements making itself permanently stationary.

But the form of life that seeks the great privilege of movement must minimize its load of the dead and must realize that life's progress should be a perfect progress of the inner life itself and not of materials and machinery; the non-living must not continue outgrowing the living, the armour deadening the skin, the armament laming the arms.

At last, when the Spirit of Life found her form in Man, the effort she had begun completed its cycle, and the truth of her mission glimmered into suggestions which dimly pointed to some direction of meaning across her own frontier. Before the end of this cycle was reached, all the suggestions had been external. They were concerned with technique, with life's apparatus, with the efficiency of the organs. This might have exaggerated itself into an endless boredom of physical progress. It can be conceded that the eyes of the bee possessing numerous facets may have some uncommon advantage which we cannot even imagine, or the glow-worm that carries an arrangement for producing light in its person may baffle our capacity and comprehension. Very likely there are creatures having certain organs that give them sensibilities which we cannot have the power to guess.

All such enhanced sensory powers merely add to the mileage in life's journey on the same road lengthening an indefinite distance. They never take us over the border of physical existence.

The same thing may be said not only about life's efficiency, but also life's ornaments. The colouring and decorative patterns on the bodies of some of the deep sea creatures make us silent with amazement. The butterfly's wings, the beetle's back, the peacock's plumes, the shells of the crustaceans, the exuberant outbreak of decoration in plant life, have reached a standard of perfection that seems to be final. And yet if it continues in the same physical direction, then, however much variety of surprising excellence it may produce, it leaves out some great element of unuttered meaning. These ornaments are like ornaments lavished upon a captive girl, luxuriously complete within a narrow limit, speaking of a homesickness for a far away horizon of emancipation, for an inner depth that is beyond the ken of the senses. The freedom in the physical realm is like the circumscribed freedom in a cage. It produces a proficiency which is mechanical and a beauty which is of the surface. To whatever degree of improvement bodily strength and skill may be developed they keep life tied to a persistence of habit. It is closed, like a mould, useful though it may be for the sake of safety and precisely standardized productions. For centuries the bee repeats its hive, the weaver-bird its nest, the spider its web; and instincts strongly attach themselves to some invariable tendencies of muscles and nerves never being allowed the privilege of making blunders. The physical functions, in order to be strictly reliable, behave like some model schoolboy, obedient, regular, properly repeating lessons by rote without mischief or mistake in his conduct, but also without spirit and initiative. It is the flawless perfection of rigid limits, a cousin—possibly a distant cousin—of the inanimate.

Instead of allowing a full paradise of perfection to continue its tame and timid rule of faultless regularity the Spirit of Life boldly declared for a further freedom and decided to eat of the fruit of the Tree of Knowledge. This time her struggle was not against the Inert, but against the limitation of her own overburdened agents. She fought against the tutelage of her prudent old prime minister, the faithful instinct. She adopted a novel method of experiment, promulgated new laws, and tried her hand at moulding Man through a history which was immensely different from that which went before. She took a bold step in throwing open her gates to a dangerously explosive factor which she had cautiously introduced into her council—the element of Mind. I should not say that it was ever absent, but only that at a certain stage some curtain was removed and its play was made evident, even like the dark heat which in its glowing intensity reveals itself in a contradiction of radiancy.

Essentially qualitative, like life itself, the Mind does not occupy space. For that very reason it has no bounds in its mastery of space. Also, like Life, Mind has its meaning in freedom, which it missed in its earliest dealings with Life's children. In the animal, though the mind is allowed to come out of the immediate limits of livelihood, its range is restricted, like the freedom of a child that might run out of its room but not out of the house; or, rather, like the foreign ships to which only a certain port was opened in Japan in the beginning of her contact with the West in fear of the danger that might befall if the strangers had their uncontrolled opportunity of communication. Mind also is a foreign element for Life; its laws are different, its weapons powerful, its moods and manners most alien.

Like Eve of the Semitic mythology, the Spirit of Life risked the happiness of her placid seclusion to win her freedom. She listened to the whisper of a temper who promised her the right to a new region of mystery, and was urged into a permanent alliance with the stranger. Up to this point the interest of life was the sole interest in her own kingdom, but another most powerfully parallel interest was created with the advent of this adventurer Mind from an unknown shore. Their interests clash, and complications of a serious nature arise. I have already referred to some vital organs of Man that are suffering from neglect. The only reason has been the diversion created by the Mind interrupting the sole attention which Life's functions claimed in the halcyon days of her undisputed monarchy. It is no secret that Mind has the habit of asserting its own will for its expression against life's will to live and enforcing sacrifices from her. When lately some adventurers accepted the dangerous enterprise to climb Mount Everest, it was solely through the instigation of the arch-rebel Mind. In this case Mind denied its treaty of cooperation with its partner and ignored Life's claim to help in her living. The immemorial privileges of the ancient sovereignty of Life are too often flouted by the irreverent Mind; in fact, all through the course of this alliance there are constant cases of interference with each other's functions, often with unpleasant and even fatal results. But in spite of this, or very often because of this antagonism, the new current of Man's evolution is bringing a wealth to his harbour infinitely beyond the dream of the creatures of monstrous flesh.

The manner in which Man appeared in Life's kingdom was in itself a protest and a challenge, the challenge of Jack to the Giant. He carried in his body the declaration of mistrust against the crowding of burdensome implements of physical progress. His Mind spoke to the naked man, 'Fear not'; and he stood alone facing the menace of a heavy brigade of formidable muscles. His own puny muscles cried out in despair, and he had to invent for himself in a novel manner and in a new spirit of evolution. This at once gave him his promotion from the passive destiny of the animal to the aristocracy of Man. He began to create his further body, his outer organs—the workers which served him and yet did not directly claim a share of his life. Some of the earliest in his list were bows and arrows. Had this change been undertaken by the physical process of evolution, modifying his arms in a slow and gradual manner, it might have resulted in burdensome and ungainly apparatus. Possibly, however, I am unfair, and the dexterity and grace which Life's technical instinct possesses might have changed his arm into a shooting medium in a perfect manner and with a beautiful form. In that case our lyrical literature today would have sung in praise of its fascination, not only for a consummate skill in hunting victims, but also for a similar mischief in a metaphorical sense. But even in the service of lyrics it would show some limitation. For instance, the arms that would specialize in shooting would be awkward in wielding a pen or stringing a lute. But the great advantage in the latest method of human evolution lies in the fact that Man's additional new limbs, like bows and arrows, have become detached. They never tie his arms to any exclusive advantage of efficiency.

The elephant's trunk, the tiger's paws, the claws of the mole, have combined their best expressions in the human arms, which are much weaker in their original capacity than those limbs I have mentioned. It would have been a hugely cumbersome practical joke if the combination of animal limbs had had a simultaneous location in the human organism through some overzeal in biological inventiveness.

The first great economy resulting from the new programme was the relief of the physical burden, which means the maximum efficiency with the minimum pressure of taxation upon the vital resources of the body. Another mission of benefit was this, that it absolved the Spirit of Life in Man's case from the necessity of specialization for the sake of limited success. This has encouraged Man to dream of the possibility of combining in his single person the fish, the bird and the fleet-footed animal that walks on land. Man desired in his completeness to be the one great representative of multiform life, not through wearisome subjection to the haphazard gropings of natural selection, but by the purposeful selection of opportunities with the help of his reasoning mind. It enables the schoolboy who is given a pen-knife on his birthday to have the advantage over the tiger in the fact that it does not take him a million years to obtain its possession, nor another million years for its removal, when the instrument proves unnecessary or dangerous. The human mind has compressed ages into a few years for the acquisition of steel-made claws. The only cause of anxiety is that the instrument and the temperament which uses it may not keep pace in perfect harmony. In the tiger, the claws and the temperament which only a tiger should possess have had a synchronous development, and in no single tiger is any maladjustment possible between its nails and its tigerliness. But the human boy, who grows a claw in the form of a pen-knife, may not at the same time develop the proper temperament necessary for its use which only a man ought to have. The new organs that today are being added as a supplement to Man's original vital stock are too quick and too numerous for his inner nature to develop its own simultaneous concordance with them, and thus we see everywhere innumerable schoolboys in human society playing pranks with their own and other people's lives and welfare by means of newly acquired pen-knives which have not had time to become humanized.

One thing, I am sure, must have been noticed—that the original plot of the drama is changed, and the mother Spirit of Life has retired into the background, giving full prominence, in the third act, to the Spirit of Man—though the dowager queen, from her inner apartment, still renders necessary help. It is the consciousness in Man of his own creative personality which has ushered in this new regime in Life's kingdom. And from now onwards Man's attempts are directed fully to capture the government and make his own Code of Legislation prevail without a break. We have seen in India those who are called mystics, impatient of the continued regency of mother Nature in their own body, winning for their will by a concentration of inner forces the vital regions with which our masterful minds have no direct path of communication.

But the most important fact that has come into prominence along with the change of direction in our evolution, is the possession of a Spirit which has its enormous capital with a surplus far in excess of the requirements of the biological animal in Man. Some overflowing influence led us over the strict boundaries of living, and offered to us an open space where Man's thoughts and dreams could have their holidays. Holidays are for gods who have their joy in creation. In Life's primitive paradise, where the mission was merely to live, any luck which came to the creatures entered in from outside by the donations of chance; they lived on perpetual charity, by turns petted and kicked on the back by physical Providence. Beggars never can have harmony among themselves; they are envious of one another, mutually suspicious, like dogs living upon their master's favour, showing their teeth, growling, barking, trying to tear one another. This is what Science describes as the struggle for existence. This beggar's paradise lacked peace; I am sure the suitors for special favour from fate lived in constant preparedness, inventing and multiplying armaments.

But above the din of the clamour and scramble rises the voice of the Angel of Surplus, of leisure, of detachment from the compelling claim of physical need, saying to men, 'Rejoice'. From his original serfdom as a creature Man takes his right seat as a creator. Whereas, before, his incessant appeal has been to get, now at last the call comes to him to give. His God, whose help he was in the habit of asking, now stands Himself at his door and asks for his offerings. As an animal, he is still dependent upon Nature; as a Man, he is a sovereign who builds his world and rules it.

And there, at this point, comes his religion, whereby he realizes himself in the perspective of the infinite. There is a remarkable verse in the Atharva Veda which says: 'Righteousness, truth, great endeavours, empire, religion, enterprise, heroism and prosperity, the past and the future, dwell in the surpassing strength of the surplus.'

What is purely physical has its limits like the shell of an egg; the liberation is there in the atmosphere of the infinite, which is indefinable, invisible. Religion can have no meaning in the enclosure of mere physical or material interest; it is in the surplus we carry around our personality—the surplus which is like the atmosphere of the earth, bringing to her a constant circulation of light and life and delightfulness.

I have said in a poem of mine that when the child is detached from its mother's womb it finds its mother in a real relationship whose truth is in freedom. Man in his detachment has realized himself in a wider and deeper relationship with the universe. In his moral life he has the sense of his obligation and his freedom at the same time, and this is goodness. In his spiritual life his sense of the union and the will which is free has its culmination in love. The freedom of opportunity he wins for himself in Nature's region by uniting his power with Nature's forces. The freedom of social relationship he attains through owning responsibility to his community, thus gaining its collective power for his own welfare. In the freedom of consciousness he realizes the sense of his unity with his larger being, finding fulfilment in the dedicated life of an ever-progressive truth and ever-active love.

The first detachment achieved by Man is physical. It represents his freedom from the necessity of developing the power of his senses and limbs in the limited area of his own physiology, having for itself an unbounded background with an immense result in consequence. Nature's original intention was that Man should have the allowance of his sight-power ample enough for his surroundings and a little over. But to have to develop an astronomical telescope on our skull would cause a worse crisis of bankruptcy than it did to the Mammoth whose densely foolish body indulged in an extravagance of tusks. A snail carries its house on its back and therefore the material, the shape and the weight have to be strictly limited to the capacity of the body. But fortunately Man's house need not grow on the foundation of his bones and occupy his flesh. Owing to this detachment, his ambition knows no check to its daring in the dimension and strength of his dwellings. Since his shelter does not depend upon his body, it survives him. This fact greatly affects the man who builds a house, generating in his mind a sense of the eternal in his creative work. And this background of the boundless surplus of time encourages architecture, which seeks a universal value overcoming the miserliness of the present need.

I have already mentioned a stage which Life reached when the units of single cells formed themselves into larger units, each consisting of a multitude. It was not merely an aggregation, but had a mysterious unity of interrelationship, complex in character, with differences within of forms and function. We can never know concretely what this relation means. There are gaps between the units, but they do not stop the binding force that permeates the whole. There is a future for the whole which is in its growth, but in order to bring this about each unit works and dies to make room for the next worker. While the unit has the right to claim the glory of the whole, yet individually it cannot share the entire wealth that occupies a history yet to be completed.

Of all creatures Man has reached that multicellular character in a perfect manner, not only in his body but in his personality. For centuries his evolution has been the evolution of a consciousness that tries to be liberated from the bonds of individual separateness and to comprehend in its relationship a wholeness which may be named Man. This relationship, which has been dimly instinctive, is ever struggling to be fully aware of itself. Physical evolution sought for efficiency in a perfect communication with the physical world; the evolution of Man's consciousness sought for truth in a perfect harmony with the world of personality.

There are those who will say that the idea of humanity is an abstraction, subjective in character. It must be confessed that the concrete objectiveness of this living truth cannot be proved to its own units. They can never see its entireness from outside; for they are one with it. The individual cells of our body have their separate lives; but they never have the opportunity of observing the body as a whole with its past, present and future. If these cells have the power of reasoning (which they may have for aught we know) they have the right to argue that the idea of the body has no objective foundation in fact, and though there is a mysterious sense of attraction and mutual influence running through them, these are nothing positively real; the sole reality which is provable is in the isolation of these cells made by gaps that can never be crossed or bridged.

We know something about a system of explosive atoms whirling separately in a space which is immense compared to their own dimension. Yet we do not know why they should appear to us a solid piece of radiant mineral. And if there is an onlooker who at one glance can have the view of the immense time and space occupied by innumerable human individuals engaged in evolving a common history, the positive truth of their solidarity will be concretely evident to him and not the negative fact of their separateness.

The reality of a piece of iron is not provable if we take the evidence of the atom; the only proof is that I see it as a bit of iron, and that it has certain reactions upon my consciousness. Any being from, say, Orion, who has the sight to see the atoms and not the iron, has the right to say that we human beings suffer from an age-long epidemic of hallucination. We need not quarrel with him but go on using the iron as it appears to us. Seers there have been who have said *Vēdāhamētam*, 'I see', and lived a life according to that vision. And though our own sight may be blind we have ever bowed our head to them in reverence.

However, whatever name our logic may give to the truth of human unity, the fact can never be ignored that we have our greatest delight when we realize ourselves in others, and this is the definition of love. This love gives us the testimony of the great whole, which is the complete and final truth of man. It offers us the immense field where we can have our release from the sole monarchy of hunger, of the growling voice, snarling teeth and tearing claws, from the dominance of the limited material means, the source of cruel envy and ignoble deception, where the largest wealth of the human soul has been produced through sympathy and co-operation; through disinterested pursuit of knowledge that recognizes no limit and is unafraid of all time-honoured *taboos*; through a strenuous cultivation of intelligence for service that knows no distinction of colour and clime. The Spirit of Love, dwelling in the boundless realm of the surplus, emancipates our consciousness from the illusory bond of the separateness of self; it is ever trying to spread its illumination in the human world. This is the spirit of civilization, which in all its best endeavour invokes our supreme Being for the only bond of unity that leads us to truth, namely, that of righteousness:

> *Ya ēkō varnō bahudhā saktiyogāt*
> *varnān anēkān nihitārthō dadhāti*
> *vichaitti chānte visvamādau sa dēvah*
> *sa nō budhyā subhayā samyunaktu.*

> He who is one, above all colours, and who with his manifold power supplies the inherent needs of men of all colours, who is in the beginning and in the end of the world, is divine, and may he unite us in a relationship of good will.

The Religion of the Forest

We stand before this great world. The truth of our life depends upon our attitude of mind towards it—an attitude which is formed by our habit of dealing with it according to the special circumstance of our surroundings and our temperaments. It guides our attempts to establish relations with the universe either by conquest or by union, either through the cultivation of power or through that of sympathy. And thus, in our realization of the truth of existence, we put our emphasis either upon the principle of dualism or upon the principle of unity.

The Indian sages have held in the Upanishads that the emancipation of our soul lies in its realizing the ultimate truth of unity. They said:

> *Ishāvāsyam idam sarvam yat kinch jagatyām jagat.*
> *Yéna tyakténa bhunjithā mā gradha kasyasvit dhanam.*
>
> (Know all that moves in this moving world as enveloped by God; and find enjoyment through renunciation, not through greed of possession.)

The meaning of this is, that, when we know the multiplicity of things as the final truth, we try to augment ourselves by the external possession of them; but, when we know the Infinite Soul as the final truth, then through our union with it we realize the joy of our soul. Therefore it has been said of those who have attained their fulfilment,—'sarvam evá vishanti' (they enter into all things). Their perfect relation with this world is the relation of union.

This ideal of perfection preached by the forest-dwellers of ancient India runs through the heart of our classical literature and still dominates our mind. The legends related in our epics cluster under the forest shade bearing all through their narrative the message of the forest-dwellers. Our two greatest classical dramas find their background in scenes of the forest hermitage, which are permeated by the association of these sages.

The history of the Northmen of Europe is resonant with the music of the sea. That sea is not merely topographical in its significance, but represents certain ideals of life which still guide the history and inspire the creations of that race. In the sea, nature presented herself to those men in her aspect of a danger, a barrier which seemed to be at constant war with the land and its children. The sea was the challenge of untamed nature to the indomitable human soul. And man did not flinch; he fought and won, and the spirit of fight continued in him. This fight he still maintains; it is the fight against disease and poverty, tyranny of matter and of man.

This refers to a people who live by the sea, and ride on it as on a wild, champing horse, catching it by its mane and making it render service from shore to shore. They find delight in turning by force the antagonism of circumstances into obedience. Truth appears to them in her aspect of dualism, the perpetual conflict of good and evil, which has no reconciliation, which can only end in victory or defeat.

But in the level tracts of Northern India men found no barrier between their lives and the grand life that permeates the universe. The forest entered into a close living relationship with their work and leisure, with their daily necessities and contemplations. They could not think of other surroundings as separate or inimical. So the view of the truth, which these men found, did not make manifest the difference, but rather the unity of all things. They uttered their faith in these words: *Yadidam kinch sarvam prāna éjati nihsratam* (All that is vibrates with life, having come out from life). When we know this world as alien to us, then its mechanical aspect takes prominence in our mind; and then we set up our machines and our methods to deal with it and make as much profit as our knowledge of its mechanism allows us to do. This view of things does not play us false, for the machine has its place in this world. And not only this material universe, but human beings also, may be used as machines and made to yield powerful results. This aspect of truth cannot be ignored; it has to be known and mastered. Europe has done so and has reaped a rich harvest.

The view of this world which India has taken is summed up in one compound Sanskrit word, *Sacchidānanda*. The meaning is that Reality, which is essentially one, has three phases. The first is *sat*; it is the simple fact that things are, the fact which relates us to all things through the relationship of common existence. The second is *chit*; it is the fact that we know, which relates us to all things through the relationship of knowledge. The third is *ānanda*; it is the fact that we enjoy, which unites us with all things through the relationship of love.

According to the true Indian view, our consciousness of the world, merely as the sum total of things that exist, and as governed by laws, is imperfect. But it is perfect when our consciousness realizes all things as spiritually one with it, and therefore capable of giving us joy. For us the highest purpose of this world is not merely living in it, knowing it and making use of it, but realizing our own selves in it through expansion of sympathy; not alienating ourselves from it and dominating it, but comprehending and uniting it with ourselves in perfect union.

II

When Vikramaditya became king, Ujjayini a great capital, and Kālidāsa its poet, the age of India's forest retreats had passed. Then we had taken our stand in the midst of the great concourse of humanity. The Chinese and the Hun, the Scythian and the Persian, the Greek and the Roman, had crowded round us. But, even in that age of pomp and prosperity, the love and reverence with which its poet sang about the hermitage shows what was the dominant ideal that occupied the mind of India; what was the one current of memory that continually flowed through her life.

In Kālidāsa's drama, *Shakuntalā,* the hermitage, which dominates the play, overshadowing the king's palace, has the same idea running through it—the recognition of the kinship of man with conscious and unconscious creation alike.

A poet of a later age, while describing a hermitage in his *Kādambari,* tells us of the posture of salutation in the flowering lianas as they bow to the wind; of the sacrifice offered by the trees scattering their blossoms; of the grove resounding with the lessons chanted by the neophytes, and the verses repeated by the parrots, learnt by constantly hearing them; of the wild-fowl enjoying *vaishva-deva-bali-pinda* (the food offered to the divinity which is in all creatures); of the ducks coming up from the lake for their portion of the grass seed spread in the cottage yards to dry; and of the deer caressing with their tongues the young hermit boys. It is again the same story. The hermitage shines out, in all our ancient literature, as the place where the chasm between man and the rest of creation has been bridged.

In the Western dramas, human characters drown our attention in the vortex of their passions. Nature occasionally peeps out, but she is almost always a trespasser, who has to offer excuses, or bow apologetically and depart. But in all our dramas which still retain their fame, such as *Mrit-Shakatikā, Shakuntalā, Uttara-rāmacharita,* Nature stands on her own right, proving that she has her great function, to impart the peace of the eternal to human emotions.

The fury of passion in two of Shakespeare's youthful poems is exhibited in conspicuous isolation. It is snatched away, naked, from the context of the age, it has not the green earth or the blue sky around it; it is there ready to bring to our view the raging fever which is in man's desires, and not the balm of health and repose which encircles it in the universe.

Ritusambhāra is clearly a work of Kālidāsa's immaturity. The youthful love-song in it does not reach the sublime reticence which is in *Shakuntalā* and *Kumāra-Sambhava.* But the tune of these voluptuous outbreaks is set to the varied harmony of Nature's symphony. The moonbeams of the summer evening, resonant with the flow of fountains, acknowledge it as a part of its own melody. In its rhythm sways the Kadamba forest, glistening in the first cool rain of the season; and the south breezes, carrying the scent of the mango blossoms, temper it with their murmur.

In the third canto *of Kumāra-Sambhava,* Madana, the God Eros, enters the forest sanctuary to set free a sudden flood of desire amid the serenity of the ascetics' meditation. But the boisterous outbreak of passion so caused was shown against a background of universal life. The divine love-thrills of Sati and Shiva found their response in the world-wide immensity of youth, in which animals and trees have their life-throbs.

Not only its third canto but the whole of the *Kumāra-Sambhava* poem is painted upon a limitless canvas. It tells of the eternal wedding of love, its wooing and sacrifice, and its fulfilment, for which the gods wait in suspense. Its inner idea is deep and of all time. It answers the one question that humanity asks through all its endeavours: 'How is the birth of the hero to be brought about, the brave one who can defy and vanquish the evil demon laying waste heaven's own kingdom?'

It becomes evident that such a problem had become acute in Kālidāsa's time, when the old simplicity of Hindu life had broken up. The Hindu kings, forgetful of their duties, had become self-seeking epicureans, and India was being repeatedly devastated by the Scythians. What answer, then, does the poem give to the question it raises? Its message is that the cause of weakness lies in the inner life of the soul. It is in some break of harmony with the Good, some dissociation from the True. In the commencement of the poem we find that the God Shiva, the Good, had remained for long lost in the self-centred solitude of his asceticism, detached from the world of reality. And then Paradise was lost. But *Kumāra-Sambhava* is the poem of Paradise Regained. How was it regained? When Sati, the Spirit of Reality, through humiliation, suffering, and penance, won the Heart of Shiva, the Spirit of Goodness. And thus, from the union of the freedom of the real with the restraint of the Good, was born the heroism that released Paradise from the demon of Lawlessness.

Viewed from without, India, in the time of Kālidāsa, appeared to have reached the zenith of civilization excelling as she did in luxury, literature and the arts. But from the poems of Kālidāsa it is evident that this very magnificence of wealth and enjoyment worked against the ideal that sprang and flowed forth from the sacred solitude of the forest. These poems contain the voice of warnings against the gorgeous unreality of that age, which, like a Himalayan avalanche, was slowly gliding down to an abyss of catastrophe. And from his seat beside all the glories of Vikramaditya's throne the poet's heart yearns for the purity and simplicity of India's past age of spiritual striving. And it was this yearning which impelled him to go back to the annals of the ancient Kings of Raghu's line for the narrative poem, in which he traced the history of the rise and fall of the ideal that should guide the rulers of men.

King Dilipa, with Queen Sudakshinā, has entered upon the life of the forest. The great monarch is busy tending the cattle of the hermitage. Thus the poem opens, amid scenes of simplicity and self-denial. But it ends in the palace of magnificence, in the extravagance of self-enjoyment. With a calm restraint of language the poet tells us of the kingly glory crowned with purity. He begins his poem as the day begins, in the serenity of sunrise. But lavish are the colours in which he describes the end, as of the evening, eloquent for a time with the sumptuous splendour of sunset, but overtaken at last by the devouring darkness which sweeps away all its brilliance into night.

In this beginning and this ending of his poem there lies hidden that message of the forest which found its voice in the poet's words. There runs through the narrative the idea that the future glowed gloriously ahead only when there was in the atmosphere the calm of self-control, of purity and renunciation. When downfall had become imminent, the hungry fires of desire, aflame at a hundred different points, dazzled the eyes of all beholders.

Kālidāsa in almost all his works represented the unbounded impetuousness of kingly splendour on the one side and the serene strength of regulated desires on the other. Even in the minor drama of *Mālavikāgnimitra* we find the same thing in a different manner. It must never be thought that, in this play, the poet's deliberate object was to pander to his royal patron by inviting him to a literary orgy of lust and passion. The very introductory verse indicates the object towards which this play is directed. The poet begins the drama with the prayer, *Sanmārgālókayan vyapanayatu sa nastāmasi vritimishah* (Let God, to illumine for us the path of truth, sweep away our passions, bred of darkness). This is the God Shiva, in whose nature Parvati, the eternal Woman, is ever commingled in an ascetic purity of love. The unified being of Shiva and Parvati is the perfect symbol of the eternal in the wedded love of man and woman. When the poet opens his drama with an invocation of this Spirit of the Divine Union it is evident that it contains in it the message with which he greets his kingly audience. The whole drama goes to show the ugliness of the treachery and cruelty inherent in unchecked self-indulgence. In the play the conflict of ideals is between the King and the Queen, between Agnimitra and Dhārini, and the significance of the contrast lies hidden in the very names of the hero and the heroine. Though the name Agnimitra is historical, yet it symbolizes in the poet's mind the destructive force of uncontrolled desire—just as did the name Agnivarna in *Raghuvamsha*. Agnimitra, 'the friend of the fire', the reckless person who in his love-making is playing with fire, not knowing that all the time it is scorching him black. And what a great name is Dhārini, signifying the fortitude and forbearance that comes from majesty of soul! What an association it carries of the infinite dignity of love, purified by a self-abnegation that rises far above all insult and baseness of betrayal!

In *Shakuntalā* this conflict of ideals has been shown, all through the drama, by the contrast of the pompous heartlessness of the king's court and the natural purity of the forest hermitage. The drama opens with a hunting scene, where the king is in pursuit of an antelope. The cruelty of the chase appears like a menace symbolizing the spirit of the king's life clashing against the spirit of the forest retreat, which is *sharanyam sarva-bhūtānām* (where all creatures find their protection of love). And the pleading of the forest-dwellers with the king to spare the life of the deer, helplessly innocent and beautiful, is the pleading that rises from the heart of the whole drama. 'Never, oh, never is the arrow meant to pierce the tender body of a deer, even as the fire is not for the burning of flowers.'

In the Rāmāyana, Rāma and his companions, in their banishment, had to traverse forest after forest; they had to live in leaf-thatched huts, to sleep on the bare ground. But as their hearts felt their kinship with woodland, hill, and stream, they were not in exile amidst these. Poets, brought up in an atmosphere of different ideals, would have taken this opportunity of depicting in dismal colours the hardship of the forest-life in order to bring out the martyrdom of Rāmachandra with all the emphasis of a strong contrast. But, in the Rāmāyana, we are led to realise the greatness of the hero, not in a fierce struggle with Nature, but in sympathy with it, Sitā, the daughter-in-law of a great kingly house, goes along the forest paths. We read:

> 'She asks Rāma about the flowering trees, and shrubs and creepers which she has not seen before. At her request Lakshmana gathers and brings her plants of all kinds, exuberant with flowers, and it delights her heart to see the forest rivers, variegated with their streams and sandy banks, resounding with the call of heron and duck.'
>
> 'When Rāma first took his abode in the Chitrakuta peak, that delightful Chitrakuta, by the Mālyavati river, with its easy slopes for landing, he forgot all the pain of leaving his home in the capital at the sight of those woodlands, alive with beast and bird.'

Having lived on that hill for long, Rāma, who was *giri-vana-priya* (lover of the mountain and the forest), said one day to Sitā:

> 'When I look upon the beauties of this hill, the loss of my kingdom troubles me no longer, nor does the separation from my friends cause me any pang.'

Thus passed Rāmachandra's exile, now in woodland, now in hermitage. The love which Rāma and Sitā bore to each other united them, not only to each other, but to the universe of life.

That is why, when Sitā was taken away, the loss seemed to be so great to the forest itself.

III

Strangely enough, in Shakespeare's dramas, like those of Kālidāsa, we find a secret vein of complaint against the artificial life of the king's court—the life of ungrateful treachery and falsehood. And almost everywhere, in his dramas, foreign scenes have been introduced in connection with some working of the life of unscrupulous ambition. It is perfectly obvious in *Timon of Athens*—but there Nature offers no message or balm to the injured soul of man. In *Cymbeline* the mountainous forest and the cave appear in their aspect of obstruction to life's opportunities. These only seem tolerable in comparison with the vicissitudes of fortune in die artificial court life. In *As You Like It* the forest of Arden is didactic in its lessons. It does not bring peace, but preaches, when it says:

> Hath not old custom made this life more sweet
> Than that of painted pomp? Are not these woods
> More free from peril than the envious court?

In the *Tempest,* through Prospero's treatment of Ariel and Caliban we realize man's struggle with Nature and his longing to sever connection with her. In *Macbeth,* as a prelude to a bloody crime of treachery and treason, we are introduced to a scene of barren heath where the three witches appear as personifications of Nature's malignant forces; and in *King Lear* it is the fury of a father's love turned into curses by the ingratitude born of the unnatural life of the court that finds its symbol in the storm on the heath. The tragic intensity of *Hamlet* and *Othello* is unrelieved by any touch of Nature's eternity. Except in a passing glimpse of a moonlight night in the love scene in the *Merchant of Venice,* Nature has not been allowed in other dramas of this series, including *Romeo and Juliet* and *Antony and Cleopatra,* to contribute her own music to the music of man's love. In *The Winter's Tale* the cruelty of a king's suspicion stands bare in its relentlessness, and Nature cowers before it, offering no consolation.

I hope it is needless for me to say that these observations are not intended to minimize Shakespeare's great power as a dramatic poet, but to show in his works the gulf between Nature and human nature owing to the tradition of his race and time. It cannot be said that beauty of nature is ignored in his writings; only he fails to recognize in them the truth of the interpenetration of human life with the cosmic life of the world. We observe a completely different attitude of mind in the later English poets like Wordsworth and Shelley, which can be attributed in the main to the great mental change in Europe, at that particular period, through the influence of the newly discovered philosophy of India which stirred the soul of Germany and aroused the attention of other Western countries.

In Milton's *Paradise Lost,* the very subject—Man dwelling in the garden of Paradise—seems to afford a special opportunity for bringing out the true greatness of man's relationship with Nature. But though the poet has described to us the beauties of the garden, though he has shown to us the animals living there in amity and peace among themselves, there is no reality of kinship between them and man. They were created for man's enjoyment; man was their lord and master. We find no trace of the love between the first man and woman gradually surpassing themselves and overflowing the rest of creation, such as we find in the love scenes in *Kumāra-Sambhava* and *Shakuntalā.* In the seclusion of the bower, where the first man and woman rested in the garden of Paradise—

> Bird, beast, insect or worm
> Durst enter none, such was their awe of man.

Not that India denied the superiority of man, but the test of that superiority lay, according to her, in the comprehensiveness of sympathy, not in the aloofness of absolute distinction.

IV

India holds sacred, and counts as places of pilgrimage, all spots which display a special beauty or splendour of nature. These had no original attraction on account of any special fitness for cultivation or settlement. Here, man is free, not to look upon Nature as a source of supply of his necessities, but to realise his soul beyond himself. The Himalayas of India are sacred and the Vindhya Hills. Her majestic rivers are sacred. Lake Mānasa and the confluence of the Ganges and the Jamuna are sacred. India has saturated with her love and worship the great Nature with which her children are surrounded, whose light fills their eyes with gladness, and whose water cleanses them, whose food gives them life, and from whose majestic mystery comes forth the constant revelation of the infinite in music, scent, and colour, which brings its awakening to the soul of man. India gains the world through worship, through spiritual communion; and the idea of freedom to which she aspired was based upon the realization of her spiritual unity.

When, in my recent voyage to Europe, our ship left Aden and sailed along the sea which lay between the two continents, we passed by the red and barren rocks of Arabia on our right side and the gleaming sands of Egypt on our left. They seemed to me like two giant brothers exchanging with each other burning glances of hatred, kept apart by the tearful entreaty of the sea from whose womb they had their birth.

There was an immense stretch of silence on the left shore as well as on the right, but the two shores spoke to me of the two different historical dramas enacted. The civilization which found its growth in Egypt was continued across long centuries, elaborately rich with sentiments and expressions of life, with pictures, sculptures, temples, and ceremonials. This was a country whose guardian-spirit was a noble river, which spread the festivities of life on its banks across the heart of the land. There man never raised the barrier of alienation between himself and the rest of the world.

On the opposite shore of the Red Sea the civilization which grew up in the inhospitable soil of Arabia had a contrary character to that of Egypt. There man felt himself isolated in his hostile and bare surroundings. His idea of God became that of a jealous God. His mind naturally dwelt upon the principle of separateness. It roused in him the spirit of fight, and this spirit was a force that drove him far and wide. These two civilizations represented two fundamental divisions of human nature. The one contained in it the spirit of conquest and the other the spirit of harmony. And both of these have their truth and purpose in human existence.

The characters of two eminent sages have been described in our mythology. One was Vashishtha and another Vishvāmitra. Both of them were great, but they represented two different types of wisdom; and there was conflict between them. Vishvāmitra sought to achieve power and was proud of it; Vashishtha was rudely smitten by that power. But his hurt and his loss could not touch the illumination of his soul; for he rose above them and could forgive. Rāmachandra, the great hero of our epic, had his initiation to the spiritual life from Vashishtha, the life of inner peace and perfection. But he had his initiation to war from Vishvāmitra, who called him to kill the demons and gave him weapons that were irresistible.

Those two sages symbolize in themselves the two guiding spirits of civilization. Can it be true that they shall never be reconciled? If so, can ever the age of peace and co-operation dawn upon the human world? Creation is the harmony of contrary forces—the forces of attraction and repulsion. When they join hands, all the fire and fight are changed into the smile of flowers and the songs of birds. When there is only one of them triumphant and the other defeated, then either there is the death of cold rigidity or that of suicidal explosion.

Humanity, for ages, has been busy with the one great creation of spiritual life. Its best wisdom, its discipline, its literature and art, all the teachings and self-sacrifice of its noblest teachers, have been for this. But the harmony of contrary forces, which give their rhythm to all creation, has not yet been perfected by man in his civilization, and the Creator in him is baffled over and over again. He comes back to his work, however, and makes himself busy, building his world in the midst of desolation and ruins. His history is the history of his aspiration interrupted and renewed. And one truth of which he must be reminded, therefore, is that the power which accomplishes the miracle of creation, by bringing conflicting forces into the harmony of the One, is no passion, but a love which accepts the bonds of self-control from the joy of its own immensity—a love whose sacrifice is the manifestation of its endless wealth within itself.

City and Village

21

The standard of living in modern civilization has been raised far higher than the average level of our necessity. The strain, which such rise of standard makes us exert, increases in the beginning our physical and mental alertness. The claim upon our energy, again, accelerates its growth; and this, in its turn, produces activity that expresses itself by the raising of life's standard still higher.

When this standard attains a degree a great deal above the normal, it encourages the passion of greed. The temptation of inordinately high living, normally confined to a negligibly small section of the community, becomes widespread. This evergrowing burden is sure to prove fatal to any civilization, that puts no restraint on the emulation of self-indulgence.

In the geography of our economic world, the ups and downs produced by the inequality of fortune are healthy only within a moderate range. In a country divided by the constant interruption of steep mountains no great civilization is possible, because therein the natural flow of communication becomes difficult. Large fortunes and luxurious living, like the mountains, form high walls of segregation; they produce worse divisions in society than any physical barriers.

There are some who believe that in the eradication of the idea of property the solution is to be found, for then, and then only, will the communal spirit find its full freedom. But we must know that the urging which has given rise to property, is something fundamental in human nature. If you have the power, you may tyrannically do violence to all that constitutes property; but you cannot change the constitution of mind itself.

Property is a medium for the expression of our personality. If we look at the negative aspect of this personality, we see in it the limits which separate one person from another. And when, in some men, this sense of separateness takes on an intense emphasis, we call them selfish. But its positive aspect reveals the truth, that it is the only medium through which men can communicate with one another. Therefore, all through the course of human history, men have tried to cultivate the sentiments that give our personality its greatest significance, thereby enabling it to bring us close together in bonds of sympathy.

If we kill our individuality because it is apt to be selfish, then human communion itself loses its meaning. But if we allow it to remain and develop, then being creative by nature, it must fashion its own world. Most often and for most men, property is the only frame that can give a foundation for such creation of a personal world. It is not merely money, not merely furniture; it does not represent merely acquisitiveness, but is an objective manifestation of our taste, our imagination, our constructive faculties, our desire for self-sacrifice.

Through this creative limitation which is our personality, we receive, we give, we express. Our highest social training is to make our property the richest expression of the best in us, of that which is universal, of our individuality whose greatest illumination is love. As individuals are the units that build the community, so property is the unit of wealth that makes for communal prosperity, when it is alive to its function. Our wisdom lies not in destroying separateness of units, but in maintaining the spirit of unity in its full strength.

When life is simple, wealth does not become too exclusive, and individual property finds no great difficulty in acknowledging its communal responsibility, rather, it becomes its vehicle. In former days, in India, public opinion levied heavy taxes upon wealth and most of the public works of the country were voluntarily supported by the rich. The water-supply, medical help, education and amusement were naturally maintained by men of property through a spontaneous adjustment of mutual obligation. This was made possible, because the limits set to the individual right of self-indulgence were narrow, and surplus wealth easily followed the channel of social responsibility. In such a society, property was the pillar that supported its civilization, and wealth gave opportunity to the fortunate for self-sacrifice.

But with the rise of the standard of living, property changes its aspect. It shuts the gate of hospitality, which is the best means of social intercommunication. It displays its wealth in an extravagance which is self-centred. It begets envy and irreconcilable class division. In short, property becomes antisocial. Because, with what is called material progress, property has become intensely individualistic, the method of gaining it has become a matter of science and not of social ethics. It breaks social bonds; it drains the life sap of the community. Its unscrupulousness plays havoc all over the world, generating forces that can coax or coerce peoples to deeds of injustice and wholesale horror.

The forest-fire feeds upon the living world, from which it springs, till it is completely exhausted along with the fuel. When a passion, like greed, breaks loose from the barrier of social control, it acts in like manner, feeding upon the life of society, and the end is annihilation. It had ever been the object of the spiritual training of man to fight those passions that are anti-social and keep them chained. But lately some abnormal temptation has set them free and they are fiercely devouring all that is affording them shelter.

There are always insects in our harvest field which, in spite of their robbery, leave a sufficient surplus for the tillers of the soil, and it does not pay to try to exterminate them. But when some pest, that has enormous powers of self-multiplication, attacks our food crop, it has to be dealt with as a calamity. In human society, in normal circumstances, there are a number of causes that make for wastage, yet it does not cost us too much to ignore them. But today the blight, that has fallen on our social life and its resources, is disastrous, because it is not restricted to limited regions. It is an epidemic of voracity that has infected the total area of civilization.

We all now-a-days claim our right of freedom to be extravagant in our enjoyment, to the extent that we can afford it. Not to be able to waste as much upon individual gratification, as my rich neighbour does, merely proves a poverty of which I am ashamed, and against which my womenfolk and my parasites are permitted to cherish their grievance. Ours has become a society in which, through its tyrannical standard of respectability, all the members are goading one another to spoil themselves to the uttermost limit.

There is a continual screwing up of the ideal of convenience and comfort, the results of which, however, inevitably fall short of the energy spent by reason of the wastage involved. The very shriek of advertisement itself, which must constantly accompany the progress of production, means the squandering of an immense quantity of material and life force, and merely helps to swell the sweepings of time.

Civilization today has turned into a vast catering establishment. It maintains constant feasts for a whole population of gluttons. The intemperance, which could safely have been tolerated in a few, has spread its contagion to the multitude. The universal greed, produced as a consequence, is the cause of the meanness, cruelty and lies, in politics and commerce, that vitiate the whole human atmosphere. A civilization with such an unnatural appetite must depend for its existence upon numberless victims, and these are being sought in those parts of the world where human flesh is cheap. In Asia and Africa a bartering goes on, whereby the future hope and happiness of entire peoples are sold for the sake of providing fastidious fashion with an endless train of respectable rubbish.

The consequence of such material and moral drain is more evident when one studies the conditions manifested in the fatness of the cities and the physical and mental anaemia of the villages, almost everywhere in the world. For cities have become inevitably important. They represent energy and materials concentrated for the satisfaction of that exaggerated appetite, which is the characteristic symptom of modern civilization. Such abnormal devouring process cannot be carried on, unless certain parts of the social body conspire and organize to feed upon the whole. This is suicidal; but, before its progressive degeneracy ends in death, the disproportionate enlargement of the particular section looks formidably great, and conceals the starved pallor of the entire body,—the sacrifice of the great maintaining the small in its enormity, and creating for the time being an illusion of wealth.

The living relationship, in a physical or social body, is the sympathetic mutuality of help among its members and organs, whereby a perfect balance of communication between them is maintained, so that the consciousness of unity is not obstructed. The resulting health and wealth are of secondary importance,—the unity is ultimate in itself. The perfect rhythm of reciprocity which generates and maintains this unity is disturbed whenever some ambition of power establishes its dominance in life's republic.

What in the West is called democracy can never be true in a society where greed grows, uncontrolled, encouraged, even admired by the populace. In such an atmosphere, a constant struggle goes on among individuals to capture public organizations for the satisfaction of their own personal ambition, and democracy becomes like an elephant whose one purpose in life is to give joy rides to the clever and the rich.

In this kind of Body-politic, the organs of information and expression, through which opinions are manufactured, together with the machinery of administration, are all openly or secretly manipulated by those prosperous few, who have been compared of old to the camel, which can never pass through a needle's eye,—the gate that leads to the kingdom of ideals. Such a society necessarily becomes inhospitable and suspicious, and callously cruel against those who preach their faith in spiritual freedom. In such a society, people are intoxicated through the constant stimulation of what they call progress, a progress which they are willing to buy at the cost of civilization itself, like the man for whom wine has more attraction than food.

Villages are like women. In their keeping is the cradle of the race. They are nearer to nature than towns; and are therefore in closer touch with the fountain of life. They have the atmosphere which possesses a natural power of healing. It is the function of the village, like that of woman, to provide people with their elemental needs, with food and joy, with the simple poetry of life, and with those ceremonies of beauty which the village spontaneously produces and in which she finds delight. But when constant strain is put upon her through the extortionate claim of ambition; when her resources are exploited through the excessive stimulus of temptation, then she becomes poor in life, her mind becomes dull and uncreative; and from her time-honoured position of the wedded partner of the city, she is degraded to that of maid-servant. While, in its turn, the city, in its intense egotism and pride, remains unconscious of the devastation it constantly works upon the very source of its life and health and joy.

Those who are familiar with the Hindu Pantheon know that in our mythology there is a demi-god named Kuvera, similar in character to Mammon. He represents the multiplication of money whose motive force is greed. His figure is ugly and gross with its protuberant belly, comic in its vulgarity of self-exaggeration. He is the genius of property that knows no moral responsibility. But the goddess, Lakshmi, who is the Deity of Prosperity, is beautiful. For prosperity is for all. It dwells in that property which, though belonging to the individual, generously owns its obligation to the community. Lakshmi is seated on a lotus, the lotus which is the symbol of the universal heart. It signifies that she presides over that wealth which means happiness for all men, which is hospitable.

By some ill-luck, Lakshmi has been deprived of her lotus throne in the present age, and Kuvera is worshipped in her place. Modern cities represent his protuberant stomach, and ugliness reigns unashamed. About one thing we have to be reminded, that there is no cause for rejoicing in the fact that this ugliness has an enormous power of growth and that it is prolific of its progeny. Its growth is not true progress; it is a disease which keeps the body swelling while it is being killed.

The sunshine that is diffuse maintains life in a whole forest of trees; and the sunshine of wealth is symbolised in Lakshmi. The sunshine, when it is focussed through a burning glass on a narrow spot, can reduce the same forest of trees to ashes; this hungry fire of concentrated wealth is symbolised in Kuvera, and he is the presiding deity of our modern cities.

Modern cities are continually growing bigger only because no central spirit of Unity exercises vital control over their growth of dimension. There can be no end to their addition of hugeness, because their object is not to modulate human relationships into some beauty of truth, but to gain convenience.

When in the Sanskrit poem, *Meghaduta,* we follow the path of the cloud messenger and in imagination pass over the old-world towns mentioned in it, with their beautiful names, we feel that the poet in reciting them was giving voice to his hungering delight of some remembrance; we instinctively know that these towns expressed more than anything else the love and hope of man, treasuring some of the splendour of his soul in their houses and temples with their auspicious decoration daily accomplished by women, and even in the picturesque bartering that went on in their market places.

We can imagine what Delhi and Agra must have been in the time to which they belonged. They manifested in their development some creatively human aspect of a great empire. Whatever might have been its character, these cities even in their decay still retain in their magnificence the true product of the self-respect of man. But modern cities merely give opportunities, not ideals.

Cities there must be in man's civilization, just as in higher organisms there must be organized centres of life, such as the brain, heart, or stomach. These never overwhelm the living wholeness of the body; on the contrary, by a perfect federation of their functions, they maintain its richness. But a tumour round which the blood is congested, is the enemy of the whole body upon which it feeds as it swells. Our modern cities, in the same way feed upon the whole social organism that runs through the villages; they continually drain away the life stuff of the community, and slough off a huge amount of dead matter, while assuming a lurid counterfeit of prosperity.

Thus, unlike a living heart, these cities imprison and kill the blood and create poison centres filled with the accumulation of death. When a very large body of men comes together for the sake of some material purpose, then it is as a congestion and not a congregation. When men are close together and yet develop no intimate bond of human relationship, there ensues moral putrefaction. Wherever in the world, this modern civilization is spreading its dominion, the life principle of society, which is the principle of personal relationship, is injured at the root.

All this is the result of an almost complete substitution of true civilization by what the West calls Progress. I am never against progress, but when, for its sake, civilization is ready to sell its soul, then I choose to remain primitive in my material possessions, hoping to achieve my civilization in the realm of the spirit.

People, as a whole, do and must live in the village, for it is their natural habitation. But the professions depend upon their special appliances and environment, and therefore barricade themselves with particular purposes, shutting out the greater part of universal nature, which is the cradle of life. The city, in all civilizations, represents this professionalism,—some concentrated purpose of the people. That is to say, people have their home in the village and their offices in the city.

We all know that the office is for serving and enriching the home, and not for banishing it into insignificance. But we also know that when goaded by greed, the gambling spirit gets hold of a man, he is willing to rob his home of all its life and joy and to pour them into the hungry jaws of the office. For a time such a man may prosper, but his prosperity is gained at the cost of happiness. His wife may shine in a blaze of jewelry, rousing envy along the path of her economic triumph, but her spirit withers in secret, thirsting for love and the simple delights of life.

Society encourages the professions only because they are of service to the people at large. They find their truth when they belong to the people. But the professions, because they get all power into their hands, begin to believe that people live to maintain them. Thus we often see that a lawyer thrives by taking advantage of the weaknesses of his clients, their helpless dread of loss, their dishonest love of gain. The proportion between the help rendered and its reward demanded, loses its legitimate limit, when it is not guided by any standard of social ethics.

Such a moral perversion has come to its extreme length today in the relationship of the city and the village. The city, which is the professional aspect of society, has gradually come to believe that the village is its legitimate field for exploitation, that the village must at the cost of its own life maintain the city in all its brilliance of luxuries and excesses; that its wealth must be magnified even though that should involve the bankruptcy of happiness.

True happiness is not at all expensive, because it depends upon that natural spring of beauty and life which is harmony of relationship. Ambition pursues its path of self-seeking by breaking this bond of harmony, cutting gaps, creating dissensions. It feels no hesitation in trampling under foot the harvest field, which is for all, in order to snatch away in haste the object of its craving. Today this ambition, wasteful and therefore disruptive of social life, the greatest enemy of civilization, has usurped the helm of society.

In India we had our family system, large and complex, each family a miniature society in itself. I do not wish to discuss the question of its desirability. But its rapid decay in the present day clearly points out the nature and process of the principle of destruction which is at work in modern civilization. When life was simple and its needs normal, when selfish passions were under control, such a domestic system was perfectly natural and fully productive of happiness. The family resources were sufficient for all and the claims on them were never excessive on the part of one or more of its individual members. But such a group can never survive, if the personal ambition of a single member begins separately to clamour for a great deal more than is necessary for him. When emulation in augmenting private possession, and the enjoyment of exclusive advantage runs ahead of the common good and general happiness, the bond of harmony, which is the bond of sustenance, must give way and brothers must separate, nay, even become enemies.

The passion that rages in the heart of modern civilization is, like a volcanic flame, constantly struggling to throw up eruptions of individual bloatedness. The stream of production, which thereupon gushes forth, may give one the impression of a huge, indefinite, gain. But such interruption needs must disturb man's creative mind. We forget that it is only the spirit of creation evolving out of its own inner abundance, that adds to our true wealth; and that the spirit of production but consumes our resources in the process of building and filling it storehouses. Therefore our needs which stimulate production must observe the limits of the normal. If we go on poking them into a bigger and bigger flame, the conflagration will no doubt dazzle our sight, but its splendour will leave on its debit side a black heap of charred remains.

When our wants are moderate, the rations we claim do not exhaust the common store of nature and the pace of their restoration does not hopelessly fall behind that our consumption of them. This moderation, moreover, leaves us leisure to cultivate happiness, the happiness which is the artist soul of the human world, creating beauty of form and rhythm of life. But man today forgets that the divinity in him is revealed by the halo of his happiness.

The Germany of the period of Goethe was considered to be poor by the Germany of the period of Bismarck. Possibly the standard of civilization, illumined by the mind of Plato, or by the life of the Emperor Asoka, is underrated by the proud children of modern times who compare it with the present age of progress, an age dominated by millionaires, diplomats and warlords. Many things that are of common use today were absolutely lacking in those days. But are those who lived then to be pitied by the young boys of our time, who have more of the printing press, but less of the mind?

I often imagine that the moon, being smaller in size than the earth, begat life on her soil earlier than was possible on that of her companion. Once, she too had her constant festival of colour, music, movement; her storehouse was perpetually replenished with food for her children who were already there and who were to come. Then in course of time, some race was born to her, gifted with a furious energy of intelligence, which began greedily to devour its surroundings. It produced beings, who, because of the excess of their animal spirit coupled with intellect lacked the imagination to realize that the mere process of addition did not create fulfilment; that acquisition because of its bigness did not produce happiness; that movement did not constitute progress merely because of its velocity; that progress could have meaning only in relation to some ideal of completeness. Through machinery of tremendous power, they made such an addition to their natural capacity for gathering and holding, that their career of plunder outstripped nature's power of recuperation. Their profit-makers created wants which were unnatural and dug big holes in the stored capital of nature, forcibly to extract provision for them. When they had reduced the limited store of material, they waged furious wars among their different sections for the special allotment of the lion's share. In their scramble for the right of self-indulgence they laughed at moral law and took it to be a sign of racial superiority to be ruthless in the satisfaction of their desires. They exhausted the water, cut down the trees, reduced the surface of the planet into a desert riddled with pits. They made its interior a rifled pocket, emptied of its valuables. At last one day, like a fruit whose pulp has been completely eaten by insects which it sheltered, the moon became a lifeless shell, a universal grave for the voracious creatures who had consumed the world to which they were born.

My imaginary selenites behaved exactly in the way that human beings are behaving on this earth, fast exhausting the stores of sustenance not because they must live their normal life, but because they strain their capacity of life to a pitch of monstrous excess. Mother Earth has enough for the healthy appetite of her children and something extra for rare cases of abnormality. But she has not nearly enough for the sudden growth of a whole world of spoilt and pampered children.

Man has been digging holes into the very foundations, not only of his livelihood, but also of his life; he is feeding upon his own body. The reckless wastage of humanity which ambition produces, is best seen in the villages, where the light of life is being dimmed, the joy of existence dulled, the natural threads of social communion snapped every day. It should be our mission to restore the full circulation of life's blood into these maltreated limbs of society; to bring to the villages health and knowledge; wealth of space in which to live; wealth of time in which to work and to rest and to enjoy; respect which will give them dignity; sympathy which will make them realize their kinship with the world of men, and not merely their survient position.

Streams, lakes and oceans are there on this earth. They exist not for the hoarding of water exclusively within their own areas. They send up the vapour which forms into clouds and helps towards a wider distribution of water. Cities have their functions of maintaining wealth and knowledge in concentrated forms of opulence, but this also, should not be for their own sake; they should be centres of irrigation; they should gather in order to distribute; they should not magnify themselves, but should enrich the entire commonwealth. They should be like lamp-posts, and the light they support must transcend their own limits.

Such a relationship of mutual benefit between the city and the village can remain strong only so long as the spirit of co-operation and self-sacrifice is a living ideal in society. When some universal temptation overcomes this ideal, when some selfish passion gains ascendancy, then a gulf is formed and goes on widening between them; then the mutual relationship of ciry and village becomes that of exploiter and victim. This is a form of perversity whereby the body-politic becomes its own enemy and whose termination is death.

We have started in India, in connection with our Visva-bharati, work of village reconstruction, the mission of which is to retard this process of race suicide. If I try to give you the details of our work, they will look small. But we are not afraid of this appearance of smallness, for we have confidence in life. We know that if as a seed it represents the truth that is in us, it will overcome opposition and conquer space and time. According to us, the poverty problem is not the most important, the problem of unhappiness is the great problem. Wealth, which is the synonym for the production and collection of things, men can make use of ruthlessly. They can crush life out of the earth and flourish. But, happiness, which may not compete with wealth in its list of materials, is final, it is creative; therefore it has its source of riches within itself.

Our object is to try to flood the choked bed of village life with the stream of happiness. For this the scholars, the poets, the musicians, the artists, have to collaborate, to offer their contributions. Otherwise they must live like parasites, sucking life from the people and giving nothing back to them. Such exploitation gradually exhausts the soil of life, which needs constant replenishing, by the return to it of life, through the completion of the cycle of receiving and giving back.

Most of us, who try to deal with the poverty problem, think of nothing but a greater intensive effort to production, forgetting that this only means a greater exhaustion of materials as well as of humanity. This only means giving exaggerated opportunity for profit to a few, at the cost of the many. It is food which nourishes, not money; it is fulness of life which makes one happy, not fulness of purse. Multiplying materials intensifies the inequality between those who have and those who have not, and this deals a fatal wound to the social system, through which the whole body is eventually bled to death.

(1924)

Judgment

22

The young generation of men in the East are everywhere attracted by what they imagine is modern. And they have convinced themselves that Western life is modern. They are seeking from its manners and mentality the magic formula of how to grow modern. They believe that what is called modern represents the principle of indefinite growth and freedom,—it is youth, it is life.

If that is the definition of modern, then we must know that its essential element does not consist in a particular time, but in a particular truth, lacking which a thing of the latest pattern and polish may in reality be out of date and condemned to perish. A number of nations have so perished who were too late in realizing that the raft of time, to which they clung believing it to be modern, had already become of the past. Are we sure that the same thing has not happened to the West, and that the atmosphere of turmoil which we find there is not due to the conflict between, their present history, which is no longer modern, and the messenger of the future, which was come with its sovereign claim?

Even the paling darkness of the dawn is immensely distant from the morning light, though they are in immediate contact; and who knows if the present history of the West is not already as old as the day of the deluge?

All that is deeply human is never old. It has the perpetual freshness of imperishable life. Only the acquisitiveness which is not of growth but of hoarding, the cleverness which wins in the game of life with false cards up its sleeve, is crabbed and wrinkled. The business of slave hunting, however up-to-date in form and profitable in practice, is old; cannibalism, crude or subtle, direct or indirect, with Christian surname or heathen, is never modern, not even in its beginning.

How can we ever believe that the spirit of the hungry Nation from the west, which for over a century has robbed and humiliated us in the eastern hemisphere, has found the secret of everlasting life in its reckless power? Have we lost all faith in the teaching of the wise: that the passions which mock the eternal and things that defiantly grow out of proportion with their surroundings, can never be lasting?

However that may be, the fact cannot be denied that the outstanding feature of the present age is the way of which the West has spread its physical dominance over the whole world, and is still imposing its mind upon other continents. All the great countries of the East, in some period or other of their history, had to submit to foreign invasion and foreign rule, but such alien contact was either milder in its driving force, or was more in harmony with local tradition and environment, and therefore did not attack the inner bonds of unity which maintained the personality of the people.

A complete change of condition has been brought about by the easy means of communication effected by modern science. It is no longer some resourceful individual, who comes like a comet with a host of mercenary soldiers forming his tail, suddenly crossing the path of a strange people and eventually getting entangled and assimilated; but an entire predatory nation which is able to clutch in its titanic grip the vitals of other races for whom it has no feeling of kinship.

Men who do not come as representatives of some organization, political, commercial or religious, have their simple human sentiments; they are not like ghosts who haunt human habitations and yet do not dwell in them, who obsess living beings and yet do not live their life. Such real individuals naturally tend to establish personal relationships with their neighbours and gradually attain their common unity. But Europe's connection with Asiatic countries has not yet developed that personal character in its organizations,—it is like the pressure of some callous outgrowth of her nature, which has not the creative touch of life, but only mechanical skilfulness.

The West has come to us like an engineer who lays stone-paved roads across our meadows and orchards, over our trampled verdure, with the primary object of making easy his work of exploitation. However marvellous and convenient this may be, the overwhelming dominance of mere method and skill in our surroundings is demoralising. It so often makes us forget that, compared to life, the machine is too simple, its action too obvious its results measurable in an indubitably definite manner, its concentrated influence directed only towards the surface of our nature.

For the same reason we often witness in western countries the demonstration of immense esteem, approaching hero-worship, for some winner in a game of skill or strength. This has increased to such an inordinate degree, that a professional organizer of such games can claim better remuneration than a cultured teacher, even in an educational institution. The very superficiality inherent in mere proficiency, produces its immediate impression upon the multitude, hiding from them the higher manifestation of truth that has no definite standard of measurement.

The barbarous in us occupies a large place in human nature; it is idolatrous in its instincts, ready to prostrate itself before all representations of power that are external, that compel us to acknowledge them through our greed, or our fear, or our primitive crudity of thought and feeling. In fact the constant sight and contemplation of any success that has colossal magnitude produces the same mentality in us, as in the savage does the fetish, made emphatically apparent by its barbarity of decoration.

However, the West, which has thrust itself upon us, is the utilitarian adventurer, imbued with the idolatry of the Nation; it carries an elaborate paraphernalia of self worship, and claims other continents for its victims of sacrifice. The loudest of all the messages that it has brought to ourselves is: *You are none of us*. For this reason, even its best gifts carry for us an insult, and it is for this very reason that, when we cannot help accepting them, we feel so small. The West has hurt us deeply with the shock of its greatness. Its very magnificence faces us with its stony gesture of refusal, allowing us to approach it as the earth does the meteorites, merely to feed with them its own dust.

The moral distance which we impose upon men to whose physical proximity we come for exploitation, is immense. This makes them appear so ridiculously diminutive as to be but dimly recognizable by our conscience. It smooths our path of self-seeking to be able to think that others are absolutely other than ourselves, that their human value is represented in coins that have an utterly different mintage from those which we claim for our own. The West, in its relationship with non-western peoples, has for its constant meditation-text: *They are radically and eternally different from ourselves.* Its cult of separateness, which is the cult of the Nation, bristles with doctrines of disdain. It displays its system of canine teeth in the barbed wire fencing round its inhospitable world, in the name of the inborn right to be supercilious, characteristic of a superior civilization.

Asia, in its dignity of age-long tradition, at first refused to acknowledge Europe's claim of superiority. But gradually it had to own defeat at the hand of the organized power and indomitable self-assertion of the Nation, the latest-born progeny of the West. The spectacle of gigantic success with its unsheathed claws and teeth sank deeper and deeper into Eastern consciousness. The contemptuous sneer which accompanied it rankled in Asia's heart, never allowing it for a moment to remain in forgetfulness of this apparition; till a day has arrived when Asia, overcome by the stupendous coil of muscle, has gradually yielded itself to the licking tongue of this monster: Organization of Power.

There has been related in one of our Bengali epics the legend of a merchant who was a devout worshipper of Shiva the Good, the Pure,—Shiva who represents the principle of renunciation and the power of self-control. This man was perpetually persecuted by a deity, the fierce Snake-goddess, who in order to divert his allegiance to herself inflicted the endless power of her malignance upon her victim. Through a series of failures, deaths and disasters he was at last compelled to acknowledge the superior merit of the divinity of frightfulness. The tragedy does not lie in the external fact of the transfer of homage from one shrine to the other, but in the moral defeat implied in the ascribing of a higher value of truth to the goddess of success,—the personification of unscrupulous egotism,—rather than to the god of moral perfection.

So long as the West herself believed in this latest evolution of her indomitable self-assertion, and was certain that it was going to give her an indefinite extension of the monopoly of all earthly privileges, we in Asia also humbly believed in her. The western people convinced us at the point of their bayonets that they were the chosen people of God, and that the right to inherit the earth was inherent in their race because of a quality which was contrary to that of meekness. We bowed our head to the belief that external success was the ultimate criterion of truth, and I still remember the shock of surprise I felt when a rumour first came to India about Japan's readiness to accept Christianity because it was the religion of a triumphant success, the religion that had unlimited cash in the banks of its devotees and frightful machines of destruction in their arsenal. The moral humiliation of Asia could go on further, and for a moment I was frightened at the prospect of a whole world some day bringing its homage to the shrine of the Snake-goddess, deserting that of Shiva, the Good.

At that time it was difficult for western people to realize that there was anything lacking in their civilization,—for they were so fatuously prosperous and comfortable, so smugly respectable in their behaviour among their own kinsmen. They were never tired of smiling at themselves and saying that they were good, because their drawing rooms were crowded with irrelevancy, their roads geometrically straight, their minds clever, methods efficient, arrangements convenient; because their women had pet dogs, pet schemes of benevolence and head-dresses for which creatures of rare beauty from the most inaccessible regions of the earth had paid toll with their lives.

We, who belong to other continent than theirs, dwell in the obscurity of their shadow, which swallows up our hemisphere, giving us very little chance to bask in the sunshine of their success. For the attitude of success is exclusive, it is by nature suspicious and arrogant. They do not care to come into the heart of our humanity, for it is not needful for their purpose; and they can be excruciatingly funny when they talk about the peculiarity of the smell of our dwelling places, the inscrutability of our countenances, some mannerisms in our code of behaviour, or any exaggerations in our language or gesture which are different from the exaggerations customary with them and therefore unconscious. Even after this they become sincerely amazed when their energetic acquaintance with us fails to evoke in our mind a grateful feeling of adoration, on when their victims show signs of unhappiness. These they ascribe either to the machination of some interested third party, or to the incomprehensible idiosyncrasies of the people with whom they deal.

It is because we are so imperfectly real to them that they try to boast of their beneficence by making a long list of the railway lines, telegraph posts, coal mines, tea plantations, and the law and order inflicted upon our lands. Their minds are so densely callous to the needs of our humanity that they are ready to punish us when we do not bless them for what they have done to ourselves, in the way of helping us with the commodities which we hardly need and which they vomit forth because they are a great deal more than they can consume themselves.

Let me quote some lines from an article on 'Christian Missions' which came to my notice:

> The last century has contained instance after instance, in the Far East, in Africa, and in the islands of the sea, in which the preaching of the Gospel has seemed to the natives only preliminary to political or economic outrage. Sometimes the two have gone hand in hand. Not soon will educated Chinese forget that the charter under which the Christian missionary operates in his land was a part of that same Treaty of Nanking that legalised the importation of opium. So it is that these peoples wonder in bewilderment why the bodies that proclaim their devotion to the setting up of the rule of God can be content with the individual type of missions,

while sins that give the very Christian concept of God the lie grow luxuriant.

About the political relations of West and East the writer quotes Tyler Dennet who says:

> No nation has escaped the valid charge of bad faith. The guilt of all parties being clearly proven, it has seemed profitless to continue the discussion of guilt with a view to determining the relative degree of wickedness. Each Nation, the United States not excepted, has made its contribution to the welter of evil which now comprises the Far Eastern Question.

Speaking of economic exploitation the same writer observes:

> The ruthless manner in which the ancient handicrafts of India were destroyed to favour the mill-owners of England is a matter of parliamentary record. And the tale of the developing industrial life of India, China and Africa is being written in blood. Western business demands, and secures, all sorts of governmental exemptions and favours to ensure its profits when it goes abroad. And again and again, when there, it follows a policy of inhuman hours and starvation wages that is sowing the wind against the future. It is probable that the West thinks of Sir John Bowring—when it thinks of him at all—as the man who wrote:
>
> In the Cross of Christ I glory
>
> Towering o'er the wrecks of time.
>
> But the East remembers him as the indefatigable diplomat whose labours contributed so much to the legalisation of the opium traffic in China.

I agree with the author when he says that 'This is the sort of international sin that most grievously besets the future—political injustice, economic exploitation, racial discrimination, material standards of success.' But what to my mind is the source of a greater mischief is the fact that bribery on a prodigious scale is being used to persuade whole peoples in the East to sell their future. As the opium has shackled the mind of the coming generation of China in fetters of stupor, the silver narcotic injected into the people's constitution is creating a chronic national helplessness, inducing a habit which will make the motherland sell her own children. The bribery which has the sanctimonious appearance of benevolence is the most dangerous form of banditry; for through its unctuous exuberance a huge load of ransom noiselessly drags the country to a bottomless insolvency.

We have seen in the late war the moral camouflage creates useful delusion not only in the minds of the opponents but in those of one's own party, and for the same reason a vast ethical department is necessary as an adjunct to the organization of exploitation. For the hand that draws blood is greatly helped if it is guided by the idea that it is translating some Sunday School lesson into a beautiful practice. In olden times there were tribes of men who throve upon other people's possessions. Not having that sense of decency which wears a protective decoration they used very little material or moral clothing. They are described in history as savage tribes with criminal tendencies. They remained isolated; no respectable peoples copied their manners. Such narrowness of seclusion itself made their mischievous power short-lived and restricted it to a small area.

In modern times they have changed their names and methods, and even while a great portion of the world is being, ripped open by the iron claws of their organization they have no hesitation in believing in the sure foundation of their civilization and the perfection of its superstructure. It produces such a moral confusion that even we, who are their victims, are willing to copy them.

In fact we are beginning to be ashamed of our trust in what we call *dharma*, the sovereignty of the inner world of ideals. We think that it is a sign of the possession of some brand-new type of cleverness, shiningly up-to-date; to be able to join in the chorus of cynical laughter at a faith in the reality of moral truth.

So we watched for long the outer horizon and there saw no portent of storm-clouds overtaking the fair weather in the West; in fact, all our meteorological misgivings pointed their arrow-heads to the thunder-bearing forces from the West carrying menace in other directions. We had been witnessing for too long the triumph in human history of the law of natural selection prevalent in the biological world, the elbowing out of the less offensive by the aggressive pressure of a superior pushfulness. All our calculations come to be based upon the working of that law till, at last, the man in us made his final obeisance to the brute in us and uttered in awe: *Hail, unholy Might!*

While such a hymn of praise was being raised in all the countries of the world, both by the victors and the vanquished, while the races favoured by fortune dreamt of nothing else but the sharpening of their military fangs and the lengthening of their commercial suckers; while the defeated peoples were cherishing the hope, and secretly preparing, to be able one day to contribute their own share of devilry to the political nightmare of the modern cult of nationalism; the most devastating war that ever happened tore into tatters the enormous self-satisfaction of Europe. She has lately been startled into realizing that its origin was not from outside.

Up to this moment she had been at the zenith of her power and brilliancy; to outward seeming she had conquered endless time for her boundless prosperity, while she had been moulding with a pitiless success the destiny of millions of alien people fashion her own footstool and keep it permanently secure. The barometer which recorded the external condition of the atmosphere foreboded a perpetual monotony of fair weather. There had been, no doubt, angry flashes of lightning from the friction created by colliding greeds, but it was firmly believed that the urging of an intelligent self-interest was itself sufficient to check any of these violent gestures from ending in a catastrophe.

Then came the day when everything that had given her supremacy in the world seemed to turn against her and the Science which she had tamed for a hunting expedition tore ugly rents in her own limbs, which still show no sign of healing. So her proud mind has had to come to the conclusion that her present suffering is not due to any lack of intellectual attainment or material advantage, but to some cancerous growth within her own moral nature.

This has, at length, given us in Asia the opportunity of judging Europe with our mind freed from the hypnotism of success,—an opportunity necessary for our own salvation. This judgment must not be in a spirit of retaliation, which chuckles at the chance of hurling back at the West some part of the evil-smelling mud which she was never tired of flinging at the unprotected Orient. Nevertheless we must have the courage to judge. For the standard of moral judgment is the true helm of our life. Lately it has been laughed at by the modern young person for being stationary, and our hold upon it has been slackened. We must regain our confidence in it, knowing that this helm is more necessary for us today than ever before, because we are overtaken by a current that is sudden and swift, by winds that are changing, and because we must move among breakers.

Fight there must be in this world. We cannot make truce with impunity. Our evolution towards the perfect has been and has to be through a series of fights. Our moral judgment is the best weapon we have in the warfare for the preservation of humanity. With it we have to resist, and even to hurt, for the cause of justice.

Have we not noticed in the modern East how the people, who have a highly developed instinct for turning out things of perfect beauty for their daily life show utter crudity in their selection of western articles for show or for use? They completely forget the dignity of the true born aristocracy which they possess in the world of craftsmanship when they try to acquire or imitate the furniture and other western appliances that bear the brand of the outcast. They carelessly allow the aggression of weeds into their garden where flowers have been nourished by the love and the sensitive understanding of generations of their forefathers. It has been made possible because they have blindly surrendered their judgment of excellence overwhelmed by the spectacle of a robust success. In their infatuation they rob Apollo of his homage in order to offer it to the image of Hercules.

My heart was filled with shame and pain when I passed by the ruined mounds of the Summer Palace of Peking, brought to the dust by those who were furiously loud in their condemnation of the destruction of some ancient cathedrals of Europe by their enemies. Yet they can be forgiven, for they knew not what they had been doing. They merely personated an unintelligent storm of fury which had a scientific thoroughness of brutality, and they wantonly destroyed buildings, pictures and objects of art the like of which was never seen before nor will be in the future.

But it fills my heart with despair when I realize that the modern Chinese are themselves helping in the devastation of the genius of China, daily growing used to things that are merely convenient and forgetting the miracle of creative touch which their fingers have acquired. It shows a laziness of apathy which is uncivilized. True civilization knows the value of things that belong to the higher nature of man and is ever ready to take trouble to produce them, use them, and maintain them in their excellence. To succumb to the temptation of cheap production and hasty utility is the sign of the shallow mind that seeks its release from the strenuous claim of high aspiration in the vulgar comfort of standardised respectability. The educated China of today seems to have surrendered its judgment of taste and through this defeat is threatened with a desert of white monotony swallowing up the colours and features of its civilization.

The surrender of moral judgment is also a defeat through which the invasion of the West is laying its stony road across the soul of the East, leading most of its traffic of ideas to the gambling den of commerce and politics, to the furious competition of suicide in the arena of military lunacy. Shady paths that ran into various avenues of life carrying the invitation of hearts and the call of co-operation, are one by one being closed. This also is helping the monotonous extension of that aspect of the West which is not fruit-bearing.

But we must not allow this to go on. We must find our voice to be able to say to the West: 'You may force your things into our homes, you may obstruct our prospects of life,—but *we judge you*. You may ignore our judgment. Materially it will not injure you, nor check you in your climbing up the dizzy precipice of profit and power, but it will save us from moral degradation. We refuse to humiliate ourselves by saying that you are worthy of obedience because you are strong, worthy of respect because you are rich.'

What I have discussed above only shows that in its relation to the eastern peoples the aspect of western character which has come uppermost is not only insulting to us but to the West itself. Nothing could have been more unfortunate in the history of man than this. For all meetings of men should reveal some great truth which is worthy of a permanent memorial, such, as for instance, had been the case of India's meeting with China in the ancient time.

At the moment when the West came to our door, the whole of Asia was asleep, the darkness of night had fallen over her life. Her lights were dim, her voice mute. She had stored up in her vaults her treasure, no longer growing. She had her wisdom shut in her books. She was not producing living thoughts of fresh forms of beauty. She was not moving forward but endlessly revolving round her past. She was not ready to receive the West in all her majesty of soul.

The best in us attracts the best in others: our weakness attracts violence to our neighbourhood, as thinness in the air attracts a storm. To remain in the fulness of our manifestation is our duty, not only for ourselves but for others. We have not seen the great in the West because we have failed to bring out the great that we have in us and we delude ourselves into thinking that we can hide this deficiency behind borrowed feathers.

Yet, through all our shame and our suffering, we have to acknowledge that the West is great. With her science she has offered a grand illumination to the path of reason. Some people in the East are in the habit of reviling science, calling it materialistic. They may as well say that incendiarism is in the fire. Science is truth. It is immaterial. It gives us freedom in the realm of matter. It brings our mind into touch with the eternal at the uttermost brink of the finite. What if science can help some temperaments solely to cultivate materialism,—cannot religion do the same? We have witnessed in the East the grossest form of materialism and the cruellest form of inhumanity stalking abroad in our society wearing the uniform of spiritual culture. We constantly see the epicureanism of religious emotion, indulged in by self-centred individuals, admired by simple-minded people as piety in full blossom.

On the other hand, the usual form of spiritual expression we find in the lives of the best individuals in western countries is their love of humanity, their spirit working through their character; their keen intellect and their indomitable will leaguing together for human welfare. In their individuals it reveals itself in loyalty to the cause of truth for which so many of them are ready to suffer martyrdom, often standing heroically alone against some fury of their national insanity. When their wide human interest, which is intellectual, takes a moral direction, it grows into a fulness of intelligent service of man that can ignore all geographical limits and racial habits of tradition. The goodness which is undaunted in its chivalrous adventure, and love of truth, variedly active and widespread in its ministration, we do not see in the East.

But, because in their individual lives the western peoples have raised the tower of their moral standard so high, the ravage of their national unrighteousness at the base is fraught with dangerous consequence. Bespattering the whole world with their diplomatic lies, continually adding to the number of victims for their man-eating prosperity, scientifically crushing the human rights of large continents of races, spreading a contagion of ugly carbuncles all over the earth with the impurity of their utilitarian touch, keeping their snarling nastiness bared at the entrance of their miserly national mansion,—they have, in all these, an ever increasing gravitational pull against the top of their greatness. The fall will be terrific.

But what is most unfortunate for us in Asia is the fact that the advent of the West into our continent has been accompanied not only by science, which is truth and therefore welcome, but by an impious use of truth for the violent purpose of self-seeking which converts it into a disruptive force. It is producing in the countries with which it is in contact a diseased mentality that refuses moral ideals, considering them to be unworthy of those who aspire to be rulers of men, and who must furiously cultivate their fitness to survive. That such a philosophy of survival, fit for the world of tigers, cannot but bring a fatal catastrophe in the human world, they do not see. They become violently angry at those who protest against it, fearing that such a protest might weaken in them the animal that should be allowed to survive for eternity.

Doctors know that infusion of animal blood into human veins does not give vigour to man but produces death, and the intrusion of the animal into humanity will never be for its survival. But faith in man is weakening even in the East, for we have seen that science has enabled the inhuman to prosper, the lie to thrive, the machine to rule in the place of *Dharma*. Therefore in order to save us from the anarchy of weak faith we must stand up today and judge the West.

But we must guard against antipathy that produces blindness. We must not disable ourselves from receiving truth. For the West has appeared before the present-day world not only with her dynamite of passion and cargo of things but with her gift of truth. Until we fully accept it in a right spirit we shall never even discover what is true in our own civilization and make it generously fruitful by offering it to the world. The culture, the humanity of the West do not belong to the Nation but to the People.

While nations fight for their exclusive possessions, the peoples share with one another their true wealth. And the highest spirit of the peoples of the West, their loyal love of truth and active love of man, we must try to make our own in order to impart to our life a movement and to our ideals a vitality that shall give them the impulse to produce new flower and fruit.

(1925)

23 The Teacher

I have already described how the nebulous idea of the divine essence condensed in my consciousness into a human realization. It is definite and finite at the same time, the Eternal Person manifested in all persons. It may be one of the numerous manifestations of God, the one in which is comprehended Man and his Universe. But we can never know or imagine him as revealed in any other inconceivable universe so long as we remain human beings. And therefore, whatever character our theology may ascribe to him, in reality he is the infinite ideal of Man towards whom men move in their collective growth, with whom they seek their union of love as individuals, in whom they find their ideal of father, friend and beloved.

I am sure that it was this idea of the divine Humanity unconsciously working in my mind; which compelled me to come out of the seclusion of my literary career and take my part in the world of practical activities. The solitary enjoyment of the infinite in meditation no longer satisfied me, and the texts which I used for my silent worship lost their inspiration without my knowing it. I am sure I vaguely felt that my need was spiritual self-realization in the life of Man through some disinterested service. This was the time when I founded an educational institution for our children in Bengal. It has a special character of its own which is still struggling to find its fulfilment; for it is a living temple that I have attempted to build for my divinity. In such a place education necessarily becomes the preparation for a complete life of man which can only become possible by living that life, through knowledge and service, enjoyment and creative work. The necessity was my own, for I felt impelled to come back into a fulness of truth from my exile in a dream-world.

This brings to my mind the name of another poet of ancient India, Kālidāsa, whose poem of Meghaduta reverberates with the music of the sorrow of an exile.

It was not the physical home-sickness form which the poet suffered, it was something far more fundamental, the home-sickness of the soul. We feel from almost all his works the oppressive atmosphere of the kings' palaces of those days, dense with things of luxury, and also with the callousness of self-indulgence, albeit an atmosphere of refined culture based on an extravagant civilization.

The poet in the royal court lived in banishment—banishment from the immediate presence of the eternal. He knew it was not merely his own banishment, but that of the whole age to which he was born, the age that had gathered its wealth and missed its well-being, built its storehouse of things and lost its background of the great universe. What was the form in which his desire for perfection persistently appeared in his drama and poems? It was the form of the *tapovana*, the forest-dwelling of the patriarchal community of ancient India. Those who are familiar with Sanskrit literature will know that this was not a colony of people with a primitive culture and mind. They were seekers after truth, for the sake of which they lived in an atmosphere of purity but not of Puritanism, of the simple life but not the life of self-mortification. They never advocated celibacy and they had constant intercommunication with other people who lived the life of worldly interest. Their aim and endeavour have briefly been suggested in the Upanishad in these lines:

Te sarvagam sarvatah prapya dhira
yuktatmanah sarvamevavisanti.

Those men of serene mind enter into the All, having realized and being in union everywhere with the omnipresent Spirit.

It was never a philosophy of renunciation of a negative character, but a realization completely comprehensive. How the tortured mind of Kālidāsa in the prosperous city of Ujjaini, and the glorious period of Vikramaditya, closely pressed by all-obstructing things and all-devouring self, let his thoughts hover round the vision of a *tapovana* for his inspiration of life!

It was not a deliberate copy but a natural coincidence that a poet of modern India also had the similar vision when he felt within him the misery of a spiritual banishment. In the time of Kālidāsa the people vividly believed in the ideal of *tapovana,* the forest colony, and there can be no doubt that even in the late age there were communities of men living in the heart of nature, not ascetics fiercely in love with a lingering suicide, but men of serene sanity who sought to realize the spiritual meaning of their life. And, therefore, when Kālidāsa sang of the *tapovana,* his poems found their immediate communion in the living faith of his hearers. But today the idea has lost any definite outline of reality, and has retreated into the far away phantom-land of legend. Therefore the Sanskrit word in a modern poem would merely be poetical, its meaning judged by a literary standard of appraisement. Then, again, the spirit of the forest-dwelling in the purity of its original shape would be a fantastic anachronism in the present age, and therefore, in order to be real, it must find its reincarnation under modern conditions of life. It must be the same in truth, but not identical in fact. It was this which made the modern poet's heart crave to compose his poem in a language of tangible words.

But I must give the history in some detail. Civilized man has come far away from the orbit of his normal life. He has gradually formed and intensified some habits that are like those of the bees for adapting himself to his hive-world. We often see men suffering from ennui, from world-weariness, from a spirit of rebellion against their environment for no reasonable cause whatever. Social revolutions are constantly ushered in with a suicidal violence that has its origin in our dissatisfaction with our hive-wall arrangement—the too exclusive enclosure that deprives us of the perspective which is so much needed to give us the proper proportion in our art of living. All this is an indication that man has not been moulded on the model of the bee and therefore he becomes recklessly anti-social when his freedom to be more than social is ignored.

In our highly complex modern condition mechanical forces are organized with such efficiency that materials are produced that grow far in advance of man's selective and assimilative capacity to simplify them into harmony with his nature and needs.

Such an intemperate overgrowth of things, like rank vegetation in the tropics, creates confinement for man. The nest is simple, it has an early relationship with the sky; the cage is complex and costly; it is too much itself excommunicated from whatever lies outside. And man is building his cage, fast developing his parasitism on the monster Thing, which he allows to envelop him on all sides. He is always occupied in adapting himself to its dead angularities, limits himself to its limitations, and merely becomes a part of it.

This may seem contrary to the doctrine of those who believe that a constant high pressure of living, produced by an artificially cultivated hunger of things, generates and feeds the energy that drives civilization upon its endless journey. Personally, I do not believe that this has ever been the principal driving force that has led to eminence any great civilization of which we know in history.

I was born in what was once the metropolis of British India. My own ancestors came floating to Calcutta upon the earliest tide of the fluctuating fortune of the East India Company. The unconventional code of life for our family has been a confluence of three cultures, the Hindu, Mohammedan and British. My grandfather belonged to that period when the amplitude of dress and courtesy and a generous leisure were gradually being clipped and curtailed into Victorian manners, economical in time, in ceremonies, and in the dignity of personal appearance. This will show that I came to a world in which the modern citybred spirit of progress had just begun driving its triumphal car over the luscious green life of our ancient village community. Though the trampling process was almost complete round me, yet the wailing cry of the past was still lingering over the wreckage.

Often I had listened to my eldest brother describing with the poignancy of a hopeless regret a society hospitable, sweet with the old-world aroma of natural kindliness, full of simple faith and the ceremonial-poetry of life. But all this was a vanishing shadow behind me in the dusky golden haze of a twilight horizon—the all-pervading fact around my boyhood being the modern city newly built by a company of western traders and the spirit of the modern time seeking its unaccustomed entrance into our life, stumbling against countless anomalies.

But it always is a surprise to me to think that though this closed-up hardness of a city was my only experience of the world, yet my mind was constantly haunted by the home-sick fancies of an exile. It seems that the subconscious remembrance of a primeval dwelling-place, where, in our ancestor's minds, were figured, and voiced the mysteries of the inarticulate rocks, the rushing water and the dark whispers of the forest, was constantly stirring my blood with its call. Some shadow-haunting living reminiscence in me seemed to ache, for the pre-natal cradle and playground it shared with the primal life in the illimitable magic of the land, water and air. The shrill, thin cry of the high-flying kite in the blazing sun of the dazed Indian midday sent to a solitary boy the signal of a dumb distant kinship. The few coconut plants growing by the boundary wall of our house, like some war captives from an older army of invaders of this earth, spoke to me of the eternal companionship which the great brotherhood of trees has ever offered to man.

Looking back upon those moments of my boyhood days, when all my mind seemed to float poised upon a large feeling of the sky, of the light, and to tingle with the brown earth in its glistening grass, I cannot help believing that my Indian ancestry had left deep in my being the legacy of its philosophy—the philosophy which speaks of fulfilment through our harmony with all things. The founding of my school had its origin in the memory of that longing for the freedom of consciousness, which seems to go back beyond the skyline of my birth.

Freedom in the mere sense of independence has no content, and therefore no meaning. Perfect freedom lies in a perfect harmony of relationship, which we realize in this world not through our response to it in knowing, but in being. Objects of knowledge maintain an infinite distance from us who are the knowers. For knowledge is not union. Therefore the further world of freedom awaits us there where we reach truth, not through feeling it by our senses or knowing it by our reason, but through the union of perfect sympathy.

Children with the freshness of their senses come directly to the intimacy of this world. This is the first great gift they have. They must accept it naked and simple and must never again lose their power of immediate communication with it. For our perfection we have to be vitally savage and mentally civilized; we should have the gift to be natural with nature and human with human society. My banished soul sitting in the civilized isolation of the town-life cried within me for the enlargement of the horizon of its comprehension. I was like the torn-away line of a verse, always in a state of suspense, while the other line, with which it rhymed and which could give it fulness, was smudged by the mist away in some undecipherable distance. The inexpensive power to be happy which, along with other children, I brought to this world, was being constantly worn away by friction with the brick-and-mortar arrangement of life, by monotonously mechanical habits and the customary code of respectability.

In the usual course of things I was sent to school, but possibly my suffering was unusually greater than that of most other children. The non-civilized in me was sensitive; it had the great thirst for colour, for music, for movement of life. Our city-built education took no heed of that living fact. It had its luggage-van waiting for branded bales of marketable result. The relative proportion of the non-civilized to the civilized in man should be in the proportion of the water and the land in our globe, the former predominating. But the school had for its object a continual reclamation of the civilized. Such a drain in the fluid element causes an aridity which may not be considered deplorable under city conditions. But my nature never got accustomed to those conditions, to the callous decency of the pavement. The non-civilized triumphed in me only too soon and drove me away from school when I had just entered my teens. I found myself stranded on a solitary island of ignorance, and had to rely solely upon my own instincts to build up my education from the very beginning.

This reminds me that when I was young I had the great good fortune of coming upon a Bengali translation of *Robinson Crusoe*. I still believe that it is the best book for boys that has ever been written. There was a longing in me when young to run away from my own self and be one with everything in Nature. This mood appears to be particularly Indian, the outcome of a traditional desire for the expansion of consciousness. One has to admit that such a desire is too subjective in its character; but this is inevitable in the geographical circumstances which we have to endure. We live under the extortionate tyranny of the tropics, paying heavy toll every moment for the barest right of existence. The heat, the damp, the unspeakable fecundity of minute life feeding upon big life, the perpetual sources of irritation, visible and invisible, leave very little margin of capital for extravagant experiments. Excess of energy seeks obstacles for its self-realization. That is why we find so often in Western literature a constant emphasis upon the malignant aspect of Nature, in whom the people of the West seem to be delighted to discover an enemy for the sheer enjoyment of challenging her to fight. The reason which made Alexander express his desire to find other worlds to conquer, when his conquest of the world was completed, makes the enormously vital people of the West desire, when they have some respite in their sublime mission of fighting against objects that are noxious, to go out of their way to spread their coat-tails in other people's thoroughfares and to claim indemnity when these are trodden upon. In order to make the thrilling risk of hurting themselves they are ready to welcome endless trouble to hurt others who are inoffensive, such as the beautiful birds which happen to know how to fly away, the timid beasts, which have the advantage of inhabiting inaccessible regions, and—but I avoid the discourtesy of mentioning higher races in this connection.

Life's fulfilment finds constant contradictions in its path; but those are necessary for the sake of its advance. The stream is saved from the sluggishness of its current by the perpetual opposition of the soil through which it must cut its way. It is this soil which forms its banks. The spirit of fight belongs to the genius of life. The tuning of an instrument has to be done, not because it reveals a proficient perseverance in the face of difficulty, but because it helps music to be perfectly realized. Let us rejoice that in the West life's instrument is being tuned in all its different chords owing to the great fact that the West has triumphant pleasure in the struggle with obstacles. The spirit of creation in the heart of the universe will never allow, for its own sake, obstacles to be completely removed. It is only because positive truth lies in that ideal of perfection, which has to be won by our own endeavour in order to make it our own, that the spirit of fight is great. But this does not imply a premium for the exhibition of a muscular athleticism or a rude barbarism of ravenous rapacity.

In *Robinson Crusoe*, the delight of the union with Nature finds its expression in a story of adventure in which the solitary Man is face to face with solitary Nature, coaxing her, co-operating with her, exploring her secrets, using all his faculties to win her help.

This is the heroic love-adventure of the West, the active wooing of the earth. I remember how, once in my youth, the feeling of intense delight and wonder followed me in my railway journey across Europe from Brindisi to Calais, when I realized the chaste beauty of this continent everywhere blossoming in a glow of health and richness under the age-long attention of her chivalrous lover, Western humanity. He had gained her, made her his own, unlocked the inexhaustible generosity of her heart. And I had intently wished that the introspective vision of the universal soul, which an Eastern devotee realizes in the solitude of his mind, could be united with this spirit of its outward expression in service, the exercise of will in unfolding the wealth of beauty and well-being from its shy obscurity to the light.

I remember the morning when a beggar woman in a Bengal village gathered in the loose end of her *sari* the stale flowers that were about to be thrown away from the vase on my table; and with an ecstatic expression of tenderness buried her face in them, exclaiming, 'Oh, Beloved of my Heart!' Her eyes could easily pierce the veil of the outward form and reach the realm of the infinite in these flowers, where she found the intimate touch of her Beloved, the great, the universal Human. But in spite of it all she lacked that energy of worship, that Western form of direct divine service, the service of man, which helps the earth to bring out her flowers and spread the reign of beauty on the desolate dust. I refuse to think that the twin spirits of the East and the West, the Mary and Martha, can never meet to make perfect the realization of truth. And in spite of our material poverty in the East and the antagonism of time I wait patiently for this meeting.

Robinson Crusoe's island comes to my mind when I think of some institution where the first great lesson in the perfect union of Man and Nature, not only through love, but through active communication and intelligent ways, can be had unobstructed. We have to keep in mind the fact that love and action are the only intermediaries through which perfect knowledge can be obtained; for the object of knowledge is not pedantry but wisdom. The primary object of an institution should not be merely to educate one's limbs and mind to be in efficient readiness for all emergencies, but to be in perfect tune in the symphony of response between life and world, to find the balance of their harmony which is wisdom. The first important lesson for children in such a place would be that of improvization, the constant imposition of the ready-made having been banished from here. It is to give occasions to explore one's capacity through surprises of achievement. I must make it plain that this means a lesson not in simple life, but in creative life. For life may grow complex, and yet if there is a living personality in its centre, it will still have the unity of creation; it will carry its own weight in perfect grace, and will not be a mere addition to the number of facts that only goes to swell a crowd.

I wish I could say that I had fully realized my dream in my school. I have only made the first introduction towards it and have given an opportunity to the children to find their freedom in Nature by being able to love it. For love is freedom; it gives us that fulness of existence which saves us from paying with our soul for objects that are immensely cheap. Love lights up this world with its meaning and makes life feel that it has that 'enough' everywhere which truly is its 'feast'. I know men who preach the cult of simple life by glorifying the spiritual merit of poverty. I refuse to imagine any special value in poverty when it is a mere negation. Only when the mind has the sensitiveness to be able to respond to the deeper call of reality is it naturally weaned away from the lure of the fictitious value of things. It is callousness which robs us of our simple power to enjoy, and dooms us to the indignity of a snobbish pride in furniture and the foolish burden of expensive things. But the callousness of asceticism pitted against the callousness of luxury is merely fighting one evil with the help of another, inviting the pitiless demon of the desert in place of the indiscriminate demon of the jungle.

I tried my best to develop in the children of my school the freshness of their feeling for Nature, a sensitiveness of soul in their relationship with their human surroundings, with the help of literature, festive ceremonials and also the religious teaching which enjoins us to come to the nearer presence of the world through the soul, thus to gain it more than can be measured—like gaining an instrument in truth by bringing out its music.

24

Ideals of Education

The greatest man of modern India, Raja Rammohun Roy was born in Bengal and was the best friend of my grandfather. He had courage to overcome the prohibition against sea-voyage which we had in our country at the time; and he crossed the sea, and came into touch with the great western minds.

My father was fortunate in coming under the influence of Rammohun Roy from his early years which helped him to free himself from the sectarian barriers, from traditions of worldly and social ideas that were very rigid, in many aspects very narrow and not altogether beneficial. My father drew from our ancient scriptures, from the *Upanishads,* truths which had universal significance, and not anything that were exclusive to any particular age or any particular people. We were ostracized by society and this liberated us from the responsibility of conforming to all those conventions that had not the value of truth, that were mere irrational habits bred in the inertia of the racial mind. In my boyhood's dreams I claimed such freedom that we had tasted, for all humanity.

Nations are kept apart not merely by international jealousy but also by their own past, handicapped by the burden of the dead and decaying, the breeding ground of diseases that attack the spiritual man. I could not believe that generations of peoples, century after century, must have their birth chamber in a moral and intellectual coffin which has its restricted space regulation for a body that has lost its movements. Civilization has its inevitable tendency to accumulate dead materials and to make elaborate adjustments for their accommodation, leaving less and less room for life with its claim to grow in freedom.

There are signs of that in India, and I know today that it is more or less true in all races, for our mind has its inclination to grow lazy as it grows old and to shirk its duty to make changes in the rhythm of the changing times. In the very heart of this rigid rule of the dead, I was brought up in an atmosphere of aspiration, aspiration for the expansion of the human spirit. We in our home sought freedom of power in our language, freedom of imagination in our literature, freedom of soul in our religious creeds and that of mind in our social environment. Such an opportunity has given me confidence in the power of education which is one with life and only which can give us real freedom, the highest that is claimed for man, his freedom of moral communion in the human world. The ghosts of ideals which no longer have a living reality have become the obsession of all nations that carry an overwhelming past behind them perpetually overshadowing their future.

The reign of the ghost has strewn the path of our history lessons with mischief, with prejudices that ever obstruct the mutual understanding of nations, that helps in the cultivation of the thorny crop of national vanity and unscrupulousness in international relationship. From our young days our minds are deliberately trained with the aid of untrue words and unholy symbolism in the name of patriotism, to a collective moral attitude, which we condemn in individuals.

Persons who have no faith in human nature are apt to think that such conditions are eternal in man—that the moral ideals are only for individuals but the race belongs to that primitive nature which is for the animal. And according to them, in the racial life, it is necessary that the animal should have its full scope of training in the cult of suspicion, jealousy, fierce destructiveness, cruel rapacity. They contemptuously brand optimism as sentimental weakness, and yet in spite of that virulent scepticism an enormous change has worked itself out in course of the growth of civilization from the darkest abyss of savagery. I refuse to believe that human society has reached its limit of moral possibility. And we must work all our strength for the seemingly impossible, and must believe that there is a constant urging in the depth of human soul for the attainment of the perfect, the urging which secretly helps us in all our endeavour for the good. This faith has been my only asset in the educational mission which I have made my life's work, and almost unaided and alone, I struggle along my path. I try to assert in my words and works that education has its only meaning and object in freedom—freedom from ignorance about the laws of universe, and freedom from passion and prejudice in our communication with the human world. In my institution I have attempted to create an atmosphere of naturalness in our relationship with strangers, and the spirit of hospitality which is the first virtue in men that made civilization possible.

I invited thinkers and scholars from foreign lands to let our boys know how easy it is to realize our common fellowship, when we deal with those who are great, and that it is the puny who with their petty vanities set up barriers between man and man.

I am glad that I have the opportunity today of letting my friends in Japan know something of my life-long cause and to assure them that it is not special to India but it will ever wait for acceptance by other races.

We in India are unfortunate in not having the chance to give expression to the best in us in creating intimate relations with the powerful peoples of the world. The bond between the nations today is made of the links of mutual menace, its strength depending upon the force of panic, and leading to an enormous waste of resources in a competition of browbeating and bluff. Some great voice is waiting to be heard which will usher in the sacred light of truth in the dark region of the nightmare of politics. But we in India have not yet had the chance. Yet we have our own human voice which truth demands. Even in the region where we are not invited to act we have our right to judge and to guide the mind of man to a proper point of view, to the vision of ideality in the heart of the real.

The activity represented in human education is a worldwide one, it is a great movement of universal co-operation interlinked by different ages and countries. And India, though defeated in her political destiny, has her responsibility to hold up the cause of truth, even to cry in the wilderness, and offer her lessons to the world in the best gifts which she could produce. The messengers of truth have ever joined their hands across centuries, across the seas, across historical barriers, and they help to form the great continent of human brotherhood. Education in all its different forms and channels has its ultimate purpose in the evolving of a luminous sphere of human mind from the nebula that has been rushing round ages to find in itself an eternal centre of unity. We individuals, however small may be our power and whatever corner of the world we may belong to, have the claim upon us to add to the light of the consciousness that comprehends all humanity. And for this cause I ask your co-operation, not merely because co-operation gives us strength in our work but because co-operation itself is the best aspect of the truth we represent, it is an end and not merely the means.

My friends, you are new converts to western ideals, in other words, the ideals belonging to the scientific view of life and the world. This is great and it is foolish to belittle its importance by wrongly describing it as materialism. For truth is spiritual in itself, and truly materialistic is the mind of the animal which is unscientific and therefore unable to cross the dark screen of appearance, of accidents, and reach the deeper region of universal laws. Science means intellectual probity in our dealings with the material world. This conscientiousness of mind is spiritual, for it never judges its results from the standard of external profits. But in science the oft-used half truth that honesty is the best policy has proved itself to be completely true. Science being mind's honesty in its relation to the physical universe never fails to bring us the best profit for our living. And mischief finds its entry through this backdoor of utility, and Satan has had his ample chance of making use of the divine fruit of knowledge for bringing shame upon humanity. Science as the best policy is tempting the primitive in man bringing out his evil passions through the respectable cover that it has supplied him. And this is why it is all the more needed today that we should have faith in ideals that have matured in the spiritual field through ages of human endeavour after perfection, the golden crops that have developed in different forms and in different soils but whose food value for man's spirit has the same composition. These are not for the local markets but for the universal hospitality, for sharing life's treasure with each other and realizing that human civilization is a spiritual feast the invitation to which is open to all, it is never for the ravenous orgies of carnage where the food and the feeders are being torn to pieces.

The legends of nearly all human races carry man's faith in a golden age which appeared as the introductory chapter in human civilization. It shows that man has his instinctive belief in the objectivity of spiritual ideals though this cannot be proved. It seems to him that they have already been given to him and that this gift has to be proved through his history against obstacles. The idea of millennium so often laughed at by the clever is treasured as the best asset by man in his mythology as complete truth realized for ever in some ageless time. Admitting that it is not a scientifical fact we must at the same time know that the instinct cradled and nourished in these primitive stories has its eternal meaning. It is like the instinct of a chick which dimly feels that an infinite world of freedom is already given to it, that it is not a subjective dream but an objective reality, even truer than its life within the egg. If a chick has a rationalistic tendency of mind it ought not to believe in a freedom which is difficult to imagine and contradictory to all its experience, but all the same it cannot help pecking at its shell and ever accepting it as ultimate. The human soul confined in its limitation has also dreamt of a millennium and striven for an emancipation which seems impossible of attainment, and it felt its reverence for some great source of inspiration in which all its experience of the true, good and beautiful finds its reality though it cannot be proved, the reality in which our aspiration for freedom in truth, freedom in love, freedom in the unity of man is ideally realized for ever.

(1929)

Spiritual Union

25

When Man's preoccupation with the means of livelihood became less insistent he had the leisure to come to the mystery of his own self, and could not help feeling that the truth of his personality had both its relationship and its perfection in an endless world of humanity. His religion, which in the beginning had its cosmic background of power, came to a higher stage when it found its background in the human truth of personality. It must not be thought that in this channel it was narrowing the range of our consciousness of the infinite.

The negative idea of the infinite is merely an indefinite enlargement of the limits of things; in fact, a perpetual postponement of infinitude. I am told that mathematics has come to the conclusion that our world belongs to a space which is limited. It does not make us feel disconsolate. We do not miss very much and need not have a low opinion of space even if a straight line cannot remain straight and has an eternal tendency to come back to the point from which it started. In the Hindu Scripture the universe is described as an egg; that is to say, for the human mind it has its circular shell of limitation. The Hindu Scripture goes still further and says that time also is not continuous and our world repeatedly comes to an end to begin its cycle once again. In other words, in the region of time and space infinity consists of ever-revolving finitude.

But the positive aspect of the infinite is in *advaitam*, in an absolute unity, in which comprehension of the multitude is not as in an outer receptacle but as in an inner perfection that permeates and exceeds its contents, like the beauty in a lotus which is ineffably more than all the constituents of the flower. It is not the magnitude of extension but an intense quality of harmony which evokes in us the positive sense of the infinite in our joy, in our love. For *advaitam* is *anandam*; the infinite One is infinite Love. For those among whom the spiritual sense is dull, the desire for realization is reduced to physical possession, an actual grasping in space. This longing for magnitude becomes not an aspiration towards the great, but a mania for the big. But true spiritual realization is not through augmentation of possession in dimension or number. The truth that is infinite dwells in the ideal of unity which we find in the deeper relatedness. This truth of realization is not in space, it can only be realized in one's own inner spirit.

Ekadhaivanudrashtavyam etat aprameyam dhruvam.

This infinite and eternal has to be known as One.

Ākasat aja ātmā—'this birthless spirit is beyond space.' For it is *Purushah,* it is the '*Person*'.

The special mental attitude which India has in her religion is made clear by the word *Yoga*, whose meaning is to effect union. Union has its significance not in the realm of *to have*, but in that of *to be*. To *gain* truth is to admit its separateness, but to *be* true is to become one with truth. Some religions, which deal with our relationship with God, assure us of reward if that relationship be kept true. This reward has an objective value. It gives us some reason outside ourselves for pursuing the prescribed path. We have such religions also in India. But those that have attained a greater height aspire for their fulfilment in union with *Narayana*, the supreme Reality of Man, which is divine.

Our union with this spirit is not to be attained through the mind. For our mind belongs to the department of economy in the human organism. It carefully husbands our consciousness for its own range of reason, within which to permit our relationship with the phenomenal world. But it is the object of *Yoga* to help us to transcend the limits built up by Mind. On the occasions when these are overcome, our inner self is filled with joy, which indicates that through such freedom we come into touch with the Reality that is an end in itself and therefore is bliss.

Once man had his vision of the infinite in the universal Light, and he offered his worship to the sun. He also offered his service to the fire with oblations. Then he felt the infinite in Life, which is Time in its creative aspect, and he said, *Yat kincha yadidam sarvam prana ejati nihsritam*, 'all that there is comes out of life and vibrates in it'. He was sure of it, being conscious of Life's mystery immediately in himself as the principle of purpose, as the organized will, the source of all his activities. His interpretation of the ultimate character of truth relied upon the suggestion that Life had brought to him, and not the non-living which is dumb. And then he came deeper into his being and said '*Raso vai sah*', 'the infinite is love itself',—the eternal spirit of joy. His religion, which is in his realization of the infinite, began its journey from the impersonal *dyaus*, 'the sky', wherein light had its manifestation; then came to Life, which represented the force of self-creation in time, and ended in *purushah*, the 'Person', in whom dwells timeless love. It said, *Tam vedyam purusham vedah*, 'Know him the Person who is to be realized', *Yatha ma vo mrityug parivyathah*—'So that death may not cause you sorrow.' For this Person is deathless in whom the individual person has his immortal truth. Of him it is said: *Esha devo visvakarmā mahātmā sadā janānam hridaye sannivishatah*. 'This is the divine being, the world-worker, who is the Great Soul ever dwelling inherent in the hearts of all people.'

Ya etad vidur amritas te bhavanti. 'Those who realize him, transcend the limits of mortality'—not in duration of time, but in perfection of truth.

Our union with a Being whose activity is world-wide and who dwells in the heart of humanity cannot be a passive one. In order to be united with Him we have to divest our work of selfishness and become *visvakarmā*, 'the world-worker', we must work for all. When I use the words 'for all', I do not mean for a countless number of individuals. All work that is good, however small in extent, is universal in character. Such work makes for a realization of *Visvakarmā*, 'the World-Worker' who works for all. In order to be one with this Mahatma, 'the Great Soul', one must cultivate the greatness of soul which identifies itself with the soul of all peoples and not merely with that of one's own. This helps us to understand what Buddha has described as *Brahmavihāra*, 'living in the infinite'. He says:

> 'Do not deceive each other, do not despise anybody anywhere, never in anger wish anyone to suffer through your body, words or thoughts. Like a mother maintaining her only son with her own life, keep thy immeasurable loving thought for all creatures.
>
> 'Above thee, below thee, on all sides of thee, keep on all the world thy sympathy and immeasurable loving thought which is without obstruction, without any wish to injure, without enmity.
>
> 'To be dwelling in such contemplation while standing, walking, sitting or lying down, until sleep overcomes thee, is called living in Brahma.'

This proves that Buddha's idea of the infinite was not the idea of a spirit of an unbounded cosmic activity, but the infinite whose meaning is in the positive ideal of goodness and love, which cannot be otherwise than human. By being charitable, good and loving, you do not realize the infinite, in the stars or rocks, but the infinite revealed in Man. Buddha's teaching speaks of Nirvana as the highest end. To understand its real character we have to know the path of its attainment, which is not merely through the negation of evil thoughts and deeds but through the elimination of all limits to love. It must mean the sublimation of self in a truth which is love itself, which unites in its bosom all those to whom we must offer our sympathy and service.

When somebody asked Buddha about the original cause of existence he sternly said that such questioning was futile and irrelevant. Did he not mean that it went beyond the human sphere as our goal—that though such a question might legitimately be asked in the region of cosmic philosophy or science, it had nothing to do with man's *dharma*, man's inner nature, in which love finds its utter fulfilment, in which all his sacrifice ends in an eternal gain, in which the putting out of the lamplight is no loss because there is the all-pervading light of the sun. And did those who listened to the great teacher merely hear his words and understand his doctrines? No, they directly felt in him what he was preaching, in the living language of his own person, the ultimate truth of Man.

It is significant that all great religions have their historic origin in persons who represented in their life a truth which was not cosmic and unmoral, but human and good. They rescued religion from the magic stronghold of demon force and brought it into the inner heart of humanity, into a fulfilment not confined to some exclusive good fortune of the individual but to the welfare of all men. This was not for the spiritual ecstasy of lonely souls, but for the spiritual emancipation of all races. They came as the messengers of Man to men of all countries and spoke of the salvation that could only be reached by the perfecting of our relationship with Man the Eternal, Man the Divine. Whatever might be their doctrines of God, or some dogmas that they borrowed from their own time and tradition, their life and teaching had the deeper implication of a Being who is the infinite in Man, the Father, the Friend, the Lover, whose service must be realized through serving all mankind. For the God in Man depends upon men's service and men's love for his own love's fulfilment.

The question was once asked in the shade of the ancient forest of India:

> *Kasmai devāya havishā vidhema?*
>
> Who is the God to whom we must bring our oblation?

That question is still ours, and to answer it we must know in the depth of our love and the maturity of our wisdom what man is—know him not only in sympathy but in science, in the joy of creation and in the pain of heroism; *tena tyaktena bhunjitha,* 'enjoy him through sacrifice'—the sacrifice that comes of love; *ma gridhah,* 'covet not'; for greed diverts your mind to that illusion in you which you represent the *parama purushah,* 'the supreme Person'.

Our greed diverts our consciousness to materials away from that supreme value of truth which is the quality of the universal being. The gulf thus created by the receding stream of the soul we try to replenish with a continuous stream of wealth, which may have the power to fill but not the power to unite and recreate. Therefore the gap is dangerously concealed under the glittering quicksand of things, which by their own weight cause a sudden subsidence while we are in the depths of sleep.

The real tragedy, however, does not lie in the risk of our material security but in the obscuration of Man himself in the human world. In the creative activities of his soul Man realizes his surroundings as his larger self, instinct with his own life and love. But in his ambition he deforms and defiles it with the callous handling of his voracity. His world of utility assuming a gigantic proportion, reacts upon his inner nature and hypnotically suggests to him a scheme of the universe which is an abstract system. In such a world there can be no question of *mukti*, the freedom in truth, because it is a solidly solitary fact, a cage with no sky beyond it. In all appearance our world is a closed world of hard facts; it is like a seed with its tough cover. But within this enclosure is working our silent cry of life for *mukti*, even when its possibility is darkly silent. When some huge overgrown temptation tramples into stillness this living aspiration then does civilization die like a seed that has lost its urging for germination. And this *mukti* is in the truth that dwells in the ideal man.

The Man of My Heart

26

At the outburst of an experience, which is unusual, such as happened to me in the beginning of my youth, the puzzled mind seeks its explanation in some settled foundation of that which is usual, trying to adjust an unexpected inner message to an organized belief which goes by the general name of a religion. And, therefore, I naturally was glad at that time of youth to accept from my father the post of secretary to a special section of the monotheistic church of which he was the leader. I took part in its services mainly by composing hymns which unconsciously took the many-thumbed impression of the orthodox mind, a composite smudge of tradition. Urged by my sense of duty I strenuously persuaded myself to think that my new mental attitude was in harmony with that of the members of our association, although I constantly stumbled upon obstacles and felt constraints that hurt me to the quick.

At last I came to discover that in my conduct I was not strictly loyal to my religion, but only to the religious institution. This latter represented an artificial average, with its standard of truth at its static minimum, jealous of any vital growth that exceeded its limits. I have my conviction that in religion, and also in the arts, that which is common to a group is not important. Indeed, very often it is a contagion of mutual imitation. After a long struggle with the feeling that I was using a mask to hide the living face of truth, I gave up my connection with our church.

About this time, one day I chanced to hear a song from a beggar belonging to the Baül sect of Bengal. We have in the modern Indian Religion deities of different names, forms and mythology, some Vedic and others aboriginal. They have their special sectarian idioms and associations that give emotional satisfaction to those who are accustomed to their hypnotic influences. Some of them may have their aesthetic value to me and others philosophical significance overcumbered by exuberant distraction of legendary myths. But what struck me in this simple song was a religious expression that was neither grossly concrete, full of crude details, nor metaphysical in its rarified transcendentalism. At the same time it was alive with an emotional sincerity. It spoke of an intense yearning of the heart for the divine which is in Man and not in the temple, or scriptures, in images and symbols. The worshipper addresses his songs to the Man the ideal, and says:

> Temples and mosques obstruct thy path,
> and I fail to hear thy call or to move,
> when the teachers and priest angrily crowd round me.

He does not follow any tradition of ceremony, but only believes in love. According to him:

> Love is the magic stone, that transmutes by its touch greed into sacrifice.

He goes on to say:

> For the sake of this love heaven longs to become earth and gods to become man.

Since then I have often tried to meet these people, and sought to understand them through their songs, which are their only form of worship. One is often surprised to find in many of these verses a striking originality of sentiment and diction; for, at their best, they are spontaneously individual in their expressions. One such song is a hymn to the Ever Young. It exclaims:

> O my flower buds, we worship the Young;
> for the Young is the source of the holy Ganges of life;
> from the Young flows the supreme bliss

And it says:

> We never offer ripe corn in the service of the Young,
> nor fruit, nor seed,

but only the lotus bud which is of our own mind.
The young hour of the day, the morning,
is our time for the worship of Him.
from whose contemplation has sprung the Universe.

It calls the Spirit of the Young the *Brahma Kamal*, 'the infinite lotus'. For it is something which has perfection in its heart and yet ever grows and unfolds its petals.

There have been men in India who never wrote learned texts about the religion of Man but had an overpowering desire and practical training for its attainment. They bore in their life the testimony of their intimacy with the Person who is in all persons, of Man the formless in the individual forms of men. Rajjab, poet-saint of medieval India, says of Man:

> God-man (*nara-nārāyana*) is thy definition, it is not a delusion but truth. In thee the infinite seeks the finite, the perfect knowledge seeks love, and when the form and the Formless (the individual and the universal) are united love is fulfilled in devotion.

Ravidas, another poet of the same age, sings:

> Thou seest me, O Divine Man (*narahari*), and I see thee, and our love becomes mutual.

Of this God-man a village poet of Bengal says:

> He is within us, an unfathomable reality. We know him when we unlock our own self and meet in a true love with all others.

A brother poet of his says:

> Man seeks the man in me and I lose myself and run out.

And another singer sings of the Ideal Man, and says:

> How could the scripture know the meaning of the Lord who has his play in the world of human forms?
>
> Listen, O brother man (declares Chandidas), the truth of man is the highest truth, there is no other truth above it.

All these are proofs of a direct perception of humanity as an objective truth that rouses a profound feeling of longing and love. This is very unlike what we find in the intellectual cult of humanity, which is like a body that has tragically lost itself in the purgatory of shadows.

Wordsworth says:

> We live by admiration, hope and love,
> And ever as these are well and wisely fixed
> In dignity of being we ascend.

It is for dignity of being that we aspire through the expansion of our consciousness in a great reality of man to which we belong. We realize it through admiration and love, through hope that soars beyond the actual, beyond our own span of life into an endless time wherein we live the life of all men.

This is the infinite perspective of human personality where man finds his religion. Science may include in its field of knowledge the starry world and the world beyond it; philosophy may try to find some universal principle which is at the root of all things, but religion inevitably concentrates itself on humanity, which illumines our reason, inspires our wisdom, stimulates our love, claims our intelligent service. There is an impersonal idea, which we call law, discoverable by an impersonal logic in its pursuit of the fathomless depth of the hydrogen atom and the distant virgin worlds clothed in eddying fire. But as the physiology of our beloved is not our beloved, so this impersonal law is not our God, the *Pitritamah pitrinam,* the Father who is ultimate in all fathers and mothers, of him we cannot say:

> *Tad viddhi pranipatena pariprasnena sevayā—*
>
> Realize him by obeisance, by the desire to know, by service—

For this can only be relevant to the God who is God and man at the same time; and if this faith be blamed for being anthropomorphic, then Man is to be blamed for being Man, and the lover for loving his dear one as a person instead of as a principle of psychology. We can never go beyond Man in all that we know and feel, and a mendicant singer of Bengal has said:

> Our world is as it is in our comprehension; the thought and existence are commingled. Everything would be lost in unconsciousness if man were nought; and when response comes to your own call you know the meaning of reality.

According to him, what we call nature is not a philosophical abstraction not cosmos, but what is revealed to *man* as nature. In fact it is included in himself and therefore there is a commingling of his mind with it, and in that he finds his own being. He is truly lessened in humanity if he cannot take it within him and through it feel the fulness of his own existence. His arts and literature are constantly giving expression to this intimate communion of man with his world. And the Vedic poet exclaims in his hymn to the sun:

> Thou who nourishest the earth, who walkest alone, O Sun, withdraw thy rays, reveal thy exceeding beauty to me and let me realize that the Person who is there is the One who I am.

It is for us to realize the Person who is in the heart of the All by the emancipated consciousness of our own personality. We know that the highest mission of science is to find the universe enveloped by the human comprehension; to see man's *visvarupa*, his great mental body, that touches the extreme verge of time and space, that includes the whole world within itself.

The original Aryans who came to India had for their gods the deities of rain, wind, fire, the cosmic forces which singularly enough found no definite shapes in images. A time came when it was recognized that individually they had no separate, unrelated power of their own, but there was one infinite source of power which was named Brahma. The cosmic divinity developed into an impersonal idea; what was physical grew into a metaphysical abstraction, even as in modern science matter vanishes into mathematics. And Brahma, according to those Indians, could neither be apprehended by mind nor described by words, even as matter in its ultimate analysis proves to be.

However satisfactory that idea might be as the unknowable principle relating to itself all the phenomena that are non-personal, it left the personal man in a void of negation. It cannot be gain-said that we can never realize things in this world from inside, we can but know how they appear to us. In fact, in all knowledge we know our own self in its condition of knowledge. And religion sought the highest value of man's existence in this self. For this is the only truth of which he is immediately conscious from within. And he said:

Purushānna parā kinchit
sā kāshthtā sā para gātih

Nothing is greater than the Person; he is the supreme, he is the ultimate goal.

It is a village poet of East Bengal who preaches in a song the philosophical doctrine that the universe has its reality in its relation to the Person, which I translate in the following lines:

The sky and the earth are born of mine own eyes,
The hardness and softness, the cold and the heat are the products of mine own body.
The sweet smell and the bad are of my own nostrils.

This poet sings of the Eternal Person within him, coming out and appearing before his eyes, just as the Vedic Rishi speaks of the Person, who is in him, dwelling also in the heart of the sun:

I have seen the vision,
the vision of mine own revealing itself,
coming out from within me.

In India, there are those whose endeavour is to merge completely their personal self in an impersonal entity which is without any quality or definition; to reach a condition wherein mind becomes perfectly blank, losing all its activities. Those who claim the right to speak about it say that this is the purest state of consciousness, it is all joy and without any object or content. This is considered to be the ultimate end of *Yoga*, the cult of union, thus completely to identify one's being with the infinite Being who is beyond all thoughts and words. Such realization of transcendental consciousness accompanied by a perfect sense of bliss is a time-honoured tradition in our country, carrying in it the positive evidence which cannot be denied by any negative argument of refutation. Without disputing its truth I maintain that it may be valuable as a great psychological experience but all the same it is not religion, even as the knowledge of the ultimate state of the atom is of no use to an artist who deals in images in which atoms have taken forms. A certain condition of vacuum is needed for studying the state of things in its original purity, and the same may be said of the human spirit; but the original state is not necessarily the perfect state. The concrete form is a more perfect manifestation than the atom, and man is more perfect as a man than where he vanishes in an original indefiniteness. This is why the Ishopanishat says: 'Truth is both finite and infinite at the same time, it moves and yet moves not, it is in the distant, also in the near, it is within all objects and without them.'

This means that perfection as the ideal is immovable, but in its aspect of the real it constantly grows towards completion, it moves. And I say of the Supreme Man, that he is infinite in his essence, he is finite in his manifestation in us the individuals. As the Ishopanishat declares, a man must live his full term of life and work without greed, and thus realize himself in the Being who is in all beings. This means that he must reveal in his own personality the Supreme Person by his disinterested activities.

27 I Am He

In the *Bṛhadāraṇyaka* Upaniṣad there is a remarkable verse:

> अथ योऽन्यां देवताम् उपास्ते
> अन्योऽसौ अन्योऽहम् अस्मीति
> न स वेद, यथा पशुरेवं स देवतानाम्।

> A person who worships God as exterior to himself does not know him, he is like an animal belonging to the gods.

The statement may rouse angry remonstrance. Should man then worship his own self? Is it possible to offer oneself in self-devotion? Then the whole process of worship becomes a mere magnification of the ego.

The truth is quite opposite. Glorification of ego is the prerogative even of the animals, but it is only man who can realize *Bhūmā*, immensity, within his own soul as detached from his ego. It is easy to place one's God outside and worship him through traditional ceremonies, observance of injunctions and taboos but the difficulty comes when we have to realize and acknowledge the divine man in our own thoughts and actions. Therefore is it said:

> नायमात्मा बलहीनेन लभ्यः।

> They who are weak cannot attain the truth of the Eternal Spirit.

> य आत्मा अपहतपाप्मा विजरो
> विमृत्युर्विशोकोऽविजिघत्सोऽपिपासः
> सत्यकामः सत्यसंकल्पः सोऽन्वेष्टव्यः स विजिज्ञासितव्यः।

> The great soul who is within me, who is beyond age and death and sorrow, beyond hunger and thirst, He who is true in thought and in action, Him we must seek, Him we must know.

This seeking and knowing him is not seeking and knowing outside oneself. It is knowing through becoming, receiving through being true within.

As man is essentially a spirit this principle of unity holds good in all departments of his life. He must identify himself with his family and then in his service to it there can be no indignity. The mother is spiritually one with her child, otherwise she would become a maidservant. When our government is not foreign to us, when it represents our own will, then we are saved from humiliation in our relation to it. And in our Indian philosophy we realize the dignity of man in our spiritual identification with God himself, for it is truth, and man is never पशुरेव देवतानाम्, 'like an animal belonging to the gods'. The true freedom is not in isolation, it is in the profound union which is perfect.

I have already said that the knowledge of things which man attains by overcoming personal idiosyncrasies and prejudices is called science. It is valuable, because it is acceptable to all men. Similarly, the self in man which transcends his self-interest finds its infinite truth in union with All. Its actions are विश्वकर्मा, universal actions. The functions of the isolated self are a bondage, the functions of the universal self are unfettered. The Upaniṣad has said:

> युक्तात्मान: सर्वमेवाविशन्ति
>
> The individual souls united with the Supreme Soul enter everywhere.

And this is the freedom of spirit which we must attain.

The truth which has been acknowledged by our scriptures, known as 'I am He'—सोऽहं, sounds like a prodigious egoism but it is not so. It has not exaggerated the small self which is isolated but expressed the great soul which comprehends all.

This word सोऽहं, carries assurance of the truth of a grand unity which waits to be realized and justified by the individual.

Man's passions come in between and divide the realization of सोऽहं, 'I am He,' into a duality, and our ego becomes disproportionately augmented. Therefore the *Upaniṣad* says मा गृध: 'Covet not.' Greed tempts the world-man and turns him into a worldly man. The enjoyment which is fit for human beings is an enjoyment which is shared with all, it is universal. It is expressed in man's art, his literature, it is manifested in his social doings, in the hospitality of his love. Therefore our scripture says अतिथिदेवो भव the guest is divine. Because into the house of the individual man comes the guest, the representative of the universal man, he extends the limits of the home towards the world. If this invitation is obstructed, then it is penury even for a royal household. In this hospitality lies the philosophy of सोऽहं, that is to say, I am in union with him who is mine and who is more than me. In our country there are some *sanyasis* who translate in their lives the philosophy of सोऽहं, into extreme inactivity and callousness. They torture the body in order to cross the boundaries of animal existence, they also discard the independent responsibility of man in their presumption to deny and transcend humanity. They give up the ego which is attached to materials, they also disregard the soul which is united with all souls. That which they call *Bhūmā* is not the *Iśa* of the *Upaniṣad* who dwells in the union of all, their *Bhūmā* is divorced from all others and therefore has no responsibilities of action. They do not recognize him is पौरुषं नृषु, who is humanity in man, who is *mahatma* and *viśvakarma*, in whom work is not fragmentary work but world-work.

Man was once a barbarian, he lived on the plane of the animal; his mind, his work, then, were confined within the limits of his bare physical existence. And then he was पशुरेव देवतानाम्, 'like an animal belonging to the gods'; he was in a servile manner afraid of his gods and tried to appease them with flattery and incantations; the divine in himself remained self-oblivious. When his mind was illumined his awakened consciousness journeyed along widening avenues of life, crossing the frontiers of individual life into the universal life of humanity. From my friend Kshtimohan's rich storehouse of medieval Indian poetry I have got these precious words of the seer Rajjab. He says:

> सब सांच मिलै सो सांच है ना मिलै सो झूठ।
> जन रज्जव सांच कही भावइ रिझिभि भावै रूठ।।

> That which conforms to all truth is truth, that which does not conform is false, this is wisdom, says Rajjab, whether it angers or pleases you.

It is evident that Rajjab knew that the majority of men would be angry at his words. Their opinions and customs were at variance with universal truth, yet they could claim them to be true and lie enmeshed in coils of unreality; indeed the very consciousness of an inner disharmony roused their excitement to an aggressive pitch. Trying to refute truth by angry remonstrance is like trying to pierce the flame with a knife. The knife cannot kill truth, it can kill man himself. Yet standing before that fury one has to say:

> सब सांच मिलै सो सांच है
> ना मिलै सो झूठ।

> That which conforms to all truth is truth, that which does not conform is false.

When one day a solitary scientist declared that the earth revolves round the sun, through his own intellect he revealed the mind of the Universal Man. On that day millions of people were bitterly angry at his words, by the terrorism of force they wanted to make him say that it is the sun itself which revolves round the earth. But however numerous those other people may have been, by denying truth they at once denounced their eternal humanity. On that day alone in the midst of fierce opponents the man of truth declared सोऽहं, 'I am He', that is to say, my individual knowledge and that of the eternal man are one.

Even if many millions of men say that because of some special combination of certain stars and planets in the immeasurable distance of space some supernatural force is generated in the river of a particular province of this earth, and that by bathing in its waters sins of the bather along with those of his forefathers are washed away, then we must stand up and say:

> सब सांच मिलै सो सांच है
> ना मिलै सो झूठ।

> With the universal mind of man this does not agree, therefore it is untrue.

But where it has been said अदिभर्गात्राणि शुध्यन्ति मनः सत्येन शुध्यति 'by water the body only can be cleansed, the mind can be cleansed only with truth', this conforms to the standard of the universal mind.

Similarly it has been said:

> कृत्वा पापं हि सन्तप्य तस्मात् पापात् प्रमुच्यते
> नैवं कुर्य्यां पुनरिति निवृत्त्या पूयते तु सः।

> If one is penitent after having committed sin then through that penitence the sin is purified; by resolving never again to repeat the sin man can again be pure.

By saying this man acknowledges in his own mind the truth of the universal mind of man, the God within us whom we know in our soul and who reveals to us our own truth.

One day the Brahmin Ramananda leaving his disciples went and embraced the *chandal* Nabha, the Mahomedan weaver Kabir, the sweeper Ravidas. The society of his day made Ramananda an out-caste. But he alone really rose to the highest caste, the caste of the universal man. On that day standing in the midst of the curses of his community, Ramananda alone had said सोऽहं 'I am He'. But that truth alone he had transgressed the limits of petty conventions and contempt which cruelly dividing man and man in the name of social stability strike at the roots of social morality.

One day Jesus Christ said सोऽहं—'I and my Father are one.' For, in the light of love and goodwill for all men, he crossed the boundary of his ego and realized himself as one with the supreme man.

Lord Buddha preached, 'Cherish towards the whole universe immeasurable *maitrī* in a spirit devoid of distinctions of hatred, of enmity. While standing, sitting, walking, lying down till you are asleep, remain established in this spirit of *maitrī*'—this is called ब्रह्मविहार।

Such great message can be given only to man, for deep in man lies the truth of सोऽहं, 'I am He'. The Buddha knew this in himself. That is why he has said that it is through immeasurable love that man reveals the immeasurable truth within himself.

The Atharva Veda says:

तस्मात् वै विद्वान् पुरुषमिदं ब्रह्मेति मन्यते

> He who is wise knows man to be greater than he appears to be.

ये पुरुषे ब्रह्म विदुस्ते विदुः परमेष्टिनम्

> They, who know the Great in man know the Supreme Being himself.

It was because he realized the divine man in humanity, that Buddha could say:

माता यथा नियं पुत्तं
आयुसा एकपुत्तमनुरक्खे
एवमपि सब्बभूतेसु
मानसंभावये अपरिमाणं

> Cultivate the spirit of immeasurable love within you even as the love the mother feels for her one child.

We should not by counting the number of heads try to find out how many men can actually follow this advice. In such computation does not lie the test of truth.

He who realized man's infinitude within himself never had to wait for statistical assurance. Without hesitation he demanded that man may reveal through immeasurable love the divine within himself. By giving this message with perfect faith to all men he offered his true reverence for humanity.

I have already referred to the saying of the *Atharva Veda* that man is spiritually much more than his apparent self, he lives in his infinite surplus. In that surplus is all that is supreme in man, his ऋतं, righteousness, his सत्यं, his truth.

The atmosphere around the earth far transcends its mass in extension. Through that invisible atmosphere comes its light, its colour, flows its life. In this atmosphere gathers its cloud, showers its rain, through its influence the eternal mystery of beauty reveals itself on earth in ever-varied form. From this atmosphere comes that which is most glorious on earth, its loveliness, its life itself. Through the open window of this atmosphere comes every night crossing regions of darkness the message of radiant kinship from the starry Universe. This atmosphere can be described as the surplus, the soul of the earth, just as the complete man has been described as 'त्रिपादस्यामृतं'—in one part he is apparent, in the other three he is infinite. It is because this intangible atmosphere is so intimately an extension of the earth itself that exuberant wealth of life manifests itself on the very dust, a wealth which is immeasurably more precious than the dust itself.

The *Upaniṣad* says that when we know united in a completeness असम्भूति, the unmanifested infinite, and सम्भूति, the manifested finite, we know truth, in a reconciliation of the duality. He who is infinite in man must be expressed in the finitude of human life, of human society. Man must translate this idea in his action. So *Īsa Upaniṣad* says, 'You have to live a hundred years, you must act.' Fulfil your hundred years of life by work, such work as can truly be claimed through belief and result to express the truth of सोऽहं 'I am He'. Not by turning up one's eye-balls and sitting with closed breath and staying far away from man do we gain this Truth.

This work, this toil is not for earning livelihood. In which truth then is the source of its constant energy? What is it that gives man this strength to sacrifice his life, to embrace suffering, to defy ruthless power without material safeguard, to endure without submitting the constant torture of injustice and cruelty with such amazing fortitude? The reason is man has within himself not only life but immensity. From Kshitimohan's priceless collection we get this message of the Baüls जीवेजीवे चाइया देखि सब इ ये तार अवतार 'When I see through men I find in them the divine incarnation.' Innumerable men in knowledge, in love, in self-giving, in various forms and ways are revealing the immeasurable within them. History does not record their names; from their individual lives they pour into the living stream of humanity the immortal energy of Him—

यश्चायमस्मिन् तेजोमयोऽमृतमयः पुरुषः सर्व्वानुभूः

Who is the immortal Purusha of in-exhaustible light dwelling within our soul, who comprehends the All.

If through the plants the universal energy were not converted into the stuff of life then this living world would have been converted into a desert. Similarly if with or without our knowing men and women had not through the centuries, in different lands, transformed their indwelling, immeasurable energy of the Supreme Man into love and knowledge, work and welfare to be absorbed endlessly into the living texture of human society, their society, being devoid of the truth of सोऽहं 'I am He', would have been reduced to that status of the animal world. Not only so, by being severed from its own truth, society would not at all be able to live. Physicians tell us that by infusion of animal-blood into human body we do not increase its life but cause death. Herds of animals can live for ever according to animal laws, but human society cannot live at all like animals. It may be said in contradiction that many brute-like men seem to thrive very well indeed in human society. Boils on the skin also thrive on the body, their growth is indeed more vigorous than the rest of their surroundings. If the power of health in the body does not transcend the boil, then it hurts and in killing the boil kills itself. Society in its normal stage can endure many sins but when its degeneration becomes emphatic, then by absorbing animal blood in its thought, behaviour, literature and art, human society seals its own death.

The greatness born of a vast surplus about which the *Atharva Veda* has spoken is not in any particular kind of fulfilment. The greatness comprehends all the efforts of humanity, all the bravery, grace and strength of man. Perhaps there is a deep self-forgetful joy in the ascetic when he succeeds in concentrating the various powers of his mind on one immovable point of his consciousness. But ततः किम्, 'what then'? So long as there is any suffering and insult in humanity, no individual man can ever win his escape. Great men who have desired the freedom of humanity, have therefore told us सम्भवामि युगे युगे. From age to age indeed are they born in different lands. Today this very moment they are being born, tomorrow also we will see their birth. The stream of that birth flows through history, bearing this message सोऽहं. सोऽहं is the *mantram* of the united evolution of Man, not of one particular individual.

In the midst of the vast nebulae where new worlds are being fashioned appears from time to time a star; it clearly indicates the creative ferment of the vast fires which stir in the heart of the nebulae. Similarly in the firmament of history now and again we see manifestations of the Supreme Man. From them we understand that in the heart of all men is constantly working the urge of evolution. Man in human society is all the while striving to realize himself in the world-man by breaking through the shell of his ego. In fact, it is in this process that the whole cosmic universe seeks its own truth, the supreme truth of the ever growing, ever-becoming Humanity. After billions of years since the beginning of the world first appeared man. Some scholars are overwhelmed by the mathematics of number and comparing the massiveness of time and space to the smallness of man indulge in the luxury of our humiliation. But it is a mere illusion to consider quantity to be greater than

Truth which cannot be measured at all by quantity. That which we call matter or unrevealed life, lay slumbering for unnumbered Ages. But when one day a single cell of life appeared on this earth the whole evolution of the universe reached a great meaning. Amidst the externality of matter appeared the truth which is internal. For life is internal, organic. Who can despise the speck of life because it has been born recently after aeons time and because in comparison to the mass of matter it seems to be small? Man first realized the truth of infinite life when from the heart of the dumb matter comes the Great voice of life, यदिदं किञ्च सर्व्वं प्राण एजति निःसृतम् 'From life is born all-that-is and trembles in the vibrating life.' Matter we know as a fact because it is external to us; but life we know as truth from within ourselves. The expression of life is internal, the whole of it is pure movement. Therefore the language of movement is immediately real to us, it is the language of our life. The reality of this endless movement we have known as truth in relation to our own inner self. The urge of incessant movement we may call heat or electricity or something else; yet all these are mere words. If we say that in this movement there is life, then we indicate something which has meaning in our immediate experience. At the same time we realize that this life of mine which is moving is also comprehended in the larger movement of Universal Life. That the urge of life's movement is nowhere else in the universe excepting, accidentally, only in living beings, is a statement which our mind cannot accept because our mind can offer its homage to truth only in its background of wholeness.

The *Upaniṣad* says:

कोह्येवान्यात् कः प्राण्यात् यदेष आकाश आनन्दो न स्यात्

With what assurance would a single insect desire for life if the joy of life did not pervade the whole of the infinite space? How can the flame burn for a single moment on the tip of the match-stick if the whole sky did not sustain its truth of ignition? Within life we find an inner meaning of the entire creation—that meaning we call Will. Matter remained dumb—it could not express the language of will,—Life came and expressed its will. That message which was implicit so long found at last its voice.

The student after much effort and time first learns the alphabet, then the spelling, then the grammar; he wastes paper and ink scribbling incomplete and meaningless sentences, he uses and discards much acquisition of materials; at last when as a poet he is able to write his first utterance, that very moment in that composition all his inexpressive accumulations of words first find their glimmer of a significance. In the great evolution of the Universe we have found its first significance in a cell of life, then in an animal, then in Man. From the outer universe gradually we come to the inner realm and one by one the gates of freedom are unbarred. When the screen is lifted on the appearance of Man on earth we realize the great and mysterious truth of relatedness, of the supreme unity of all that is. Only can Man declare that those who know Truth can enter into the heart of the All—Only man can open our heart with this aspiration.

> सव्वे सत्ता सुखिता होन्तु अवेरा होन्तु
> अब्यापज्झो होन्तु सुखी अत्तानं परिहरन्तु।
> सव्वे सत्ता दुक्खा पमुञ्चन्तु। सव्वे सत्ता मा
> यथालब्द्धसम्पत्तितो विगच्छन्तु-

> May all beings be happy, may they have no enemies, may they be indestructible, may they spend time in joyousness. May all living beings be free from suffering and not be denied of their dues.

We can only pray, let sorrow come if it has to come, let there be death, let there be loss, but let Man declare across all space and time 'I am He'.

Spiritual Freedom

28

There are injuries that attack our life; they hurt the harmony of life's functions through which is maintained the harmony of our physical self with the physical world; and these injuries are called diseases. There are also factors that oppress our intelligence. They injure the harmony of relationship between our rational mind and the universe of reason; and we call them stupidity, ignorance or insanity. They are uncontrolled exaggerations of passions that upset all balance in our personality. They obscure the harmony between the spirit of the individual man and the spirit of the universal Man; and we give them the name sin. In all these instances our realization of the universal Man, in his physical, rational and spiritual aspects, is obstructed, and our true freedom in the realms of matter, mind and spirit is made narrow or distorted.

All the higher religions of India speak of the training for *Mukti*, the liberation of the soul. In this self of ours we are conscious of individuality, and all its activities are engaged in the expression and enjoyment of our finite and individual nature. In our soul we are conscious of the transcendental truth in us, the Universal, the Supreme Man; and this soul, the spiritual self, has its enjoyment in the renunciation of the individual self for the sake of the supreme soul. This renunciation is not in the negation of self, but in the dedication of it. The desire for it comes from an instinct which very often knows its own meaning vaguely and gropes for a name that would define its purpose. This purpose is in the realization of its unity with some objective ideal of perfections, some harmony of relationship between the individual and the infinite man. It is of this harmony, and not of a barren isolation that the Upanishad speaks, when it says that truth no longer remains hidden in him who finds himself in the All.

Once when I was on a visit to a remote Bengali village, mostly inhabited by Mahomedan cultivators, the villagers entertained me with an operatic performance the literature of which belonged to an obsolete religious sect that had wide influence centuries ago. Though the religion itself is dead, its voice still continues preaching its philosophy to a people, who, in spite of their different culture, are not tired of listening. It discussed according to its own doctrine the different elements, material and transcendental, that constitute human personality, comprehending the body, the self and the soul. Then came a dialogue, during the course of which was related the incident of a person who wanted to make a journey to Brindaban, the Garden of Bliss, but was prevented by a watchman who startled him with an accusation of theft. The thieving was proved when it was shown that inside his clothes he was secretly trying to smuggle into the garden the self, which only finds its fulfilment by its surrender. The culprit was caught with the incriminating bundle in his possession which barred for him his passage to the supreme goal. Under a tattered canopy, supported on bamboo poles and lighted by a few smoking kerosene lamps, the village crowd, occasionally interrupted by howls of jackals in the neighbouring paddy fields, attended with untired interest, till the small hours of the morning, the performance of a drama that discussed the ultimate meaning of all things in a seemingly incongruous setting of dance, music and humorous dialogue.

This illustration will show how naturally, in India, poetry and philosophy have walked hand in hand, only because the latter has claimed its right to guide men to the practical path of their life's fulfilment. What is that fulfilment? It is our freedom in truth, which has for its prayer:

> Lead us from the unreal to reality.
> For *satyam* is *anandam*, the Real is Joy.

In the world of art, our consciousness being freed from the tangle of self-interest, we gain an unobstructed vision of unity, the incarnation of the real, which is a joy for ever.

As in the world of art, so in the spiritual world, our soul waits for its freedom from the ego to reach that disinterested joy which is the source and goal of creation. It cries for its *mukti*, its freedom in the unity of truth. The idea of *mukti* has affected our lives in India, touched the springs of pure emotions and supplications; for it soars heavenward on the wings of poesy. We constantly hear men of scanty learning and simple faith singing in their prayer to Tara, the Goddess Redeemer:

'For what sin should I be compelled to remain in this dungeon of the world of appearance?'

They are afraid of being alienated from the world of truth, afraid of perpetual drifting amidst the froth and foam of things, of being tossed about by the tidal waves of pleasure and pain and never reaching the ultimate meaning of life. Of these men, one may be a carter driving his cart to market, another a fisherman playing his net. They may not be prompt with an intelligent answer if they are questioned about the deeper import of the song they sing, but they have no doubt in their mind, that the abiding cause of all misery is not so much in the lack of life's furniture as in the obscurity of life's significance. It is a common topic with such to decry an undue emphasis upon 'me' and 'mine', which falsifies the perspective of truth. For have they not often seen men, who are not above their own level in social position or intellectual acquirement, going out to seek Truth, leaving everything that they have behind them?

They know that the object of these adventurers is not betterment in worldly wealth and power—it is *mukti*, freedom. They possibly know some poor fellow villager of their own craft, who remains in the world carrying on his daily vocation and yet has the reputation of being emancipated in the heart of the Eternal. I myself have come across a fisherman singing with an inward absorption of mind, while fishing all day in the Ganges, who was pointed out to me by my boatman, with awe, as a man of liberated spirit. He is out of reach of the conventional prices that are set upon men by society, and which classify them like toys arranged in the shop-windows according to the market standard of value.

When the figure of this fisherman comes to my mind, I cannot but think that their number is not small who with their lives sing the epic of the unfettered soul, but will never be known in history. These unsophisticated Indian peasants know that an Emperor is merely a decorated slave, remaining chained to his Empire, that a millionaire is kept pilloried by his fate in the golden cage of his wealth, while this fisherman is free in the realm of light. When, groping in the dark, we stumble against objects, we cling to them believing them to be our only hope. When light comes, we slacken our hold, finding them to be mere parts of the All to which we are related. The simple man of the village knows what freedom is—freedom from the isolation of self, from the isolation of things, which imparts a fierce intensity to our sense of possession. He knows that this freedom is not the mere negation of bondage, in the bareness of our belongings, but in some positive realization which gives pure joy to our being, and he sings: 'To him who sinks into the deep, nothing remains unattained.' He says again:

> Let my two minds meet and combine,
>
> And lead me to the city Wonderful.

When that one mind of ours which wanders in search of things in the outer region of the varied, and the other which seeks the inward vision of unity, are no longer in conflict, they help us to realize the *ajab*, the *anirvachaniya*, the ineffable. The poet saint Kabir has also the same message when he sings:

> By saying that Supreme Reality only dwells in the inner realm of spirit, we shame the outer world of matter; and also when we say that he is only in the outside, we do not speak the truth.

According to these singers, truth is in unity, and therefore freedom is in its realization. The texts of our daily worship and meditation are for training our mind to overcome the barrier of separateness from the rest of existence and to realize *advaitam*, the Supreme Unity which is *anantam*, infinitude. It is philosophical wisdom, having its universal radiation in the popular mind in India, that inspires our prayer, our daily spiritual practices. It has its constant urging for us to go beyond the world of appearances, in which facts as facts are alien to us, like the mere sounds of foreign music; it speaks to us of an emancipation in the inner truth of all things, where the endless *Many* reveal the *One*.

Freedom in the material world has also the same meaning expressed in its own language. When nature's phenomena appeared to us as irrelevant, as heterogeneous manifestations of an obscure and irrational caprice, we lived in an alien world never dreaming of our *swaraj* within its territory. Through the discovery of the harmony of its working with that of our reason, we realize our unity with it, and therefore our freedom.

Those who have been brought up in a misunderstanding of this world's process, not knowing that it is one with themselves through the relationship of knowledge and intelligence, are trained as cowards by a hopeless faith in the ordinance of a destiny darkly dealing its blows. They submit without struggle when human rights are denied them, being accustomed to imagine themselves born as outlaws in a world constantly thrusting upon them incomprehensible surprises of accidents.

Also in the social or political field, the lack of freedom is based upon the spirit of alienation, on the imperfect realization of the One. There our bondage is in the tortured link of union. One may imagine that an individual who succeeds in dissociating himself from his fellow attains real freedom, inasmuch as all ties of relationship imply obligation to others. But we know that, though it may sound paradoxical, it is true that in the human world only a perfect arrangement of interdependence gives rise to freedom. The most individualistic of human beings who own no responsibility are the savages who fail to attain their fulness of manifestation. They live immersed in obscurity, like an ill-lighted fire that cannot liberate itself from its envelope of smoke. Only those may attain their freedom from the segregation of an eclipsed life who have the power to cultivate mutual understanding and co-operation. The history of the growth of freedom is the history of the perfection of human relationship.

It has become possible for men to say that existence is evil, only because in our blindness we have missed something wherein our existence has its truth. If a bird tries to soar with only one of its wings, it is offended with the wind for buffeting it down to the dust. All broken truths are evil. They hurt because they suggest something they do not offer. Death does not hurt us, but disease does, because disease constantly reminds us of health and yet withholds it from us. And life in a halfworld is evil because it feigns finality when it is obviously incomplete, giving us the cup but not the draught of life. All tragedies result from truth remaining a fragment, its cycle not being completed. That cycle finds its end when the individual realize the universal and thus reaches freedom.

But because this freedom is in truth itself and not in an appearance of it, no hurried path of success, forcibly cut out by the greed of result, can be a true path. And an obscure village poet, unknown to the world of recognized respectability, sings:

> O cruel man of urgent need, must you scorch with fire the mind which still is a bud? You will burst it into bits, destroy its perfume in your impatience. Do you not see that my Lord, the Supreme Teacher, takes ages to perfect the flower and never is in a fury of haste? But because of your terrible greed, you only rely on force, and what hope is there for you, O man of urgent need? 'Prithi', says Madan the poet, 'Hurt not the mind of my Teacher. Know that only he who follows the simple current and loses himself, can hear the voice, O man of urgent need.'

This poet knows that there is no external means of taking freedom by the throat. It is the inward process of losing ourselves that leads to it. Bondage in all its forms has its stronghold in the inner self and not in the outside world; it is in the dimming of our consciousness, in the narrowing of our perspective, in the wrong valuation of things.

Let me conclude this chapter with a song of the Baül sect in Bengal, over a century old, in which the poet sings of the eternal bond of union between the infinite and the finite soul, from which there can be no *mukti*, because love is ultimate, because it is an interrelation which makes truth complete, because absolute independence is the blankness of utter servility. The song runs thus:

> It goes on blossoming for ages, the soul-lotus, in which I am bound, as well as thou, without escape. There is no end to the opening of its petals, and the honey in it has so much sweetness that thou, like an enchanted bee, canst never desert it, and therefore thou art bound, and I am, and *mukti* is nowhere.

The Message of the Forest

29

The past not only contains, in its depths, the unrealized future, but in part the realized future itself. Everybody admits the truth, that, in the grandfather, lies dormant the potential grandson, who is to carry the growth of his ancestry to a further stage, or in a new direction. But it is also true that the grandson is practically born in the grandfather. New additions are made and modifications effected, but some keynote, that is to dominate the racial life, has already been achieved in the life of the grandfather.

This is the reason, why every race of people has its tradition of the Golden Age in the past, because we never can trust our future, if it does not carry some great promise bequeathed to it. It is not enough for us to know, that our future is growing out clearer from the nebulous adumbration of a primitive age, we must also be assured that it has already shown itself distinct in its achievements in the past. Every great people hold its history so valuable because of this, because, it contains not mere memories, but hope, and therefore the image of the future. Man has his instinctive faith in heredity. He feels, that, in heredity, that which is to come has been proved in that which has been,—in great heredity, the great conclusion is perpetually present in the process. And all history is man's credential of his future, signed and sealed by his past.

The physical organization of the race has certain vital memories, which are persistent, which fashion its nose and eyes in a particular shape, regulate its stature and deal with the pigment of its skin. In the ideal of a race, there also run memories that remain constant, or, in case of alien mixture, come back repeatedly, even after the lapse of long intervals.

These are the compelling forces, that secretly and inevitably fashion the future of a people and give characteristic shape to its civilization. In our Shastras, it is held that our desires are the creative factors which originate and guide our future births. Likewise every race has its innate desires, of its former days, leading it through the repeated new births of its history. Any people which lacks, in its racial mind, these inherited aspirations, merely drifts, till it sinks in the current of time; it never creates its own history. In a word, it does not renew its birth, but is merged in the amorphous vagueness of a ghostly existence.

Therefore, it is of great importance for us to know, whether, as a people, we carry in our subconscious mind some primal aspiration, which alone can guarantee us a definite future of our own. If we still have that, strong and living, it will save us from extinction, or from the perpetual shame,—worse than death,—of the life of imitation, or parasitism. When we are threatened with loss of self-respect; when our mind is overwhelmed with the idea, that there can be only one type of civilization worth the name, and that a foreign one; when our one conscious desire is to strive with all our might, by begging, borrowing or stealing, towards some ideal of perfection which can only be related to us, as a mask to a face, or a wig to a head,—then our only hope lies in discovering some profound creative desire persistent in the heart of our race, in the subconscious mind of our people. For, in the long run, it is our subconscious nature which wins, and it is the deeper unseen current of the mind which secretly cuts its own path and reaches its own goal,—not the conscious waves on the surface, which clamorously make themselves obvious and vigorously storm at the present time.

I have said elsewhere, that the environment, in which we see the past of India, is the forest, the memory of which permeates our classical literature and still haunts our minds. The legends related in our great epics cluster under the sublime shade of those ancient forests; and, in the forest, the most intense pathos of human life found its background in the greatest of our romantic dramas. The memory of these sacred forests is the one great inheritance which India ever cherishes through all her political vicissitudes and economic disturbances.

But we must know, that these forests were not merely topographical in their significance. We have seen that the history of the Northmen of Europe is resonant with the association of the sea. That sea, also, is not a mere physical fact, but represents certain ideals of life which still guide their history and inspire all their creations. In the sea, Nature presented herself to these men in her aspect of a danger, of a barrier, which seemed to be at constant war with the land and its children. The sea was the challenge of untamed Nature to the indomitable human soul. And man did not flinch; he fought and won; and the spirit of fight continued in him. He looked upon his place in the world as extorted from a hostile scheme of things, retained in the teeth of opposition. His cry is the cry of triumph of defiant Man against the rest of the universe.

This is about the people who lived by the sea, and rode on it as on a wild champing horse, clutching it by its mane and making it render service from shore to shore. But in the level tracts of *Aryavarta* men found no barrier between their lives and the Grand Life that permeates the Universe. The forest gave them shelter and shade, fruit and flower, fodder and fuel; it entered into a close living relation with their work and leisure and necessity, and in this way made it easy for them to know their own lives as associated with the larger life. They could not think of their surroundings as lifeless, separate, or inimical. So the view of the Truth, which these men found, was distinctly different from that of those of whom we have spoken above; and their relationship with this world also took a different turn, as they came to realize that the gifts of light and air, of food and drink, did not come from either sky or tree or soil, but had their fount in the all-pervading consciousness and joy of universal life. They uttered quite simply and naturally यदिदम् किञ्च सर्व्वम् प्राण एजति निष्टतम्—"All that is, vibrates with life, having emerged from the Supreme Life."

When we know this world as alien to us then we know it as a thing mechanical, built by a divine mechanic or by a chance combination of blind forces. Then our relation to it becomes the relation of utility, and we set up our own machines or mechanical methods to deal with it and make as much profit as our knowledge of its mechanism allows us to do. Then we are apt to say that Knowledge is power. This view of things does not altogether play us false, for the machine has its place in this world. And therefore, not only this material universe, but also human beings can be used as machines and made to yield results. But the view of the world which India has taken is summed up in one compound word—सच्चिदानन्द. Its meaning is that Reality, which is essentially one, has three aspects. The first is *sat,* the principle of Being, whose first information comes to us through our senses; it relates us to all things through the relationship of common existence. The second is *chit,* the principle of Knowing; it relates us to all things through the relationship of mind. The third is *ananda*—the principle of Enjoying—which unites us with all things through the relationship of love. Our consciousness of the world as that of the sum total of things that exist or that are governed by universal laws is imperfect according to the true Indian view,—but it is perfect when our consciousness realizes all things as spiritually one with it and therefore capable of giving us joy. Our text of daily meditation contains the truth of the one and the same creative force appearing in an undivided stream of manifestation in our consciousness and in the world of which we are conscious. They are one, as the East and the West are one, which only our self divides into contradictions. For us the highest purpose of this world is not merely living in it, knowing it and making use of it, but realizing our own selves in it through expansion of sympathy and emancipation of consciousness, not alienating and dominating it but comprehending and uniting it with us in blissful union. The Man whom you only use is a machine; the Man whom you only study is a material for your knowledge. But your friend is neither a machine to you nor a psychological curiosity, (though consciously or unconsciously he does take his part as a machine of work and as an object of study for you), his ultimate value lies in his giving you opportunity to lose yourself in his love. This is his aspect of *ananda*—his truest aspect for you, which comprehends his other two aspects in harmony. And to know the highest truth of all existence as that of a friend is truly Indian. This view of the world as the world of life and love, as the manifestation of the Supreme Soul whose nature is to realize his unity in the endlessness of the varied, has come to us from the great peace of our ancient forest.

When Vikramāditya became king, Ujjain a great capital, and Kālidāsa its poet, the age of India's forest retreats had passed. Then we had taken our stand in the midst of the great concourse of humanity, and the Chinese and the Hun, the Scythian and the Persian, the Greek and the Roman, had crowded round us. But even in this age of pride and prosperity, the longing love and awe of reverence with which its poet sang about the hermitage, shows what was the dominant ideal that occupied the mind of India, what was the one current of memory that continually flowed back through her life.

In Kālidāsa's drama *Shakuntala*, also, the hermitage, which dominates the play, overshadowing even the king's palace, has the same idea running through,—the recognition of the kinship of man with conscious and unconscious creation alike.

A poet of a later age, while describing a hermitage in his *Kadambari*, tells of the posture of devoutness in the flowering lianas as they bow to the wind; of the sacrifice offered by the trees scattering their blossoms; of the grove sounding with the lessons chanted by the neophytes, and the *mantras* which the parrots, constantly hearing, had learned to pronounce; of the wild fowl enjoying *Vaishva-deva-bali-pinda*—the food offered to the divinity which is in all creatures,—and of the ducks coming up from the lake, nearby, for their portion of the grass-seed, spread in the cottage yards to dry; of the deer caressing with their tongues the young hermit boys. It is again the same story. The hermitage shines out, in all our ancient literature, as the place where the chasm between man and the rest of creation has been bridged.

In the drama of other countries, where the human characters violently drown our attention in the vortex of their passions, Nature occasionally peeps in, but she is almost always a trespasser, who has to submit urgent excuses, or bow apologetically and depart. But in all our dramas, which still retain their fame, such as *Mrichchhakatika, Shakuntala, Uttara-Rama-Charita*, Nature stands on her own right, proving that she has her great function, to impart the peace of the eternal to the human passions and to mitigate their violent agitations which often come from the instability of spiritual lameness.

The frenzied fury of passion, described in two of Shakespeare's youthful poems, stands isolated upon its own pedestal of unashamed conspicuity. It is wrenched away naked from the cover of the All; it has not the green earth or the blue sky around it; the many-coloured veil of nature has been impatiently swept away from its face, bringing to our view the fever which is in man's desires, and not the healing balm which encircles it in the universe.

Ritusamhara is clearly a work of Kālidāsa's immaturity. The song of youthful love sung in it sounds from the fundamental bass notes of human passion,—it does not reach the sublime height of reticence that there is in *Shakuntala* or *Kumara-Sambhava.* But the tune of these voluptuous outbreaks, being set to the varied harmony of Nature's symphony, loses its delirious shrillness in the expanse of the open sky. The moon-beams of the summer evening, resonant with the murmuring flow of fountains, add to it their own melody; in its rhythm sways the *Kadamba* grove, glistening in the first cool rain of the season; and the south breezes waft into its heart the wistfulness of the scent of the mango flowers.

In the third canto of *Kumara Sambhava,* while describing the boisterous emergence of youth at the sudden coming of *Madana* (Eros), Kālidāsa has been careful to avoid giving this outburst of passion an abnormal supremacy within the narrow field of view of exclusive humanity. His genius basked in the sunshine of the human spirit, where it pervades the spring flower and the harvest of the autumn; and that genius never played at focusing it into a point of ignition upon the naked fluttering heart. Kālidāsa has shown a true reverence to the divine love-making of Sati by making his narration of it as a central white lotus floating on the world-wide immensity of youth, in which the animals and trees have their rhythm of life-throbs. It is a sacred flame of longing whose lamp is the universe.

Not only its third canto, but the whole of the *Kumara Sambhava* poem is painted upon a limitless canvas. Its inner idea is deep and of all time. It answers the one question that humanity asks through all its endeavours: How is the birth of the hero to be brought about,—the brave one who can defy and vanquish the evil demon, when he sweeps upon the scene, laying waste heaven's own kingdom? This is the greatest of all problems for each individual, and it forces itself in ever-new, ever-recurring forms upon each race and nation, and this is the one problem which persists in most of our poet's works,—in his *Shakuntala, Raghuvamsha* and *Kumara-Sambhava.*

It becomes evident that such a problem had become acute in Kālidāsa's time, when the old simplicity of Hindu life had broken up. The Hindu kings, forgetful of their kingly duties, had become self-seeking epicureans, and India was being repeatedly devastated by the Shakas.

But what answer does the poem give to the question it raises?—Not that more armaments were needed, or that a league of powers should be formed, or that some mechanical adjustment of political balance had to be effected. Its message is that the cause of weakness lies in the inner life of the soul. It is in some break of harmony with the Good, some dissociation from the True. When gain is completed by giving up, when love is fulfilled by self-sacrifice, when passion is purified by the penance of the soul, then only is heroism born,—the heroism which can save mankind from all defeat and disaster. When the ascetic Shiva—the Good—was lost in the passive immensity of his solitude, heaven was in peril. And when beautiful Sati—the Real—was all by herself, in her unwedded self-seclusion, the demons were triumphant. Only from the union of the exuberant freedom of the Real with the tranquil restraint of the Good comes the fullest strength.

Viewed from the outside, India, in the time of Kālidāsa, appeared to have reached the zenith of civilization, excelling as she did in luxury, literature and the arts. Kālidāsa himself was not free from the prevailing tone, and the outer embellishment of his poetry is as daintily luxurious as must have been the decorative art of the period. This, however, is only one aspect in which his age influenced the poet.

But what sudden passion for sacrifice, for the austere discipline of the life of aspiration, troubled our Goddess of Poesy amidst the luxury of her golden bower? It was the eternal message of the forest, that can never be silenced, and like a refrain, simple in its purity, comes up again and again, through all noisy distractions of discord,—the message to free our consciousness from the accumulations of desire, to win our immortality, by breaking through the sheath of self, the self which belongs to death. From his seat beside all the glories of Vikramaditya's throne, the poet's heart yearned for the purity of India's past age of spiritual striving. And it was this yearning which took shape and impelled him to go back to the annals of the ancient kings of Raghu's line.

'I fain would sing,' says Kālidāsa, in his prologue, 'of those whose purity went back to the day of their birth, whose striving went forward till attainment, whose empire knew no bounds but the seas, whose adventurous journeys reached up to the high heaven, who offered oblations to the sacred fire in accordance with injunctions, made gifts to the needy in accordance with their wants, awarded punishments in accordance with the crime, and regulated every wakeful activity in accordance with the hour,—who accumulated treasure for the sake of redistribution, tempered their utterance for the sake of truth, desired victories for the sake of glory, entered into wedlock for the sake of progeny,—who practised learning in their childhood, attended to wealth in their youth, took to the hermitage in their old age, cast away their bodies when they had attained the supreme union. Of these would I sing, though I lack all wealth of language; for their great merits, entering my ears, have disturbed my heart.'

But it was not in a paean of praise that his poem ended. What had troubled his heart becomes clear, when we come to the end of his *Raghuvamsha.* What was the life story of the founder of this line of Kings? Where did it begin?

The heroic life of Raghu had its prologue in a hermitage, showing that its origin was in a life of purity and self-restraint, led there by Raghu's royal parents. The poem is not ushered in with the pomp and circumstance befitting the history of a great kingly line. King Dilip, with his consort, Queen Sudakshina, has entered upon the life of the forest. The great monarch is busy tending the cattle of the hermitage. Thus opens the *Raghuvamsha* amidst scenes of simplicity and self-denial. But it ends in the palace of magnificence, in the wealth and luxury which divert the current of energy from the truth of life to the heaps of things. There is brilliance in this ending, as there is in the conflagration which destroys and devastates. Peaceful as the dawn, radiant as the tawny-haired hermit boy, is the calm strength of the restrained language in which the poet tells us of the kingly glory crowned with the halo of purity,—beginning his poem, as the day begins, in the serene solemnity of its sunrise. And lavish are the colours in which he describes the end, as of the evening, eloquent for a time with its sumptuous splendour of sunset, but overtaken at last by the devouring darkness which sweeps away all its brilliance into the fathomless abyss of night.

In this beginning and this ending of his poem, lies hidden the message of the forest which found its voice in the poet's words. With a suppressed sigh he is saying: 'Look on that which was and that which is! In the days when the future glowed gloriously ahead, self-discipline was esteemed as the highest path, self-renunciation the greatest treasure, but when downfall had become imminent, the hungry fires of desire aflame at a hundred different points, dazzled the eyes of all beholders.'

When the lust of self-aggrandizement is unbridled, the harmony between enjoyment and renunciation is destroyed. By concentrating our pride or desire upon a limited field, the field of the animal life, we seek to exaggerate a portion at the expense of the whole, the wholeness which is in man's life of the spirit. From this results evil. That is why renunciation becomes necessary,—not to lead to destitution, but to restoration, to win back the All.

Kālidāsa in almost all his works, has depicted this break of harmony between enjoyment and renunciation, between the life that loses itself in the sands of the self and the life that seeks its sea of eternity. And this is characteristically represented by the unbounded impetuousness of kingly splendour on one side and the serene strength of regulated desires on the other. I have already given above an illustration of this from the *Raghuvamsha.* Even in the minor drama of *Malavikagnimitra* we find the same thing in a different manner. It must never be thought that, in this play, the poet's deliberate object was to pander to his royal patron by inviting him to a literary orgy of lasciviousness. The very *Nandi* contradicts this and shows the object towards which this play is directed. The poet begins the drama with the prayer, 'सम्मार्गालोकयन् व्यपनयतु स नस्तामसौष्ठत्तिभोग:' 'Let God, to illumine for us the path of truth, sweep away our passions, bred of darkness.' The God, to whom this prayer is uttered, says the poet, is one in whose nature Eternal Woman is ever commingled, in an ascetic purity of love,—who stands in the sacred simplicity of barenness in the midst of his infinite wealth. The unified being of Hara and Parvati is the perfect symbolism of the eternal in the wedded love of man and woman. The poet opens his drama with the invocation of this spirit of the Divine Union. It is quite evident that this invocation carries the message in it with which he greeted his kingly audience. The whole drama is to show in vivid colour the utter ugliness of the treacherous falsehoods and cruelties inherent in all passions that are unchecked. In this play the conflict of ideals is between the king and the queen,—between Agnimitra and Dharini, between the insolent offence against all that is good and true, and the unlimited peace of forgiveness that dwells deep in the self-sacrifice of love. The great significance of this contrast lies hidden in the very names of the hero and the heroine of the drama. Though the name '*Agnimitra*' is historical, yet it symbolises in the poet's mind the desolating destructiveness of uncontrolled desire,—just as did the name of *Agnivarna* in *Raghuvamsha*. *Agnimitra,*—'the friend of the fire',—the reckless person, who in his love-making is playing with fire, not knowing that, all the time, it is scorching him black, till the seed of immortality perishes at the core of his being. And what a great name is *Dharini,* signifying the fortitude and forbearance that comes of the majesty of soul! What association it carries of the infinite dignity of love purified by the sacrificial fire of self-abnegation rising far above all insult of base betrayal! Can anybody doubt what effect the performance of this drama produced upon the royal looker-on, what searching of heart, what humility, what reverence for the love that claims our best worship by the offer of its patient worship of service!

In Shakuntala, this conflict of ideals has been shown all through the drama, by the contrast of the pompous heartlessness of the king's court and the natural purity of the hermitage, the contrast of the arrogance displaying itself upon the hollow eminence of convention, and the simplicity standing upon the altitude of truth. The message of the poet is uttered by the two hermit boys, when they enter the king's palace, just before the impending catastrophe of Shakuntala's life, the naked cruelty of which is skilfully hidden by the episode of the curse, though it was unbarred a moment before through the shameless self-confession of fickleness by the king, when he listened to the lamentation of Hamsapadika, one of his numerous victims. The message is:

> अभ्यक्तमिव स्नातः शुचिरशुचिमिव प्रवुच इव सुप्तम्
> वचामिव स्वैरगतिर्जनमिह सुखसडिंगतम् अवैमि।

> We look upon these devotees of pleasure as he, who has bathed, looks upon the unclean, as the pure in heart upon the polluted, as the wide awake soul looks upon the slothful slumberer, and as the one, who is free to move, looks upon the shackled.

And what is the inner meaning of the curse that follows the hermit girl in this drama, till she is purified by her penance? I am sure, according to the poet, it is the same curse from which his country at that time suffered. There were two guests who knocked at the gate of Shakuntala of whom one was accepted and the other refused. The king, as an embodiment of passion and worldliness, came to her and she readily yielded to his allurements. But when after that the duty of the higher life, the spirit of the forest ideal, stood before her in the guise of an ascetic, she in her absent-mindedness did not notice him. And what was the result? She lost her world of desire for which she had forsaken her truth. And in order to regain that world as her own by right she had to follow through suffering the path of self-conquest. The poet was aware of the two guests who sought entrance into the heart of his country,—the devotee of pleasure and power who comes secretly without giving his real name and insinuates himself into trustful acceptance, and the seeker of spiritual perfection who announces himself in a master's voice, in clear notes, अयमहं भो—'I am here!' And to his dismay he found his country baring her heart to the former to be betrayed by him. It is evident that kings of that period were deeply drawn into the eddy of self-indulgence and were fighting each other for power, the love of which leads men into the insanity of suicide. The fatal curse of falsehood is always generated when power and success are pursued for their own sake, when our baser passions shamelessly refuse all claims of justice and self-control. The poet had one lingering ray of hope in his heart. He could not but believe that his country had not lost her reverence for her *tapaswi*, the guest who brings to her door the message of everlasting life: only her mind was distracted by some temporary outbreak of temptation. He was certain that she would wake up in sanctifying sorrow, and give birth to her Bharata, the hero who would bring to her life unity and strength of truth. There was a note of assurance in the poet's voice when through his great poems Kumara-Sambhava and Shakuntala he called her to come back once again to her purity of life and realization of soul, the call which is true for other times and other countries also. For the curse still remains to be worked off by humanity for the inhospitable insult offered to the Eternal in Man.

The drama of Shakuntala opens with a hunting scene, where the king is in pursuit of an antelope. This indulgence in sport appears like a menace symbolising the spirit of the king's life clashing against the spirit of the forest-retreat, where all creatures find their protection of love. And the pleading of the forest-dwellers to the king, to spare the life of the deer, helplessly innocent and beautiful, is the pleading that rises from the heart of the whole drama.

> न खलु न खलु बाणः सन्निपात्योऽयमस्मिन्।
> मृदुनि मृगशरीरे पुष्प राशाविवाग्निः॥
>
> Never, oh never is the arrow meet for piercing the tender body of a deer, as the fire is not for burning flowers.

The living beauty, whose representative in this drama is Shakuntala, is not aggressively strong like the callous destructiveness of lust, but, through its frailness, it is sublimely great. And it is the poet's pleading which still rings in our ears against the ugly greed of commercialism in the modern age, against its mailed fist of earth-hunger, against the lust of the strong, which is grossly intent upon killing the Beautiful and piercing the heart of the Good to the quick. Once again sounds the warning of the forest, at the conclusion of the first act, when the king is engaged in fateful dalliance with the hermit girl: 'O *Tapaswis*, hasten to rescue the living spirit of the sacred forest, for Dushyanta, the lord of earth, whose pleasure is in hunting, is come.' It is the warning of India's past, and that warning still continues against the reckless carnival of the present time, celebrated by the lords of Earth, whose pleasure is in hunting to death with their ruthless machines all that is beautiful with the delicacy of life.

In *Kumara-Sambhava,* the friend and ally of Indra, the king of the Gods, is Madana, the god of desire. And he, in his blindness, imagines that he can unite Shiva and Parvati by the delusion created by the madness of the senses. It is the same as when we try to reach our perfection through wealth and power, through the intensity of boisterous self-seeking. That is not to be. At last Parvati's love was crowned with fulfilment through her penance of self-sacrifice. The moral of the *Kumara-Sambhava* is the same as the teaching of the Upanishad: त्यक्तकेन भुञ्जी, 'enjoy through renunciation'. मा गृध: कस्यस्विञ्जनम्, 'Enjoyment not be through greed.'

One thing which we must remember is, that the life in ancient India was not all forest life,—nor is the heart the only organ we possess in our vital organism. But the heart lies in the centre of our body; it purifies our blood and sends our life-current through the ramifications of all the channels in our body to the extremities of our limbs. Our *tapovana* was just such a vital centre of our social body. In it throbbed the rhythm of our life's ebb and flow: it gave truth to our thoughts, right impulse to our feelings, and guiding force to our work. We distinctly see, from the works of our poet, that the teaching of the forest was not towards the inertia of passivity, but towards true heroism and victory. It was not towards suppression of action, but its purification, towards giving it freedom of life by removing obstructions.

We know of other great systems in which there is a special insistence upon sacrifice and resignation. Just as heat is an important factor in the process of creation, so is pain an essential reagent in the formation of man's life. It melts the intractable hardness of his spirit, and wears away the unyielding crust which confines his heart. But the Upanishad enjoins renunciation, not by way of acceptance of pain, but for the purpose of enjoyment of truth. Such renunciation means an expansion into the Universal, a union with the Supreme. It is the renunciation of the cocoon for the freedom of the living wings. So that the ideal hermitage of ancient India was not a theatre where the spirit should wrestle with the flesh, or where the monastic order should try conclusions with the social order,—it was to establish a harmony between all our energies and the eternal reality. That is why the relations of Indian humanity with beast and bird and tree had attained an intimacy which may seem strange to people of other lands. Our poets have told us that the *tapovana* is *shantarasaspadam*,—

that the emotional quality peculiar to the forest-retreat is Peace, the peace which is the emotional counterpart of perfection. Just as the mingling of the colours of the spectrum gives us white light, so when the faculties of our mind, instead of being scattered, flow in a united stream, in harmony with the universal purpose, then does peace result—the peace which pervaded India's forest retreats, where man was not separate from, and had no quarrel with, the rest of his surroundings.

The two hermitages, which we have in the drama of Shakuntala, serve to give a magnitude to her joy and sorrow. One of these hermitages was on earth, the other on the border of the abode of immortals. In the first, we see the daughter of the hermitage watching in delight the union of the sweet flowering creeper with the mango tree round which it has twined; or busy rearing motherless young deer with handfuls of grass-seed, and picking the spear-grass out from their tender mouths, soothing the pricks with healing oil. This hermitage serves to make simple, natural and beautiful the love of the king for the hermit girl. The other hermitage was on the great cloud-like massive Hemakuta peak, standing like Shiva, with his locks of forest-growths and tangled creepers, lost in meditation, its gaze fixed on the sun. In this, Marichi, the revered preceptor of both Gods and Titans, together with his wife, was engaged in the pursuit of self-realization. There, when the young hermit boys would playfully snatch from the lioness her suckling cub, its distress would greatly exercise the tāpasa Mother. The second hermitage, in turn, serves to mellow with a great peace and purity the sorrow and insult which had driven Shakuntala there.

It has to be realized, that the former is of the earth, the region of the mortals, the latter of heaven, the region of the immortals. In other words, the one represents, 'what is', the other 'what should be'. The unceasing movement of 'what is' is towards 'what should be'. It finds its true freedom in that movement. The first is Sati—the Real—the last Shiva, the Good. In the life of Shakuntala, likewise, the 'what is' had to find its fulfilment in the 'what should be'. What was of the earth had to come, through the path of sorrow, to the border of heaven.

Those who have followed the evolution of the principal idea in this drama,—its seed-life in the soil of passion, its deliverance of harvest in the sunlight of the purity of self-abnegation,—will understand the great poet Goethe's criticism of Shakuntala, so tersely expressed in a single verse:

> Wouldst thou the flower of the spring and fruit of the mature year,
> Wouldst thou what charms and enraptures and what feeds and nourishes,
> Wouldst thou heaven and earth in one name entwined,
> I name thee, O Shakuntala, and all is said.

For in Shakuntala the reconciliation is given, through the penance of pain and sacrifice, to the pair of contraries, that which attracts and that which gives freedom, the limitation of self and the dedication of self to the Eternal. Goethe's own drama Faust, in its first and in its second part, tries to show the same separation and then reconciliation between the Real and the Good, between Sati and Shiva.

However, my point is this, that the scene of such reconciliation is depicted, both in *Shakuntala* and in *Kumara-Sambhava*, upon the background of the *tapovana,* showing whence the spring of the ideal harmony welled forth, the harmony between Nature and man, between the life in the individual and life in the All.

In the Ramayana, Rama and his companions, in their banishment, had to traverse forest after forest; they had to live in leaf-thatched huts, to sleep on the bare ground. But as their hearts felt their kinship with woodland, hill and stream, they were not in exile amidst these. Poets, brought up in an atmosphere of different ideals, would have taken this opportunity of depicting in dismal colours the hardship of the forest-life in order to bring out the martyrdom of Ramachandra in the strong emphasis of contrast. But, in the Ramayana, we are led to realize the greatness of the hero, not in an inimical struggle with nature, but in sympathy with it.

Sita, the daughter-in-law of a great kingly house, goes along the forest paths.

> एकैकं पादपं गुल्मं लतां वा पुष्पशालिनीम्
> अदृष्ठरूपां पश्यन्तौ रामं पप्रच्छ सावला।
> रमणीयान् बहुविधान् पादपान् कुसुमोत्करान्
> सीतावचनसंरब्ध आनयामास लक्ष्मणः।
> विचित्रवालुकाजलां हंससारसनादिताम्
> रेमे जनकराजस्य सुता प्रेक्षा तदा नदीम्।।

She asks Rama about the flowering trees and shrubs and creepers which she has not seen before. At her request, Lakshmana gathers and brings her plants of all kinds exuberant with flowers, and it delights her heart to see the forest rivers, variegated with their streams and sandy bank, resounding with the calls of heron and duck.

> सुरभ्यमासाद्य तु चित्रकूटम्
> मदीञ्च तां मालयवती सुतीर्थाम्
> ननन्द दृष्टो मृगपक्षिजुष्टाम्
> अहो च दुःखं पुरविप्रवासात्।।

When Rama first took his abode in the Chitrakuta peak, that delightful Chitrakuta, by the Malyavati river, with its easy slopes for landing, he forgot all the pain of leaving his home in the capital at the sight of these woodlands, alive with beast and bird.

दीर्घकालोषितस्तस्मिनौ गिरी गिरिवनप्रियः having lived on that hill for long, Rama, who was गरिवनप्रिय, lover of the mountain and the forest, said one day to Sita:

> न राजामंशमं भद्रे न कुचदिंभर्विनाभवः
> मनो मे बाधते दष्टा रमणीयमिमं गिरिम्
>
> When I look upon the beauties of this hill, the loss of my kingdom troubles me no longer, no does the separation from my friends cause me any pang.

When they went over to the Dandaka forest, they saw there a hermitage with a halo round it caused by the sacrificial fires blazing like the sun itself. This ashram was शरण्यम् सर्व्वभूतानाम् the refuge of all creatures; it was enfolded by *Brahmi Lakshmi*, the Spirit of the Infinite.

Thus passed Ramachandra's exile, now in woodland, now in hermitage scenes. The love which Rama and Sita bore each other united them, not only to each other, but to the Universe of life. That is why, when Sita was taken away, the loss seemed to be very great to the forest itself. The extinction of a star is doubtless a mighty event in the world of stars; and we would know, if we had pure vision, that any infliction of injury in the heart of a true lover gives rise to suffering which belongs to all the world. Sita's abduction robbed the forest of the most beautiful of its blossoms, the ineffable tenderness of human love,—that which imparted the mystery of a spiritual depth to all its sounds and forms.

Strangely enough, in Shakespeare's dramas, like those of Kālidāsa, we find a secret vein of complaint against the artificial life of the king's court, the life of ungrateful treachery and falsehood. And almost everywhere, in his dramas, forest scenes have been introduced in connection with some working of the life of unscrupulous ambition. It is perfectly obvious in 'Timon of Athens'—but there Nature offers no message or balm to the injured soul of man. In 'Cymbeline' the mountainous forest and the cave appear in their aspect of obstruction to life's opportunities—which only seem tolerable in comparison with the vicissitudes of fortune in the artificial court life, as expressed by Belarius:

> 'Did you but know the city's usuries,
> And felt them knowingly, the art o the court,
> As hard to leave as keep; whose top to climb
> Is certain falling, or so slippery that
> The fear's as bad as falling:'

In 'As You Like It' the Forest of Arden is didactic in its lessons,—It does not bring peace, but it preaches when it says:

> Hath not old custom made this life more sweet
> Than that of painted pomp? Are not these woods
> More free from peril than the envious court?

In the 'Tempest' in Prospero's treatment of Ariel and Caliban we realize man's struggle with nature and his longing to sever connection with her. In 'Macbeth', as a prelude to a bloody crime of treachery and treason, we are introduced to a scene of barren heath where the three witches appear as the personification of Nature's malignant forces; and in 'King Lear', it is the fury of a father's love turned into curses by the ingratitude born of the unnatural life of the court, that finds its symbol in the storm in the heath. The extreme tragic intensity of 'Hamlet' and 'Othello' is unrelieved by any touch of Nature's eternity. Excepting in a passing glimpse of a moonlight night in the love scene in the 'Merchant of Venice' Nature has not been allowed in other dramas of this series, including 'Romeo and Juliet' and 'Antony and Cleopatra', to contribute her own music to the music of man's love. In 'The Winter's Tale' the suspicious cruelty of a king's love stands bare in its relentlessness, and Nature cowers before it offering no consolation. I hope it is needless for me to say that these observations of mine are not for criticizing Shakespeare's great power as a dramatic poet, but to show in his works the gulf between nature and human nature owing to the tradition of his race and time. It cannot be said that beauty of nature is ignored in his writings; only he fails to recognize in them the truth of the interpenetration of human life and the cosmic life of the world. When literature takes for its object the exhibition of the explosiveness of a human passion, then necessarily that passion is made detached from its great context of the universe and is shown in its extreme violence generated by the instability of equilibrium. And this is what we find in Elizabethan dramas,—the clash of passions in their fury of self-assertion. We observe a sudden and a completely different attitude of mind in the later English poets, like Wordsworth and Shelley, which can only be attributed to the great mental change in Europe, at that particular period, through the influence of the newly-discovered philosophy of India which stirred the soul of Germany and strongly roused the attention of other Western countries.

In Milton's 'Paradise Lost', the very subject,—Man dwelling in the garden of Paradise,—seems to afford a special opportunity for bringing out the true greatness of man's relationship with Nature. But though the poet has described to us the beauties of the garden, though he has shown us the animals living there in amity and peace among themselves, there is no reality of kinship between them and man. They were created for man's enjoyment; man was their lord and master. We find no trace of the love of the first man and woman surpassing themselves and over-flowing the rest of creation, such as we find in the love scenes in *Kumara-Sambhava* and *Shakuntala* and in our Vaishnava lyrics, where love finds its symbols in the beauty of all natural objects. But in the seclusion of the bower, where the first man and woman rested in the garden of paradise,

Bird, beast, insect or worm
Durst enter none, such was their awe of man.

At the bottom of this gulf between man and Nature there is the lack of the message,—ईशावास्यमिदम् सर्व्वम् 'know all that is, as enveloped by God'. According to this epic of the West, God remains aloof to receive glorification from his creatures. The same idea persists in the case of man's relation to the rest of creation.

Not that India denied the superiority of man, but the test of that superiority lies, according to her, in the comprehensiveness of sympathy,—not in the aloofness of absolute distinction.

The love of Rama and Sita, in the *Uttara Rama Charita* has permeated the surrounding earth, water and sky with its exuberance. When Rama, for the second time, finds himself on the banks of the Godavari, he exclaims: यत्र द्रुमा अपि मृगा अपि बान्धवो मे 'this is the place even whose deer and whose trees are my friends'. When after Sita's exile he comes across some former haunt of theirs, he laments that his heart, even though turned to stone, melts when he sees the trees and the deer and the birds which Sita's own hands used to nourish with water, seed and grass.

In the *Meghaduta,* the exiled Yaksha is not shut up within himself in his grief. The very agony of his separation from his loved one serves to scatter his heart over the woods and streams, enriched by the prodigality of the rains. And so the casual longing of a love-sick individual has become part of the symphony of the universe. And this is the outcome of the spirit of teaching which springs from the ancient forest.

India holds sacred, and counts as places of pilgrimage, all spots which display a special beauty or splendour of nature. These had no original attraction, or account of any special fitness to be cultivated, or lived upon. Here, man is free, not to look upon nature as a source of supply of his necessities but to realize his soul beyond himself. The Himalayas of India are sacred and the Vindhya Hills. Her majestic rivers are sacred. Like Manasa and the confluence of the Ganges and the Jamuna are sacred. India has saturated with her love and worship the great nature with which her children are surround, whose light fills their eyes with gladness, whose water cleanses them, whose food gives them life, and from whose majestic mystery come forth constant messages of the infinite in music, scent, and colour, bringing awakening to their souls. India has gained the world through worship,—through communion of soul. And this is her heritage from her forest sanctuary.

Learning does not depend on the school alone. Much more does it depend upon the receptive mind of the pupil. There are scholars who win diplomas, but fail to learn. So do many of us frequent-places of pilgrimage, but come away from the door of the invisible shrine, where dwells the Eternal spirit of the place. They imagine that the mere journey to a place held sacred is sanctifying, that some peculiar virtues reside in particular soils and waters. Their minds do not shrink at the unspeakable pollution of the water and the air of those places, the pollution to which they themselves contribute, and the moral filth which they allow to accumulate there. The salutation of worship to the all-pervading divinity in the fire, water and plants, in all creation, has been bequeathed to us by our ancestors in the following immortal verse:

यो देवोऽग्नो योऽप्सु यो विश्वम् भुवनमाविवेश

य ओषधिषु यो वनस्यतिषु तस्मै देवाय नमो नमः।

But we seem to have forgotten that all worship has also its duty of service, and in order truly to realize and approach the divine presence in the water and the air we have reverently to keep them clean and pure and healthful. The more our country has lost its powers of soul, the more elaborate have become its outward practices. The inner illumination of consciousness which is not only the object, but also the means of all true worship has, in our case, given place to the grossness of the senses and deadness of mere repetition of habits. But, even in these days of our spiritual sluggishness, I am unwilling to accept these mechanical practices as a permanent feature of India. It is absurd to believe as well-founded the idea, that a bath in a particular stream procures for the bather and millions of his ancestors a more favourable circumstance and desirable accommodation in the after life. Nor am I able to respect such a belief as something admirable. But my reverence goes out to the man, who when taking an immersion, can receive the water upon his body, and into his mind as well, in a devout spirit;—for him the grimy touch of habit has not been able to tarnish the everlasting mystery which is in fire and earth, water and food; he has overcome, by the sensitiveness of his soul, the gross materialism,—the spirit of contempt, of the average man, which impels the latter to look upon water as mere liquid matter.

So long as man was unable to realize an all-pervading law in the material world, his knowledge remained petty and unfruitful. But the modern man feels himself united to the universe by physical laws governing all. This is Science's great achievement.

The quest which India set to herself was to realize the same unity in the realm of the spirit, that is to say, in its completeness. Such union enables us to see Him in all who is above all else. And the wisdom, which grew up in the quiet of the forest shade, came out of the realization of this Greater-than-all in the heart of the all.

Let no one think that I desire to extol this achievement, as the one and the only consummation. I would rather insist on the inexhaustible variety of the human race, which does not grow straight up, like a Palmyra tree, on a single stem, but like a banian tree spreads itself in ever-new trunks and branches. Man's history is organic, and deep-seated life-forces work towards its growth. It is hopeless to cater to some clamorous demand of the moment, by endeavouring to fashion the history of one people on the model of another,—however flourishing the latter may be. A small foot may be the sign of aristocratic descent, but the Chinese woman's artificial attempt has only resulted in cramped feet. For India to force herself along European lines of growth would not make her Europe, but only a distorted India.

That is why we must be careful today to try to find out the principles, by means of which India will be able for certain to realize herself. That principle is neither commercialism, nor nationalism. It is universalism. It is not merely self-determination, but self-conquest and self-dedication. This was recognized and followed in India's forests of old; its truth was declared in the Upanishad and expounded in the Gita; the Lord Buddha renounced the world that he might make this truth a household word for all mankind; Kabir, Nanak and other great spirits of India continued to proclaim its message. India's grand achievement, which is still stored deep within her heart, is waiting, to unite within itself Hindu, Moslem, Buddhist, and Christian, not by force, not by the apathy of resignation, but in the harmony of active co-operation.

An almost impossible task has been set to India by her Providence, a task given to no other great countries in the world. Among her children and her guests differences in race and language, religion and social ideals are as numerous as great, and she has to achieve the difficult unity which has to be true in spite of the separateness that is real. The best and the greatest of her sons have called us in immortal words to realize the unity of souls in all human beings and thus fulfil the highest mission of our history; but we have merely played with their words, and we have rigidly kept apart man from man, and class from class, setting up permanent barriers of indignity between them. We remained unconscious of the suicidal consequence of such divisions, so long as we lay stationary in the torpor of centuries, but when the alien world suddenly broke upon our sleep and dragged us on in its impetus of movement, our disjointed heterogeneity set up in its lumbering unwieldiness an internal clash and crush and unrhythmic stagger which is both ludicrous and tragic at the same moment. So long as we disregard or misread the message of our ancient forest, the message of all-pervading truth in humanity, the message of all-comprehensive union of souls which rises above all differences and goes deeper than mere expediency, we shall have to go on suffering sorrow after sorrow and endless humiliation, and in all things futility.

(1919)

30 Nationalism in the West

Man's history is being shaped according to the difficulties it encounters. These have offered us problems and claimed their solutions from us, the penalty of non-fulfilment being death or degradation.

These difficulties have been different in different peoples of the earth, and in the manner of our overcoming them lies our distinction.

The Scythians of the earlier period of Asiatic history had to struggle with the scarcity of their natural resources. The easiest solution that they could think of was to organize their whole population, men, women, and children, into bands of robbers. And they were irresistible to those who were chiefly engaged in the constructive work of social cooperation.

But fortunately for man the easiest path is not his truest path. If his nature were not as complex as it is, if it were as simple as that of a pack of hungry wolves, then, by this time, those hordes of marauders would have overrun the whole earth. But man, when confronted with difficulties, has to acknowledge that he is man, that he has his responsibilities to the higher faculties of his nature, by ignoring which he may achieve success that is immediate, perhaps, but that will become a death trap to him. For what are obstacles to the lower creatures are opportunities to the higher life of man.

To India has been given her problem from the beginning of history—it is the race problem. Races ethnologically different have come in this country in close contact. This fact has been and still continues to be the most important one in our history. It is our mission to face it and prove our humanity in dealing with it in the fullest truth. Until we fulfil our mission all other benefits will be denied us.

There are other peoples in the world who have obstacles in their physical surroundings to overcome, or the menace of their powerful neighbours. They have organized their power till they are not only reasonably free from the tyranny of Nature and human neighbours, but have a surplus of it left in their hands to employ against others. But in India, our difficulties being internal, our history has been the history of continual social adjustment and not that of organized power for defence and aggression.

Neither the colourless vagueness of cosmopolitanism, nor the fierce self-idolatry of nation-worship is the goal of human history. And India has been trying to accomplish her task through social regulation of differences, on the one hand, and the spiritual recognition of unity, on the other. She has made grave errors in setting up the boundary walls too rigidly between races, in perpetuating the results of inferiority in her classifications; often she has crippled her children's minds and narrowed their lives in order to fit them into her social forms; but for centuries new experiments have been made and adjustments carried out.

Her mission has been like that of a hostess to provide proper accommodation to her numerous guests whose habits and requirements are different from one another. It is giving rise to infinite complexities whose solution depends not merely upon tactfulness but sympathy and true realization of the unity of man. Towards this realization have worked from the early time of the Upanishads up to the present moment, a series of great spiritual teachers, whose one object has been to set at naught all differences of man by the overflow of our consciousness of God. In fact, our history has not been of the rise and fall of kingdoms, of fights for political supremacy. In our country records of these days have been despised and forgotten. For they in no way represent the true history of our people. Our history is that of our social life and attainment of spiritual ideals.

But we feel that our task is not yet done. The world-flood has swept over our country, new elements have been introduced, and wider adjustments are waiting to be made.

We feel this all the more, because the teaching and example of the West have entirely run counter to what we think was given to India to accomplish. In the West the national machinery of commerce and politics turns out neatly compressed bales of humanity which have their use and high market value; but they are bound in iron hoops, labelled and separated off with scientific care and precision. Obviously God made man to be human; but this modern product has such marvellous square-cut finish, savouring of gigantic manufacture, that the Creator will find it difficult to recognize it as a thing of spirit and a creature made in his own divine image.

But I am anticipating. What I was about to say is this, take it in whatever spirit you like, here is India, of about fifty centuries at least, who tried to live peacefully and think deeply, the India devoid of all politics, the India of no nations, whose one ambition has been to know this world as of soul, to live here every moment of her life in the meek spirit of adoration, in the glad consciousness of an eternal and personal relationship with it. This is the remote portion of humanity, childlike in its manner, with the wisdom of the old, upon which burst the Nation of the West.

Through all the fights and intrigues and deceptions of her earlier history India had remained aloof. Because her homes, her fields, her temples of worship, her schools, where her teachers and students lived together in the atmosphere of simplicity and devotion and learning, her village self-government with its simple laws and peaceful administration—all these truly belonged to her. But her thrones were not her concern. They passed over her head like clouds, now tinged with purple gorgeousness, now black with the threat of thunder. Often they brought devastations in their wake, but they were like catastrophes of nature whose traces are soon forgotten.

But this time it was different. It was not a mere drift over her surface of life,—drift of cavalry and foot soldiers, richly caparisoned elephants, white tents and canopies, strings of patient camels bearing the loads of royalty, bands of kettledrums and flutes, marble domes of mosques, palaces and tombs, like the bubbles of the foaming wine of extravagance; stories of treachery and loyal devotion, of changes of fortune, of dramatic surprises of fate. This time it was the Nation of the West driving its tentacles of machinery deep down into the soil.

Therefore, I say to you, it is we who are called as witnesses to give evidence as to what the Nation has been to humanity. We had known the hordes of Moghals and Pathans who invaded India, but we had known them as human races, with their own religions and customs, likes and dislikes,—we had never known them as a nation. We loved and hated them as occasions arose; we fought for them and against them, talked with them in a language which was theirs as well as our own, and guided the destiny of the Empire in which we had our active share. But this time we had to deal, not with kings, not with human races, but with a nation,—we, who are no nation ourselves.

Now let us from our own experience answer the question, What is this Nation?

A nation, in the sense of the political and economic union of a people, is that aspect which a whole population assumes when organized for a mechanical purpose. Society as such has no ulterior purpose. It is an end in itself. It is a spontaneous self-expression of man as a social being. It is a natural regulation of human relationships, so that men can develop ideals of life in cooperation with one another. It has also a political side, but this is only for a special purpose. It is for self-preservation. It is merely the side of power, not of human ideals. And in the early days it had its separate place in society, restricted to the professionals. But when with the help of science and the perfecting of organization this power begins to grow and brings in harvests of wealth, then it crosses its boundaries with amazing rapidity. For then it goads all its neighbouring societies with greed of material prosperity, and consequent mutual jealousy, and by the fear of each other's growth into powerfulness. The time comes when it can stop no longer, for the competition grows keener, organization grows vaster, and selfishness attains supremacy. Trading upon the greed and fear of man, it occupies more and more space in society, and at last becomes its ruling force.

It is just possible that you have lost through habit consciousness that the living bonds of society are breaking up, and giving place to merely mechanical organization. But you see signs of it everywhere. It is owing to this that war has been declared between man and woman, because the natural thread is snapping which holds them together in harmony; because man is driven to professionalism, producing wealth for himself and others, continually turning the wheel of power for his own sake or for the sake of the universal officialdom, leaving woman alone to wither and to die or to fight her own battle unaided. And thus there where cooperation is natural has intruded competition. The very psychology of men and women about their mutual relation is changing and becoming the psychology of the primitive fighting elements rather than of humanity seeking its completeness through the union based upon mutual self-surrender. For the elements which have lost their living bond of reality have lost the meaning of their existence. They, like gaseous particles, forced into a too narrow space, come in continual conflict with each other till they burst the very arrangement which holds them in bondage.

Then look at those who call themselves anarchists, who resent the imposition of power, in any form whatever, upon the individual. The only reason for this is that power has become too abstract—it is a scientific product made in the political laboratory of the Nation, through the dissolution of the personal humanity.

And what is the meaning of these strikes in the economic world, which like the prickly shrubs in a barren soil shoot up with renewed vigour each time they are cut down? What, but that the wealth-producing mechanism is incessantly growing into vast stature, out of proportion to all other needs of society,—and the full reality of man is more and more crushed under its weight. This state of things inevitably gives rise to eternal feuds among the elements freed from the wholeness and wholesomeness of human ideals, and interminable economic war is waged between capital and labour. For greed of wealth and power can never have a limit, and compromise of self-interest can never attain the final spirit of reconciliation. They must go on breeding jealousy and suspicion to the end—the end which only comes through some sudden catastrophe or a spiritual rebirth.

When this organization of politics and commerce, whose other name is the Nation, becomes all powerful at the cost of the harmony of the higher social life, then it is an evil day for humanity. When a father becomes a gambler and his obligations to his family take the secondary place in his mind, then he is no longer a man, but an automaton led by the power of greed. Then he can do things which, in his normal state of mind, he would be ashamed to do. It is the same thing with society. When it allows itself to be turned into a perfect organization of power, then there are few crimes which it is unable to perpetrate. Because success is the object and justification of a machine, while goodness only is the end and purpose of man. When this engine of organization begins to attain a vast size, and those who are mechanics are made into parts of the machine, then the personal man is eliminated to a phantom, everything becomes a revolution of policy carried out by the human parts of the machine, requiring no twinge of pity or moral responsibility. It is not unusual that even through this apparatus the moral nature of man tries to assert itself, but the whole series of ropes and pulleys creak and cry, the forces of the human heart become entangled among the forces of the human automaton, and only with difficulty can the moral purpose transmit itself into some tortured shape of result.

This abstract being, the Nation, is ruling India. We have seen in our country some brand of tinned food advertised as entirely made and packed without being touched by hand. This description applies to the governing of India, which is as little touched by the human hand as possible. The governors need not know our language, need not come into personal touch with us except as officials; they can aid or hinder our aspirations from a disdainful distance, they can lead us on a certain path of policy and then pull us back again with the manipulation of office red tape; the newspapers of England, in whose columns London street accidents are recorded with some decency of pathos, need but take the scantiest notice of calamities happening in India over areas of land sometimes larger than the British Isles.

But we, who are governed, are not a mere abstraction. We, on our side, are individuals with living sensibilities. What comes to us in the shape of a mere bloodless policy may pierce into the very core of our life, may threaten the whole future of our people with a perpetual helplessness of emasculation, and yet may never touch the chord of humanity on the other side, or touch it in the most inadequately feeble manner. Such wholesale and universal acts of fearful responsibility man can never perform, with such a degree of systematic unawareness, where he is an individual human being. These only become possible where the man is represented by an octopus of abstractions, sending out its wriggling arms in all directions of space, and fixing its innumerable suckers even into the faraway future. In this reign of the nation, the governed are pursued by suspicions; and these are the suspicions of a tremendous mass of organized brain and muscle. Punishments are meted out, leaving a trail of miseries across a large bleeding tract of the human heart; but these punishments are dealt by a mere abstract force, in which a whole population of a distant country has lost its human personality.

I have not come here, however, to discuss the question as it affects my own country, but as it affects the future of all humanity. It is not about the British Government, but the government by the Nation—the Nation which is the organized self-interest of a whole people, where it is the least human and the least spiritual. Our only intimate experience of the Nation is with the British Nation, and as far as the government by the Nation goes there are reasons to believe that it is one of the best. Then again we have to consider that the West is necessary to the East. We are complementary to each other because of our different outlooks upon life which have given us different aspects of truth. Therefore if it be true that the spirit of the West has come upon our fields in the guise of a storm it is all the same scattering living seeds that are immortal. And when in India we shall be able to assimilate in our life what is permanent in Western civilization we shall be in the position to bring about a reconciliation of these two great worlds. Then will come to an end the one-sided dominance which is galling. What is more, we have to recognize that the history of India does not belong to one particular race but is of a process of creation to which various races of the world contributed—the Dravidians and the Aryans, the ancient Greeks and the Persians, the Mohamedans of the West and those of central Asia. At last now has come the turn of the English to become true to this history and bring to it the tribute of their life, and we neither have the right nor the power to exclude this people from the building of the destiny of India. Therefore what I say about the Nation has more to do with the history of Man than specially with that of India.

This history has come to a stage when the moral man, the complete man, is more and more giving way, almost without knowing it, to make room for the political and the commercial man, the man of the limited purpose. This, aided by the wonderful progress in science, is assuming gigantic proportion and power, causing the upset of man's moral balance, obscuring his human side under the shadow of soul-less organization. Its iron grip we have felt at the root of our life, and for the sake of humanity we must stand up and give warning to all, that this nationalism is a cruel epidemic of evil that is sweeping over the human world of the present age, eating into its moral vitality.

I have a deep love and a great respect for the British race as human beings. It has produced great-hearted men, thinkers of great thoughts, doers of great deeds. It has given rise to a great literature. I know that these people love justice and freedom, and hate lies. They are clean in their minds, frank in their manners, true in their friendships; in their behaviour they are honest and reliable. The personal experience which I have had of their literary men has roused my admiration not merely for their power of thought or expression but for their chivalrous humanity. We have felt the greatness of this people as we feel the sun; but as for the Nation, it is for us a thick mist of a stifling nature covering the sun itself.

This government by the Nation is neither British nor anything else; it is an applied science and therefore more or less similar in its principles wherever it is used. It is like a hydraulic press, whose pressure is impersonal and on that account completely effective. The amount of its power may vary in different engines. Some may even be driven by hand, thus leaving a margin of comfortable looseness in their tension, but in spirit and in method their differences are small. Our government might have been Dutch, or French, or Portuguese, and its essential features would have remained much the same as they are now. Only perhaps, in some cases, the organization might not have been so densely perfect, and, therefore, some shreds of the human might still have been clinging to the wreck, allowing us to deal with something which resembles our own throbbing heart.

Before the Nation came to rule over us we had other governments which were foreign, and these, like all governments, had some element of the machine in them. But the difference between them and the government by the Nation is like the difference between the hand loom and the power loom. In the products of the hand loom the magic of man's living fingers finds its expression, and its hum harmonizes with the music of life. But the power loom is relentlessly lifeless and accurate and monotonous in its production.

We must admit that during the personal government of the former days there have been instances of tyranny, injustice and extortion. They caused sufferings and unrest from which we are glad to be rescued. The protection of law is not only a boon, but it is a valuable lesson to us. It is teaching us the discipline which is necessary for the stability of civilization and continuity of progress. We are realizing through it that there is a universal standard of justice to which all men irrespective of their caste and colour have their equal claim.

This reign of law in our present Government in India has established order in this vast land inhabited by peoples different in their races and customs. It has made it possible for these peoples to come in closer touch with one another and cultivate a communion of aspiration.

But this desire for a common bond of comradeship among the different races of India has been the work of the spirit of the West, not that of the Nation of the West. Wherever in Asia the people have received the true lesson of the West it is in spite of the Western Nation. Only because Japan had been able to resist the dominance of this Western Nation could she acquire the benefit of the Western Civilization in fullest measure. Though China has been poisoned at the very spring of her moral and physical life by this Nation, her struggle to receive the best lessons of the West may yet be successful if not hindered by the Nation. It was only the other day that Persia woke up from her age-long sleep at the call of the West to be instantly trampled into stillness by the Nation. The same phenomenon prevails in this country also, where the people are hospitable but the nation has proved itself to be otherwise, making an Eastern guest feel humiliated to stand before you as a member of the humanity of his own motherland.

In India we are suffering from this conflict between the spirit of the West and the Nation of the West. The benefit of the Western civilization is doled out to us in a miserly measure by the Nation trying to regulate the degree of nutrition as near the zero point of vitality as possible. The portion of education allotted to us is so raggedly insufficient that it ought to outrage the sense of decency of a Western humanity. We have seen in these countries how the people are encouraged and trained and given every facility to fit themselves for the great movements of commerce and industry spreading over the world, while in India the only assistance we get is merely to be jeered at by the Nation for lagging behind. While depriving us of our opportunities and reducing our education to a minimum required for conducting a foreign government, this Nation pacifies its conscience by calling us names, by sedulously giving currency to the arrogant cynicism that the East is east and the

West is west and never the twain shall meet. If we must believe our schoolmaster in his taunt that after nearly two centuries of his tutelage, India not only remains unfit for self-government but unable to display originality in her intellectual attainments, must we ascribe it to something in the nature of Western culture and our inherent incapacity to receive it or to the judicious niggardliness of the Nation that has taken upon itself the white man's burden of civilizing the East? That Japanese people have some qualities which we lack we may admit, but that our intellect is naturally unproductive compared to theirs we cannot accept even from them whom it is dangerous for us to contradict.

The truth is that the spirit of conflict and conquest is at the origin and in the centre of the Western nationalism; its basis is not social cooperation. It has evolved a perfect organization of power but not spiritual idealism. It is like the pack of predatory creatures that must have its victims. With all its heart it cannot bear to see its hunting grounds converted into cultivated fields. In fact, these nations are fighting among themselves for the extension of their victims and their reserve forests. Therefore the Western Nation acts like a dam to check the free flow of the Western civilization into the country of the No-Nation. Because this civilization is the civilization of power, therefore it is exclusive, it is naturally unwilling to open its sources of power to those whom it has selected for its purposes of exploitation.

But all the same moral law is the law of humanity, and the exclusive civilization which thrives upon others who are barred from its benefit carries its own death sentence in its moral limitations. The slavery that it gives rise to unconsciously drains its own love of freedom dry. The helplessness with which it weighs down its world of victims exerts its force of gravitation every moment upon the power that creates it. And the greater part of the world which is being denuded of its self-sustaining life by the Nation will one day become the most terrible of all its burdens ready to drag it down into the bottom of destruction. Whenever Power removes all checks from its path to make its career easy, it triumphantly rides into its ultimate crash of death. Its moral brake becomes slacker every day without its knowing it, and its slippery path of ease becomes its path of doom.

Of all things in Western civilization, those which this Western Nation has given us in a most generous measure are law and order. While the small feeding bottle of our education is nearly dry, and sanitation sucks its own thumb in despair, the military organization, the magisterial offices, the police, the Criminal Investigation Department, the secret spy system, attain to an abnormal girth in their waists, occupying every inch of our country. This is to maintain order. But is not this order merely a negative good? Is it not for giving people's life greater opportunities for the freedom of development? Its perfection is the perfection of an egg-shell whose true value lies in the security it affords to the chick and its nourishment and not in the convenience it offers to the person at the breakfast table. Mere administration is unproductive, it is not creative, not being a living thing. It is a steam-roller, formidable in its weight and power, having its uses, but it does not help the soil to become fertile. When after its enormous toil it comes to offer us its boon of peace we can but murmur under our breath that 'peace is good but not more so than life which is God's own great boon'.

On the other hand, our former governments were woefully lacking in many of the advantages of the modern government. But because those were not the governments by the Nation, their texture was loosely woven, leaving big gaps through which our own life sent its threads and imposed its designs. I am quite sure in those days we had things that were extremely distasteful to us. But we know that when we walk barefooted upon a ground strewn with gravel, gradually our feet come to adjust themselves to the caprices of the inhospitable earth; while if the tiniest particle of a gravel finds its lodgment inside our shoes we can never forget and forgive its intrusion. And these shoes are the government by the Nation,—it is tight, it regulates our steps with a closed up system, within which our feet have only the slightest liberty to make their own adjustments. Therefore, when you produce your statistics to compare the number of gravels which our feet had to encounter in former days with the paucity in the present régime, they hardly touch the real points. It is not the numerousness of the outside obstacles but the comparative powerlessness of the individual to cope with them. This narrowness of freedom is an evil which is more radical not because of its quantity but because of its nature. And we cannot but acknowledge this paradox, that while the spirit of the West marches under its banner of freedom, the Nation of the West forges its iron chains of organization which are the most relentless and unbreakable that have ever been manufactured in the whole history of man.

When the humanity of India was not under the government of the Organization, the elasticity of change was great enough to encourage men of power and spirit to feel that they had their destinies in their own hands. The hope of the unexpected was never absent, and a freer play of imagination, both on the part of the governor and the governed, had its effect in the making of history. We were not confronted with a future which was a dead white wall of granite blocks eternally guarding against the expression and extension of our own powers, the hopelessness of which lies in the reason that these powers are becoming atrophied at their very roots by the scientific process of paralysis. For every single individual in the country of the no-nation is completely in the grip of a whole nation,—whose tireless vigilance, being the vigilance of a machine, has not the human power to overlook or to discriminate. At the least pressing of its button the monster organization becomes all eyes, whose ugly stare of inquisitiveness cannot be avoided by a single person amongst the immense multitude of the ruled. At the least turn of its screw, by the fraction of an inch, the grip is tightened to the point of suffocation around every man, woman and child of a vast population, for whom no escape is imaginable in their own country, or even in any country outside their own.

It is the continual and stupendous dead pressure of this unhuman upon the living human under which the modern world is groaning. Not merely the subject races, but you who live under the delusion that you are free, are every day sacrificing your freedom and humanity to this fetish of nationalism, living in the dense poisonous atmosphere of world-wide suspicion and greed and panic.

I have seen in Japan the voluntary submission of the whole people to the trimming of their minds and clipping of their freedom by their government, which through various educational agencies regulates their thoughts, manufactures their feelings, becomes suspiciously watchful when they show signs of inclining toward the spiritual, leading them through a narrow path not toward what is true but what is necessary for the complete welding of them into one uniform mass according to its own recipe. The people accept this all-pervading mental slavery with cheerfulness and pride because of their nervous desire to turn themselves into a machine of power, called the Nation, and emulate other machines in their collective worldliness.

When questioned as to the wisdom of its course the newly converted fanatic of nationalism answers that 'so long as nations are rampant in this world we have not the option freely to develop our higher humanity. We must utilize every faculty that we possess to resist the evil by assuming it ourselves in the fullest degree. For the only brotherhood possible in the modern world is the brotherhood of hooliganism.' The recognition of the fraternal bond of love between Japan and Russia, which has lately been celebrated with an immense display of rejoicing in Japan, was not owing to any sudden recrudescence of the spirit of Christianity or of Buddhism,—but it was a bond established according to the modern faith in a surer relationship of mutual menace of bloodshedding. Yes, one cannot but acknowledge that these facts are the facts of the world of the Nation, and the only moral of it is that all the peoples of the earth should strain their physical, moral and intellectual resources to the utmost to defeat one another in the wrestling match of powerfulness. In the ancient days Sparta paid all her attention to becoming powerful—and she did become so by crippling her humanity, and she died of the amputation.

But it is no consolation to us to know that the weakening of humanity from which the present age is suffering is not limited to the subject races, and that its ravages are even more radical because insidious and voluntary in peoples who are hypnotized into believing that they are free. This bartering of your higher aspirations of life for profit and power has been your own free choice, and I leave you there, at the wreckage of your soul, contemplating your protuberant prosperity. But will you never be called to answer for organizing the instincts of self-aggrandizement of whole peoples into perfection, and calling it good? I ask you what disaster has there ever been in the history of man, in its darkest period, like this terrible disaster of the Nation fixing its fangs deep into the naked flesh of the world, taking permanent precautions against its natural relaxation?

You, the people of the West, who have manufactured this abnormality, can you imagine the desolating despair of this haunted world of suffering man possessed by the ghastly abstraction of the organizing man? Can you put yourself into the position of the peoples, who seem to have been doomed to an eternal damnation of their own humanity, who not only must suffer continual curtailment of their manhood, but even raise their voices in paeans of praise for the benignity of a mechanical apparatus in its interminable parody of providence?

Have you not seen, since the commencement of the existence of the Nation, that the dread of it has been the one goblin-dread with which the whole world has been trembling? Wherever there is a dark corner, there is the suspicion of its secret malevolence; and people live in a perpetual distrust of its back where it has no eyes. Every sound of footstep, every rustle of movement in the neighbourhood, sends a thrill of terror all around. And this terror is the parent of all that is base in man's nature. It makes one almost openly unashamed of inhumanity. Clever lies become matters of self-congratulation. Solemn pledges become a farce,—laughable for their very solemnity. The Nation, with all its paraphernalia of power and prosperity, its flags and pious hymns, its blasphemous prayers in the churches, and the literary mock thunders of its patriotic bragging, cannot hide the fact that the Nation is the greatest evil for the Nation, that all its precautions are against it, and any new birth of its fellow in the world is always followed in its mind by the dread of a new peril. Its one wish is to trade on the feebleness of the rest of the world, like some insects that are bred in the paralyzed flesh of victims kept just enough alive to make them toothsome and nutritious. Therefore it is ready to send its poisonous fluid into the vitals of the other living peoples, who, not being nations, are harmless. For this the Nation has had and still has its richest pasture in Asia. Great China, rich with her ancient wisdom and social ethics, her discipline of industry and self-control, is like a whale awakening the lust of spoil in the heart of the Nation. She is already carrying in her quivering flesh harpoons sent by the unerring aim of the Nation, the creature of science and selfishness. Her pitiful attempt to shake off her traditions of humanity, her social ideals, and spend her last exhausted resources to drill herself into modern efficiency, is thwarted at every step by the Nation. It is tightening its financial ropes round her, trying to drag her up on the shore and cut her into pieces, and then go and offer public thanksgiving to God for supporting the one existing evil and shattering the possibility of a new one. And for all this the Nation has been claiming the gratitude of history, and all eternity for its exploitation; ordering its band of praise to be struck up from end to end of the world, declaring itself to be the salt of the earth, the flower of humanity, the blessing of God hurled with all his force upon the naked skulls of the world of no nations.

I know what your advice will be. You will say, form yourselves into a nation, and resist this encroachment of the Nation. But is this the true advice? that of a man to a man? Why should this be a necessity? I could well believe you, if you had said, Be more good, more just, more true in your relation to man, control your greed, make your life wholesome in its simplicity and let your consciousness of the divine in humanity be more perfect in its expression. But must you say that it is not the soul, but the machine, which is of the utmost value to ourselves, and that man's salvation depends upon his disciplining himself into a perfection of the dead rhythm of wheels and counterwheels? That machine must be pitted against machine, and nation against nation, in an endless bullfight of politics?

You say, these machines will come into an agreement, for their mutual protection, based upon a conspiracy of fear. But will this federation of steam-boilers supply you with a soul, a soul which has her conscience and her God? What is to happen to that larger part of the world, where fear will have no hand in restraining you? Whatever safety they now enjoy, those countries of no nation, from the unbridled license of forge and hammer and turn-screw, results from the mutual jealousy of the powers. But when, instead of being numerous separate machines, they become riveted into one organized gregariousness of gluttony, commercial and political, what remotest chance of hope will remain for those others, who have lived and suffered, have loved and worshipped, have thought deeply and worked with meekness, but whose only crime has been that they have not organized?

But, you say, 'That does not matter, the unfit must go to the wall—they shall *die,* and this is science.'

No, for the sake of your own salvation, I say, they shall *live,* and this is truth. It is extremely bold of me to say so, but I assert that man's world is a moral world, not because we blindly agree to believe it, but because it is so in truth which would be dangerous for us to ignore. And this moral nature of man cannot be divided into convenient compartments for its preservation. You cannot secure it for your home consumption with protective tariff walls, while in foreign parts making it enormously accommodating in its free trade of license.

Has not this truth already come home to you now, when this cruel war has driven its claws into the vitals of Europe? When her hoard of wealth is bursting into smoke and her humanity is shattered into bits on her battlefields? You ask in amazement what has she done to deserve this? The answer is, that the West has been systematically petrifying her moral nature in order to lay a solid foundation for her gigantic abstractions of efficiency. She has all along been starving the life of the personal man into that of the professional.

In your medieval age in Europe, the simple and the natural man, with all his violent passions and desires, was engaged in trying to find out a reconciliation in the conflict between the flesh and the spirit. All through the turbulent career of her vigorous youth the temporal and the spiritual forces both acted strongly upon her nature, and were moulding it into completeness of moral personality. Europe owes all her greatness in humanity to that period of discipline,—the discipline of the man in his human integrity.

Then came the age of intellect, of science. We all know that intellect is impersonal. Our life is one with us, also our heart, but our mind can be detached from the personal man and then only can it freely move in its world of thoughts. Our intellect is an ascetic who wears no clothes, takes no food, knows no sleep, has no wishes, feels no love or hatred or pity for human limitations, who only reasons, unmoved through the vicissitudes of life. It burrows to the roots of things, because it has no personal concern with the thing itself. The grammarian walks straight through all poetry and goes to the root of words without obstruction. Because he is not seeking reality, but law. When he finds the law, he is able to teach people how to master words. This is a power,—the power which fulfils some special usefulness, some particular need of man.

Reality is the harmony which gives to the component parts of a thing the equilibrium of the whole. You break it, and have in your hands the nomadic atoms fighting against one another, therefore unmeaning. Those who covet power try to get mastery of these aboriginal fighting elements and through some narrow channels force them into some violent service for some particular needs of man.

This satisfaction of man's needs is a great thing. It gives him freedom in the material world. It confers on him the benefit of a greater range of time and space. He can do things in a shorter time and occupies a larger space with more thoroughness of advantage. Therefore he can easily outstrip those who live in a world of a slower time and of space less fully occupied.

This progress of power attains more and more rapidity of pace. And, for the reason that it is a detached part of man, it soon outruns the complete humanity. The moral man remains behind, because it has to deal with the whole reality, not merely with the law of things, which is impersonal and therefore abstract.

Thus, man with his mental and material power far outgrowing his moral strength, is like an exaggerated giraffe whose head has suddenly shot up miles away from the rest of him, making normal communication difficult to establish. This greedy head, with its huge dental organization, has been munching all the topmost foliage of the world, but the nourishment is too late in reaching his digestive organs, and his heart is suffering from want of blood. Of this present disharmony in man's nature the West seems to have been blissfully unconscious. The enormity of its material success has diverted all its attention toward self-congratulation on its bulk. The optimism of its logic goes on basing the calculations of its good fortune upon the indefinite prolongation of its railway lines toward eternity. It is superficial enough to think that all tomorrows are merely todays with the repeated additions of twenty-four hours. It has no fear of the chasm, which is opening wider every day, between man's ever-growing storehouses and the emptiness of his hungry humanity. Logic does not know that, under the lowest bed of endless strata of wealth and comforts, earthquakes are being hatched to restore the balance of the moral world, and one day the gaping gulf of spiritual vacuity will draw into its bottom the store of things that have their eternal love for the dust.

Man in his fulness is not powerful, but perfect. Therefore, to turn him into mere power, you have to curtail his soul as much as possible. When we are fully human, we cannot fly at one another's throats; our instincts of social life, our traditions of moral ideals stand in the way. If you want me to take to butchering human beings, you must break up that wholeness of my humanity through some discipline which makes my will dead, my thoughts numb, my movements automatic, and then from the dissolution of the complex personal man will come out that abstraction, that destructive force, which has no relation to human truth, and therefore can be easily brutal or mechanical. Take away man from his natural surroundings, from the fulness of his communal life, with all its living associations of beauty and love and social obligations, and you will be able to turn him into so many fragments of a machine for the production of wealth on a gigantic scale. Turn a tree into a log and it will burn for you, but it will never bear living flowers and fruit.

This process of dehumanizing has been going on in commerce and politics. And out of the long birth-throes of mechanical energy has been born this fully developed apparatus of magnificent power and surprising appetite, which has been christened in the West as the Nation. As I have hinted before, because of its quality of abstraction it has, with the greatest ease, gone far ahead of the complete moral man. And having the conscience of a ghost and the callous perfection of an automaton, it is causing disasters of which the volcanic dissipations of the youthful moon would be ashamed to be brought into comparison. As a result, the suspicion of man for man stings all the limbs of this civilization like the hairs of the nettle. Each country is casting its net of espionage into the slimy bottom of the others, fishing for their secrets, the treacherous secrets brewing in the oozy depths of diplomacy. And what is their secret service but the nation's underground trade in kidnapping, murder and treachery and all the ugly crimes bred in the depth of rottenness? Because each nation has its own history of thieving and lies and broken faith, therefore there can only flourish international suspicion and jealousy, and international moral shame becomes anaemic to a degree of ludicrousness. The nation's bagpipe of righteous indignation has so often changed its tune according to the variation of time and to the altered groupings of the alliances of diplomacy, that it can be enjoyed with amusement as the variety performance of the political music hall.

I am just coming from my visit to Japan, where I exhorted this young nation to take its stand upon the higher ideals of humanity and never to follow the West in its acceptance of the organized selfishness of Nationalism as its religion, never to gloat upon the feebleness of its neighbours, never to be unscrupulous in its behaviour to the weak, where it can be gloriously mean with impunity, while turning its right cheek of brighter humanity for the kiss of admiration to those who have the power to deal it a blow. Some of the newspapers praised my utterances for their poetical qualities while adding with a leer that it was the poetry of a defeated people. I felt they were right. Japan had been taught in a modern school the lesson how to become powerful. The schooling is done and she must enjoy the fruits of her lessons. The West in the voice of her thundering cannon had said at the door of Japan: Let there be a Nation—and there was a Nation. And now that it *has* come into existence, why do you not feel in your heart of hearts a pure feeling of gladness and say that it is good? Why is it that I saw in an English paper an expression of bitterness at Japan's boasting of her superiority of civilization—the thing that the British, along with other nations, has been carrying on for ages without blushing? Because the idealism of selfishness must keep itself drunk with a continual dose of self-laudation. But the same vices which seem so natural and innocuous in its own life make it surprised and angry at their unpleasantness when seen in other nations. Therefore when you see the Japanese nation, created in your own image, launched in its career of national boastfulness you shake your head and say it is not good. Has it not been one of the causes that raise the cry on these shores for preparedness to meet one more power of evil with a greater power of injury? Japan protests that she has her *bushido,* that she can never be treacherous to America to whom she owes her gratitude. But you find it difficult to believe her,—for the wisdom of the Nation is not in its faith in humanity but in its complete distrust. You say to yourself that it is not with Japan of the *bushido,* the Japan of the moral ideals, that you have to deal—it is with the abstraction of the popular selfishness, it is with the Nation; and Nation can only trust Nation where their interests coalesce, or at least do not conflict. In fact your instinct tells you that the advent of another people into the arena of nationality makes another addition to the evil which contradicts all that is highest in Man and proves by its success that unscrupulousness is the way to prosperity,—and goodness is good for the weak and God is the only remaining consolation of the defeated.

Yes, this is the logic of the Nation. And it will never heed the voice of truth and goodness. It will go on in its ring-dance of moral corruption, linking steel unto steel, and machine unto machine; trampling under its tread all the sweet flowers of simple faith and the living ideals of man.

But we delude ourselves into thinking that humanity in the modern days is more to the front than ever before. The reason of this self-delusion is because man is served with the necessaries of life in greater profusion and his physical ills are being alleviated with more efficacy. But the chief part of this is done, not by moral sacrifice, but by intellectual power. In quantity it is great, but it springs from the surface and spreads over the surface. Knowledge and efficiency are powerful in their outward effect, but they are the servants of man, not the man himself. Their service is like the service in a hotel, where it is elaborate, but the host is absent; it is more convenient than hospitable.

Therefore we must not forget that the scientific organizations vastly spreading in all directions are strengthening our power, but not our humanity. With the growth of power the cult of the self-worship of the Nation grows in ascendency; and the individual willingly allows the nation to take donkey rides upon his back; and there happens the anomaly which must have its disastrous effects, that the individual worships with all sacrifices a god which is morally much inferior to himself. This could never have been possible if the god had been as real as the individual.

Let me give an illustration of this in point. In some parts of India it has been enjoined as an act of great piety for a widow to go without food and water on a particular day every fortnight. This often leads to cruelty, unmeaning and inhuman. And yet men are not by nature cruel to such a degree. But this piety being a mere unreal abstraction completely deadens the moral sense of the individual, just as the man who would not hurt an animal unnecessarily, would cause horrible suffering to a large number of innocent creatures when he drugs his feelings with the abstract idea of 'sport'. Because these ideas are the creations of our intellect, because they are logical classifications, therefore they can so easily hide in their mist the personal man.

And the idea of the Nation is one of the most powerful anesthetics that man has invented. Under the influence of its fumes the whole people can carry out its systematic programme of the most virulent self-seeking without being in the least aware of its moral perversion,—in fact feeling dangerously resentful if it is pointed out.

But can this go on indefinitely? Continually producing barrenness of moral insensibility upon a large tract of our living nature? Can it escape its nemesis forever? Has this giant power of mechanical organization no limit in this world against which it may shatter itself all the more completely because of its terrible strength and velocity? Do you believe that evil can be permanently kept in check by competition with evil, and that conference of prudence can keep the devil chained in its makeshift cage of mutual agreement?

This European war of Nations is the war of retribution. Man, the person, must protest for his very life against the heaping up of things where there should be the heart, and systems and policies where there should flow living human relationship. The time has come when, for the sake of the whole outraged world, Europe should fully know in her own person the terrible absurdity of the thing called the Nation.

The Nation has thriven long upon mutilated humanity. Men, the fairest creations of God, came out of the National manufactory in huge numbers as war-making and money-making puppets, ludicrously vain of their pitiful perfection of mechanism. Human society grew more and more into a marionette show of politicians, soldiers, manufacturers and bureaucrats, pulled by wire arrangements of wonderful efficiency.

But the apotheosis off selfishness can never make its interminable breed of hatred and greed, fear and hypocrisy, suspicion and tyranny, an end in themselves. These monsters grow into huge shapes but never into harmony. And this Nation may grow on to an unimaginable corpulence, not of a living body, but of steel and steam and office buildings, till its deformity can contain no longer its ugly voluminousness,—till it begins to crack and gape, breathe gas and fire in gasps, and its death-rattles sound in cannon roars. In this war, the death-throes of the Nation have commenced. Suddenly, all its mechanism going mad, it has begun the dance of the furies, shattering its own limbs, scattering them into the dust. It is the fifth act of the tragedy of the unreal.

Those who have any faith in Man cannot but fervently hope that the tyranny of the Nation will not be restored to all its former teeth and claws, to its far-reaching iron arms and its immense inner cavity, all stomach and no heart; that man will have his new birth, in the freedom of his individuality, from the enveloping vagueness of abstraction.

The veil has been raised, and in this frightful war the West has stood face to face with her own creation, to which she had offered her soul. She must know what it truly is.

She had never let herself suspect what slow decay and decomposition were secretly going on in her moral nature, which often broke out in doctrines of scepticism, but still oftener and in still more dangerously subtle manner showed itself in her unconsciousness of the mutilation and insult that she had been inflicting upon a vast part of the world. Now she must know the truth nearer home.

And then there will come from her own children those who will break themselves free from the slavery of this illusion, this perversion of brotherhood founded upon self-seeking, those who will own themselves as God's children and as no bondslaves of machinery, which turns souls into commodities and life into compartments, which, with its iron claws, scratches out the heart of the world and knows not what it has done.

And we of no nations of the world, whose heads have been bowed to the dust, will know that his dust is more sacred than the bricks which build the pride of power. For this dust is fertile of life, and of beauty and worship. We shall thank God that we were made to wait in silence through the night of despair, had to bear the insult of the proud and the strong man's burden, yet all through it, though our hearts quaked with doubt and fear, never could we blindly believe in the salvation which machinery offered to man, but we held fast to our trust in God and the truth of the human soul. And we can still cherish the hope, that, when power becomes ashamed to occupy its throne and is ready to make way for love, when the morning comes for cleansing the bloodstained steps of the Nation along the highroad of humanity, we shall be called upon to bring our own vessel of sacred water—the water of worship—to sweeten the history of man into purity, and with its sprinkling make the trampled dust of the centuries blessed with fruitfulness.

The Nation

31

The peoples are living beings. They have their distinct personalities. But nations are organizations of power, and therefore their inner aspects and outward expressions are everywhere monotonously the same. Their differences are merely differences in degree of efficiency.

In the modern world the fight is going on between the living spirit of the people and the methods of nation-organizing. It is like the struggle that began in Central Asia between cultivated areas of man's habitation and the continually encroaching desert sands, till the human region of life and beauty was choked out of existence. When the spread of higher ideals of humanity is not held to be important, the hardening method of national efficiency gains a certain strength; and for some limited period of time, at least, it proudly asserts itself as the fittest to survive. But it is the survival of that part of man which is the least living. And this is the reason why dead monotony is the sign of the spread of the Nation. The modern towns, which present the physiognomy due to this dominance of the Nation, are everywhere the same, from San Francisco to London, from London to Tokyo. They show no faces, but merely masks.

The peoples, being living personalities, must have their self-expression, and this leads to their distinctive creations. These creations are literature, art, social symbols and ceremonials. They are like different dishes at one common feast. They add richness to our enjoyment and understanding of truth. They are making the world of man fertile of life and variedly beautiful.

But the nations do not create, they merely produce and destroy. Organizations for production are necessary. Even organizations for destruction may be so. But when, actuated by greed and hatred, they crowd away into a corner the living man who creates, then the harmony is lost, and the people's history runs at a break-neck speed towards some fatal catastrophe.

Humanity, where it is living, is guided by inner ideals; but where it is a dead organization it becomes impervious to them. Its building process is only an external process, and in its response to the moral guidance it has to pass through obstacles that are gross and non-plastic.

Man as a person has his individuality, which is the field where his spirit has its freedom to express itself and to grow. The professional man carries a rigid crust around him which has very little variation and hardly any elasticity. This professionalism is the region where men specialize their knowledge and organize their power, mercilessly elbowing each other in their struggle to come to the front. Professionalism is necessary, without doubt; but it must not be allowed to exceed its healthy limits, to assume complete mastery over the personal man, making him narrow and hard, exclusively intent upon pursuit of success at the cost of his faith in ideals.

In ancient India professions were kept within limits by social regulation. They were considered primarily as social necessities, and in the second place as the means of livelihood for individuals. Thus man, being free from the constant urging of unbounded competition, could have leisure to cultivate his nature in its completeness.

The Cult of the Nation is the professionalism of the people. This cult is becoming their greatest danger, because it is bringing them enormous success, making them impatient of the claims of higher ideals. The greater the amount of success, the stronger are the conflicts of interest and jealousy and hatred which are aroused in men's minds, thereby making it more and more necessary for other peoples, who are still living, to stiffen into nations. With the growth of nationalism, man has become the greatest menace to man. Therefore the continual presence of panic goads that very nationalism into ever-increasing menace.

Crowd psychology is a blind force. Like steam and other physical forces, it can be utilized for creating a tremendous amount of power. And therefore rulers of men, who, out of greed and fear, are bent upon turning their peoples into machines of power, try to train this crowd psychology for their special purposes. They hold it to be their duty to foster in the popular mind universal panic, unreasoning pride in their own race, and hatred of others. Newspapers, school-books, and even religious services are made use of for this object; and those who have the courage to express their disapprobation of this blind and impious cult are either punished in the law-courts, or are socially ostracized. The individual thinks, even when he feels; but the same individual, when he feels with the crowd, does not reason at all. His moral sense becomes blurred. This suppression of higher humanity in crowd minds is productive of enormous strength. For the crowd mind is essentially primitive; its forces are elemental. Therefore the Nation is for ever watching to take advantage of this enormous power of darkness.

The people's instinct of self-preservation has been made dominant at particular times of crisis. Then, for the time being, the consciousness of its solidarity becomes aggressively wide-awake. But in the Nation this hyper-consciousness is kept alive for all time by artificial means. A man has to act the part of a policeman when he finds his house invaded by burglars. But if that remains his normal condition, then his consciousness of his household becomes acute and over-wrought, making him fly at every stranger passing near his house. This intensity of self-consciousness is nothing of which a man should feel proud; certainly it is not healthful. In like manner, incessant self-consciousness in a nation is highly injurious for the people. It serves its immediate purpose, but at the cost of the eternal in man.

When a whole body of men train themselves for a particular narrow purpose, it becomes a common interest with them to keep up that purpose and preach absolute loyalty to it. Nationalism is the training of a whole people for a narrow ideal; and when it gets hold of their minds it is sure to lead them to moral degeneracy and intellectual blindness. We cannot but hold firm the faith that this Age of Nationalism, of gigantic vanity and selfishness, is only a passing phase in civilization, and those who are making permanent arrangements for accommodating this temporary mood of history will be unable to fit themselves for the coming age, when the true spirit of freedom will have sway.

With the unchecked growth of Nationalism the moral foundation of man's civilization is unconsciously undergoing a change. The ideal of the social man is unselfishness, but the ideal of the Nation, like that of the professional man, is selfishness. This is why selfishness in the individual is condemned, while in the nation it is extolled, which leads to hopeless moral blindness, confusing the religion of the people with the religion of the nation. Therefore, to take an example, we find men more and more convinced of the superior claims of Christianity, merely because Christian nations are in possession of the greater part of the world. It is like supporting a robber's religion by quoting the amount of his stolen property. Nations celebrate their successful massacre of men in their churches. They forget that Thugs also ascribed their success in manslaughter to the favour of their goddess. But in the case of the latter their goddess frankly represented the principle of destruction. It was the criminal tribe's own murderous instinct deified—the instinct, not of one individual, but of the whole community, and therefore held sacred. In the same manner, in modern churches, selfishness, hatred and vanity in their collective aspect of national instincts do not scruple to share the homage paid to God.

Of course, pursuit of self-interest need not be wholly selfish; it can even be in harmony with the interest of all. Therefore, ideally speaking, the nationalism, which stands for the expression of the collective self-interest of a people, need not be ashamed of itself if it maintains its true limitations. But what we see in practice is, that every nation which has prospered has done so through its career of aggressive selfishness either in commercial adventures or in foreign possessions, or in both. And this material prosperity not only feeds continually the selfish instincts of the people, but impresses men's minds with the lesson that, for a nation, selfishness is a necessity and therefore a virtue. It is the emphasis laid in Europe upon the idea of the Nation's constant increase of power, which is becoming the greatest danger to man, both in its direct activity and its power of infection.

We must admit that evils there are in human nature, in spite of our faith in moral laws and our training in self-control. But they carry on their foreheads their own brand of infamy, their very success adding to their monstrosity. All through man's history there will be some who suffer, and others who cause suffering. The conquest of evil will never be a fully accomplished fact, but a continuous process like the process of burning in a flame.

In former ages, when some particular people became turbulent and tried to rob others of their human rights, they sometimes achieved success and sometimes failed. And it amounted to nothing more than that. But when this idea of the Nation, which has met with universal acceptance in the present day, tries to pass off the cult of collective selfishness as a moral duty, simply because that selfishness is gigantic in stature, it not only commits depredation, but attacks the very vitals of humanity. It unconsciously generates in people's minds an attitude of defiance against moral law. For men are taught by repeated devices the lesson that the Nation is greater than the people, while yet it scatters to the winds the moral law that the people have held sacred.

It has been said that a disease becomes most acutely critical when the brain is affected. For it is the brain that is constantly directing the siege against all disease forces. The spirit of national selfishness is that brain disease of a people which shows itself in red eyes and clenched fists, in violence of talk and movements, all the while shattering its natural restorative powers. But the power of self-sacrifice, together with the moral faculty of sympathy and cooperation, is the guiding spirit of social vitality. Its function is to maintain a beneficent relation of harmony with its surroundings. But when it begins to ignore the moral law which is universal and uses it only within the bounds of its own narrow sphere, then its strength becomes like the strength of madness which ends in self-destruction.

What is worse, this aberration of a people, decked with the showy title of 'patriotism', proudly walks abroad, passing itself off as a highly moral influence. Thus it has spread its inflammatory contagion all over the world, proclaiming its fever flush to be the best sign of health. It is causing in the hearts of peoples, naturally inoffensive, a feeling of envy at not having their temperature as high as that of their delirious neighbours and not being able to cause as much mischief, but merely having to suffer from it.

I have often been asked by my Western friends how to cope with this evil, which has attained such sinister strength and vast dimensions. In fact, I have often been blamed for merely giving warning, and offering no alternative. When we suffer as a result of a particular system, we believe that some other system would bring us better luck. We are apt to forget that all systems produce evil sooner or later, when the psychology which is at the root of them is wrong. The system which is national today may assume the shape of the international tomorrow; but so long as men have not forsaken their idolatry of primitive instincts and collective passions, the new system will only become a new instrument of suffering. And because we are trained to confound efficient system with moral goodness itself, every ruined system makes us more and more distrustful of moral law.

Therefore I do not put my faith in any new institution, but in the individuals all over the world who think clearly, feel nobly, and act rightly, thus becoming the channels of moral truth. Our moral ideals do not work with chisels and hammers. Like trees, they spread their roots in the soil and their branches in the sky, without consulting any architect for their plans.

The Call of Truth

32

Parasites have to pay for their readymade victuals by losing the power of assimilating food in its natural form. In the history of man this same sin of laziness has always entailed degeneracy. Man becomes parasitical, not only when he fattens on others' toil, but also when he becomes rooted to a particular set of outside conditions and allows himself helplessly to drift along the stream of things as they are; for the outside is alien to the inner self, and if the former be made indispensable by sheer habit, man acquires parasitical characteristics, and becomes unable to perform his true function of converting the impossible into the possible.

In this sense all the lower animals are parasites. They are carried along by their environment; they live or die by natural selection; they progress or retrogress as nature may dictate. Their mind has lost the power of growth. The bees, for millions of years, have been unable to get beyond the pattern of their hive. For that reason, the form of their cell has attained a certain perfection, but their mentality is confined to the age-long habits of their hive-life and cannot soar out of its limitations. Nature has developed a cautious timidity in the case of her lower types of life; she keeps them tied to her apron strings and has stunted their minds, lest they should stray into dangerous experiments.

But Providence displayed a sudden accession of creative courage when it came to man; for his inner nature has not been tied down, though outwardly the poor human creature has been left naked, weak and defenceless. In spite of these disabilities, man in the joy of his inward freedom has stood up and declared; 'I shall achieve the impossible.' That is to say, he has consistently refused to submit to the rule of things as they always have been, but is determined to bring about happenings that have never been before. So when, in the beginning of his history, man's lot was thrown in with monstrous creatures, tusked and taloned, he did not, like the deer, simply take refuge in flight, nor, like the tortoise, take refuge in hiding, but set to work with flints to make even more efficient weapons. These, moreover, being the creation of his own inner faculties, were not dependent on natural selection, as were those of the other animals, for their development. And so man's instruments progressed from flint to steel. This shows that man's mind has never been helplessly attached to his environment. What came to his hand was brought under his thumb. Not content with the flint on the surface, he delved for the iron beneath. Not satisfied with the easier process of chipping flints, he proceeded to melt iron ore and hammer it into shape. That which resisted more stubbornly was converted into a better ally. Man's inner nature not only finds success in its activity, but there it also has its joy. He insists on penetrating further and further into the depths, from the obvious to the hidden, from the easy to the difficult, from parasitism to self-determination, from the slavery of his passions to the mastery of himself. That is how he has won.

But if any section of mankind should say, 'The flint was the weapon of our revered forefathers; by departing from it we destroy the spirit of the race', then they may succeed in preserving what they call their race, but they strike at the root of the glorious tradition of humanity which was theirs also. And we find that those, who have steadfastly stuck to their flints, may indeed have kept safe their pristine purity to their own satisfaction, but they have been outcasted by the rest of mankind, and so have to pass their lives slinking away in jungle and cave. They are, as I say, reduced to a parasitic dependence on outside nature, driven along blindfold by the force of things as they are. They have not achieved Swaraj in their inner nature, and so are deprived of Swaraj in the outside world as well. They have ceased to be even aware, that it is man's true function to make the impossible into the possible by dint of his own powers; that it is not for him to be confined merely to what has happened before; that he must progress towards what ought to be by rousing all his inner powers by means of the force of his soul.

Thirty years ago I used to edit the Sādhanā magazine, and there I tried to say this same thing. Then English-educated India was frightfully busy begging for its rights. And I repeatedly endeavoured to impress on my countrymen, that man is not under any necessity to beg for rights from others, but must create them for himself; because man lives mainly by his inner nature, and there he is the master. By dependence on acquisition from the outside, man's inner nature suffers loss. And it was my contention, that man is not so hard oppressed by being deprived of his outward rights as he is by the constant bearing of the burden of prayers and petitions.

Then, when the Bangadarshan magazine came into my hands, Bengal was beside herself at the sound of sharpening of the knives for her partition. The boycott of Manchester, which was the outcome of her distress, had raised the profits of the Bombay mill-owners to a super-foreign degree. And I had then to say, 'This will not do, either; for it is also of the outside. Your main motive is hatred of the foreigner, not love of country.' It was then really necessary for our countrymen to be made conscious of the distinction, that the Englishman's presence is an external accident,—mere *māyā*—but that the presence of our country is an internal fact which is also an eternal truth. *Māyā* looms with an exaggerated importance, only when we fix our attention exclusively upon it, by reason of some infatuation— be it of love, or of hate. Whether in our passion we rush to embrace it, or attack it; whether we yearn for it, or spurn it; it equally fills the whole field of our blood-shot vision.

Māyā is like the darkness. No steed, however swift, can carry us beyond it; no amount of water can wash it away. Truth is like a lamp; even as it is lit *māyā* vanishes. Our Shastras tell us that Truth, even when it is small, can rescue us from the terror which is great. Fear is the atheism of the heart. It cannot be overcome from the side of negation. If one of its heads be struck off, it breeds, like the monster of the fable, a hundred others. Truth is positive: it is the affirmation of the soul. If even a little of it be roused, it attacks negation at the very heart and overpowers it wholly.

Alien government in India is a veritable chameleon. Today it comes in the guise of the Englishman; tomorrow perhaps as some other foreigner; the next day, without abating a jot of its virulence, it may take the shape of our own countrymen. However determinedly we may try to hunt this monster of foreign dependence with outside lethal weapons, it will always elude our pursuit by changing its skin, or its colour. But if we can gain within us the truth called our country, all outward *māyā* will vanish of itself. The declaration of faith that my country it there, to be realized, has to be attained by each one of us. The idea that our country is ours, merely because we have been born in it, can only be held by those who are fastened, in a parasitic existence, upon the outside world. But the true nature of man is his inner nature, with its inherent powers. Therefore that only can be a man's true country, which he can help to create by his wisdom and with his love and his actions. So in 1905, I called upon my countrymen to *create* their own country by putting forth their own powers from within. For the act of creation itself is the realization of truth.

The Creator gains Himself in His universe. To gain one's own country means to realize one's own soul more fully expanded within it. This can only be done when we are engaged in building it up with our service, our ideas and our activities. Man's country being the creation of his own inner nature, when his soul thus expands within it, it is more truly expressed, more fully realized. In my paper called 'Swadeshi Samaj', written in 1905, I discussed at length the ways and means by which we could make the country of our birth more fully our own. Whatever may have been the shortcomings of my words then uttered, I did not fail to lay emphasis on the truth, that we must win our country, not from some foreigner, but from our own inertia, our own indifference. Whatever be the nature of the boons we may be seeking for our country at the door of the foreign Government, the result is always the same,—it only makes our inertia more densely inert. Any public benefit done by the alien Government goes to their credit, not to ours. So whatever outside advantage such public benefit might mean for us, our country will only get more and more completely lost to us thereby. That is to say, we shall have to pay out in soul value for what we purchase as material advantage. The Rishi has said: 'Then son is dear, not because we desire a son, but because we desire to realize our own soul in him.' It is the same with our country. It is dear to us, because it is the expression of our own soul. When we realize this, it will become impossible for us to allow our service of our country to wait on the pleasure of others.

These truths, which I then tried to press on my countrymen, were not particularly new, nor was there anything therein which need have grated on their ears; but, whether anyone else remembers it or not, I at least am not likely to forget the storm of indignation which I roused. I am not merely referring to the hooligans of journalism whom it pays to be scurrilous. But even men of credit and courtesy were unable to speak of me in restrained language.

There were two root causes of this. One was anger, the second was greed.

Giving free vent to angry feelings is a species of self-indulgence. In those days there was practically nothing to stand in the way of the spirit of destructive revel, which spread all over the country. We went about picketing, burning, placing thorns in the path of those whose way was not ours, acknowledging no restraints in language or behaviour,—all in the frenzy of our wrath. Shortly after it was all over, a Japanese friend asked me: 'How is it you people cannot carry on your work with calm and deep determination? This wasting of energy can hardly be of assistance to your object.' I had no help but to reply: 'When we have the gaining of the object clearly before our minds, we can be restrained, and concentrate our energies to serve it; but when it is a case of venting our anger, our excitement rises and rises till it drowns the object, and then we are spend-thrift to the point of bankruptcy.'

However that may be, there were my countrymen encountering, for the time being, no check to the overflow of their outraged feelings. It was like a strange dream. Everything seemed possible. Then all of a sudden it was my misfortune to appear on the scene with my doubts and my attempts to divert the current into the path of self-determination. My only success was in diverting their wrath on to my own devoted head.

Then there was our greed. In history, all people have won valuable things by pursuing difficult paths. We had hit upon the device of getting them cheap, not even through the painful indignity of supplication with folded hands, but by proudly conducting our beggary in threatening tones. The country was in ecstasy at the ingenuity of the trick. It felt like being at a reduced price sale. Everything worth having in the political market was ticketed at half-price. Shabby-genteel mentality is so taken up with low prices that it has no attention to spare for quality, and feels inclined to attack anybody who has the hardihood to express doubts in that regard. It is like the man of worldly piety who believes that the judicious expenditure of coin can secure, by favour of the priest, a direct passage to heaven. The dare-devil who ventures to suggest that not heaven but dreamland is likely to be his destination must beware of a violent end.

Anyhow, it was the outside *māyā* I which was our dream and our ideal in those days. It was a favourite phrase of one of the leaders of the time that we must keep one hand at the feet and the other at the throat of the Englishman,—that is to say, with no hand left free for the country! We have since perhaps got rid of this ambiguous attitude. Now we have one party that has both hands raised to the foreigner's throat, and another party which has both hands down at his feet; but whichever attitude it may be, these methods still appertain to the outside *māyā*. Our unfortunate minds keep revolving round and round the British Government, now to the left, now to the right; our affirmations and denials alike are concerned with the foreigner.

In those days, the stimulus from every side was directed towards the heart of Bengal. But emotion by itself, like fire, only consumes its fuel and reduces it to ashes; it has no creative power. The intellect of man must by itself, with patience, with skill, with foresight, in using this fire to melt that which is hard and difficult into the object of its desire. We neglected to rouse our intellectual forces, and so were unable to make use of this surging emotion of ours to create any organization of permanent value. The reason of our failure, therefore, was not in anything outside, but rather within us. For a long time past we have been in the habit, in our life and endeavour, of setting apart one place for our emotions and another for our practices. Our intellect has all the time remained dormant, because we have not dared to allow it scope. That is why, when we have to rouse ourselves to action, it is our emotion which has to be requisitioned, and our intellect has to be kept from interfering by the hypnotism of some magical formula,—that is to say we hasten to create a situation absolutely inimical to the free play of our intellect.

The loss which is incurred by this continual deadening of our mind cannot be made good by any other contrivance. In our desperate attempts to do so we have to invoke the magic of *māyā* and our impotence jumps for joy at the prospect of getting hold of Aladin's lamp. Of course everyone has to admit that there is nothing to beat Aladin's lamp, its only inconvenience being that it beats one to get hold of. The unfortunate part of it is that the person, whose greed is great, but whose powers are feeble, and who has lost all confidence in his own intellect, simply will not allow himself to dwell on the difficulties of bespeaking the services of some of the lamp. He can only be brought to exert himself at all by holding out the speedy prospect of getting at the wonderful lamp. If any one attempts to point out the futility of his hopes, he fills the air with wailing and imprecation, as at a robber making away with his all.

In the heat of the enthusiasm of the partition days, a band of youths attempted to bring about the millennium through political revolution. Their offer of themselves as the first sacrifice to the fire which they had lighted makes not only their own country, but other countries as well, bare the head to them in reverence. Their physical failure shines forth as the effulgence of spiritual glory. In the midst of their supreme travail, they realized at length that the way of bloody revolution is not the true way; that where there is no politics, a political revolution is like taking a short cut to nothing; that the wrong way may appear shorter, but it does not reach the goal, and only grievously hurts the feet. The refusal to pay the full price for a thing leads to the loss of the price without the gain of the thing. These impetuous youths offered their lives as the price of their country's deliverance; to them it meant the loss of their all, but alas! the price offered on behalf of the country was insufficient. I feel sure that those of them who still survive must have realized by now, that the country must be the creation of all its people, not of one section alone. It must be the expression of all their forces of heart, mind and will.

The creation can only be the fruit of that *yoga,* which gives outward form to the inner faculties. Mere political or economical *yoga* is not enough; for that all the human powers must unite.

When we turn our gaze upon the history of other countries, the political steed comes prominently into view; on it seems to depend wholly the progress of the carriage. We forget that the carriage also must be in a fit condition to move; its wheels must be in agreement with one another and its parts well fitted together; with which not only have fire and hammer and chisel been busy but much thought and skill and energy have also been spent in the process. We have seen some countries which are externally free and independent; when, however, the political carriage is in motion, the noise which it makes arouses the whole neighbourhood from slumber and the jolting produces aches and pains in the limbs of the helpless passengers. It comes to pieces in the middle of the road, and it takes the whole day to put it together again with the help of ropes and strings. Yet however loose the screws and however crooked the wheels, still it is a vehicle of some sort after all. But for such a thing as is our country,—a mere collection of jointed logs, that not only have no wholeness amongst themselves, but are contrary to one another,—for this, to be dragged along a few paces by the temporary pull of some common greed or anger, can never be called by the name of political progress. Therefore, is it not, in our case, wiser to keep for the moment our horse in the stable and begin to manufacture a real carriage?

From the writings of the young men, who have come back out of the valley of the shadow of death, I feel sure some such thoughts must have occurred to them. And so they must be realizing the necessity of the practice of *yoga* as of primary importance;—that form which is the union in a common endeavour of all the human faculties. This cannot be attained by any outside blind obedience, but only by the realization of self in the light of intellect. That which fails to illumine the intellect, and only keeps it in the obsession of some delusion, is its greatest obstacle.

The call to make the country our own by dint of our own creative power, is a great call. It is not merely inducing the people to take up some external mechanical exercise; for man's life is not in making cells of uniform pattern like the bee, nor in incessant weaving of webs like the spider; his greatest powers are within, and on these are his chief reliance. If by offering some allurement we can induce man to cease from thinking so that he may go on and on with some mechanical piece of world, this will only result in prolonging the sway of *Māyā*, under which our country has all along been languishing. So far, we have been content with surrendering our greatest right—the right to reason and to judge for ourselves—to the blind forces of shastric injunctions and social conventions. We have refused to cross the seas, because Manu has told us not to do so. We refuse to eat with the Mussulman, because prescribed usage is against it. In other words, we have systematically pursued a course of blind routine and habit, in which the mind of man has no place. We have thus been reduced to the helpless condition of the master who is altogether dependent on his servant. The real master, as I have said, is the internal man; and he gets into endless trouble, when he becomes his own servant's slave—a mere automaton, manufactured in the factory of servitude. He can then only rescue himself from one master by surrendering himself to another. Similarly, he who glorifies inertia by attributing to it a fanciful purity, becomes, like it, dependent on outside impulses, both for rest and motion. The inertness of mind, which is the basis of all slavery, cannot be got rid of by a docile submission to being hoodwinked, nor by going through the motions of a wound up mechanical doll.

The movement, which has now succeeded the Swadeshi agitation, is ever so much greater and has moreover extended its influence all over India. Previously, the vision of our political leaders had never reached beyond the English-knowing classes, because the country meant for them only that bookish aspect of it which is to be found in the pages of the Englishman's history. Such a country was merely a mirage born of vapourings in the English language, in which flitted about thin shades of Burke and Gladstone, Mazzini and Garibaldi. Nothing resembling self-sacrifice or true feeling for their countrymen was visible. At this juncture, Mahatma Gandhi came and stood at the cottage door of the destitute millions, clad as one of themselves, and talking to them in their own language. Here was the truth at last, not a mere quotation out of a book. So the name of Mahatma, which was given to him, is his true name. Who else has felt so many men of India to be of his own flesh and blood? At the touch of Truth the pent-up forces of the soul are set free. As soon as true love stood at India's door, it flew open: all hesitation and holding back vanished. Truth awakened truth.

Stratagem in politics is a barren policy,—this was a lesson of which we were sorely in need. All honour to the Mahatma, who made visible to us the power of Truth. But reliance on tactics is so ingrained in the cowardly and the weak, that, in order to eradicate it, the very skin must be sloughed off. Even today, our worldly-wise men cannot get rid of the idea of utilizing the Mahatma as a secret and more ingenious move in their political gamble. With their minds corroded by untruth, they cannot understand what an important thing it is that the Mahatma's supreme love should have drawn forth the country's love. The thing that has happened is nothing less than the birth of freedom. It is the gain by the country of itself.

In it there is no room for any thought, as to where the Englishman is, or is not. This love is self-expression. It is pure affirmation. It does not argue with negation; it has no need for argument.

Some notes of the music of this wonderful awakening of India by love, floated over to me across the seas. It was a great joy to me to think that the call of this festivity of awakening would come to each one of us; and that the true *shakti* of India's spirit, in all its multifarious variety, would at last find expression. This thought came to me because I have always believed that in such a way India would find its freedom. When Lord Buddha voiced forth the truth of compassion for all living creatures, which he had obtained as the fruit of his own self-discipline, the manhood of India was roused and poured itself forth in science and art and wealth of every kind. True, in the matter of political unification the repeated attempts that were then made as often failed; nevertheless India's mind had awakened into freedom from its submergence in sleep, and its overwhelming force would brook no confinement within the petty limits of country. It overflowed across ocean and desert, scattering its wealth of the spirit over every land that it touched. No commercial or military exploiter, today, has ever been able to do anything like it. Whatever land these exploiters have touched has been agonized with sorrow and insult, and the fair face of the world has been scarred and disfigured. Why? Because not greed but love is true. When love gives freedom it does so at the very centre of our life. When greed seeks unfettered power, it is forcefully impatient. We saw this during the partition agitation. We then compelled the poor to make sacrifices, not always out of the inwardness of love, but often by outward pressure. That was because greed is always seeking for a particular result within a definite time. But the fruit which love seeks is not of today of tomorrow, nor for a time only: it is sufficient unto itself.

So, in the expectation of breathing the buoyant breezes of this new found freedom, I came home rejoicing. But what I found in Calcutta when I arrived depressed me. An oppressive atmosphere seemed to burden the land. Some outside compulsion seemed to be urging one and all to talk in the same strain, to work at the same mill. When I wanted to inquire, to discuss, my well-wishers clapped their hands over my lips, saying: 'Not now, not now. Today, in the atmosphere of the country, there is a spirit of persecution, which is not that of armed force, but something, still more alarming, because it is invisible.' I found, further, that those who had their doubts as to the present activities, if they happened to whisper them out, however cautiously, however guardedly, felt some admonishing hand clutching them within. There was a newspaper which one day had the temerity to disapprove, in a feeble way, of the burning of cloth. The very next day the editor was shaken out of his balance by the agitation of his readers. How long would it take for the fire which was burning cloth to reduce his paper to ashes? The sight that met my eye was, on the one hand, people immensely busy; on the other, intensely afraid. What I heard on every side was, that reason, and culture as well, must be closured. It was only necessary to cling to an unquestioning obedience. Obedience to whom? To some *mantra*, some unreasoned creed!

And why this obedience? Here again comes that same greed, our spiritual enemy. There dangles before the country the bait of getting a thing of inestimable value, dirt cheap and in double-quick time. It is like the faqir with his goldmaking trick. With such a lure men cast so readily to the winds their independent judgment and wax so mightily wroth with those who will not do likewise. So easy is it to overpower, in the name of outside freedom, the inner freedom of man. The most deplorable part of it is that so many do not even honestly believe in the hope that they swear by. 'It will serve to make our countrymen, do what is necessary'—say they. Evidently, according to them, the India which once declared: 'In truth is Victory, not in untruth'—that India would not have been fit for *Swaraj*.

Another mischief is that the gain, with the promise of which obedience is claimed, is indicated by name, but is not defined. Just as when fear is vague it becomes all the more strong, so the vagueness of the lure makes it all the more tempting; inasmuch as ample room is left for each one's imagination to shape, it to his taste. Moreover there is no driving it into a corner because it can always shift from one shelter to another. In short, the object of the temptation has been magnified through its indefiniteness, while the time and method of its attainment have been made too narrowly definite. When the reason of man has been overcome in this way, he easily consents to give up all legitimate questions and blindly follows the path of obedience. But can we really afford to forget so easily that delusion is at the root of all slavery—that all freedom means freedom from *māyā*? What if the bulk of our people have unquestioningly accepted the creed, that by means of sundry practices *swaraj* will come to them on a particular date in the near future, and are also ready to use their clubs to put down all further argument,—that is to say, they have surrendered the freedom of their own minds and are prepared to deprive other minds of their freedom likewise,—is not this by itself a reason for profound misgiving? We were seeking the exorciser to drive out this very ghost; but if the ghost itself comes in the guise of exorciser then the danger is only heightened.

The Mahatma has won the heart of India with his love; for that we have all acknowledged his sovereignty. He has given us a vision of the *shakti* of truth; for that our gratitude to him is unbounded. We read about truth in books: we talk about it: but it is indeed a red-letter day, when we see it face to face. Rare is the moment, in many a long year, when such good fortune happens. We can make and break Congresses every other day. It is at any time possible for us to stump the country preaching politics in English. But the golden rod which can awaken our country in Truth and Love is not a thing which can be manufactured by the nearest goldsmith. To the wielder of that rod our profound salutation! But if, having seen truth, our belief in it is not confirmed, what is the good of it all? Our mind must acknowledge the truth of the intellect, just as our heart does the truth of love. No Congress or other outside institution succeeded in touching the heart of India. It was roused only the touch of love. Having had such a clear vision of this wonderful power of Truth, are we to cease to believe in it, just where the attainment of *Swaraj* is concerned? Has the truth, which was needed in the process of awakenment, to be got rid of in the process of achievement?

Let me give an illustration. I am in search of a Vina player. I have tried East and I have tried West, but have not found the man of my quest. They are all experts, they can make the strings resound to a degree, they command high prices, but for all their wonderful execution they can strike no chord in my heart. At last I come across one whose very first notes melt away the sense of oppression within. In him is the fire of the *shakti* of joy which can light up all other hearts by its touch. His appeal to me is instant, and I hail him as Master. I then want a Vina made. For this, of course, are required all kinds of material and a different kind of science. If, finding me to be lacking in the means, my master should be moved to pity and say: 'Never mind, my son, do not go to the expense in workmanship and time which a Vina will require. Take rather this simple string tightened across a piece of wood and practice on it. In a short time you will find it to be as good as a Vina.' Would that do? I am afraid not. It would, in fact, be a mistaken kindness for the master thus to take pity on my circumstances. Far better if he were to tell me plainly that such things cannot be had cheaply. It is he who should teach me that merely one string will not serve for a true Vina; that the materials required are many and various; that the lines of its moulding must be shapely and precise; that if there be anything faulty, it will fail to make good music, so that all laws of science and technique of art must be rigorously and intelligently followed. In short, the true function of the master player should be to evoke a response from the depths of our heart, so that we may gain the strength to wait and work till the true end is achieved.

From our master, the Mahatma,—may our devotion to him never grow less!—we must learn the truth of love in all its purity, but the science and art of building up *Swaraj* is a vast subject. Its pathways are difficult to traverse and take time. For this task, aspiration and emotion must be there, but no less must study and thought be there likewise. For it, the economist must think, the mechanic must labour, the educationist and statesman must teach and contrive. In a word, the mind of the country must exert itself in all directions. Above all, the spirit of Inquiry throughout the whole country, must be kept intact and untrammeled, its mind not made timid or inactive by compulsion, open or secret.

We know from past experience that it is not any and every call to which the country responds. It is because no one has yet been able to unite in *Yoga* all the forces of the country in the work of its creation, that so much time has been lost over and over again. And we have been kept waiting and waiting for him who has the right and the power to make the call upon us. In the old forests of India, our *Gurus,* in the fulness of their vision of the Truth had sent forth such a call saying: 'As the rivers flow on their downward course, as the months flow on to the year, so let all seekers after truth come from all sides.' The initiation into Truth of that day has borne fruit, undying to this day, and the voice of its message still rings in the ears of the world.

Why should not our *Guru* of today, who would lead us on the paths of *Karma,* send forth such a call? Why should he not say: 'Come yet from all sides and be welcome. Let all the forces of the land he brought into action, for then alone shall the country awake. Freedom is in complete awakening, in full self-expression.' God has given the Mahatma the voice that can call, for in him there is the Truth. Why should this not be our long-awaited opportunity?

But his call came to one narrow field alone. To one and all he simply says: Spin and weave, spin and weave. Is this the call: 'Let all seekers after truth come from all sides?' Is this the call of the New Age to new creation? When nature called to the Bee to take refuge in the narrow life of the hive, millions of bees responded to it for the sake of efficiency, and accepted the loss of sex in consequence. But this sacrifice by way of self-atrophy led to the opposite of freedom. Any country, the people of which can agree to become neuters for the sake of some temptation, or command, carries within itself its own prison-house. To spin is easy, therefore for all men it is an imposition hard to bear. The call to the ease of mere efficiency is well enough for the Bee. The wealth of power, that is Man's can only become manifest when his utmost is claimed.

Sparta tried to gain strength by narrowing herself down to a particular purpose, but she did not win. Athens sought to attain perfection by opening herself out in all her fulness,—and she did win. Her flag of victory still flies at the masthead of man's civilization. It is admitted that European military camps and factories are stunting man, that their greed is cutting man down to the measure of their own narrow purpose, that for these reasons joylessness darkly lowers over the West. But if man be stunted by big machines, the danger of his being stunted by small machines must not be lost sight of. The *charka* in its proper place can do no harm, but will rather do much good. But where, by reason of failure to acknowledge the differences in man's temperament, it is in the wrong place, there thread can only be spun at the cost of a great deal of the mind itself. Mind is no less valuable than cotton thread.

Some are objecting: 'We do not propose to curb our minds for ever, but only for a time.' But why should it be even for a time? Is it because within a short time spinning will give us Swaraj? But where is the argument for this? Swaraj is not concerned with our apparel only—it cannot be established on cheap clothing; its foundation is in the mind, which, with its diverse powers and its confidence in those powers, goes on all the time creating Swaraj for itself. In no country in the world is the building up of Swaraj completed. In some part or other of every nation, some lurking greed or illusion still perpetuates bondage. And the root of such bondage is always within the mind. Where then, I ask again, is the argument, that in our country Swaraj can be brought about by everyone engaging for a time in spinning? A mere statement, in lieu of argument, will surely never do. If once we consent to receive fate's oracle from human lips, that will add one more to the torments of our slavery, and not the least one either. If nothing but oracles will serve to move us, oracles will have to be manufactured, morning, noon and night, for the sake of urgent needs, and all other voices would be defeated. Those for whom authority is needed in place of reason, will invariably accept despotism in place of freedom. It is like cutting at the root of a tree while pouring water on the top. This is not a new thing, I know. We have enough of magic in the country,—magical revelation, magical healing, and all kinds of divine intervention in mundane affairs. That is exactly why I am so anxious to re-instate reason on its throne. As I have said before, God himself has given the mind sovereignty in the material world. And I say today, that only those will be able to get and keep Swaraj in the material world who have realized the dignity of self-reliance and self-mastery in the spiritual world, those whom no temptation, no delusion, can induce to surrender the dignity of intellect into the keeping of others.

Consider the burning of cloth, heaped up before the very eyes of our motherland shivering and ashamed in her nakedness. What is the nature of the call to do this? Is it not another instance of a magical formula? The question of using or refusing cloth of a particular manufacture belongs mainly to economic science. The discussion of the matter by our countrymen should have been in the language of economics. If the country has really come to such a habit of mind that precise thinking has become impossible for it, then our very first fight should be against such a fatal habit, to the temporary exclusion of all else if need be. Such a habit would clearly be the original sin from which all our ills are flowing. But far from this, we take the course of confirming ourselves in it by relying on the magical formula that foreign cloth is 'impure'. Thus economics is bundled out and a fictitious moral dictum dragged into its place.

Untruth is impure in any circumstances, not merely because it may cause us material loss, but even when it does not; for it makes our inner nature unclean. This is a moral law and belongs to a higher plane. But if there be anything wrong in wearing a particular kind of cloth, that would be an offence against economics, or hygiene, or aesthetics, but certainly not against morality. Some urge that any mistake which brings sorrow to body or mind is a moral wrong. To which I reply that sorrow follows in the train of every mistake. A mistake in geometry may make a road too long, or a foundation weak, or a bridge dangerous. But mathematical mistakes cannot be cured by moral maxims. If a student makes a mistake in his geometry problem and his exercise book is torn up in consequence the problem will nevertheless remain unsolved until attacked by geometrical methods. But what if the schoolmaster comes to the conclusion that unless the exercise books are condemned and destroyed, his boys will never realize the folly of their mistakes? If such conclusion be well-founded, then I can only repeat that the reformation of such moral weakness of these particular boys should take precedence over all other lessons, otherwise there is no hope of their becoming men in the future.

The command to burn our foreign clothes has been laid on us. I, for one, am unable to obey it. Firstly, because I conceive it to be my very first duty to put up a valiant fight against this terrible habit of blindly obeying orders, and this fight can never be carried on by our people being driven from one injunction to another. Secondly, I feel that the clothes to be burnt are not mine, but belong to those who most sorely need them. If those who are going naked should have given us the mandate to burn, it would, at least, have been a case of self-immolation and the crime of incendiarism would not lie at our door. But how can we expiate the sin of the forcible destruction of clothes which might have gone to women whose nakedness is actually keeping them prisoners, unable to stir out of the privacy of their homes?

I have said repeatedly and must repeat once more that we cannot afford to lose our mind for the sake of any external gain. Where Mahatma Gandhi has declared war against the tyranny of the machine which is oppressing the whole world, we are all enrolled under his banner. But we must refuse to accept as our ally the illusion-haunted magic-ridden slave-mentality that is at the root of all the poverty and insult under which our country groans. Here is the enemy itself, on whose defeat alone Swaraj within and without can come to us.

The time, moreover, has arrived when we must think of one thing more, and that is this. The awakening of India is a part of the awakening of the world. The door of the New Age has been flung open at the trumpet blast of a great war. We have read in the Mahabharata how the day of self-revelation had to be preceded by a year of retirement. The same has happened in the world today. Nations had attained nearness to each other without being aware of it, that is to say, the outside fact was there, but it had not penetrated into the mind. At the shock of the war, the truth of it stood revealed to mankind. The foundation of modern, that is Western, civilization was shaken; and it has become evident that the convulsion is neither local nor temporary, but has traversed the whole earth and will last until the shocks between man and man, which have extended from continent to continent, can be brought to rest, and a harmony be established.

From now onward, any nation which takes an isolated view of its own country will run counter to the spirit of the New Age, and know no peace. From now onward, the anxiety that each country has for its own safety must embrace the welfare of the world. For some time the working of the new spirit has occasionally shown itself even in the Government of India, which has had to make attempts to deal with its own problems in the light of the world problem. The war has torn away a veil from before our minds. What is harmful to the world, is harmful to each one of us. This was a maxim which we used to read in books. Now mankind has seen it at work and has understood that wherever there is injustice, even if the external right of possession is there, the true right is wanting. So that it is worthwhile even to sacrifice some outward right in order to gain the reality. This immense change, which is coming over the spirit of man raising it from the petty to the great, is already at work even in Indian politics. There will doubtless be imperfections and obstacles without number. Self-interest is sure to attack enlightened interest at every step. Nevertheless it would be wrong to come to the decision that the working of self-interest alone is honest, and the larger-hearted striving is hypocritical.

After sixty years of self-experience, I have found that out and out hypocrisy is an almost impossible achievement, so that the pure hypocrite is a rarity indeed. The fact is, that the character of man has always more or less of duality in it. But our logical faculty, the trap-door of our mind, is unable to admit opposites together. So when we find the good with the bad, the former is promptly rejected as spurious. In the universal movement, as it becomes manifest in different parts of the world, this duality of man's character cannot but show itself. And whenever it does, if we pass judgment from past experience, we are sure to pronounce the selfish part of it to be the real thing; for the spirit of division and exclusion did in fact belong to the past age. But if we come to our judgment in the light of future promise, then shall we understand the enlightened large-heartedness to be the reality, and the counsel which will unite each to each to be the true wisdom.

I have condemned, in unsparing terms, the present form and scope of the League of Nations and the Indian Reform Councils. I, therefore, fell certain that there will be no misunderstanding when I state that, even in these, I find signs of the Time Spirit, which is moving the heart of the West. Although the present form is unacceptable, yet there is revealed an aspiration, which is towards the truth, and this aspiration must not be condemned. In this morning of the world's awakening, if in only our own national striving there is no response to its universal aspiration, that will betoken the poverty of our spirit. I do not say for a moment that we should belittle the work immediately to hand. But when the bird is roused by the dawn, all its awakening is not absorbed in its search for food. Its wings respond unweariedly to the call of the sky, its throat pours forth songs for joy of the new light. Universal humanity has sent us its call today. Let our mind respond in its own language; for response is the only true sign of life. When of old we were immersed in the politics of dependence on others, our chief business was the compilation of others' shortcomings. Now that we have decided to dissociate our politics from dependence, are we still to establish and maintain it on the same recital of others' sins? The state of mind so engendered will only raise the dust of angry passion, obscuring the greater world from our vision, and urge us more and more to take futile short cuts for the satisfaction of our passions. It is a sorry picture of India, which we shall display if we fail to realize for ourselves the greater India. This picture will have no light. It will have in the foreground only the business side of our aspiration. Mere business talent, however, has never created anything.

In the West, a real anxiety and effort of their higher mind to rise superior to business considerations, is beginning to be seen. I have come across many there whom this desire has imbued with the true spirit of the *Sannyasin,* making them renounce their home-world in order to achieve the unity of man, by destroying the bondage of nationalism; men who have within their own soul realized the *Advaita* of humanity. Many such have I seen in England who have accepted persecution and contumely from their fellow countrymen in their struggles to free other peoples from the oppression of their own country's pride of power. Some of them are amongst us here in India. I have seen *sannyasins* too in France—Romain Rolland for one, who is an outcast from his own people. I have also seen them in the minor countries of Europe. I have watched the faces of European students all a glow with the hope of a united mankind, prepared manfully to bear all the blows, cheerfully to submit to all the insults, of the present age for the glory of the age to come. And are we alone to be content with telling the beads of negation, harping on others faults and proceeding with the erection of *swaraj* on a foundation of quarrelsomeness? Shall it not be our first duty in the dawn to remember Him, who is One, who is without distinction of class or colour, and who with his varied *shakti* makes true provision for the inherent need of each and every class; and to pray to the Giver of Wisdom to unite us all in right understanding—

Yo ekōvarno vahudhā shakti yōgāt
Varnānanekān nihitārthodadhāti
Vichaiti chānte vishvamādau
Sa no buddhyā subhayā samyunaktu!

(1921)

The Way to Unity

33

Now that mutual intercourse has become easy, and the different peoples and nations of the world have come to know one another in various relations, one might have thought that the time had arrived to merge their differences in a common unity. But the significant thing is, that the more the doors are opening and the walls breaking down outwardly, the greater is the force which the consciousness of individual distinction is gaining within. There was a time when we believed that men were remaining separate, because of the obstacles between them; but the removal of these to the largest possible extent, is not seen to have the effect of doing away with the differences between diverse sections of mankind.

The smaller nations, who had been content to remain attached to one or other of the greater powers, have become restlessly anxious to be established on their own separate bases. Norway and Sweden have become divided from each other. Ireland has been struggling unweariedly through many a long year to achieve her separateness; her people, meanwhile, also being busy with the revival of their own literature. The Flemings have become enthusiastic about winning a distinct place for their original language and culture in Belgium, where so long French had reigned undisputed. The minor peoples who lived side by side within the Empire of Austria, have burst their bonds and are happy to have their separate existence. Russia in its frantic efforts to absorb Finland discovered that it was easier to swallow than to assimilate. For all the blood which flowed in Turkey, in her day of undisputed Empire, the differences of her subject races could not be washed away. For England, the desire to consolidate her overseas dominions into integral parts of a truly imperial body, has become an obsession; but none of the proposals for facilitating centralised control has met with favour in her colonies, who protest vigorously whenever any specific freedom of theirs is at stake.

The shibboleths, that unification means strength, or that bulk means greatness, do not hold today. Where there is a true distinction, its truth does not admit of being blindly overlooked for the sake of expediency, or in the hope of greater solidarity. Suppressed distinctions are dangerously explosive, and if allowed to remain suppressed may burst out in a revolution at the slightest shock. The true way to maintain a harmonious unity is by according due respect to the true distinctness of the different parts.

When man realises his own individuality, it stimulates his desire to grow greater. This growth of greatness for an individual can only become real by establishing wide relationship with a large number of other individuals. He who has no conscious regard for his own personality, lets go the helm of self and becomes merged in the crowd. In this he does not attain greatness, because one's relation to a crowd is a superficial relation of mere propinquity, with no scope for that ever-active voluntary adjustment which is living and creative. The differences of sleeping men are hardly perceptible, but these loudly assert themselves in the waking state. In the bud, the petals are compressed into oneness: only when each petal attains its separate distinctness, does it find its perfect unity in a flower and can help to attain the common object, which is fruition. Today the clash of the different parts of the world coming into contact, has brought about a general awakening, and under the law of manifestation each part is seeking its own self-unfoldment. No living thing, whose vital force is awake can feel itself any the greater by merging into something else, however large; it stakes its very life to be saved from being assimilated into something bigger, however superior that may be to itself.

What then is to be the end of such sectional movements? Nothing more or less than this, that the consciousness of the dignity of separate individuality will impel man to accept suffering for the sake of becoming greater; and true greatness can only be achieved by each section of mankind finding its field of self-realization in the great world of man. Only then can be attained real Unity, harmonious in structure, and therefore permanent. The artificial consolidation of the mangled in spirit, the crippled in life, the dependent and the hard-pressed, can only remain a jumble of incongruent parts.

At the period of the Swadeshi movement in Bengal, we experienced a desire to make the Moslems one with ourselves, but we did not succeed in doing so. Doubtless a coalition with them would have been very convenient for us, but it is not enough that a thing should be convenient for it to be feasible. If there are differences between Hindu and Moslem which are real, they cannot be spirited away by any jugglery. If, in our anxiety to secure some convenience, we ignore the facts, the facts will ignore our convenience. We failed because the invitation which we extended to the Moslems was for serving a purpose, not because it was inevitable, as is the invitation of mutual good feeling in common service.

True, in the immediate past, the consciousness of differences in the two communities was not obtrusively strong. Both of us then lived as neighbours under conditions which did not tend to bring out our divergence so acutely as to make us aware of it to the degree of active opposition. But, after all, the lack of consciousness, whether of differences or anything else, does not point to any superiority in our former circumstances; it merely shows that something then was wanting in ourselves, namely, vigour of life. Along with the arousing of our political aspiration, the movement of Hindu revivalism was started as a protest against the western influence on our life and mind. When, with the new age, the Hindu rose to a sense of the dignity of his Hinduism, if the Moslem had simply acquiesced therein, that would doubtless have suited us admirably; but the same causes likewise roused the Moslem to a sense of the dignity of Islam.

What is disconcerting in this circumstance is the fact that, while it lasts, peace between the two sections of the population can only be had either through apathy and forgetfulness, or through fear of foreign rule and common hatred against it. They may form an alliance for some such immediate object of mutual self-interest; but these alliances, like political alliances between countries which have traditions of antagonism, are not only transitory, but in constant danger of ending in violent re-action. For, the bond which depends upon some special expectation, either becomes a menace at the slightest sign of disappointment, or ceases to exist when that expectation is fulfilled. The most difficult problem for India is, that both Hindus and Mohamedan, when they reach the full consciousness of their individuality, become, in the natural course of things as they exist today, mutually exclusive and antagonistic.

There must be something radically wrong in our mental and social life when such can be the case. It must be the result of some narrowness of vision, some distrust of human nature in its universal aspect, which distracts our sympathy from the great course of its development that is to comprehend all humanity.

Individuality is precious, because only through it we can realize the universal. If it were a prison-house to shut us in for ever within a strictly circumscribed range of truth, devoid of movement or growth, then our existence itself would become an insult to us who have a living soul, just as a cage is to winged creatures. Unfortunately there are people who take enormous pride in magnifying their speciality and proclaiming to the world that they are fixed for ever on their pedestal of uniqueness. They forget that only discords are unique and therefore can claim their own separate place outside the universal world of music.

It should be the function of religion to provide us with this universal ideal of truth and maintain it in its purity. But men have often made perverse use of their religion, building with it permanent walls to ensure their own separateness. In the region of worldly interest, our individual boundaries, in spite of their strength, are adjustable; they are ever changing their lines of demarcation. A man who, in the natural course of things, is a stranger to me may establish intimate kinship with me tomorrow; one who has been my enemy may become my best friend in time. But if we use religion itself for the delimitation of our mutual relationships, then these boundaries become rigidly unalterable.

Religion must only deal with things that belong to the spiritual realm of the eternal, and with sentiments that are self-luminous, carrying their ultimate value in themselves. It should allow a great part of human existence to lie outside its direct interference, so that life may enjoy its freedom of growth guided by laws of reason, or rhythm of beauty. The guidance of reason constantly varies its course, in its perpetual process of adjustment with unforeseen circumstances; its scope is ever being widened by contact with new data. But if religion, which is to give us emancipation in the realm of the infinite, tries also to usurp the place of reason in the world of the finite, then it brings about utter stagnation and sterility.

There was a time in the middle age in Europe when religion acted like a wall surrounding the whole life of the people. We know how it tried to keep its sway over the western world through persecution, excommunication and even suppression of science. By the sheer vigour of their intellect the western people have broken through this imprisonment of their mind and have achieved in their life a freedom which makes it possible for them to approach and receive truth in its various phases and forms.

Intercourse between men is not merely external its deepest channel is through the freedom of mind. When religion instead of emancipating mind, fetters it within the narrow confinement of creeds and conventions, then it becomes the greatest barrier against a true meeting of races. Christianity, when it minimises its spiritual truth which is universal and emphasises its dogmatic side which is a mere accretion of time has the same effect of creating a mental obstruction which leads to the misunderstanding of people who are outside its pale. A great deal of the unmerited contempt and cruelty, which the non-western peoples have suffered in their political, commercial or other relations at the hands of the West, is owing to sectarian calumnies with which even the western children's textbooks are contaminated. Nevertheless this sectarian religion does not occupy the greater part of the western life and therefore in its heart still remains the possibility of a better human relationship than what prevails now between the races.

We have seen Europe cruelly unscrupulous in its politics and commerce, widely spreading slavery over the face of the earth in various names and forms. And yet, in this very same Europe, protest is always alive against its own iniquities. Martyrs are never absent whose lives of sacrifice are the penance for the wrongs done by their own kindred. The individuality which is western is not to be designated by any sect-name of a particular religion, but is distinguished by its eager attitude towards truth, in two of its aspects, scientific and humanistic. This openness of mind to Truth has also its moral value and so in the West it has often been noticed that, while those who are professedly pious have sided with tyrannical power, encouraging repression of freedom, the men of intellect, the sceptics, have bravely stood for justice and the rights of man.

I do not mean to say that those who seek truth always find truth, and we know that men in the West are apt to borrow the sanction of science under false pretences to give expression to their passions and prejudices. To many thinkers there has appeared a clear connection between Darwin's theories and the 'imperialism', Teutonic and other, which was so marked a feature during the 'sixties. We have also read western authors who, admirably mimicking scientific mannerism, assert that only the so-called Nordic race has the proper quality and therefore the right to rule the world, extolling its characteristic ruthlessness as giving it the claim to universal dominance. But we must not forget that such aberrations of science, padded with wrong or imperfect data, will be knocked down by science itself. The stream of water in a river does carry sand, but so long as the stream is fluent it will push away that sand from its own path. If the mental attitude is right we need not be afraid of mistakes. That is why the individual in the West has no unsurpassable barrier between himself and the rest of humanity. He may have his prejudices, but no irrational injunctions to keep him in internment away from the wide world of men.

A Mahomedan is defined by his religion. But a religion does not consist merely in its spiritual essence; a great deal of it is formal, the outcome of special historical circumstances. All things that constitute mere forms of religion are exclusive,—no man belonging to a different creed can claim them as his own. These are, therefore, fences that separate; and are, moreover, constant causes of conflict so long as they are more valued than the essential truths of religion. Therefore the people who are chiefly recognised by their religion, whose behaviour and intellect itself is dominated by the externals of that religion, must find it difficult to establish channels of intimate relationship with neighbours belonging to a different religion.

Men often are unreasonable, but their unreason is as fluid in character as life itself; it is constantly mitigated by experience and education. But when religion stands against reason in the region which by right belongs to the latter, then it becomes a fixed screen of darkness against all communication of light. Truth finds no permanent antagonism in our passion or stupidity, just as sunshine is not perpetually obstructed by mist. But when religion, with its own material and authority, builds a barricade against truth, then woe to the men who bend their knees to such a power, terrible because it is the power of light that has blinded itself.

On the other side, a Hindu also is known by his speciality, which is not so much his religion as his social conventions. A Mahomedan is comparatively free in matters of his personal life, as to his food, companionship or occupation. Therefore he has more freedom of opportunity in the choice of his vocation than an orthodox Hindu. A narrow range of vocation not only curtails for men their field of livelihood, but also limits their chance of coming into close touch with others in the active pursuit of common objects. Surrounded in his personal life by prohibitions of all kinds about the most insignificant details of his daily career, an orthodox Hindu lives insulated in the confinement of his conventional solitary cell. His is a world which has its one gate of entrance, the gate of birth, though those of departure are innumerable. The strict code of Hinduism is, in every way, inhospitable to the world at large, which cannot but react upon the mind of the orthodox Hindu by narrowing and deadening his human interest, detracting from his power of forming great combinations.

We have to realize this in India, and know that the religion, chiefly based upon a fixed code of custom, which we have allowed to fasten upon the entire region of our life, has been the one radical cause of the separateness of our races, and has made the cracks from which comes out the poisonous gas of degeneracy. The problem of untouchability is merely one of the numerous symptoms of this fatal malady. By suppressing these through external means we do not cure the disease. The thorny bushes of evil are overspreading our social soil, made barren by the obsession of a religion that insults reason. Uprooting a few of these will not help us in improving the soil, the impoverishment of which is the real origin of our futility.

Civilization is that which gives individuals the best facility to deal with the greatest number of human beings in the noblest spirit of truth. Unfortunately for India, the latter development of Hinduism has been the product of a history of reaction. It represents the most powerfully organized effort of a people, not only to withdraw itself from contact with the larger world, but also to separate its own component parts so that they become out of touch with each other. The greater portion of the world is branded by it with impurity. Defilement is waiting for it at every turn, against which its only security is the strict system of segregation built up by itself. In order to build this effectively, it has not been content with forbidding its members to cross the sea, but has nearly obliterated from its annals and literature all mention of foreign contact. For, though from Greek, Tibetan, Chinese and other sources we find; materials for that great period of India's history when her influence transcended her geographical limits and spread civilization over peoples completely alien to her own children, we find no mention in the Indian scriptures about what those outside countries were to her. So much so, that all the records of the greatest of India's sons were banished for centuries from her memory, till they were brought back to her by foreigners. The mentality produced by such a contemptuous ignoring of the world outside her own immediate surroundings, still persists in the life and culture of India's people.

No doubt, in all parts of the world we have such restrictions of narrowness, under different names. Societies in all countries have their irrational conventions and traditions that have outlived their original meaning, clogging the path of human intercourse with incongruities. Everywhere such social holes and ditches are the breeding places of moral disease and callousness of heart. The spirit of nationalism itself in the West is another such confinement, which raises a barrier against the large human world and gives rise to degeneracy of soul. How, in the end, it becomes disastrous to its own cause, has been proved in the frank brutality of the late War, and perhaps more so in the sinister manoeuvres of the Peace conferences.

I know how reluctant it makes us feel to give any credit for humanity to the western civilization when we observe the brutalities into which this nationalism of theirs breaks out, instances of which are so numerous all the world over,—in the late war, in the lynching of Negroes, in cowardly outrages allowed to be committed by European soldiers upon helpless Indians, in the rapacity and vandalism practised in Peking during the Boxer war by the very people who are never tired of vulgarly applying the epithet of Hun to one section of their own confederates. But while I have never sought to gloss over or keep out of mind any of these ugly phenomena, I still aver that in the life of the West they have a large tract where their mind is free; whence the circulation of their thought currents can surround the world. This freedom of the mind's ventilation constantly bears in it the promise of righting the wrong and purifying the noxious accumulation within.

The latter-day orthodox Hinduism of our country, on the other hand, though free from militant aggressiveness, is even more fatal in its effects on its own votaries, for it has to kill the mind first in order to make it possible for human beings to accept such deprivation of freedom and outrage on dignity as are entailed by its prohibitions and exactions. Accustomed as we are to it, we may not feel the humiliation of such restriction of life and mind, or may even glorify it in our blind pride; but in these days, when we are talking about nation-building and the uniting of the different Indian races, we must know that Hindus and Mahomedans can never effect any real union until we can cast off the shackles of our non-essentials, and free our mind from the grip of unmeaning dead tradition.

To me the mere political necessity is unimportant; it is for the sake of our humanity, for the full growth of our soul, that we must turn our mind towards the ideal of the spiritual unity of man. We must use our social strength, not to guard ourselves against the touch of others, considering it as contamination, but generously to extend hospitality to the world, taking all its risks however numerous and grave. We must manfully accept the responsibility of moral freedom, which disdains to barricade itself within dead formulae of external regulation, timidly seeking its security in utter stagnation. For, men who live in dread of the spirit of enquiry and lack courage to launch out in the adventure of truth, can never achieve freedom in any department of life. Freedom is not for those who are not lovers of freedom and who only allow it standing space in the porter's vestibule for the sake of some temporary purpose, while worshipping, in the inner shrine of their life, the spirit of blind obedience.

In India what is needed more than anything else, is the broad mind which, only because it is conscious of its own vigorous individuality, is not afraid of accepting truth from all sources. Fortunately for us we know what such a mind has meant in an individual who belongs to modern India. I speak of Rammohun Roy. He was thoroughly oriental in his early training and did not study English till he was of mature age. He was a profound scholar of Sanskrit, Persian, Arabic and he learnt Hebrew in order to study the Old Testament in its original oriental setting. He knew more of Sanskrit scriptures and Indian philosophy than any contemporary pandit. His learning, because of its depth and comprehensiveness, did not merely furnish him with materials for scholarship, but trained his mind for the free acceptance of truth. Rammohun Roy developed the courage and capacity to discriminate between things that are essential and those that are non-essential in the culture which was his by inheritance. This helped him to realise that, truth can never be foreign, that money and material may exclusively belong to the particular country which produces them, but not knowledge, or ideas, or immortal forms of art.

The spirit of orthodox Hinduism is not modern, because it is fixed in the past,—the present age does not exist for it, and therefore it goes on missing its future. Rammohun Roy received from the storehouse of his country's past, things that were living. Therefore the future for him had its reality. For, life has its growth, which means that it perpetually carries its future in its own past and present; in other words, its present is a bridge between its past and its future. Rammohun was typically modern, because in his life and work he not only built such a bridge between the past and the future of his own country, but between India and the rest of the world.

The very magnitude of mind of such men becomes almost a grievance for smaller personalities, and Rammohun has been misunderstood by his own countrymen because he had in him this modern spirit of freedom and comprehensive grasp of truth. We must, however, never make the mistake that those great men who are belittled by their contemporary compatriots do not represent their countries; for, countries are not always true to themselves.

Giordano Bruno more truly represented the spirit of the intellectual probity of Europe than the Europe herself of that period which killed him. The Judea which held her god to be the god of a chosen people did not clearly know her own ideal; her truth was represented by the prophets who realized the Kingdom of God in the unbounded realm of humanity. The true life of India has been obscured by the night which overtook her and the slightest glimmer of light on her eastern horizon is more her own than the vast darkness which contradicts it. The India which keeps her religion shackled in chains of dead custom that refuse to be responsible to reason or to conscience, is *maya,*—she reveals her soul only there, where her seers have declared that religion recognises no external bond.

We have often seen in human history that at the very time and place where facts appear overwhelming in their congregated attack against the dignity of man, there appears the prophet who discovers some sovereign truth which raises its head above the rebellious turmoil. And because in India the heterogeneity of races is a most overbearing fact that has produced such incoherence of mind, such division in life, making our present problems seem well-nigh insoluble, there is a strong hope that in the India of today will be evolved some great spiritual guidance which will lead her to an enlightened future across irrational dogmas, or nationalistic cults. For, obstacles are like blocks of marble with which those who are artists amongst men fashion the best living images of truth.

In Rammohun Roy's life we find a concrete illustration of what India seeks, the true indication of her goal. Thoroughly steeped in the best culture of his country, he was capable of finding himself at home in the larger world. His culture was not for rejection of those cultures which came from foreign sources, on the contrary, it had an uncommon power of sympathy which could adjust itself to them with respectful receptiveness. His mind had a natural reverence for Saraswati, the goddess of knowledge,—for the Truth, whose dwelling is in the hundred-petalled lotus-heart of humanity. It is an utter lack of reverence for truth which, in the name of Patriotism, can ignore the grand quest of man for knowledge because, for the time being, its field of activity happens to be in the West. And I must strenuously maintain that such irreverence is not in harmony with the spirit of our land.

The ideal I have formed of the culture which should be universal in India, has become clear to me from the life of Rammohun Roy. I have come to feel that the mind, which has been matured in the atmosphere of a profound knowledge of its own country and of the perfect thoughts that have been produced in that land, is ready to accept and assimilate the cultures that come from foreign countries. He who has no wealth of his own can only beg, and those who are compelled to follow the profession of beggary at the gate of the intellectually rich may gain occasional scraps of mental food, but they are sure to lose the strength of their intellectual character and their minds are doomed to become timid in thought and in creative endeavour.

All this time we have been receiving education on purely western lines. When this first began, western culture was imbued with a supreme contempt for that of the East. And to this day, consequently, we have been brought up in this contempt. This speaks of internal dissensions within the temple of Mother Saraswati. Her eastern sons kept closed the door leading to the western side for fear of adulteration, and her western sons barred their eastern windows through want of respect. Meanwhile the system of education in India remained, and still remains, absurdly un-Indian, making no adequate provision for our own culture. We have, here, not even anything like the facility which the German student enjoys in Germany, for the study of the lore of Hindu and Moslem. And if we have become conscious of this vital deficiency in our education, that is because of the spirit of the times.

A certain number of us do not admit that our culture has any special features of value. These good people I leave out of account. But the number of those others is not few, who while admitting this value in theory, ignore it more or less in practice. Very often, the flourishing of the banner of this culture is not for the sake of the love of truth but for that of national vaingloriousness,—like brandishing a musical instrument in athletic display before one's own admiring family, instead of using it to make music.

This section of our people while never neglecting to make proud boast of their country's glory, have an absurdly narrow conception of the ideal in which that glory consists. Their indiscriminate reverence is for the actual, not for the eternal. The habits and customs of our decadence which have set up barriers between us and the world, splitting us into mutually exclusive sections, making us weak and bowing our heads in shame at every turn of our later history,—these are the idols of their special worship, which they endow with endless virtues of their own imagining. They consider it to be their sacred mission to retain in perpetuity the waste matter sloughed off by age, as the true insignia of our Hindu civilization; to extol the gleam of the will-o-the-wisp, born of the noxious miasma of decay, as more time-hallowed than the light of sun, moon and stars.

Up to now we have not been submitting our own scriptures to the same critical, historical and scientific tests to which we are accustomed in the case of western lore. As if, everywhere else in the world, the normality of universal law prevails, but the door is barred to it in India, whose history, forsooth, has no beginning and is altogether beyond the province of science! Some god is responsible for its grammar, another for its chemistry, a third for its science of medicine. Everything in this wonderland has been set going, once for all, by the co-operation of gods and sages. What critic can be allowed to pry too curiously into an arrangement of such perfection? That is why even our educated men do not feel any qualms in counting our miraculous myths as integral parts of our history.

Therefore it is reckoned as a sin to enquire into the why and wherefore of what we do as Hindus. The ordinary laws of cause and effect cannot be taken into consideration in the India of the Infallibles, where the injunctions of the *shastras* are the one cause of all action. So when we debate whether sea-voyage is good or bad, we have to look into our scriptures to find the reply; and if we want to know whether the presence of a particular person in the room will contaminate the water in our vessels, we must go to a pandit for the solution. If we dare to question why the caste, which may handle our milk or our molasses, may not come near our water, or why foreign food should destroy our caste while foreign strong drink apparently does not, our mouths may be stopped, in more senses than one, by a stoppage of all supplies.

It seems to me that one reason for the persistence of these absurdities, even in our educated circles, is, that we reserve western science and method only for our school hours, while the current traditions and beliefs are imbibed at other times when, with our school dress, we have likewise doffed the school habit of precise thinking. They are kept in separate compartments, and so never come to a mutual understanding. Thus it is no matter of difficulty for us to believe that only in our class lessons we need to be rational; for the rest, if we be but grammatical, that is enough.

In our greed for immediate political result, we are apt to ascribe the fact of our tendency towards separateness to accidental circumstances, refusing to see that a code of behaviour, which has not the sanction of reason, and yet has the support of religion, must result in the creation of irreconcilable divisions between men. In reason alone can we have our common meeting ground; for that which is against reason needs must be peculiar and exclusive, offering constant friction until worn away by the ever-active, rational mind of man. So when, for a body of men, popular custom is artificially protected by a religion which is allowed to usurp the entire range of human knowledge and conduct, it becomes a potent factor in maintaining an immense gap of aloofness and antagonism between closest neighbours.

The evolving Hindu social ideal has never been present to us as a whole, so that we have only a vague conception of what the Hindu has achieved in the past, or can attempt in the future. The partial view, before us at any moment, appears at the time to be the most important, so we can hardly bring ourselves to believe that it is this very aspect which, not only hides from us the true ideal, but tends to destroy it. And we have thus come to imagine a picture of the Hindu Samaj continually bathing, fasting and telling beads, emaciated with doing penance, shrinking into a corner away from the rest of the world.

We forget that Hindu civilization was once very much alive, crossing the seas, planting colonies, giving to and taking from all the world. It had its arts, its commerce, its vast and strenuous field of work. In its history, new ideas had their scope, social and religious revolutions their opportunity. Its women also, had their learning, their bravery, their place in the civic life. In every page of the Mahābhārata we shall find proofs that it was no rigid, cast-iron type of civilization. The men of those days did not, like marionettes, play the same set piece over and over again. They progressed through mistakes, made discoveries through experiment, and gained truth through striving. They belonged to a free and varied *samāj*, quick with life, driven into ever new enterprise by its active vigour.

This, however, was a society which orthodoxy today would hardly recognise as Hindu, because it was living and had a growth which was revealing its inner unity through outer changes. So the *dharma* of life which thinks and doubts, accepts and rejects, progresses, changes and evolves, cannot, according to orthodoxy, be a part of the Hindu Dharma. Man shows his mental feebleness when he loses his faith in life because it is difficult to govern, and is only willing to take the responsibility of the dead because they are content to lie still under an elaborately decorated tomb-stone of his own make. We must know that life carries its own weight, while the burden of the dead is heavy to bear,—an intolerable burden which has been pressing upon our country for ages. Can we really believe that with this incubus of social inertness on our bowed back we can cross the pathless wilderness and succeed in reaching the hill-top of political independence?

The fact stands out clearly today that the Divinity dwelling within the heart of man cannot be kept immured any longer in the darkness of particular temples. The day of the *Ratha-yātrā*, the Car Festival, has arrived when He shall come out on the highway of the world, into the thick of the joys and sorrows, the mutual commerce, of the throng of men. Each of us must set to work to build such car as we can, to take its place in the grand procession. The material of some may be of value, of others cheap. Some may break down on the way, others last till the end. But the day has come at last when all the cars must set out.

I feel proud that I have been born in this great age. I know that it must take time before we can adjust our minds to a condition which is not only new, but almost exactly the opposite of the old. Let us not imagine the death struggle of the doomed to be a sign of life. Let us announce to the world that the light of the morning has come, not for entrenching ourselves behind barriers, but for meeting in mutual understanding and trust on the common field of co-operation; never for nourishing a spirit of rejection, but for that glad acceptance which constantly carries in itself the giving out of the best that we have.

(1923)

Race Conflict

34

The problem of race conflict has ever been present in the history of mankind. This conflict has been at the basis of all great civilizations. It is like the clash of elements in the material world giving rise to complex combinations and evolutions of higher growth.

It was the concussion of peoples brought up in different surroundings and with different outlook upon life that started the original energy resulting in complicated social organizations. All civilizations are mixed products. Only barbarism is simple, monadic and unalloyed.

When differences have to be taken into account perforce, when there is no possible escape from them, then men are compelled to find out some central bond which can bring into unity all the diverse elements. This is really the seeking after truth, the search for the one in the many, the universal through the individuals.

Naturally, in the commencement its appearance is simple and crude. Some common visible object of worship is held as a symbol of the oneness of the people. It is very often gross and frightful. For when man has to depend upon external standards of life these have to be made as conspicuous as possible, and nothing is so compelling to primitive imagination as fear.

But, as the community grows larger and, by conquest and other means, peoples of different traditions unite, then fetishes multiply and more gods than one have to be recognized. In that case, these symbols lose their power as common bonds, and they have to be replaced by something whose appeal is not so much to the senses and whose significance is more universal.

Thus, gradually, as the problem grows more and more wide and complex, the solution of it becomes deeper and more far-reaching, and human solidarity seeks for its foundation something which is abiding and comprehensive. This is the purpose of all history, man seeking truth through complexities of experience impelled by the impetus of the immensity of evergrowing life.

There was a time when owing to the restricted means of communication different races and nations lived in a state of comparative segregation and consequently their social laws and institutions had an intensely local character. They were narrowly racial and aggressively hostile to the aliens. People did not have frequent occasion to learn how to adjust themselves with outsiders. They had to take to violent measures when they collided with alien people. They simplified the problem to its narrowest limits and either absolutely excluded and exterminated all foreign elements or completely amalgamated them.

Men have not yet outgrown this training of racial or national self-sufficiency. They are still burdened with the age-long inheritance of a suspicion of aliens which is the primitive instinct of animals. They still have a lurking ferocity ready to come out at the slightest provocation when in contact with people outside their social boundaries. They have not yet acquired fairness of mind when judging other races and dealing with them. They have not that power of adjusting their mental vision which would enable them to understand the people who are not nearest to them. They strive their utmost to prove the superiority and originality of their own religion and philosophy and they are reluctant to acknowledge that, truth, because it is truth, naturally manifests itself in different countries in different garbs. They are ever prone to put more stress on differences which are external and lose sight of the inner harmony.

This is the result of being brought up in the home training of isolation, which makes one unfit for the citizenship of the world. But this cannot continue for long and with the advent of the new age of science and commerce men have been brought nearer to each other than they ever were before and they are face to face with the highest problem of human history, the problem of race conflict.

This problem has been waiting to be solved by experience, through the expansion of history. It is not a mere matter of sentiment or of intellect. We had prophets who preached equality of man, and philosophy and literature which gave us a broader view of reality than is contained in the limits of racial traditions and habits. But this race problem with its vast complexity was never before us—we were not in living contact with it. Humanity, till now, has played with this sentiment of brotherhood of man as a girl does with her doll. It reveals the truth of the feeling which is innate in the heart of man, still it lacks the reality of life. But the playtime is passed and what was only in the sentiment has grown into our life fraught with immense responsibilities.

Of all the ancient civilizations, I think, that of India was compelled to recognize this race problem in all seriousness and for ages she has been engaged unravelling the most bafflingly complicated tangle of race-differences. Europe was fortunate in having neighbouring races more or less homogeneous, for, most of them were of the same origin. So, though in Europe there were bitter feuds between different peoples, there was not that physical antipathy between them which the difference in colour of skin and in feature tends to produce. In England it did not take long for the Norman and Saxon elements to coalesce and lose their distinctions. Not only in colour and features but in their ideals of life the western peoples are so near each other that practically they are acting as one in building up their civilization.

But it has been otherwise with India. At the beginning of Indian history the white-skinned Aryans had encounters with the aboriginal people who were dark and who were intellectually inferior to them. Then there were the Dravidians who had their own civilization and whose gods and modes of worship and social system were totally different from those of the newcomers, which must have proved a more active barrier between them than full-fledged barbarism.

In tropical countries life is not so strenuous as it is where the climate is cold. There the necessities of life are comparatively small and nature more prodigal in her bounties; therefore in those countries strifes between contending parties die away for want of incentives. So, in India, after a period of fierce struggles, men of different colours and creeds, different physical features and mental attitudes settled together side by side. As men are not inert matter but living beings, this juxtaposition of different elements became an ever-present problem for India. But with all its disadvantages this it was that stimulated men's minds to find out the essential unity in diversity of forms, to know that, however different be the symbols and rituals, God, whom they try to represent, is one without a second, and to realize him truly is to realize him in the soul of all beings.

When differences are too jarring, man cannot accept them as final; so, either he wipes them out with blood, or coerces them in some kind of superficial homogeneity, or he finds out a deeper unity which he knows is the highest truth.

India chose the last alternative; and all through the political vicissitudes that tossed her about for centuries, when her sister civilizations of Greece and Rome exhausted their life force, her spiritual vitality still continued and she still retains her dignity of soul. I do not say for a moment that the difficulties about the race differences have been altogether removed in India. On the contrary, new elements have been added, new complications introduced, and all the great religions of the world have taken their roots in the soil of India. In her attempts at bringing into order this immense mass of heterogeneity India has passed through successive periods of expansion and contraction of her ideals. And her latest has been that of setting up rigid lines of regulations to keep different sections at arm's length to prevent confusion and clash.

But such a negative attitude cannot last long, and mere mechanical contrivances can never work satisfactorily in human society. If, by any chance, men are brought together who are not products of the same history and not moulded in the same traditions, they never can rest till they can find out some broad basis of union which is positive in its nature and which makes for love. And I am sure, in India we have that spiritual ideal, if dormant but still living, which can tolerate all differences in the exterior while recognizing the inner unity. I feel sure, in India, we have that golden key forged by ancient wisdom and love which will one day open the barred gates to bring together to the feast of good fellowship men who have lived separated for generations.

From a very remote period of her history till now all the great personalities of India have been working in the same direction. The Gospel of universal love that Buddha preached was the outcome of a movement long preceding him, which endeavoured to get at the kernel of spiritual unity, breaking through all divergence of symbols and ceremonies and individual preferences.

With the advent of the Mohamedan power not only a new political situations was created in India but new ideas in religion and social customs were brought before the people with a violent force. Nevertheless, it had not the effect of generating an antagonistic fanatical movement among Hindus. On the contrary, all the great religious geniuses that were born during this period in India sought a reconciliation of the old with the new ideals in a deeper synthesis, which was possible because of the inherited spirit of toleration and accumulated wisdom of ages. In all these movements there was the repeated call to the people to forget all distinctions of castes and creeds and accept the highest privilege of brotherhood of man by uniting in love of God.

The same thing has occurred again when India has been closely brought in contact with the Christian civilization with the coming of the English. The Brahmo Samaj movement in India is the movement for the spiritual reconciliation of the East and West, the reconciliation resting upon the broad basis of spiritual wisdom laid in the Upanishads. There is again the same call to the people to rise above all artificial barriers of caste and recognise the common bond of brotherhood in the name of God.

In no other country in the world is the conflux of races different in every respect so great as in India. Therefore it never could have been possible for her to come to such a simple solution of the difficulty as national unity. The fetish of nationalism is powerless to bring her warring elements into a harmony; she must appeal to the highest power in man, the spiritual power, she must come to her God. There has been going on in India a long continued contention between rigid forms of exclusiveness which is mechanical and a recognition of the unity of mankind which is spiritual. Here, as in every land, the social convention is on the side of the pride of caste, and the higher nature and the deeper wisdom of the people assert in the lives of its greatest personalities the validity of the claims of all men to justice and love. On the one hand there is the regulation which forbids eating and drinking at the same board for men of different castes and on the other hand there comes the voice from the ancient past which preaches that he who realizes his own self in the self of all individuals realizes truly. And I have not the least doubt in my mind that it is the urging of this spiritual impulse in man which will win in the end, and will mould all the social forms in such a way that they may not hinder its purpose but become its instrument.

I bring before you this instance of Indian history to show that a problem must be a living one to rouse man's mind for its solution. It has become so in the present age. Races widely separated in their geographical position and historical growth, in their modes of thought and manners of expression have been brought near each other in closer relations. To each man the human world has been enlarged to an extent never dreamt of in former days. That we are not ready for these changed circumstances is becoming painfully evident every day. The caste feeling is running fearfully high. The western people are cultivating an arrogant exclusiveness against all other races. While keeping for themselves their prerogatives of exploiting weaker nations by threat of force they securely bar their own gates against them in a manner cruelly barbarous and inhospitable. Sentiments of humanity are openly discredited and poets of world-wide reputation are exulting in the triumph of brute force, Nations wakened from a lethargy of centuries and bravely struggling for a larger life are held back by others more fortunate, waiting to turn to their own advantage the situation created by the breaking up of old order. Want of consideration for people held to be inferior to themselves, rising into inhuman atrocities where privacy is secured, is not uncommon with the people proud of their colour and the impunity of their position.

Yet, in spite of these untoward aspects of the case I assert strongly that the solution is most assured when difficulties are greatest. It is a matter for congratulation that today the civilized man is seriously confronted with this problem of race conflict. And the greatest thing that this age can be proud of is the birth of Man in the consciousness of men. Its bed has not been provided for, it is born in poverty, its infancy is lying neglected in a wayside stall, spurned by wealth and power. But its day of triumph is approaching. It is waiting for its poets and prophets and host of humble workers and they will not tarry for long. When the call of humanity is poignantly insistent then the higher nature of man cannot but respond. In the darkest periods of his drunken orgies of power and national pride man may flout and jeer at it, daub it as an expression of weakness and sentimentalism, but in that very paroxysm of arrogance, when his attitude is most hostile and his attacks most reckless against it, he is suddenly reminded that it is the direst form of suicide to kill the highest truth that is in him. When organized national selfishness, racial antipathy and commercial self-seeking begin to display their ugly deformities in all their nakedness, then comes the time for man to know that his salvation is not in political organizations and extended trade relations, not in any mechanical rearrangement of social system, but in a deeper transformation of life, in the liberation of consciousness in love, in the realization of God in man.

(1912)

The Meeting of the East and the West

For over a century and a half India has borne a foreign rule which is western. Whether she has been benefited by it, whether her arts and industries have made progress, her wealth increased and her opportunities of self-government multiplied, are a matter of controversy which is of very little material interest to the present generation of our countrymen, as it cannot change facts. Even from the point of view of historical curiosity it has a very imperfect value, for we are not allowed to remember all facts except in strict privacy. So I am not going to enter into any discussion which is sure to lead to an unsatisfactory conclusion or consequences.

But one thing about which there has been no attempt at concealment or difference of opinion is that the East and the West have remained far apart even after these years of relationship. When two different peoples have to deal with each other and yet without forming any true bond of union, it is sure to become a burden, whatever benefit may accrue from it. And when we say that we suffer from the dead weight of mutual alienation we do not mean any adverse criticism of the motive or the system of government, for the problem is vast and it affects all mankind. It inspires in our minds awe verging upon despair when we come to think that all the world has been bared open to a civilization which has not the spiritual power in it to unite, but which can only exploit and destroy and domineer and can make even its benefits an imposition from outside while claiming its price in loyalty of heart.

Therefore it must be admitted that this civilization, while it abounds in the riches of mind, lacks in a great measure to one truth which is of the highest importance to all humanity; the truth which man even in the dimmest dawn of his history felt, however vaguely it might be. This is why, when things go against them, the peoples brought up in the spirit of modern culture furiously seek for some change in organization and system, as if the human world were a mere intellectual game of chess where winning and losing depended upon the placing of pawns. They forget that for a man winning a game may be the greatest of his losses.

Men began their career of history with a faith in a Personal Being in relation to whom they had their unity among themselves. This was no mere belief in ghost but in the deeper reality of their oneness which is the basis of their moral ideals. This was the one great comprehension of truth which gave life and light to all the best creative energies of man, making us feel the touch of the infinite in our personality.

Naturally the consciousness of unity had its beginning in the limited area of race—the race which was the seed-plot of all human ideals. And therefore, and first, men had their conception of God as a tribal God which restricted their moral obligation within the bounds of their own people.

The first Aryan immigrants came to India with their tribal gods and special ceremonials and their conflict with the original inhabitants of India seemed to have no prospect of termination. In the midst of this struggle the conception of a universal soul, the spiritual bond of unity in all creatures, took its birth in the better minds of the time. This heralded a change of heart and along with it a true basis of reconciliation.

During the Mahomedan conquest of India, behind the political turmoil our inner struggle was spiritual. Like Asoka of the Buddhist age Akbar also had his vision of spiritual unity. A succession of great men of those centuries, both Hindu saints and Mahomedan sufis, was engaged in building a kingdom of souls over which ruled the one God who was the god of Mahomedans, as well as Hindus.

In India this striving after spiritual realization still shows activity. And I feel sure that the most important event of modern India has been the birth and life-work of Rammohun Roy, for it is a matter of the greatest urgency that the East and the West should meet and unite in hearts. Through Rammohun Roy was given the first true response of India when the West knocked at her door. He found the basis of our union in our own spiritual inheritance, in faith in the reality of the oneness of man in Brahma.

Other men of intellectual eminence we have seen in our days who have borrowed their lessons from the West. This schooling makes us intensely conscious of the separateness of our people giving rise to a patriotism fiercely exclusive and contemptuous. This has been the effect of the teaching of the west everywhere in the world. It has roused up a universal spirit of suspicious antipathy. It incites each people to strain all resources for taking advantages of others by force or by cunning. This cult of organized pride and self-seeking, this deliberate falsification of moral perspective in our view of humanity, has also invaded with a new force men's minds in India. If it does contain any truth along with its falsehood we must borrow it from others to mend our defect in mental balance. But, at the same time, I feel sure India is bid to give expression to the truth belonging to her own inner life.

Today the western people have come in contact with all races of the world when their moral adjustment has not yet been made true for this tremendous experience. The reality of which they are most fervidly conscious is the reality of the Nation. It has served them up to a certain point, just as some amount of boisterous selfishness, pugnacious and inconsiderate, may serve us in our boyhood, but makes mischief when carried into our adult life of larger social responsibilities. But the time has come at last when the western people are beginning to feel nearer home what the cult of the nation has been to humanity, they who have reaped all its benefits, with a great deal of its cost thrown upon the shoulders of others.

It is natural that they should realize humanity when it is nearest themselves. It increases their sensibility to a very high pitch, within a narrow range, keeping their conscience inactive where it is apt to be uncomfortable.

But when we forget truth for our own convenience, truth does not forget us. Up to a certain limit, she tolerates neglect, but she is sure to put in her appearance, to exact her dues with full arrears, on an occasion which we grumble at as inappropriate and at a provocation which seems trivial. This makes us feel the keen sense of the injustice of providence, as does the rich man of questionable history, whose time-honoured wealth has attained the decency of respectability, if he is suddenly threatened with an exposure.

We have observed that when the West is visited by a sudden calamity, she cannot understand why it should happen at all in God's world. The question has never occurred to her, with any degree of intensity, why people in other parts of the world should suffer. But she has to know that humanity is a truth which nobody can mutilate and yet escape its hurt himself. Modern civilization has to be judged not by its balance-sheet of imports and exports, luxuries of rich men, lengths of dreadnoughts, breadth of dependencies and tightness of grasping diplomacy. In this judgment of history, we from the East are the principal witnesses, who must speak the truth without flinching, however difficult it may be for us and unpleasant for others. Our voice is not the voice of authority, with the power of arms behind it, but the voice of suffering which can only count upon the power of truth to make itself heard.

There was a time when Europe had started on her search for the soul. In spite of all digressions she was certain that man must find his true wealth by becoming true. She knew that the value of his wealth was not merely subjective, but its eternal truth was in a love ever active in man's world. Then came a time when science revealed the greatness of the material universe and violently diverted Europe's attention to gaining things in place of inner perfection. Science has its own great meaning for man. It proves to him that he can bring his reason to co-operate with nature's laws, making them serve the higher ends of humanity; that he can transcend the biological world of natural selection and create his own world of moral purposes by the help of nature's own laws. It is Europe's mission to discover that Nature does not stand in the way of our self-realization, but we must deal with her with truth in order to invest our idealism with reality and make it permanent.

This higher end of science is attained where its help has been requisitioned for the general alleviation of our wants and sufferings, where its gifts are for all men. But it fearfully fails where it supplies means for personal gains and attainment of selfish power. For its temptations are so stupendously great that our moral strength is not only overcome but fights against its own forces under the cover of such high-sounding names as patriotism and nationality. This has made the relationship of human races inhuman, burdening it with repression and restriction where it faces the weak and brandishing it with vengefulness and competition of ferocity where it meets the strong. It has made war and preparation for war the normal condition of all nations, and has polluted diplomacy, the carrier of the political pestilence, with cruelty and dishonourable deception.

Yet those who have trust in human nature cannot but feel certain that the West will come out triumphant and the fruit of the centuries of her endeavour will not be trampled under foot in the mad scrimmage for things which are not of the spirit of man. Feeling the perplexity of the present-day entanglements she is groping for a better system and a wiser diplomatic arrangement. But she will have to recognize, perhaps at the end of her series of death-lessons, that it is an intellectual Pharisaism to have faith only in building pyramids of systems, that she must realize truth in order to be saved, that continually gathering fuel to feed her desire will only lead to world-wide incendiarism. One day she will wake up to set a limit to her greed and turbulent pride and find in compensation that she has an ever-lasting life.

Europe is great. She has been dowered by her destiny with a location and climate and race combination producing a history rich with strength, beauty and tradition of freedom. Nature in her soil challenged man to put forth all his forces never overwhelming his mind into a passivity of fatalism. It imparted in the character of her children the energy and daring which never acknowledge limits to their claims and also at the same time an intellectual sanity, a restraint in imagination, a sense of proportion in their creative works, and sense of reality in all their aspirations. They explored the secrets of existence, measured and mastered them; they discovered the principle of unity in nature not through the help of meditation or abstract logic, but by boldly crossing barriers of diversity and peeping behind the screen. They surprised themselves into nature's great storehouse of powers and there they had their fill of temptation.

Europe is fully conscious of her greatness and that itself is the reason why she does not know where her greatness may fail her. There have been periods of history when great races of men forgot their own souls in the pride and enjoyment of their power and possessions. They were not even aware of this lapse because things and institutions assumed such magnificence that all their attention was drawn outside their true selves. Just as nature in her aspect of bewildering vastness may have the effect of humiliating man, so also his own accumulation may produce the self-abasement which is spiritual apathy by stimulating all his energy towards his wealth and not his welfare. Through this present war has come the warning to Europe that her things have been getting better of her truth and in order to be served she must find her soul and her God and fulfil her purpose by carrying her ideals into all continents of the earth and not sacrifice them to her greed of money and dominion.

(1918)

A Cry for Peace

36

The world is crying for peace. The West is desiring the restoration of peace through a League of Powers. But can Powers find their equilibrium in themselves? Power cannot be made secure only against power, it must also be made secure against the weak; for there lies the peril of its losing balance. The weak are as great a danger for the strong, as quicksands for an elephant. They do not assist progress, because they do not resist, they only drag down. The people who grow accustomed to wield absolute power over others are apt to forget, that by doing it they generate an unseen disruptive force, which some day rends that power into pieces. The dumb fury of the downtrodden finds its awful support from the universal law of moral balance. The air which is thin and weak gives birth to storms that nothing can resist. This has been proved in history over and over again; and stormy forces arising from the heart of insulted humanity are openly gathering in the air even in the present day. Yet the psychology of athletic might stubbornly refuses its lessons and despises to take count of the terribleness of the weak. This is the gross stupidity, that, like an unsuspected worm, burrows at the bottom of the muscular bulk of the prosperous and the proud. Have we never read of the gorgeousness of a power, supinely secure in its arrogance, in a moment dissolving in the air at the explosion of the outraged weak? Politicians calculate upon the number of mailed hands that are on the sword-hilts; they do not possess the third eye to see the great invisible hand, that clasps in silence the hand of the helpless and waits its time. The strong form their League by combination of Powers, driving the weak to form their league alone with their God. I know I am crying in the wilderness, when I raise my voice of warning; and while the West is busy in its organization for building its machine-made peace, it will still continue to nourish, with its iniquities, underground forces of earthquake in the vast bosom of the Eastern Continent. The West seems unconscious that Science, by providing it with more and more power, is tempting it to suicide, encouraging it to accept the challenge of the disarmed, not knowing that this challenge comes from a higher source.

Two prophecies about the world's salvation are cherished in the hearts of the two great religions of the world. They represent the highest expectation of man, thereby indicating his faith in a truth, which he instinctively considers as ultimate,—the truth of love. These prophecies have not for their vision the fettering of the world into tameness with a closely linked power forged in the factory of a political steel trust. One of these religions has, for its meditation, the image of Buddha who is to come, Maitreya, the Buddha of love. And he is to bring peace. The other religion waits for the coming of Christ. For Christ preached peace when he preached love, when he preached Oneness of the Father among brothers who are many. And this was the truth of peace. Christ never held that peace was the best policy. For policy is not truth. The calculation of self-interest can never successfully fight the irrational force of passion—the passion which is perversion of love, and which can only be set aright by the truth of love. So long as the Powers build a League on the foundation of their desire for safety, and for securest enjoyment of gains,—for consolidation of past injustice, for putting off reparation of wrongs, while their fingers still wriggle for grabbing and still reek of blood,—rifts will appear in their union, and conflicts in future will take greater force and magnitude. It is the national and commercial egoism, which is the evil harbinger of war; by different combinations it changes its shape and dimensions, but not its nature. This egoism is still held almost as sacred as religion; and such religion, by its mere change of temple and of committee of priests, will never save men. We must know that, as, through science and commerce, the realization of the unity of the material world gives us power, so the realization of the great spiritual unity of man only can give us peace.

(1919)

Crisis in Civilization

37

Today I complete eighty years of my life. As I look back on the vast stretch of years that lie behind me and see in clear perspective the history of my early development, I am struck by the change that has taken place both in my own attitude and in the psychology of my countrymen—a change that carries within it a cause of profound tragedy.

Our direct contact with the larger world of men was linked up with the contemporary history of the English people whom we came to know in those earlier days. It was mainly through their mighty literature that we formed our ideas with regard to these newcomers to our Indian shores. In those days the type of learning that was served out to us was neither plentiful nor diverse, nor was the spirit of scientific enquiry very much in evidence. Thus their scope being strictly limited, the educated of those days had recourse to English language and literature. Their days and nights were eloquent with the stately declamations of Burke, with Macaulay's long-rolling sentences; discussions centred upon Shakespeare's drama and Byron's poetry and above all upon the large-hearted liberalism of the nineteenth-century English politics.

At the time though tentative attempts were being made to gain our national independence, at heart we had not lost faith in the generosity of the English race. This belief was so firmly rooted in the sentiments of our leaders as to lead them to hope that the victor would of his own grace pave the path of freedom for the vanquished. This belief was based upon the fact that England at the time provided a shelter to all those who had to flee from persecution in their own country. Political martyrs who had suffered for the honour of their people were accorded unreserved welcome at the hands of the English. I was impressed by this evidence of liberal humanity in the character of the English and thus I was led to set them on the pedestal of my highest respect. This generosity in their national character had not yet been vitiated by Imperialist pride. About this time, as a boy in England, I had the opportunity of listening to the speeches of John Bright, both in and outside Parliament. The large-hearted, radical liberalism of those speeches, overflowing all narrow national bounds, had made so deep an impression on my mind that something of it lingers even today, even in these days of graceless disillusionment.

Certainly that spirit of abject dependence upon the charity of our rulers was no matter for pride. What was remarkable, however, was the whole-hearted way in which we gave our recognition to human greatness even when it revealed itself in the foreigner. The best and noblest gifts of humanity cannot be the monopoly of a particular race or country; its scope may not be limited nor may it be regarded as the miser's hoard buried underground. That is why English literature which nourished our minds in the past, does even now convey its deep resonance to the recesses of our heart.

It is difficult to find a suitable Bengali equivalent for the English word 'civilization'. That phase of civilization with which we were familiar in this country has been called by Manu '*Sadachar*' (*lit.* proper conduct), that is, the conduct prescribed by the tradition of the race. Narrow in themselves these time-honoured social conventions originated and held good in a circumscribed geographical area, in that strip of land, Brahmavarta by name, bound on either side by the rivers Saraswati and Drisadvati. That is how a pharisaic formalism gradually got the upper hand of free thought and the ideal of 'proper conduct' which Manu found established in Brahmavarta steadily degenerated into socialized tyranny.

During my boyhood days the attitude of the cultured and educated section of Bengal, nurtured on English learning, was charged with a feeling of revolt against these rigid regulations of society. A perusal of what Rajnarain Bose has written describing the ways of the educated gentry of those days will amply bear out what I have said just now. In place of these set codes of conduct we accepted the ideal of 'civilization' as represented by the English term.

In our own family this change of spirit was welcomed for the sake of its sheer rational and moral force and its influence was felt in every sphere of our life. Born in that atmosphere, which was moreover coloured by our intuitive bias for literature, I naturally set the English on the throne of my heart. Thus passed the first chapters of my life. Then came the parting of ways accompanied with a painful feeling of disillusion when I began increasingly to discover how easily those who accepted the highest truths of civilization disowned them with impunity whenever questions of national self-interest were involved.

There came a time when perforce I had to snatch myself away from the mere appreciation of literature. As I emerged into the stark light of bare facts, the sight of the dire poverty of the Indian masses rent my heart. Rudely shaken out of my dreams, I began to realize that perhaps in no other modern state was there such hopeless dearth of the most elementary needs of existence. And yet it was this country whose resources had fed for so long the wealth and magnificence of the British people. While I was lost in the contemplation of the great world of civilization, I could never have remotely imagined that the great ideals of humanity would end in such ruthless travesty. But today a glaring example of it stares me in the face in the utter and contemptuous indifference of a so-called civilized race to the well-being of crores of Indian people.

That mastery over the machine, by which the British have consolidated their sovereignty over their vast Empire, has been kept a sealed book, to which due access has been denied to this helpless country. And all the time before our very eyes Japan has been transforming herself into a mighty and prosperous nation. I have seen with my own eyes the admirable use to which Japan has put in her own country the fruits of this progress. I have also been privileged to witness, while in Moscow, the unsparing energy with which Russia has tried to fight disease and illiteracy, and has succeeded in steadily liquidating ignorance and poverty, wiping off the humiliation from the face of a vast continent. Her civilization is free from all invidious distinction between one class and another, between one sect and another. The rapid and astounding progress achieved by her made me happy and jealous at the same time. One aspect of the Soviet administration which particularly pleased me was that it provided no scope for unseemly conflict of religious difference nor set one community against another by unbalanced distribution of political favours. That I consider a truly civilized administration which impartially serves the common interests of the people.

While other imperialist powers sacrifice the welfare of the subject races to their own national greed, in the USSR I found a genuine attempt being made to harmonise the interests of the various nationalities that are scattered over its vast area. I saw peoples and tribes, who, only the other day, were nomadic savages being encouraged and indeed trained, to avail themselves freely of the benefits of civilization. Enormous sums are being spent on their education to expedite the process. When I see elsewhere some two hundred nationalities—which only a few years ago were at vastly different stages of development—marching ahead in peaceful progress and amity, and when I look about my own country and see a very highly evolved and intellectual people drifting into the disorder of barbarism, I cannot help contrasting the two systems of governments, one based on co-operation, the other on exploitation, which have made such contrary conditions possible.

I have also seen Iran, newly awakened to a sense of national self-sufficiency, attempting to fulfil her own destiny freed from the deadly grinding-stones of two European powers. During my recent visit to that country I discovered to my delight that Zoroastrians who once suffered from the fanatical hatred of the major community and whose rights had been curtailed by the ruling power were now free from this age-long repression, and that civilized life had established itself in the happy land. It is significant that Iran's good fortune dates from the day when she finally disentangled herself from the meshes of European diplomacy. With all my heart I wish Iran well.

Turning to the neighbouring kingdom of Afghanistan I find that though there is much room for improvement in the field of education and social development, yet she is fortunate in that she can look forward to unending progress; for none of the European powers, boastful of their civilization, has yet succeeded in overwhelming and crushing her possibilities.

Thus while these other countries were marching ahead, India, smothered under the dead weight of British administration, lay static in her utter helplessness. Another great and ancient civilization for whose recent tragic history the British cannot disclaim responsibility, is China. To serve their own national profit the British first doped her people with opium and then appropriated a portion of her territory. As the world was about to forget the memory of this outrage, we were painfully surprised by another event. While Japan was quietly devouring North China, her act of wanton aggression was ignored as a minor incident by the veterans of British diplomacy. We have also witnessed from this distance how actively the British statesmen acquiesced in the destruction of the Spanish Republic.

On the other hand, we also noted with admiration how a band of valiant Englishmen laid down their lives for Spain. Even though the English had not aroused themselves sufficiently to their sense of responsibility towards China in the Far East, in their own immediate neighbourhood they did not hesitate to sacrifice themselves to the cause of freedom. Such acts of heroism reminded me over again of the true English spirit to which in those early days I had given my full faith, and made me wonder how imperialist greed could bring about so ugly a transformation in the character of so great a race.

Such is the tragic tale of the gradual loss of my faith in the claims of the European nations to civilization. In India the misfortune of being governed by a foreign race is daily brought home to us not only in the callous neglect of such minimum necessities of life as adequate provision for food, clothing, educational and medical facilities for the people, but in an even unhappier form in the way the people have been divided among themselves. The pity of it is that the blame is laid at the door of our own society. So frightful a culmination of the history of our people would never have been possible, but for the encouragement it has received from secret influences emanating from high places.

One cannot believe that Indians are in any way inferior to the Japanese in intellectual capacity. The most effective difference between these two eastern peoples is that whereas India lies at the mercy of the British, Japan has been spared the shadow of alien domination. We know what we have been deprived of. That which was truly best in their own civilizations the upholding of the dignity of human relationship, has no place in the British administration of this country. If in its place they have established, with baton in hand, a reign of 'law and order', in other words a policeman's rule, such mockery of civilization can claim no respect from us. It is the mission of civilization to bring unity among people and establish peace and harmony. But in unfortunate India the social fabric is being rent into shreds by unseemly outbursts of hooliganism daily growing in intensity, right under the very aegis of 'law and order'. In India, so long as no personal injury is inflicted upon any member of the ruling race, this barbarism seems to be assured of perpetuity, making us ashamed to live under such an administration.

And yet my good fortune has often brought me into close contact with really large-hearted Englishmen. Without the slightest hesitation I may say that the nobility of their character was without parallel—in no country or community have I come across such greatness of soul. Such examples would not allow me wholly to lose faith in the race which produced them. I had the rare blessing of having Andrews—a real Englishman, a real Christian and a true man—for a very close friend. Today in the perspective of death his unselfish and courageous magnanimity shines all the brighter. The whole of India remains indebted to him for innumerable acts of love and devotion. But personally speaking, I am especially beholden to him because he helped me to retain in my old age that feeling of respect for the English race with which in the past I was inspired by their literature and which I was about to lose completely. I count such Englishmen as Andrews not only as my personal and intimate friends but as friends of the whole human race. To have known them has been to me a treasured privilege. It is my belief that such Englishmen will save British honour from shipwreck. At any rate if I had not known them, my despair at the prospect of western civilization would be unrelieved.

In the meanwhile the demon of barbarity has given up all pretence and has emerged with unconcealed fangs, ready to tear up humanity in an orgy of devastation. From one end of the world to the other the poisonous fumes of hatred darken the atmosphere. The spirit of violence which perhaps lay dormant in the psychology of the West, has at last roused itself and desecrates the spirit of Man.

The wheels of Fate will some day compel the English to give up their Indian empire. But what kind of India will they leave behind, what stark misery? When the stream of their centuries' administration runs dry at last, what a waste of mud and filth they will leave behind them! I had at one time believed that the springs of civilization would issue out of the heart of Europe. But today when I am about to quit the world that faith has gone bankrupt altogether.

As I look around I see the crumbling ruins of a proud civilization strewn like a vast heap of futility. And yet I shall not commit the grievous sin of losing faith in Man. I would rather look forward to the opening of a new chapter in his history after the cataclysm is over and the atmosphere rendered clean with the spirit of service and sacrifice. Perhaps that dawn will come from this horizon, from the East where the sun rises. A day will come when unvanquished Man will retrace his path of conquest, despite all barriers, to win back his lost human heritage.

Today we witness the perils which attend on the insolence of might; one day shall be borne out the full truth of what the sages have proclaimed:

'By unrighteousness man prospers, gains what appears desirable, conquers enemies, but perishes at the root.'

(1941)

Notes

Thirty-seven essays included in this volume cover only a fraction of the complete works of Tagore. But even this cross section is expected to give an idea of some of the basic ideas of Tagore which come up again and again in his writings and which are often embodied in characters and situations presented in his innumerable creative works.

1. The Nobel Prize Acceptance Speech

Since Tagore could not attend the Nobel Award Ceremony held in Stockholm in 1913 this speech may be regarded as "the Nobel Prize Acceptance Speech". The speech very succinctly describes "the growth of a poet's mind". The poet tells us about his early exposure to Nature, how he "used to live in utmost seclusion in the solitude of an obscure Bengali village by the river Ganges in a boat house "(5:2), his growing love for the children, his translation of the poems of *Gitanjali* "without having any desire to have them published, being diffident of my mastery of that language" (4), his enthusiastic reception in the West, his faith in the cultural heritage of India, for all its splendours and wisdom and wealth, his identification of the spirit of India as "the ideal of unity" which he considers as "the highest aim of our spiritual exertion to be able to penetrate all things with one soul, to comprehend all things as they are, and not keep out anything in the whole universe—to comprehend all things with sympathy and love" (8). The speech, in brief, gives us an idea, though in an embryonic form, of the quality and substance of Tagore's vision of man, India and the world. All his writings can be seen as elaborate manifestations of this vision, in diverse forms.

2. What is Art?

"What is Art?" is first of the eight essays included in *Sādhanā* (The Realization of Life) which was first published by Macmillan, London in 1913.

Tagore believes that man's relation with the world is twofold: physical and emotional.

The world of Art is not concerned with the physical needs of a man but his emotional involvement which finds expression in Art. "The principal creative forces, which transmute things into our living structure, are emotional forces" (4:346). The feeling of a religious person for the divine, Tagore points out, is creative while the theologian's knowledge of the divine is not. Like Oscar Wilde Tagore also believes that all art is 'useless' in the sense that art is not to be put to any use; it has no extraterritorial loyalty. Art, Tagore, says comes out of "some impulse of expression, which is the impulse of our being itself" (343). One difference of man from animal is that an animal lives an active existence; it is concerned with the "is" of a thing while a man is a moral agent and lives a passive existence where he is concerned with the "should" of a thing. He is a moral agent, "who has the inherent power to select things from his surroundings in order to make them his own" (346). Tagore says that man "has a fund of emotional energy which is not all occupied with his self-preservation. This surplus seeks its outlet in the creation of Art, for man's civilization is built upon his surplus" (345). Like Coleridge Tagore also believes that "the true principle of art is the principle of unity" (350). The debate whether in Art the manner is more important than matter is, according to Tagore, beside the point. In Art they are "indissolubly one" (350). The artist, through what Coleridge would call the esemplastic imagination, "finds out the unique, the individual, which yet is the heart of the universal" (352). A work of art though frozen in time transcends time, and though uniquely individual becomes universal through its manifestation of the universal principle of nature. A work of art is for Tagore, as it was for Aristotle, a "concrete universal." In this essay Tagore combats the view that beauty is the object of art. Tagore believes, on the other hand, that beauty is only a means to an end. The end of poetry is joy (or Aristotelian pleasure) which comes from the expression of one's personality and the creation of *rasa* through various artistic devices.

3. Construction versus Creation

"Construction Versus Creation", originally an address delivered at the Gujarat Literary Conference in 1920, was later included in *Letters and Addresses* edited by Anthony X. Soares and published in 1920. Tagore begins the essay with the statement of his thesis: "Construction is for a purpose, it expresses our wants; but creation is for itself, it expresses our very being" (6:531). The purpose of construction is to meet our material needs, but to give the construction a beautiful form is to move from construction to creation, from the utilitarian to the aesthetic. "Creation", Tagore says, "is the revelation of truth through the rhythm of forms" (531). The expression is more important than the material. The truth about the materials of the world consists in their universal relatedness. Tagore says: "This expression alone is creation; it is an end in itself. So also does our civilization find its completeness when it expresses humanity, not when it displays its power to amass materials" (532). But unfortunately, in the world of today the vital harmony is lacking as man is busy exploiting science for the fulfillment of its greed for power and money. All this means heading towards man's doom, because it runs counter to human sensibility. It is time we realized this world "not as a storehouse of mechanical power but as a habitation of man's soul with its eternal music of beauty and its inner light of a divine presence" (542).

4. The Creative Ideal

"The Creative Ideal", included in *Creative Unity* also harps on the same theme of unity: unity in diversity as manifested in the absorption and assimilation of many into one through the application of the universal principle operating in separate forms. Tagore says that the entire poem must be built up round a single idea which runs through and dominates the entire poem. But to hit upon the universal principle or development of a single idea is not enough. According to the old Sanskrit poeticians it is also necessary to attain proportion and propriety, what Kṣemendra would call *aucitya* or Horace would call *decorum*. But Tagore proceeds to point out that even that is not enough. He quotes two lines of a nursery rhyme, "Thirty days hath September, /April, June and November", and comments: "The metre is there, and it simulates the movement of life. But it finds no synchronous response in the metre of our heart-beats; it has not in its centre the *living idea* which creates for itself an *indivisible unity*" (4:570 emphasis added). In Chapter XIV of *Biographia Literaria* Coleridge while attempting a definition of poetry also cited these two lines of mnemonic verse and refused to accept them as poetry. The reasons, though differently worded, are also the same. It is a metrical composition but it is not vitalized by imagination (Tagore's *living idea*) which is "the soul that is everywhere and in each (Tagore's *indivisible unity*) and forms all into one graceful and intelligent whole". Tagore further argues that the joy that the poet experiences in the act of creation and transmits to the reader through the verbal artifact, is not pleasure nor is the beauty that the poet creates is simple prettiness. "Joy", Tagore says, "is the outcome of detachment from self and lives in freedom of spirit" (571). The idea anticipates Eliot's famous statement in "Tradition and the Individual Talent" (1919 in *Selected Essays* [1951]13-22): "What happens is a continual surrender of himself (the poet) as he is at the moment to something which is more valuable. The progress of an artist is a continual self-sacrifice, a continual extinction of personality". And again: "Poetry is not a turning loose of emotion, but an escape from emotion; it is not the expression of personality, but an escape from personality" *(Selected Essays* 21). Tagore affirms that "art gives our personality the disinterested freedom of the eternal, there to find it in its true perspective" (573). The idea also anticipates Eliot's insistence that "[...] the artistic emotion approximates to the emotion of an actual spectator [...]. But the difference between art and the event is always absolute" (*Selected Essays* 19). And here is Tagore: "To detach the individual idea from its confinement of everyday facts and to give its soaring wings the freedom of the universal: this is the function of poetry" (574).

5. The Religion of an Artist

"The Religion of an Artist" was first published in *Visva-Bharati Quarterly* in April 1926 under the title "Meaning of Art", and later a revised version was published in *Contemporary Indian Philosophy* in 1936. It was also published in book form by Visva-Bharati in 1953.

The artist referred to in this essay is none other than Tagore himself and the essay is concerned with development of Tagore as an artist who realized, like James Joyce in *The Portrait of the Artist as a Young Man,* that for an artist art is his religion. And since Tagore is primarily a poet Tagore says: "My religion is essentially a poet's religion" (7:934). Tagore begins his essay by providing the backdrop of history in 1861 when he was born. There were at that time three very important, almost revolutionary, parallel movements: religious, literary and political. During his formative years he imbibed the influence of all the three in different measures. At an early age Tagore was very much impressed by the freedom of metre and the courage of expression of the Vaishnava [*Vaiṣnava*] poems of Bengal. Although many of the songs, basically erotic in nature, were not suited to his age his "imagination was fully occupied with the beauty of their forms and music of their words; and their breath, heavily laden with voluptuousness, passed over[his] mind without distracting it" (931-32). Right from his childhood he had an eye for the beauty of nature and, like Wordsworth, he had "an intimate feeling of companionship with the trees and the clouds, and felt in tune with the musical touch of the seasons in the air" (932). In course of time he studied the European literature in translation, although he knew that a translation can never be a substitute for the original. Tagore says: "We cannot receive the smiles and glances of our sweetheart through an attorney, howsoever diligent and dutiful he may be" (932). Tagore had composed some two thousand songs and he had a training in music and he says, "I claim to be something of a musician myself" (933). He broke away from "the canons of orthodox propriety" audaciously focusing more on the feeling-content of the song than on grammar of it. In this connection what he says in course of a long Bengali essay, "*Saṅgīt o bhāb*" [Music and Feeling] in *Saṅgīt* (RR 14: 875-80) is worth recalling. In English translation it would be like this: "...the very purpose of music is to express feeling. Rhythm in itself, however sweet, is unnecessary. It is only in relation to the feeling that the rhythm is the concern of the poets and critics. Similarly a collection of notes without feeling is like a lifeless body. The body may be beautiful, but it is devoid of life". [For a translation of the entire essay one can see *Introduction to Tagore* (Visva-Bharati, 1983]). Anyway Tagore is happy that people have accepted them, because it is a vindication of his revolutionary theory. With remarkable courage of conviction Tagore says: "I do not hesitate to say that my songs have found their place in the heart of my land, along with her flowers that are never exhausted, and that the folk of the future, in days of joy or sorrow or festival, will have to sing them." (933-34). About formal religion Tagore says that the content is more important than the form manifested in rites and rituals and various technicalities. The content of religion consists in the joy of apprehending the truth in us. Tagore says that "we touch the infinite reality immediately within us only when we perceive the pure truth of love or goodness, not through the explanations of theologians, not through the erudite discussion of ethical doctrines" (935). In such a situation one realizes that "peace is in the harmony which dwells in truth, and not in any outer adjustments; and that beauty carries an eternal assurance of our spiritual relationship to reality, which waits for its perfection in the response of our love" (936).

In the second part of the essay Tagore talks about creation and reiterates his view that "man has his vital and mental energy vastly in excess of his need, which urges him to work in various lines of creation for its own sake" (937). Art is a product of imagination which "helps us to integrate desultory facts in a vision of harmony" (937). And what is rhythm? Tagore says: "It is the movement generated and regulated by harmonious restriction. This is the creative force in the hand of the artist. So long as words remain in uncadenced prose form, they do not give any lasting feeling of reality. The moment they are taken and put into rhythm they vibrate into radiance" (940). In perfect rhythm "the art-form becomes like the stars which in their seeming stillness are never still, like a motionless flame that is nothing but movement. A great picture is always speaking, but news from a news paper, even of some tragic happening, is still-born" (941). Tagore clarifies: "The unity of a poem introduces itself in a rhythmic language in a gesture of character. Rhythm is not merely in some measured blending of words, but in a significant adjustment of ideas, in a music of thought produced by a subtle principle of distribution, which is not primarily logical but evidential" (946). Tagore concludes the essay with a statement of his credo: "I believe that the vision of Paradise is to be seen in the sunlight of the green of the earth, in the beauty of the human face and the wealth of human life, even in objects that are seemingly insignificant and unprepossessing" (947).

6. The Artist

The essay, "The Artist" constitutes the ninth chapter of the book, *The Religion of Man*.

Tagore begins by reiterating his belief that as "angel of the surplus" man's great distinction lies in the use of his leisure in creating dreams, and in course of creating the dreams man "realizes his divine dignity, his great human truth" (5:173). Man is the self-revealer, who, Tagore says, "goes on exploring ages of creation to find himself in perfection" (173). The act of creation enables man to find corroboration of his consciousness of the real in the external reality. He realizes the unity, and through art he expresses his delight of this realization of the unity. In other words, art is the "objective correlative" for the manifestation of his delight. This delight is a pure delight like the delight of the Upanishadic bird watching another bird perched on the same branch feeding. The advantage of a work of art is that it is not bound by the rules of the phenomenal reality. An imaginary tiger is free to violate all the rules of nature and can still remain a tiger, with its distinctive individuality, as a product of imagination. It is more real than a real or physical tiger. It is on account of this longing to grasp the Real that man gave voices to the stones and made rocks to sing and produced infinite forms of unknown things which never existed in the phenomenal world. Tagore believes that Art is "the response of man's creative soul to the call of the Real. Once in Bengal one such call, heard through the voice of a "radiating personality" led to a feast of colours and forms and inspired *kirtan* music that emotionally swept Bengal and inculcated consciousness that was "aflame with a sense of reality that must be adequately acknowledged" (179). The reference to *kirtan* [*kīrtan*, songs about Radha and Krishna] leads Tagore to comment on the place of music in Art which evokes in our mind the profound sense of reality. Tagore says that music is "the most abstract of all the arts, as mathematics is in the region of science" (179). He goes on to discuss the nature of music as distinct from other arts. He says: "In the pictorial, plastic and literary arts, the object and our feelings with regard to it are closely associated, like the rose and its perfumes. In music, we find "the feeling distilled in sound, becoming itself an independent object. It assumes a tune-form which is definite, but a meaning which is undefinable, and yet which grips our mind with a sense of absolute truth"(180).

7. The Poet's Religion

"The Poet's Religion" is one of the ten essays included in the collection *Creative Unity* which was first published by Macmillan, New York in 1917.

Starting with the claim that to a poet poetry is his religion Tagore goes on to explain and elaborate the nature of the religiosity of poetry in "The Poet's Religion". Man does not live by bread alone; meeting the requirements of his animal existence does not satisfy his soul. He aspires after attaining "an ideal of perfection, a sense of unity, which is a harmony between parts and a harmony with surroundings". The finite man longs for "the touch of the infinite". "The quality of the infinite", Tagore says, "is not the magnitude of extension, it is in the *advaitam*, the mystery of Unity", and "wherever our heart touches the One, in the small or the big, it finds the touch of the infinite" (4:553). We have joy in our personality and when that joy of unity seeks expression one becomes creative. Keats had said "A thing of beauty is a joy for ever". Tagore says that a thing of beauty has "no question to answer; it has nothing to do, but to be" (554). This reminds one of Archibald McLeish's observation about poetry that "a poem should not mean but *be*" (emphasis added). Throughout the essay Tagore highlights the necessary aspect of unity in everything and the poet's commitment to this unity. Even elusive play of light and sound has "a language of harmony" (555). What Coleridge said in the Chapter XIII of *Biographia Literaria,* in connection with the nature of Secondary Imagination is subscribed to by Tagore. Coleridge said: "It dissolves, diffuses, dissipates, in order to re-create; or where this process is rendered impossible, yet still, at all events, it struggles to idealize and to unify". Imagination reconciles even discordant elements into a harmonious whole. And here is Tagore: "Materials aré savage; they are solitary; they are ready to hurt one another[...]. But directly an ideal of unity raises its banner in their centre, it brings these rebellious forces under its sway and creation is revealed- the creation which is peace, which is the unity of perfect relationship"(555). Tagore further says: "I know it was my imagination which transmuted the world around me into my own world—*the imagination which seeks unity* (556, emphasis added). Imagination as seen by Coleridge and by Tagore reconciles the Greek idea of *hen kai pan* (one and the many) and the Roman idea of *omne ens unum* (all in one). With many illustrative references to Keats and Shelley, among others, and fine *explication de texte* Tagore arrives at his conviction about the poet's credo: "We realize that Creation is the perpetual harmony between the infinite ideal of perfection and the eternal continuity of its realization; that so long as there is no absolute separation between the positive ideal and the material obstacle to its attainment, we need not be afraid of suffering and loss. This is the poet's religion" (560).

8. Principle of Literature

"Principle of Literature" was first published in *Visva-Bharati Quarterly* in July 1927. Tagore begins the essay with a comment on a fairy tale in which a detective, a merchant and a prince go in quest of the Princess, but while the detective and the merchant are concerned with material aspects of the Princess the king's son is concerned only with the Princess herself and with nothing else. The prince has "crossed difficult paths, not for learning, nor for riches, but for the Princess herself, whose palace is not in the laboratory, nor in the market place, but in that heart's paradise of Eternal Spring where bloom the flowers in the poet's bower of phantasy" (7:810). Then Tagore comes to the point: "That which is not known by logic, which defies definition, whose value is not in any practical use, but which can only be felt, finds its expression in Literature, is the subject of Aesthetics" (810). Quoting the Upanishad Tagore says that we cannot reach the godhead with our speech or with our mind but only by our consciousness of joy, because, according to the Upanishad the world has come into being out of joy, and it is the longing for this joy, for its immediate realization that can be satisfied only through literature or art. Only a work of art can induce that state of bliss which is the *sumum bonum* of human existence. Tagore says: "The appearances, the thoughts, the dreams which are not made manifest through reason,—these are of Literature" (812). This reminds one of Shakespeare's famous observations in *The Tempest:* "We are such stuff/ As dreams are made on; and our little life/ Is rounded with a sleep". Tagore reaffirms that anything that is of material value is "tainted by the touch of the hunger of the body" (813) and, therefore, lies outside the purview of art. Tagore says that the flower *sajinā* [*Moringa oleifera*], though beautiful "has lost prestige with the poets because it happens to figure as an article of diet" (813). In passing Tagore makes a very insightful comment on the role of sound in poetry and says that sound is the essence of poetry, for, after all, a poem is ultimately a construct of sound which also contributes to the meaning of a poem and reconciles the semantic structure and the sonic texture into a harmonious whole. In this respect Tagore subscribes to the views of Bhartrhari (6th century) elaborately enunciated in *Vākyapadīyam.*

9. The Meaning of Art

"The Meaning of Art" originally a lecture delivered at Dhaka University, was published in *Visva-Bharati Quarterly* in April 1926. In this essay Tagore reaffirms his conviction that art is the product of man as the angel of the surplus. Tagore believes that through art man expresses himself with "his vital and mental energy vastly in excess of his need, which urges him to work in various lines of creation for its own sake". Art is an end itself; it has no utilitarian purpose or ulterior motive. It is not meant to fulfill any material need. But, interestingly, art involves two contradictory forces. On the one hand it is an expression of joy, joy of the artist in discovering and expressing himself while, on the other hand it calls for rigour and sustained labour. Thus art involves both the freedom of joy and the restraint of order and discipline. Tagore here seems to be subscribing to the basic tenet of German Romanticism with which he was quite familiar. It believes that Imagination while seeing the endless flux of facts and images also discerns the controlling Form which lies dormant in the vast chamber of unborn designs. In the process of creation three factors reciprocally interplay: the Well, the Vision and the Will. When freedom and restraint are perfectly reconciled into a harmonious whole in meeting the demands of the fabric of the Vision, the composition, as an art form, achieves a movement within the stillness, the kind of dynamic quality that we find in the paintings of Turner or Hokusai or a statue by Rodin or Ramkinkar Bej, although both the pictures and the statues are empirically static. As emotional representation of facts and ideas a work of art transcends the limitations of photography which is tied to scientific objectivity only. That is why, Tagore says, Shelley's skylark is so different from Wordsworth's. Every work of art is *sui generis* and unique. In course of his discussion Tagore also comments on music and says that in music "the feeling extracted in sound, becomes itself an independent object", and it "assumes a tune-form which is definite, but a meaning which is indefinable and yet grips our mind with a sense of absolute truth" (7:796). In contradistinction to music in "the pictorial, plastic and verbal arts the object and our feelings with regard to it are closely associated, like the rose and its perfume" (796). Towards the end of the essay Tagore talks about the relation between tradition and modernity in art. He believes, like Eliot, that tradition is not a dead weight but a living, dynamic, ongoing process and it must be modified from time to time so that art can accommodate new ideas and new forces. With all due reverence for tradition Tagore emphatically says that "there is no such thing as absolute caste restriction in human cultures; they ever have the power to combine and produce new variations, and such combinations have been going on for ages proving the truth of the deep unity of human psychology" (797). "Art", Tagore argues, "is not a gorgeous sepulcher immovably brooding over a lonely eternity of vanished years. It belongs to the procession of life, making constant adjustment with surprises, exploring unknown shrines of reality along its path of pilgrimage to a future which is different from the past as the tree from the seed" (799). Art, for Tagore is "the response of man's creative soul to the call of the real" (796).

10. My Pictures

"My Pictures" was first published in *The Modern Review* in December 1930. Although this essay is a kind of "workshop criticism", the craftsman talking about his craft, in the essay which consists of three statements Tagore goes deep into the very ontology of the art of painting. He believes that the "one thing which is common to all arts is the principle of rhythm which transforms inert materials into living creations" (7:864). Tagore admits that he never underwent any training in painting but he had an instinct for rhythm and his pictures which evolved in the process of his correcting the manuscripts are "rhythmic incarnations" of lines and colours in pictures. They are, in the words of Tagore are his "versification in lines" (863). Tagore says that it is useless to look for meaning of his pictures. He says: "They have nothing ulterior behind their own appearance for the thoughts to explore and words to describe, and if that appearance carries its ultimate worth, then they remain, otherwise they are rejected and forgotten even though they may have some scientific truth or ethical justification" (868). He concludes by saying that art, like love, is inexplicable. Other things can be measured by some standard criteria but "art by nothing but itself" (868).

11. Man's Nature

"Man's Nature" constitutes the tenth chapter of the book, *The Religion of Man*. Tagore says that from the time that man became conscious of his own self he also became conscious of a "mysterious spirit of unity" (5:182) manifested through him in the society, and he also felt that it has a divine character which transcends his individual self. The word *dharma* (religion) etymologically means "that which holds something firm", which, in the case of man means, by implication, the essential qualities of man, qualities which are "inherent in the nature of Man, the Eternal" (182). The vision of the Eternal Man is not something that is created by our mind; it is only realized by our imagination. It is through the faculty of imagination that unlike birds which can only repeat certain notes, man creates his own music and infinite variety of rhythmic relationship of notes. In the process dull facts are turned into heart-felt, realized truths. All his arts and literature, all his imaginative (and not imaginary) works, for that matter, are only expressions of the Universal Man.

12. Man

"Man" is the first of the three lectures delivered at Andhra University in 1933.

The essay reaffirms and elaborates most of the ideas Tagore introduced in *Religion of Man.* The essay develops through a contrastive study of animal and man. Tagore points out that man surpasses the animal in his aspiration for what is neither evident in the material world nor is urgently necessary for his physical survival. Man realizes that beyond his individual self there lies the universal self of which he is an integral part. He is "one in spirit with the universal Man" (5:234). In his efforts to answer the question, "Who am I?", in his search for identity he becomes conscious that he "hides a mystery of depth within himself, and that he will finally know himself only when the veils of mystery have been pierced"(236). As the seat of God is in His glory, similarly the real seat of man is in his glory which is revealed in his thoughts and actions which have nothing to do with the utilitarian world, which are "extras", products of the angel of the surplus. Tagore refers to the Upanishadic distinction between *śreya* (what is good and, therefore, desirable) and *preya* (what is attractive and, therefore, desired). The glory of a man lies in his striving for the *śreya* and thus *become* something. Tagore says that real goodness lies "in realizing in oneself the humanity which is universal and of all times; degradation is in the failure to realize the Universal Man" (243). And Tagore adds, "All this would have no meaning unless man had a spiritual self over and above his natural self" (243). In this connection Tagore recalls the fragment of a song that he had heard from an illiterate villager. The song said, "Seek for the inner man in your inner heart."

13. The Surplus in Man

"The Surplus in Man" constitutes the third chapter of *The Religion of Man*. Tagore briefly traces the evolution of man from his quadruped position to biped position to come to his point that once man could stand erect he could easily look around and realize his central position in the world. Not only that. From the wider scope of his vision he gained a view not only about the location of things but also about their interrelatedness, and their unity. The freedom of view and the freedom of action led to the exercise of imagination which is a special faculty of the human kind. Imagination made man "intensely conscious of a life that we must live which transcends the individual life and contradicts the biological meaning of the instinct of self-preservation" (5:125). This consciousness, Tagore tells us, "works at the surplus" (125) and it extends beyond the necessities and reaches out to the "world-spirit of Man" (125). True freedom always helps in self-realization which transcends the mundane trivialities of life. Man asks himself "What am I?" because his real happiness largely depends on the truth of the answer. The Roman empire had its decline and fall but what has survived is "her faith in the sublimity of man" (129), the mission "to reveal her humanity on the background of the eternal" (129). What emerges is the image of man "dreaming of his own infinity" and majestically working for all time "defying danger and death" (130).

Incidentally while talking about formal religion Tagore warns us against the bigotry that often vitiates religious practices. He says that it leads to "aberrations that are intellectually blind, morally reprehensible and aesthetically repellant" (130).

14. The Music Maker

The essay, "The Music Maker" constitutes the eighth chapter of the book, *The Religion of Man*. The title is taken from a poem with slight changes in the wording of the line. The original lines are "We are the music-makers,/ We are the dreamers of dreams". Tagore quotes the two lines approvingly as a proper definition of man. An animal in his struggle for existence is narrowly confined in the present. But man with his leisure "lives in an endless future" (5:167). Man knows that he is ideally limitless and he dreams of the unattained and the unattainable, and this dream "gives character to what is attained" (167). In modern civilization when the "world is too much with us" we have lost our leisure and we have lost our dreams. The materialistic civilization and the cult of machine today have taken us back to the animal existence at the cost of the divine in man who is the music maker, the dreamer of dreams. The botanical anatomy of a rose, howsoever realistic it may be claimed, does not reveal the real identity of a rose which consists in its beauty and harmony. The morgue does not reveal the reality of the body; the body must be seen when it is vibrant with life. Similarly the reality of man consists in his realization of the ideal unity manifested in the world of which he is an integral part.

As in the previous essays here also Tagore reiterates his belief in the infinite potentialities of the finite man in his longing for the infinite and in his realization of his capacity to transcend himself.

15. Supreme Man

"Supreme Man" is the second of the three lectures Tagore delivered at Andhra University in 1933. It continues and further develops Tagore's idea of man. Tagore starts with the notion of unity that informs all scientific kinds of scientific knowledge. Even a piece of iron is "only a physical symbol revealing the mysterious spirit of relationship which cannot be seen by the bodily eye" (5:247). Similarly despite the differences between men belonging to different time and space "there is a large and deep unity encompassing all men" (247). A Supreme Man is one who can feel within himself "the one Spirit in all men" (247). Of all creatures man alone perceives this world "in the form of *his* thought within the scaffoldings of *his* Understanding and Reason" (248). Yet his perception touches the universal and becomes timeless. It is one thing to realize pure truth as the manifestation of the universal man, but can we realize the universal mind in our aesthetic experience? Tagore answers this question by commenting on Russell's observation on Beethoven's symphony. Russell said that Beethoven's symphonies cannot be regarded as creations of the universal mind. But Tagore says that facts falsify the statement. The very fact that Beethoven is universally appreciated proves that though "his creations are personal to him" (to Russell) they touch the universal mind. In this connection Tagore talks about Art and the creation of beauty. Creation of beauty does not serve any useful purpose, but, what is important for Tagore is that the influence of Art transforms our inner being, and, therefore helps us in realizing the universal man in us.

16. Woman

"Woman" is one of the six lectures delivered in America. The collection of these six lectures was published by Macmillan, New York in 1917 under the title, *Personality*.

In "Woman" Tagore compares the essential differences in the nature of man and woman and holds that a woman "is endowed with the passive qualities of chastity, modesty, devotion and power of self sacrifice in a greater measure than man" (4:432). The ideal of stability is "deeply cherished in woman's nature" (431). Tagore deplores the fact that "[a]t the present stage of history civilization is almost exclusively masculine, a civilization of power, in which woman has been thrust aside in the shade" (431). The result is that the civilization "has lost its balance and it is moving by hopping from war to war. Its motive forces are the forces of destruction, and its ceremonials are carried through by an appalling number of human sacrifices. The one-sided civilization is crashing along a series of catastrophes at a tremendous speed because of its one-sidedness" (431-32). Contrary to the widely prevalent notion that the proper place of woman is the home and woman is the "angel of the house" Tagore combats the view that the domestic life is the only life for a woman. He clarifies: "I mean that the human world is the woman's world, be it domestic or be full of the other activities of life, which are human activities, and not merely abstract efforts to organize" (434). Tagore exhorts the women: "...at last the time has arrived when woman must step in and impart her life rhythm to this reckless movement of power" (432). Tagore warns the men folk: "But woman cannot be pushed back for good into the mere region of the decorative by man's aggressiveness of power. For she is not less necessary in civilization than man but possibly more so" (436).

17. Woman and Home

In "Woman and Home", included in *Creative Unity* Tagore expresses his view that man and woman are complementary to each other, but it is the woman who has always been the source of inspiration for man, because the woman "had the instinctive wisdom to realize that it was her mission to help her mate in creating Paradise of their own on earth, whose ideal she was to supply with her life, whose materials were to be produced and gathered by her comrade" (4:633). There was harmony and balance of power when home was a great attraction for men. But in modern times man is carried away by temptations of easy pleasure and cheap luxuries in hotels, guns and gambling clubs, and consequently the woman is neglected. When her sacrifice and the loving contributions to the making of home are not recognized the home becomes for the woman, a prison house and wronged she sharply reacts and rebels. Tagore says that "the wrong is in woman's lack of freedom in her relationship with man, which compels her to turn her disabilities into attractions, and to use untruths as her allies in the battle of life, while she is suffering from the precariousness of her position." (635). Women who have always created home as an expression of their natural "poetry of life" (633) are now compelled to come out of home in search of place in the "unlimited range of society" (637). But Tagore believes that once circumstances have forced the women to come out of their segregation they will certainly restore the spiritual supremacy of all that is human in the world of humanity"(638), because their suffering "radiates through the ideal, and becomes, like sunlight, a creative force in their world." (636)

The essay shows how highly Tagore regarded women and in this essay he puts the blame squarely on men for the present predicament of women which they are sure to triumphantly get over and establish their superiority to men.

18. Man's Universe

"Man's Universe" is one of the Hibbert lectures Tagore delivered in Oxford, at Manchester College in 1930, later published as *The Religion of Man* (Allen & Unwin, 1930) with some changes. A second edition was brought out by Macmillan in 1931. The present essay is the first chapter of the second edition.

In the Preface to the volume Tagore writes:

"The fact that one theme runs through all only proves to me that the Religion of Man has been growing within my mind as a religious experience and not merely as a philosophical subject" (5:95). He further remarks that all his works and utterances are "deeply linked by a unity of inspiration" (99). Tagore, a Unitarian, an *Advaitin* in a profound sense, believes that the principle of unity has always been the principle of interrelationship of all the objects of the universe. Relationship, according to Tagore, is "the fundamental truth of this world of appearance" (104). Nothing exists in isolation; everything is related to everything else in a strange organic way. On the surface level our existence is marked by "the ever-changing phases of the individual self, but in the depth there dwells the Eternal Spirit of human unity beyond our direct knowledge" (101), and it "inspires us in works that are the expressions of a Universal Spirit" (101-02).

The realization of this unity was a religious experience for Tagore, and he first became aware of it through his perception of Nature. The relationship with Nature was not just a physical relationship. He realized that Nature "satisfies our personality with manifestations that make our life rich and stimulate our imagination in their harmony of forms, colours, sounds and movements" (102). He also realized that Nature "lavishly displays its wealth of reality to our personal self having its own perpetual reaction upon our human nature" (102). Like various objects of the universe man and Nature are also bound by a healthy, harmonious relationship. Since the world is "pervaded by one supreme entity" (105) the real enjoyment can come not through any self-centred greed or isolation but through "*the surrender of our individual self* to the Universal Self" (105, emphasis added). Tagore says that creation "has been made possible through the *continual self-surrender* of the unit to the universe" (104, emphasis added). Eliot had also said that in the creative process there is "a continual surrender [...] a continual self-sacrifice, a continual extinction of personality" of the artist. Tagore believes in the existence of "the universal human mind which comprehends all time and all possibilities of realization" (105). In this respect Tagore seems to be an exponent of Platonic idealism. Furthermore, he believes that any progress simply means progress towards the realization of the ideal—the search of the individual for the universal. Tagore believes that we share the mind of this Supreme Person whose Spirit permeates man's universe, "in all our true knowledge, love and service" and we reveal this Supreme Person in ourselves "through renunciation of self" which is "the highest end of life" (106).

19. The Creative Spirit

In "The Creative Spirit" which constitutes the second chapter of *The Religion of Man* Tagore first makes a brief critical survey of the origin of the universe and the evolution of man and argues that from the beginning of the creation of man his evolution has been "the evolution of a consciousness that tries to be liberated from the bonds of individual separateness and to comprehend in its relationship a wholeness which may be called Man" (5:120). He believes that "the evolution process of the world has made its progress towards the revelation of its *truth*—that is to say some inner value which is not the extension in space and duration of time" (109). This value which cannot be measured and analysed is related to "the mind and consciousness of self" (109-10). They are "revelations of a great meaning, the self-expression of a truth" (110). The mind does not occupy any space, and, therefore it enjoys limitless freedom. This freedom from the compelling claim of physical needs makes man "an Angel of Surplus" and enables him to realize himself "in a wider and deeper relationship with the universe" (119). This freedom finds manifestations in different fields. In moral life it helps him inculcate goodness. In spiritual life it culminates in love. The freedom of opportunity enables him to unite his power with the forces of Nature. The freedom of social relationship makes him conscious of his responsibility to the community and induces him to use the collective power for his own betterment in the betterment of the society. Finally the freedom of consciousness enables him to realize "the sense of his unity with his larger being, finding fulfillment in the dedicated life of an ever-progressive truth and ever-active love" (119). Tagore believes that it is love which "gives us the testimony of the great whole, which is the complete and final truth of man" (121).

This essay also shows how Tagore's idea of unity acts as seminal principle of his view of the world, nature and man and reinforces his Platonic idealism and his idea of man as an angel of surplus who uses his surplus energy in creative activities.

20. The Religion of the Forest

"The Religion of the Forest" is also included in *Creative Unity*. In this essay Tagore says that there are two ways of establishing our relation with the universe: conquest and union, based on the principle of dualism and the principle of unity respectively. While the history of the West is the history of the conquest of Nature the Indian approach has been from the ancient time of the Upanishads, the realization of the ultimate truth of unity by establishing a harmonious relation with Nature. The entire Sanskrit classical literature is replete with this message. This view of the world is summed up in the word, *saccidānanda* (*sat+cit+ānanda*). It means that Reality has three phases—(i) the being or the relatedness of all things that exist; (ii) the knowledge of this relatedness of being; and (iii) the joy arising out of that knowledge. Tagore says that our consciousness becomes perfect only when it realizes "all things as spiritually one with it, and therefore capable of giving us joy" (4:577).

Tagore brings out the difference between the Western view and the Indian by comparing mainly the Shakespearean plays with some Sanskrit plays. In *Timon of Athens* Nature is impervious to "the injured soul of man" (583). In *Cymbeline* Nature is a veritable "obstruction to life's opportunities" (583). In *Macbeth* the witches on the barren heath appear as "personifications of Nature's malignant forces" (583). In *Hamlet* and *Othello* the tragic intensity is "unrelieved by any touch of Nature's eternity" (583). In *Romeo and Juliet* and *Antony and Cleopatra* "Nature has not been allowed [...] to contribute her own music to the music of man's love" (583-84). In *The Winter's Tale* Nature does not offer any consolation. In *As You Like It,* Nature "does not bring peace, but preaches" (583). Tagore deplores the fact that even in Milton's *Paradise Lost* which provided an excellent opportunity to bring out the "true greatness of man's relationship with Nature" (584). Milton simply describes the beauty of the garden and the various creatures meant for the pleasure of man, but "there is no reality of kinship between them and man" (584). In contrast, in all the dramas that are still popular such as *Mritśhakatika*, *Śakuntalā* and *Uttararāmacarita* "Nature stands on her own right, proving that she has her great function, to impart peace of the eternal to human emotions" (578). In an epic, like the *Ramayana* we are made to feel that the greatness of the hero lies not in his struggle with Nature but in his "sympathy with it" (582). Going back to his theme of unity Tagore concludes that the one truth that man must remember is that the power which fuses the conflicting forces into one "is no passion, but a love which accepts the bonds of self-control from the joy of its own immensity" (587). It is the bond of love that unites man and Nature into a harmonious relation, and in the process, draws out the latent potentialities of man and enables him to realize them.

21. City and Village

"City and Village" originally a lecture delivered in Turin, Italy, was published in *Visva-Bharati Quarterly* in October 1924. Tagore believes that cities are as necessary as villages, but there should always be a healthy symbiotic relationship between the two. Tagore says: "The living relationship, in a physical or social body, is the sympathetic mutuality of help among its members and organs, whereby a perfect balance of communication between them is maintained, so that consciousness of unity is not obstructed" (7:693). He further clarifies: "The resulting health and wealth are of secondary importance,—the unity is ultimate in itself" (693). But, unfortunately, Tagore deplores that unprecedented material progress has given birth to enormous greed for property and power "at the cost of civilization itself, like the man for whom wine has more attraction than food" (693). Modern cities are growing bigger and bigger, because "no central spirit of Unity exercises vital control over their growth of dimension" (694), and the villages which are, in fact, "in closer touch with the fountain of life" (693) are ignored and exploited. It is time man realized the fatal mistake that he is committing by atrophied interest in the cities. Tagore concludes his essay with a reference to the work of village reconstruction that he has started in a modest way at Visva-Bharati, Santinketan "to retard this process of race suicide" (700).

22. Judgment

"Judgment" was published in *Visva-Bharati Quarterly* in October 1925. In this essay Tagore says that people of the East are dazed by the opulence of the West and its modernism. They are led to believe that "what is called modern represents the principle of indefinite growth and freedom, it is youth, it is life" (7:745). Tagore combats this view and holds that anything to be modern must have "the perpetual freshness of imperishable life" (744). The secret of this cannot be found in the spirit of the reckless power with which the West keeps on exploiting its colonies. The stone-paved roads across the meadows and orchards are only meant to make easy the work of exploitation. Tagore believes that deep down man is basically a beast. The barbarous that is ingrained in human nature makes us easily prostrate before the powerful and acknowledge them as great. Drunk by power and prosperity "it was difficult for the western people to realize that there was anything lacking in their civilization" (749). The war, however, which revealed their critical myopia and exposed the "cancerous growth within her moral nature" (753) gave an opportunity to Asia to sit in judgment over them. Tagore says that we must pounce upon this opportunity, because "our moral judgment is the best weapon we have in the warfare for the preservation of humanity" (754), for he believes that the "surrender of moral judgment is also a defeat through which the invasion of the west is laying its stony road across the soul of the East, leading most of its traffic of ideas to the gambling den of commerce and politics, to the furious competition of suicide in the arena of military lunacy" (755). Tagore always believed that toleration of injustice amounted to abetting injustice.

23. The Teacher

"The Teacher" constitutes the twelfth chapter of the book, *The Religion of Man*. The main purpose of the essay is to briefly give an idea of Tagore's philosophy of education that led to the establishment of a children's school at Santinketan. Early in life Tagore felt that he needed spiritual self-realization through some disinterested service. Education must prepare one for a complete life through knowledge and service, enjoyment and creative work, and above all, by establishing a perfect harmony with nature. Perfect freedom, Tagore says, is not in knowledge when truth is realized not by reason but "through the union of perfect sympathy" (5:202). According to Tagore love is freedom; "it gives us that fullness of existence which saves us from paying with our soul for objects that are immensely cheap. Love lights up this world with its meaning and makes life feel that it has that 'enough' everywhere which truly is its 'feast'" (205). That is why Tagore says he tried to develop in the children of his school "the freshness of their feeling for Nature, a sensitiveness of soul in their relationship with their surroundings, with the help of literature, festive ceremonials and also the religious teaching which enjoins us to come to the nearer presence of the world through the soul, thus to gain it more than can be measured—like gaining an instrument in truth by bringing out its music" (206).

24. Ideals of Education

"Ideals of Education", an address delivered in Tokyo in 1929, was published in *Visva-Bharati Quarterly* in April-July 1929. In this essay Tagore reminisces about his upbringing in a *Brāhmo* family which was virtually ostracized by the orthodox Hindu society of the time. As a result the family was liberated from the responsibility of conforming to the sectarian barriers and rigid social ideas which were very narrow, dogmatic and inimical to the development of the spirit of freedom so necessary for man for the realization of himself and his intimate relationship with the huge external world. The point of this autobiographical reference is that for Tagore the ideal of education is to inculcate the spirit of freedom and strive for the attainment of the perfect, "the urging which secretly helps us in all our endeavour for the good" (7:832). Thus Tagore says about the educational institution that he had established at Santiniketan: "This faith has been my only asset in the educational mission which I have made my life's work, and almost unaided and alone, I struggle along my path" (832). Ideal education must make one free. It must give him freedom from ignorance and freedom from all kinds of prejudice and untruth. Then only the mind can hit upon "some great source of inspiration in which all its experience of the true, good and beautiful finds its reality though it cannot be proved, the reality in which our aspiration for freedom in truth, freedom in love, freedom in the unity of man is ideally realized forever" (835).

25. Spiritual Union

"Spiritual Union" constitutes the fourth chapter of the book, *The Religion of Man*. In this essay Tagore continues with the same theme of the concept of unity as the living principle of the world and its role in man's realization of his highest ideal. The unity that Tagore refers to is not just the collection of all kinds of materials at one place; it is "like the beauty in a lotus which is ineffably more than all the constituents of the flower" (5:132). Tagore clarifies: "It is not the magnitude of extension but an intense quality of harmony which evokes in us the positive sense of the infinite in our joy, in our love" (132). The ideal of unity that we find in deeper relatedness of all the objects of the world is realized in one's own spirit, and it is in this ideal of unity that the infinite truth inheres. In this context the Sanskrit word *yoga* which means connection or union becomes meaningful in man's realization of the ideal in the union with the Supreme Reality. The union brings infinite joy and Tagore contends that "the infinite One is infinite Love" (132). Tagore says that all great religious teachers realized this truth in their life, and reminds us that "Buddha's idea of the infinite was not the idea of an unbounded cosmic activity, but the infinite whose meaning is in the positive ideal of goodness and love, which cannot be otherwise than human" (135). The infinite is revealed not in the external phenomenal objects but in man himself.

26. The Man of My Heart

"The Man of My Heart" constitutes the seventh chapter of the book, *The Religion of Man*. Tagore begins this essay with a biographical reference to his youth when he was entrusted by his father to work as the secretary of a special section of the monotheistic church. Soon he realized that there is a difference between the form and the content of religion. The religious institution was different from the actual religion, and people often dogmatically followed the prescribed rites and rituals without realizing the spirit of religion. The church, in practice, became an empty form without any significant content. About the job that Tagore was assigned by his father, he had a feeling, therefore, that he was "using a mask to hide the living faces of truth" (5:160), and to be true to himself soon he gave up his connection with the church.

Tagore then refers to a song of a beggar belonging to the Baul sect of Bengal. The simple folk songs of this sect carry profound religious truths in simple words and analogies. The particular song that he refers to contained an intense yearning for the divine that dwells, not in the temples or scriptures but in the heart of man. The divine in man can be reached only by love. This, in fact, sums up the essence of Tagore's idea of religion.

27. I Am He

"I Am He" is the third and last of the three lectures Tagore delivered at Andhra University in 1933. Tagore begins his essay with a quotation from the Upanishad which says that a person who worships God as something external does not know God and is like an animal belonging to the gods. Man must realize God in his own soul. A man must acknowledge and realize the divine man, the universal man, within himself, in his thoughts and actions. Man realizes his dignity in his spiritual identification with God himself, and in this union which transcends his self-interest he finds the universal truth. Truth reconciles the duality of the unmanifested infinite and the manifested finite. In this essay Tagore refers to Ramananda, Buddha and Christ and shows how each of them through their actions transcended the limits of the individual ego and realized himself as one with the supreme man. The history of the evolution of man can be seen as a movement towards realization of "the great and mysterious truth of relatedness, of the supreme unity of all that is" (5:268). "I am He", is only an unequivocal affirmation of this truth.

28. Spiritual Freedom

"Spiritual Freedom" constitutes the thirteenth chapter of the book, *The Religion of Man*. A man attains spiritual freedom when, conscious of the transcendental truth lying hidden in us, he renounces his individual self for the sake of the supreme soul. When a man realizes the harmony of relationship between the individual and the infinite or universal man, he is filled with real joy, because realization of this truth registers a movement from the unreal to the real. The unobstructed vision of unity that provides spiritual freedom, according to Tagore, is "the incarnation of the real, which is joy for ever" (5:208). Since truth is in unity, freedom consists in its realization. The texts of our daily worship and meditation, Tagore points out, train our mind to overcome our separateness from the rest of the world and constantly urge us to move on beyond the appearances till we attain emancipation and realize "the inner truth of all things, where the endless *Many* reveal the *One*" (211). And this realization, Tagore warns us, must come from within and not from without. The idea of the many and the one, we have already noted, is essentially Greek, *hen kai pan*. In this essay also we find Tagore as an exponent of Platonic idealism.

29. The Message of the Forest

"The Message of the Forest" is the published and enlarged version of a lecture originally delivered in Bangalore in 1919. In this essay Tagore reiterates unambiguously that the principle by which India can realize her is "neither commercialism, nor nationalism. It is universalism. It is not merely self-determination, but self-conquest and self-determination" (6:529). This was the message of the forest as deeply enshrined in the Upanishads, the Gita, the teachings of Buddha, Kabir, Nanak and many other savants of India. Tagore warns us that as long as we disregard this message "of all-pervading truth and humanity, the message of all-comprehensive union of souls which rises above all differences and goes deeper than expediency, we shall have to go on suffering sorrow after sorrow and endless humiliation, and in all things futility" (530).

30. Nationalism in the West

"Nationalism in the West" is one of the three lectures delivered in Japan. The lectures were first published by Macmillan, New York in 1917 under the title, *Nationalism.*

The essay, "Nationalism in the West", originally a lecture delivered in Japan shows Tagore's distrust of Western form of nationalism. Before coming to the concept of a nation Tagore calls attention to the differences between the East and the West in terms of historical development and the philosophical world-view. The history of the West is the history of the development of organizational power and gradual freedom from the tyranny of nature. But the history of India is the history of the evolution of social life and realization of spiritual ideals. What is of supreme importance is the realization of the unity of man. From the ancient times to the present, great spiritual teachers have tried "to set at naught the differences of man by the overflow of consciousness" (4:442). To Tagore society and not nation is most important for the development of personality and realization of the unity of man. He believes that "society is a spontaneous self-expression of man as a social being. It is a natural regulation of human relationships, so that men can develop ideals of life in cooperation with one another" (444). It is true that the society has political side also. But Tagore believes that this political side is only concerned with self-preservation and not with the realization of the ideals.

But when we look at the West we notice that, in sharp contrast to the Indian ideals, "the spirit of conflict and conquest is at the origin and in the centre of the Western nationalism; its basis is not social cooperation. It has evolved a perfect organization of power but not spiritual idealism. It is like a pack of predatory creatures that must have its victims" (451). The nation, Tagore points out, is "a political and economic union of people...organized for a mechanical purpose" (444). When such an organization which is called a nation, "becomes all powerful then it is an evil day for humanity" (446), because then the only object of it becomes self-aggrandizement and aggression, prompted by greed and fuelled by love of power and desire to dominate others. It kills the spirit of humanity and turns man into machine. There is a lopsided development when the intellectual and material power outgrows the moral strength of man. It then kills his soul and alienates him from his natural surroundings. Tagore says: "Take away man from his natural surroundings, from the fullness of his communal life, with all its living associations of beauty and love and social obligations, and you will be able to turn him into so many fragments of a machine for the production of wealth on a gigantic scale. Turn a tree into a log and it will burn for you but it will never bear living flowers and fruits" (460).

In brief, Tagore rejects nationalism of the West, because it dehumanizes man and is inimical to the realization of the ideals of humanity. Tagore thinks that as an organization, society is better than a nation.

31. The Nation

"The Nation" is also included in *Creative Unity.* Tagore has expressed, time and again, his distrust of the concept of Nation on account of its fundamental difference from Society as is evident in the functioning of a Nation. "The Ideal of the social man is unselfishness", Tagore points out, "but the ideal of the Nation, like that of the professional man, is selfishness" (4:630). Tagore believes that it is the living personalities of the people that give birth to distinctive creations, like literature and arts, rites and rituals, symbols and ceremonies. The guiding principle of social vitality is the power of self-sacrifice prompted by a spirit of sympathy and cooperation. All these are moves toward the creation of beauty and realization of the higher ideals of humanity. But the Nation is conceived as an organization where individual distinctions are sacrificed for the promotion of "the collective self-interest of a people" (630) which, in practice, turns out to be "aggressive selfishness either in commercial ventures or in foreign possessions, or in both" (630). And what is still worse is that "selfishness is a necessity and therefore a virtue" (631). Tagore believes that with the growth of nationalism "man has become the greatest menace to man" (628). Tagore is not an idle dreamer. He knows that "all systems produce evil sooner or later, when the psychology which is at the root of them is wrong" (632). And this is bound to be, because "evils there are in human nature, in spite of our faith in moral laws and training in self-control" (631). Tagore's conviction that evil is ingrained in the human nature looks forward to the convictions of many modern writers such as Conrad (*Heart of Darkness, Nostromo*), Golding (*Lord of the Flies*) and Arthur Miller (*View from the Bridge*), among others.

32. The Call for Truth

"The Call for Truth" was published in *The Modern Review* in 1921. After briefly discussing the difference between other animals and man whose distinction consists in his creativity Tagore comes to the question of India's freedom and the ways adopted to attain it. Very often the ways are characterized by thoughtless anger and insatiable greed. He says that sporadic violence leads to nowhere. The faith in one's country must be realized by all the countrymen. That is why in 1905 Tagore had called upon his countrymen "to *create* their own country by putting forth their own powers from within. For the act of creation itself is the realization of truth" (6:548). The English-educated arm chair politicians were seeking inspiration from the lives and works of Gladstone, Mazzini and Garibaldi, but "[n]othing resembling self-sacrifice or true feeling for their countrymen was visible" (554). It was at this time that Mahatma Gandhi appeared on the scene: "Mahatma Gandhi came and stood at the cottage door of the destitute millions, clad as one of themselves, and talking to them in their own language. Here was the truth at last, not a mere quotation out of a book." Tagore acknowledged the sovereignty of Gandhiji because he won the heart of the people with his love. Gandhiji was, to Tagore, truth incarnate. Yet Tagore could not accept the policy of boycotting of foreign goods, burning of foreign clothes or spinning of *charka* as the real means to achieve *Swaraj*. Tagore says: "*Swaraj* is not concerned with our apparel only- it cannot be established on cheap clothing; its foundation is in the mind, which with its diverse powers and its confidence in those powers, goes on all the time creating *Swaraj* for itself" (560). And again: "The question of using or refusing cloth of a particular manufacture belongs mainly to economic science" (561). Incidentally, these ideas are brilliantly embodied in characters, situations and actions in Tagore's novel, *Ghare Baire* (Home and the World) filmed be Satyajit Ray.

33. The Way to Unity

"The Way to Unity" was published in *Visva-Bharati Quarterly* in 1923. In order to drive home his idea of the way to unity Tagore first refers to what is erroneously considered as the way to unity. He says that just because in the contemporary world the nations have come closer it does not necessarily suggest any movement towards unity, because these nations are not brought together by love. Each nation tries to brandish its superiority and hold others in contempt. He then comes to the religious differences prevailing amongst the Hindus and Muslims, and argues that dogmatic adherence to "a fixed code of custom [...] has been one radical cause of the separateness of our races, and has made cracks from which comes out the poisonous gas of degeneracy" (6:619). It is such degeneration that has given birth to untouchability. According to Tagore civilization is that "which gives individuals the best facility to deal with the greatest number of human beings in the noblest spirit of truth" (620). What is needed in India is "the broad mind, which, only because it is conscious of its own vigorous individuality, is not afraid of accepting truth from all sources" (622). A profound scholar of many languages and a radical thinker Rammohun's was such a mind trained for "the free acceptance of truth" (622). He built a bridge between India and the rest of the world, on the one hand, and a bridge between India's past and present. Rammohun has shown the right way to unity, and we should follow him as our ideal guide.

Incidentally Tagore had a great admiration for Rammohun. His essay on Rammohun included in *Rabindra-Rachanavali* (*RR:11*) bears eloquent testimony to it.

34. Race Conflict

The essay, "Race Conflict", originally an address delivered at the Congress of the National Federation of Religious Liberals at Rochester, New York, in 1912 was published in *The Modern Review* in 1913.

Tagore says that the problem of race conflict is a perennial problem of mankind. Marginal differences between different kinds of people are generally absorbed into the cultural milieu of the original people. But when differences between races become very great then there are two ways of tackling the situation. In one case one race becomes aggressive and tries to force the other race or races to submit to its will. This has been the case with many western races, including the British. The other way is to "search for the one in the many, the universal through the individuals" (6:471). India has always followed the second course. India has been exposed to various kinds of race differences ranging from the Moguls and Pathans to the British, the differences amongst whom are radical and too many. But India tried "to find out the essential unity in diversity of forms, to know that, however different be the symbols and rituals, God, whom they try to represent, is one without a second, and to realize him truly is to realize him in the soul of all beings"(474). That is how the external races—Moguls and Pathans, among others, have all been assimilated into the main stream of the Indian people. Incidentally in a poem "*Bharattīrtha*"(*RR* 2:280-82) Tagore made a fine poetic evocation of the theme. However, in this essay Tagore deplores the fact that in the present time (around 1912) the world is torn by race conflict, but Tagore reaffirms his faith in the essential goodness of man. He says: that when "organized national selfishness, racial antipathy and commercial self-seeking begin to display their ugly deformities in all their nakedness, then comes the time for man to know that his salvation is not in political organizations and extended trade relations, not in any mechanical rearrangement of social system, but in a deeper transformation of life, in the liberation of consciousness in love, in the realization of God in man"(477).

35. The Meeting of the East and the West

"The Meeting of the East and the West" originally published in the *Manchester Guardian* was reprinted in *The Modern Review* in 1918.

Tagore says that although the East and the West have been in contact for many years there has been no proper assimilation of the two, because the West lacks the spiritual power to unite; it can only destroy and dominate. The Aryan immigrants conceived of a universal soul, a bond of spiritual unity in all creatures. In modern India Rammohun reaffirmed India's "spiritual inheritance in faith in the reality of the oneness of man in Brahma" (6:497). In the West the misuse of the advancement of science has made "the relationship of human races inhuman" (499) which has made "war and preparation for war the normal condition of all nations" (499). But, it is a fact that Europe has a rich cultural history "rich with strength, beauty and tradition of freedom" (499) and "they discovered the principle of unity in nature" (500). It is only in recent years that with material and scientific progress Europe became more interested in the accumulation of wealth than in the welfare of humanity. Tagore however believes that the experience of the first World War will bring Europe back to senses and she will come back to her real self and carry "her ideals into all continents of the earth and not sacrifice them to her greed for money and dominion" (500).

36. A Cry for Peace

"A Cry for Peace" was first published in *The Modern Review* in 1919.

In this essay while acknowledging the fact that the world is crying for peace and is trying to restore it through a League of Powers, Tagore observes that real peace can never be obtained by exercise of power. It can be had, as Christ and Buddha had preached, only by love of humanity, by realization of the spiritual unity of man. He declares: "We must know that, as, through science and commerce, the realization of the unity of the material world gives us power, so the realization of the great spiritual unity of man only can give us peace" (6:544).

37. Crisis in Civilization

"Crisis in Civilization", is Tagore's last public address delivered on 14 April 1941. It was subsequently published in *Visva-Bharati News*, Vol. 9, No. 2 and in *The Modern Review* in May 1941.

The essay records Tagore's early admiration amounting to almost adulation of the generosity of the English race and the large-hearted liberalism of the nineteenth century English politics. But gradually the process of disillusionment set in when he realized "how easily those who accepted the highest truths of civilization disowned them with impunity when questions of national self-interest were involved" (7:982). He also saw how while other countries like China, Japan, Iran and USSR were progressing "India, smothered under the dead weight of British administration, lay static in her utter helplessness" (984). With the outbreak of the Second World War Tagore was shocked into an awareness of the grim reality of the Western psychology. He says: "In the meanwhile the demon of barbarity has given up all pretence and has emerged with unconcealed fangs, ready to tear up humanity in an orgy of devastation. From one end of the world to the other the poisonous fumes of hatred darken the atmosphere. The spirit of violence which perhaps lay dormant in the psychology of the West, has at last roused itself and desecrates the spirit of man" (986). He sees "the crumbling ruins of a proud civilization strewn like a vast heap of futility". This is the crisis of civilization; this is the crisis of humanity. Even then Tagore refuses to lose faith in man. He declares: "And yet I shall not commit the grievous sin of losing faith in Man." An optimist and a great humanist as he is he "would rather look forward to the opening of a new chapter in his (Man's) history after the cataclysm is over and the atmosphere rendered clean with the spirit of service and sacrifice" (986). Incidentally, a few years later in 1950 William Faulkner in his Nobel Prize Speech almost echoed Tagore and said: "I believe that man will not merely endure: he will prevail. He is immortal, not because he among creatures has an inexhaustible voice, but because he has a soul, a spirit capable of compassion and sacrifice and endurance"

Poets are prophets, and Tagore's prophecy—"The wheels of Fate will some day compel the English to give up their Indian empire" (986)—came true just six years later, in 1947. Incidentally in a poem, *Orā kāj kare* ([They keep on working] RR:3 822-23) written around the same time (February 1941). Tagore had made the same prophecy- loud and clear—about the inevitable collapse of the British empire.

Bibliography

Ashcroft, Bill et al. *The Post-Colonial Studies Reader.* Routledge, 1965. Rept. 2000.

Bandyopadhyay, Hiranmay. *Rabīndra Śilpatatva* [Tagore's Theory of Art] Kolkata: Rabindra Bharati University, 1971.

Chakraborty, Biplab. ed. *Bānglā Sāhitya o Samskṛti* [Bengali Literature and Culture]. Burdwan: Academic Staff College, 2000.

Chaudhuri, Bhudeb and K.G. Subramanyan. eds. *Rabindranath Tagore and the Challenges of Today.* Shimla: Institute of Advanced Study, 1988. Cited as Chaudhuri.

Dasgupta, Uma. ed. *The Oxford India Tagore: Selected Writings on Education and Nationalism.* Oxford: OUP, 2009.

Kripalani, Krishna. *Rabindranath Tagore: A Biography.* Calcutta: Visva-Bharati, 1980.

Indian Horizons. Vol. 42. Nos 1-2. 1994. New Delhi: Indian Council for Cultural Relations.

Mitra, Sarojmohan. *Rabīndranāth o Cīn* [Rabindranath and China] Kolkata: Granthalay Private Ltd., 1987. Cited as Mitra.

O'Connell, K.M. (2003). 'Rabindranath Tagore on education', *The Encyclopaedia of* informal education. http://www.infed. org/thinkers/Tagore. htm.

Quayum, Mohammad A. 'Rabindranath Tagore's Critique of Nationalism'. http://www. mukto-mona.com/Articles/mohammad_qu.

Rabindranath Tagore: A Centenary Volume 1861-1961. New Delhi: Sahitya Akademi, 1961. Cited as Centenary Volume.

Sen, Taraknath. *A Literary Miscellany*. Calcutta: Rupa & Co., 1972.

Tagore, Rabindranath. *The English Writings of Tagore*. 8 vols. New Delhi: Atlantic Publishers & Distributors, 2007. Cited as *EWT*.

——. *Rabindra Rachanavali* [Collected Works of Tagore]. Centenary edition. Kolkata:, Government of West Bengal, 1961. Cited as *RR*.

Index

A

Advaitam, 81, 267, 268, 294
'Angel of the Surplus', 206
Antony and Cleopatra, 221, 312
Arabian Nights, 40
"Artist, The" 63, 72-80, 98, 107
'Art for Art's sake', 12, 14
As You Like It, 221, 315

B

Bankimchandra Chatterjee, 50
Baudelaire, xvii
Bertrand Russell, 166
Bibliography, 339-340
Brāhma, 60, 104, 105, 147, 155, 164, 270, 275, 277, 400, 407
Brāhmo Samāj movement, 395
Bṛkṣaropana, xvii
Buddha, 78, 112, 270, 285, 320, 395, 405

C

"Call of Truth, The", 353-373
China, 21, 28, 76, 112, 130, 150, 187, 243, 245, 248, 249, 331, 337, 410
Chinese poems, 64
Chomsky, xi
Christ, 132, 244, 285, 405
'Christian Missions', 243
"City and Village", 225-237
Civilization, 127, 228, 262, 331, 381
Conrad, xii
Construction versus Creation, 30
"Creative Ideal", 43-49
"Creative Spirit, The", 197-212
"Crisis in Civilization", 406-412
"Cry for Peace, A", 404-405
Cymbeline, 221, 315

D

Dharma, 24-28, 30-31, 123, 141, 171, 244, 250, 270, 389
Dhulāmandir, xxi

E

East India Company, 255
Egypt, 223
Eve, 183, 205
Fanon, xiii

F

Fashions in literature, 65
Foreword, iii

G

Ganges, 2, 4, 36, 37, 274, 293, 318
Garibaldi, 364
Gautam Buddha, 32
Gladstone, 362

God, 8, 9, 23, 33, 38, 40, 41, 48, 56, 62, 78, 92, 93, 94, 95, 105, 111, 116, 123, 139, 144, 150, 152, 163, 164, 167, 168, 178, 179, 186, 191, 192, 196, 209, 213, 217, 223, 242, 244, 252, 268, 271, 275, 276, 280, 281, 284, 307, 317, 323, 324, 337, 338, 343, 344, 346, 350, 367, 369, 384, 394, 397, 399, 403, 404

Goethe, 56, 234

H

Hamlet, 221, 316

Hindu Civilization, 387, 388

Hindu Scripture, The, 267

I

"I Am He", 280-290

"Ideals of Education", 262-266

Index, 442-444

Indian Reform Councils, 372

Introduction, vii-xxviii

J

"Judgment", 237-251

K

Kabir, 96, 284, 320

Kādambarī, 216, 302

Keats, 87

King Lear, 221, 316

Kīrtan music, 111

Kumāra-Sambhava, 216, 217, 222

Kyāmeliyā, xx

L

Lakshmi, 230

Lao-tze, 125, 128, 130, 131

League of Nations, The, 372

Lyric, 46, 64, 107, 130

M

Macbeth, 49, 221, 316

Mahomedan, 280, 284, 292, 399

Mālavikāgnimitra, 218, 307

Mammon, 230

"Man", 132-146

"Man of My Heart, The", 273-279

"Man's Nature", 123-131

"Man's Universe", 189-196

Manu, 361, 407

Mathematics, 79, 110

Māyā, 106

Mazzini, 362

"Meaning of Art, The", 104-116

"Meeting of the East and the West, The", 398-403

Merchant of Venice, 221, 316

"Message of the Forest, The", 298-311

Metre, 45, 54, 63, 64, 98, 319

Mṛit-Shakatikā, 216

Muktadhāra, xv

Mukti, 272, 291, 293, 297

Music, 79, 110

"Music Maker", 156-162

"My Pictures", 117-122

N

"Nation, The", 347-352

"Nationalism in the West", 322-346

"Nobel Prize Acceptance Speech", 1 -9

"*Notes*" (MKR), 413-438

O

'Oriental art', 21

Othello, 49, 221, 316

P

Paradise Lost, 222, 316

"Poet's Religion, The", 81-95

Prthwis Neogy, xxvii

"Principle of Literature, The", 96-103

R

Ravidas, 275, 284

"Race Conflict", 392-397

Rajjab, 275, 283

Rammohun Roy, 50, 262, 383, 386, 385, 400

Reality, 26, 73, 75, 76, 85, 164, 215, 217, 268, 294, 301, 339

Relationship, 194

Religion, 50, 81, 92, 123, 124, 168, 170, 171, 209, 213, 273, 378

"Religion of an Artist, The", 50-71

"Religion of the Forest, The", 213-224

Ritusamharā, 216, 303

Robinson Crusoe, 258, 259

Rome, 50, 150, 153, 394

Romeo and Juliet, 221, 316

Rudra, 172

Saguna Brahma, 164

S

Science, 10, 11, 13, 15, 17, 19, 20, 24, 27, 31, 32, 35, 39, 40, 74, 78, 102, 114, 190, 192, 193, 195, 198, 248, 250, 265, 276, 401, 405

Shakuntala, 122, 216, 302, 303, 304, 308, 309, 310, 312, 313, 317

Sisir Kumar Das, xxvi

"Spiritual Freedom", 291-297

"Spiritual Union", 267-272

"Supreme Man", 162-173

"Surplus in Man, The", 147-155

Swaraj, 354, 364, 366, 368, 370, 373

T

"Teacher, The", 252-261

Traditional Christians, 167

U

Universal Man, 60, 129, 130, 143, 145, 165, 168, 171, 173, 195, 282, 283

V

Vikramāditya, 215, 218, 255, 302

Villages, 229

Viśvakarmā, 119

W

"Way to Unity, The", 374-390

"What is Art", 10-29

Winter's Tale, The, 221, 316

"Woman", 174-182

"Woman and Home", 183-188

Woman's nature, 23, 175, 176, 178, 180, 183

Wordsworth, 66, 83, 84, 110, 222, 276, 316

Z

Zoroastrians, 409